REGNUM EDINBURGH CENTENARY SERIES
Volume 23

Global Diasporas and Mission

REGNUM EDINBURGH CENTENARY SERIES

The Centenary of the World Missionary Conference of 1910, held in Edinburgh, was a suggestive moment for many people seeking direction for Christian mission in the twenty-first century. Several different constituencies within world Christianity held significant events around 2010. From 2005, an international group worked collaboratively to develop an intercontinental and multi-denominational project, known as Edinburgh 2010, and based at New College, University of Edinburgh. This initiative brought together representatives of 20 different global Christian bodies, representing all major Christian denominations and confessions, and many different strands of mission and church life, to mark the Centenary.

Essential to the work of the Edinburgh 1910 Conference, and of abiding value, were the findings of the eight think-tanks or 'commissions'. These inspired the idea of a new round of collaborative reflection on Christian mission – but now focused on nine themes identified as being key to mission in the twenty-first century. The study process was polycentric, open-ended, and as inclusive as possible of the different genders, regions of the world, and theological and confessional perspectives in today's church. It was overseen by the Study Process Monitoring Group: Miss Maria Aranzazu Aguado (Spain, The Vatican), Dr Daryl Balia (South Africa, Edinburgh 2010), Mrs Rosemary Dowsett (UK, World Evangelical Alliance), Dr Knud Jørgensen (Norway, Areopagos), Rev John Kafwanka (Zambia, Anglican Communion), Rev Dr Jooseop Keum (Korea, World Council of Churches), Dr Wonsuk Ma (Korea, Oxford Centre for Mission Studies), Rev Dr Kenneth R Ross (UK, Church of Scotland), Dr Petros Vassiliadis (Greece, Aristotle University of Thessaloniki), and co-ordinated by Dr Kirsteen Kim (UK, Edinburgh 2010).

These publications reflect the ethos of Edinburgh 2010 and will make a significant contribution to ongoing studies in mission. It should be clear that material published in this series will inevitably reflect a diverse range of views and positions. These will not necessarily represent those of the series' editors or of the Edinburgh 2010 General Council, but in publishing them the leadership of Edinburgh 2010 hopes to encourage conversation between Christians and collaboration in mission. All the series' volumes are commended for study and reflection in both church and academy.

Series' Editors

Knud Jørgensen	Areopagos, Norway, MF Norwegian School of Theology and the Lutheran School of Theology, Hong Kong. Former Chair of Edinburgh 2010 Study Process Monitoring Group
Kirsteen Kim	Leeds Trinity University and former Edinburgh 2010 Research Co-ordinator, UK
Wonsuk Ma	Oxford Centre for Mission Studies, Oxford, UK
Tony Gray	Words by Design, Bicester, UK

REGNUM EDINBURGH CENTENARY SERIES
Volume 23

Global Diasporas and Mission

Edited by
Chandler H. Im
Amos Yong

WIPF & STOCK · Eugene, Oregon

Wipf and Stock Publishers
199 W 8th Ave, Suite 3
Eugene, OR 97401

Global Diasporas and Mission
By Im, Chandler H. and Yong, Amos

ISBN 13: 978-1-4982-0940-3
Publication date 10/15/2014
Previously published by Regnum, 2014

CONTENTS

Edinburgh 2010 Common Call

The Edinburgh 2010 Common Call emerged from the Edinburgh 2010 study process and conference to mark the centenary of the World Missionary Conference, Edinburgh 1910. The Common Call was affirmed in the Church of Scotland Assembly Hall in Edinburgh on 6 June 2010 by representatives of world Christianity, including Catholic, Evangelical, Orthodox, Pentecostal, and Protestant churches.

As we gather for the centenary of the World Missionary Conference of Edinburgh 1910, we believe the church, as a sign and symbol of the reign of God, is called to witness to Christ today by sharing in God's mission of love through the transforming power of the Holy Spirit.

1. Trusting in the Triune God and with a renewed sense of urgency, we are called to incarnate and proclaim the good news of salvation, of forgiveness of sin, of life in abundance, and of liberation for all poor and oppressed. We are challenged to witness and evangelism in such a way that we are a living demonstration of the love, righteousness and justice that God intends for the whole world.

2. Remembering Christ's sacrifice on the Cross and his resurrection for the world's salvation, and empowered by the Holy Spirit, we are called to authentic dialogue, respectful engagement and humble witness among people of other faiths – and no faith – to the uniqueness of Christ. Our approach is marked with bold confidence in the gospel message; it builds friendship, seeks reconciliation and practises hospitality.

3. Knowing the Holy Spirit who blows over the world at will, reconnecting creation and bringing authentic life, we are called to become communities of compassion and healing, where young people are actively participating in mission, and women and men share power and responsibilities fairly, where there is a new zeal for justice, peace and the protection of the environment, and renewed liturgy reflecting the beauties of the Creator and creation.

4. Disturbed by the asymmetries and imbalances of power that divide and trouble us in church and world, we are called to repentance, to critical reflection on systems of power, and to accountable use of power structures. We are called to find practical ways to live as members of One Body in full awareness that God resists the proud, Christ welcomes and empowers the poor and afflicted, and the power of the Holy Spirit is manifested in our vulnerability.

5. Affirming the importance of the biblical foundations of our missional engagement and valuing the witness of the Apostles and martyrs, we are called to rejoice in the expressions of the gospel in many nations all over

the world. We celebrate the renewal experienced through movements of migration and mission in all directions, the way all are equipped for mission by the gifts of the Holy Spirit, and God's continual calling of children and young people to further the gospel.

6. Recognizing the need to shape a new generation of leaders with authenticity for mission in a world of diversities in the twenty-first century, we are called to work together in new forms of theological education. Because we are all made in the image of God, these will draw on one another's unique charisms, challenge each other to grow in faith and understanding, share resources equitably worldwide, involve the entire human being and the whole family of God, and respect the wisdom of our elders while also fostering the participation of children.

7. Hearing the call of Jesus to make disciples of all people – poor, wealthy, marginalised, ignored, powerful, living with disability, young, and old – we are called as communities of faith to mission from everywhere to everywhere. In joy we hear the call to receive from one another in our witness by word and action, in streets, fields, offices, homes, and schools, offering reconciliation, showing love, demonstrating grace and speaking out truth.

8. Recalling Christ, the host at the banquet, and committed to that unity for which he lived and prayed, we are called to ongoing co-operation, to deal with controversial issues and to work towards a common vision. We are challenged to welcome one another in our diversity, affirm our membership through baptism in the One Body of Christ, and recognize our need for mutuality, partnership, collaboration and networking in mission, so that the world might believe.

9. Remembering Jesus' way of witness and service, we believe we are called by God to follow this way joyfully, inspired, anointed, sent and empowered by the Holy Spirit, and nurtured by Christian disciplines in community. As we look to Christ's coming in glory and judgment, we experience his presence with us in the Holy Spirit, and we invite all to join with us as we participate in God's transforming and reconciling mission of love to the whole creation.

ACKNOWLEDGEMENTS

As editors of the present volume, we are grateful first to Wonsuk Ma, editor-in-chief at Regnum Books International and Executive Director of the Oxford Centre for Mission Studies, for his initial invitation to work on and edit this volume on the topic of global diasporas and mission in the Edinburgh Centenary Series. Warm gratitude is offered to Tony Gray and other staff at the Regnum offices in Oxford, UK for their assistance in the production, printing, publication, and promotion processes. Laurie Fortunak Nichols, Director of Communications at Billy Graham Center, Wheaton College, worked diligently to copy-edit the chapters according to Regnum style. Vince Le and Enoch Charles, Amos Yong's graduate assistants at Regent University, compiled the volume's bibliography and created the index respectively, among many other minor but essential tasks that go into such a project.

In addition, Jason Chew in Singapore – through the hands of Robert Oh, a missionary in Cambodia – made a generous financial gift toward the book's initial publication costs. Korean Diaspora Forum, led by Soon K. Lee, contributed the needed funds to allow this book to be distributed to selected libraries of Christian colleges and seminaries around the globe. It is a pleasure to publish this volume in partnership with the Global Diaspora Network as well.

Finally, we would like to express our deep appreciation to the respective institutions we serve for the support that provides the broader context for our scholarship, and to the volume authors for their timely and valuable contributions to this important volume. Soli Deo gloria!

Chandler H. Im
Amos Yong

INTRODUCTION

Chandler H. Im and Tereso C. Casiño

Nearly 1,200 Protestant leaders, almost exclusively from Europe and North America, gathered at the World Missionary Conference in Edinburgh, Scotland, in 1910 to reflect on and discuss eight key mission-related themes.[1] The present volume on global diasporas and mission is published as a part of the Edinburgh Centenary Series on Christian mission in the twenty-first century.

For contemporary evangelical missiologists, God is the master conductor of the global diasporas. God has devised and orchestrated the scattering and gathering of individuals and people groups since the creation of the progenitor of the human family. Genesis 3 describes the banishment of Adam and Eve from the Garden of Eden after they willfully disobeyed God's commandment. Since then, humanity has been in a state of diaspora – physically and/or spiritually – although still under the redemptive plan of God. The overarching motif of diaspora comprises a homeland, an adopted society, and the initiating and resultant circumstances, along with their corresponding factors, events, and processes. Global diasporas and migration have been and will continue to be a significant and indispensable means by which God accomplishes his redemptive purposes in this world through Jesus Christ. The developmental process of the Church's expansion – inclusive of past, present, and future – cannot be explained without taking into consideration 'God's sovereignty, ruling over the nations, and the moving of His people' from everywhere to everywhere.[2]

Global diasporas, especially during the last five centuries, have played a major role in Christian history, including contributing to the shifting of the centers of Christianity from European and North American cities to other Majority World metropolises. Since the sixteenth-century Reformation, for instance, many Christian centers, such as Amsterdam, Geneva, London, and Paris, have become multiethnic and multi-religious, and now can hardly be regarded as exclusively 'Christian' cities any longer. On the

---

[1] The Eight Commissions of the World Missionary Conference of Edinburgh in 1910 are as follows: 1. Carrying the Gospel to all the Non-Christian World; 2. The Church in the Mission Field; 3. Education in Relation to the Christianization of National Life; 4. Missionary Message in Relation to the Non-Christian World; 5. The Preparation of Missionaries; 6. The Home Base of Missions; 7. Missions and Governments; and, 8. Co-operation and the Promotion of Unity. See www.edinburgh2010.org/en/resources/1910-conference.html (accessed 22.8.2012).

[2] Lausanne Diasporas Leadership Team (LDLT), *Scattered to Gather: Embracing the Global Trend of Diaspora* (Manila: LifeChange Publishing Inc., 2010), 17.

contrary, Majority World cities like Seoul, Nairobi, and São Paulo have been emerging as new major hubs of global Christianity.

In this volume, we endeavor to view the world through the lens of the global diasporas and their missiological implications in the twenty-first century. Combining both the numbers of their countries of birth and their current places of residence, this work's 21 contributors represent 13 nations and four continents – Asia, Europe, North America, and South America. We attempt to provide glimpses into issues of which represented diaspora communities and churches grapple. Due to space limitation, we cannot cover the countless global diasporas and myriad issues and challenges diaspora individuals, families, churches, communities, and people groups face on a daily basis. As a multi-authored volume, the chapters are eclectic in nature, with topics ranging from general overviews of the phenomenon of global diasporas to varying ethnic-specific issues of global diaspora churches.

This volume is divided into three major sections. The four chapters of the first section offer panoramic overviews of historical, theological, and biblical aspects of global diasporas. The second section includes nine chapters on global diaspora movements and churches on four continents. The third section contains six chapters on both the positive and negative missional implications and impacts of living and working within the 'God on the move and people on the move' realities of the twenty-first century.

In addition to evangelical authors, ecumenical and Catholic authors who have been recommended by the International Association of Catholic Missiologists have contributed to the volume. The book thus offers a wide spectrum of theological and missiological perspectives on diaspora and migration. It is our hope that the reader will gain something positive from this collaborative endeavor, regardless of its limitations.

Definitions: Diaspora, Diasporas, Migration, and Diaspora Missiology

The word 'diaspora' (διασπορα in Greek) comes from the Septuagint and has been translated in English Bible versions as 'removed', 'driven out', 'scattered', 'banished', 'exiled', 'dispersed', 'outcast', 'exiles', 'preserved', 'remnant [which were scattered]', and even 'horrified'.[3] In this volume, a person of diaspora is simply defined as one who lives or works in a nation outside his or her land of birth. The plural form 'diasporas' refers to many diverse people groups in the state of diaspora (e.g., the Armenian diaspora, Brazilian diaspora, Chinese diaspora, Danish diaspora, Egyptian diaspora, etc.).

Generally speaking, the terms 'diaspora' and 'migration' are assumed to bear the same linguistic currency and are used interchangeably. These two

---

[3] LDLT, *Scattered to Gather*, 11-12.

terms, however, have different definitions, meanings, and nuances in a variety of academic circles, including among Christian scholars and mission practitioners. The distinction between 'diaspora' and 'migration' is crucial to understanding the interface between people's geographic and spatial mobility and world missions. On the one hand, diaspora refers broadly to the global phenomenon of the dispersion or scattering of people in various parts of the world, occurring either by a voluntary act or coercive conditions in both domestic and global contexts. On the other hand, migration *facilitates* geographic or demographic mobility that eventually results in diasporic conditions and circumstances. Migration involves geographic and demographic flows of people or individuals, taking both internal and international directions.

The inherent connection between diaspora and migration is important because of their symbiotic relationship. Theoretically, creative tension exists between the two, although both motifs are complementary; however, they should not be taken as identical or synonymous. Diaspora refers to the overarching structure under which all forms of mobility take place; migration serves as a tool to account for diasporic movements.[4] In this strict sense, diaspora can be understood more as a grand design with migration – a specific act or effort – constituting the structure. In reference to the Great Commission, diaspora accentuates a strong, broad missiological perspective over the sociologically-oriented acts of migration. If ties to one's homeland are indicative of diasporic identity, then not all migrants could be viewed as people of diaspora. Some migrants radically severe ties with their countries of origin; however, diasporic communities revitalize their identity either by memory or physical connectivity as they go through the process of movements and displacements. Thus, the bond that continues to exist between a person outside his or her homeland highlights a diasporic identity.

As an interdisciplinary field, diaspora missiology refers to the study of the geographic or demographic mobility of people in various parts of the globe viewed through the lens of God's redemptive plan for 'all nations' (*panta ta ethne*). It also refers to the exploration of how the body of Christ can participate in this redemptive purpose and work. Enoch Wan asserts that diaspora missiology is fundamentally 'glocal' in nature because it is borderless and transnational, multicultural rather than homogenous, and both multiethnic and multi-directional.[5]

---

[4] Tereso C. Casiño, 'Why People Move', *Torch Trinity Journal* 13:1 (May 2010), 30.

[5] Enoch Wan, 'Diaspora Missiology – A Different Paradigm for the 21st Century', in Enoch Wan (ed), *Diaspora Missiology: Theory, Methodology, and Practice* (Portland, OR: Institute of Diaspora Studies, 2011), 97-100.

Basic Theological Considerations for Global Diaspora

There are at least five basic theological considerations pertaining to the phenomenon of global diaspora.[6] The first three depict diaspora negatively in relation to how God deals with his erring people. The last two express the positive aspects of people's mobility with particular respect to God's redemptive work among people on the move.

First, the permanent exile and departure of Adam and Eve from their 'original homeland' portrays *primordial diaspora* in its fullest sense. This *first order* dispersion may be perceived as a form of divine retribution. Exiles, migrations, and dispersions became irreversible after this archetypal incident. Since the beginning, involuntary migration has become a fixture in human history.[7] In contrast with many migrants today who have the capacity and resources to visit their homelands, Adam and Eve's exit from the Garden of Eden was both permanent and irreversible. Divine justice was meted out, resulting in the alteration of the first family's citizenship; disobedience prompted their sojourn outside their place of residence. This primal dispersion became the first recorded geographic mobility in biblical history. However, it should not be taken as *the* prototype for the ensuing scattering of people around the globe because not all human mobility can be attributed to divine judgment.

Second, the Jewish diaspora may be construed as a form of 'hermeneutical corrective' to check nationalistic particularism. Israel's perennial exclusivist tendency and Jewish extreme nationalism provide a backdrop to the extent of global diaspora. Some Jews were passionate about domesticating Yahweh within the territories of Israel. They thought Yahweh was confined to Israel's political and religious borders. Other Jews obstinately strived to localize Yahweh's presence within the boundaries of Israel and Judah, thinking they could suppress the redemptive plan and purpose for the nations. A good example is the prophet Jonah, who depicts the tension between Yahweh's universalism and the Jews' nationalist particularism. Called to proclaim Yahweh's message to the people in Nineveh, Jonah lamented over the universal scope of Yahweh's love and justice, even after the demonstration of God's power that swept across the nation in the aftermath of delivering God's message.[8] This misplaced exclusivist religious fervor persisted beyond the exilic and restoration

---

[6] This section is based primarily upon the original version in Casiño, 'Why People Move', 35-39, unless otherwise noted.

[7] See Enoch Wan and Sadiri Joy Tira, 'Diaspora Missiology', in Sadiri Joy Tira and Enoch Wan (eds), *Missions in Action in the 21st Century* (Toronto: Prinbridge, 2008), 44.

[8] See Uriel Simon, *Jonah,* The JPS Bible Commentary (trans. L.J. Schramm; Philadelphia: The Jewish Publication Society, 1999).

periods, although God used the Jewish diaspora even at the early stages of gospel advancement.[9]

Third, Jewish dispersion in particular and the scattering of people in general may be interpreted as a form of divine judgment. There are specific instances where the scattering of people accentuates the reality of divine justice. For example, ancient human population was distributed in various directions after the confusion of languages at the Tower of Babel. A series of spiritual and moral lapses led the Jews to exiles and countless sojourns outside their beloved homeland. Spiritual corruption, loss of moral compass, and religious and political miscalculations by many Jewish leaders led to the downfall of both Israel and Judah, resulting in the Jewish community's geographic and spatial displacement and relocation. Nevertheless, the exilic presence of the Jews in an environment of dispersion paved the way for cross-cultural engagement, multiculturalism in the host country, and eventually cultural transformation.

Fourth, diaspora functions as a divine strategy to fulfill the universal missionary mandate. As a global phenomenon, the scattering of people in many directions may signify the execution of God's grand redemptive plan for all nations. The sovereignty of God encompasses the dispersions of people from various quarters of the world for an expressed missionary intention. When people move, evangelism opportunities emerge. Migration flows can facilitate conditions and circumstances where the diasporas have direct access to the gospel without losing their ethnic identity.

Fifth, based on the triune God's revelatory nature, global diaspora can serve as a key theological framework to interpret redemptive acts in the world. Tuvya Zaretsky asserts that the diaspora motif 'has shaped Jewish identity and history'. Human identity and history in general, and the Christian identity and heritage in particular, likewise evolve through endless migration and dispersion. Geographic and spatial mobility is never a monopoly of the Jews or Christians because the rest of humanity belongs to global diaspora communities as well. Christ's incarnation stands in the center of all diasporic conditions as the universal Lord and Redeemer; it serves as a theological model of purposeful migration. Other equally important themes include the universal workings of the Spirit of God, the spiritual state of humanity, the universal reality of sin, God's salvific works around the world, the diasporic orientation of the missionary mandate, the identity and calling of the church, and the realities involving millennialism in particular and eschatology in general. These relevant themes provide a coherent framework for understanding the interface between people's mobility and world missions.

---

[9]For a fuller treatment, see Tuvya Zaretsky, 'A Missiological Study of Jewish Diaspora', a paper presented at the Global Diaspora Consultation, Taylor University College, Edmonton, Alberta, Canada, November 15-18, 2006.

Global diaspora is best construed as a 'theological form' that accentuates God's missionary intention for people on the move and the redemptive acts that go along with it, both domestically and globally. The space existing between people's original homelands and their adopted countries or societies unfolds God's convicting, yet gentle presence. Divine grace operates in and through people on the move as they face new challenges in life and maximize the creative possibilities in their diasporic environment.[11]

Ebbs and Flows around the Globe, Especially in the West and Middle East

The number of people moving from their respective homelands to other countries or from one place to another is growing. The International Organization for Migration (IOM) estimates one billion people as migrants today – 214 million internationally and 740 million internally (within countries or nation-states). This reality of global mobility translates into one out of 33 persons in the world, or 3.1% of the world's population. It is projected that by 2050, the population of international migrants alone would reach 405 million. Accordingly, Latin America and the Caribbean account for 15% of all international diasporas in the world. The region also hosts one of the three largest internally displaced peoples (IDP) in the world. In fact, Columbia has over 2.5 million displaced citizens, accounting for almost 6% of the nation's total population.[12] On the global scene, the top ten nations in 2010 that host the largest number of migrants are shown in Table 1 below.

The foreign-born populations in Europe vary widely from country to country – from over 30% in Luxembourg to less than 1% in Slovakia and Romania. However, it is evident in the table below that the demographic changes across Europe caused by the influx of the foreign-born populations are significant and will likely continue.

To a large extent, historically, the USA has been a nation *of* and *for* immigrants in pursuit of the American Dream. America continues to witness the coming together of myriads of cultures and ethnolinguistic communities. Table 3 below portrays the top 20 diaspora populations of the American ethnic mosaic based on the US Census Bureau's 2011 American Community Survey (ACS).

---

[11] One excellent example of God's redemptive work is church planting on a ship as documented in Martin Otto's *Church on the Oceans: A Missionary Vision for the 21st Century* (Carlisle, UK: Piquant, 2007).

[12] www.iom.int/cms/en/sites/iom/home/about-migration/facts--figures-1.html. Sources for these figures include UN DEAS, 2009; UNDP, 2009; UNFPA, 2009; and World Bank, 2009 (accessed 26.2.14).

Table 1: Top Ten Countries with the Largest Numbers of International Migrants, 2010 (Millions)

United States of America	42.8 Mil.
Russian Federation	12.3 Mil.
Germany	10.8 Mil.
Saudi Arabia	7.3 Mil.
Canada	7.2 Mil.
France	6.7 Mil.
United Kingdom	6.5 Mil.
Spain	6.4 Mil.
India	5.4 Mil.
Ukraine	5.3 Mil.

Sources: United Nations, Department of Economic and Social Affairs, Population Division (2009). International Migration, 2009 Wallchart (United Nations publication, Sales No. E.09.XIII.8).

Table 2: Foreign-born Populations in European Countries, 2009

European Country	**Percent of Foreign-Born Population**
Luxembourg	32.2%
Estonia	16.4%
Latvia	15.6%
Austria	15.2%
Ireland	14.1%
Spain	13.8%
Sweden	13.8%
Belgium	13.0% (2007)
Slovenia	12.0%
Germany	11.6%
United Kingdom	11.3%
Greece	11.1%
France	11.0%
Netherlands	10.9%
Denmark	8.8%
Portugal	7.4%
Italy	7.1%
Lithuania	6.6%
Hungary	4.1%
Finland	4.0%
Czech Republic	3.7%
Poland	2.7%
Slovakia	0.9%
Romania	0.8%

Sources: The Migration Policy Institute, Eurostat, et al. (quoted in National Geographic, March 2012, 148-9).

Table 3: Estimates of the Top 20 Largest Diaspora Populations in the USA in 2011 (in Millions)[13]

Rank & Origin	Pop Size	Rank & Origin	Pop Size	Rank & Origin	Pop Size
1. Germany	48.1 Mil.	8. Puerto Rico	5.4 Mil.	15. Canada	3.2 Mil.
2. Ireland	39.3 Mil.	9. Netherlands	4.5 Mil.	16. El Salvador	2.3 Mil.
3. Mexico	34.8 Mil.	10. China	4.4 Mil.	17. Cuba	2.1 Mil.
4. UK	33.2 Mil.	11. Norway	4.4 Mil.	18. Vietnam	2.0 Mil.
5. Italy	17.4 Mil.	12. Sweden	4.0 Mil.	19. S. Korea	1.8 Mil.
6. Poland	9.5 Mil.	13. Philippines	3.6 Mil.	20. Dominican Republic	1.8 Mil.
7. France	8.6 Mil.	14. India	3.5 Mil.	**TOTAL**	**230.9 Mil.**

Every year, over one million people immigrate to the USA. As of July 1, 2010, 12.9% (39,956,000) of the US population was foreign-born.[14] The average annual arrival of refugees in the USA from 2001 to 2010 was 52,789.[15] The total ceiling allocated for refugee admissions in 2009, 2010, and 2011 was 80,000 per year.[16] According to US Census data, it is projected that the non-Anglo population in the USA would become the majority by 2043.[17] This trend in cultural and ethnic diversity is expected to continue in the USA and in other Western and developed countries in the twenty-first century. Recent data show the US population has 197.5 million non-Hispanic whites (63.3%). Hispanics are second with 52 million

---

[13] Adapted from the Migration Policy Institute Data Hub, 'Estimates of the Top 20 Diaspora Groups in the United States, 2011', www.migrationinformation.org/datahub/historicaltrends.cfm#Diaspora (accessed 19.5.13). It is important to note that the ACS asks two questions, namely, country of birth *and* country of ancestry.

[14] US Census Bureau, American Community Survey 2010, Table 1. Population by Nativity Status and Citizenship.

[15] US Dept. of State, Bureau of Population, Refugees, and Migration, Worldwide Admissions Processing System, Fiscal Years 1980 to 2010, and 2010 Yearbook of the Immigration Statistics. Table 13. Refugee Arrivals Fiscal Years 1980 to 2010. The number of refugees admitted each year into the USA has been fluctuating from 1980 to 2010: the highest in 1980 (207,116) and the lowest in 2002 (26,785), after 9/11 in 2001.

[16] US Dept. of State, Proposed Refugee Admissions FY 2012 Report to Congress.

[17] *Huffington Post*, 12 December 2012; www.huffingtonpost.com/2012/12/12/census-hispanics-and-black-unseat-whites-as-majority-in-united-states-population_n_2286105.html (accessed 26.2.14).

(16.7%), and non-Hispanic blacks now rank third with 38.3 million (12.3%).[18]

While Hispanics have grown dramatically, surpassing the African American community in the USA, they are not the fastest-growing ethnic groups in the country. Asian American communities are now the fastest-growing ethnolinguistic communities in the USA, and they are also highly educated, with an average annual income higher than the rest of their American compatriots.[19] In 2011, the total population of Asian Americans – foreign-born and US-born – rose to a record high of 18.2 million, representing 5.8% of the total US population, up from less than 1% in 1965.[20]

According to a 2011 survey released by Statistics Canada, 20.6% (6.8 million) of the Canadians were born outside the country. Canada plans to welcome about 250,000 immigrants each year. About 1.2 million immigrants, 56.9% from Asia, came to Canada between 2006 and 2011. It is also interesting to note that the Muslim population in Canada nearly doubled from 2001 to 2011. About 1.1 million strong in 2011, Muslims constitute 3.2% of the Canadian population; this number was just 2% in 2001.[21]

By 2017, Canada's 150th anniversary, Canada's national statistical agency, Statistics Canada, projects that immigrants would account for 22% of the population. By 2031, 46% of Canadians aged 15 and over will be foreign-born, or have at least one foreign-born parent, up from 39% in 2006. In 2001, about 70% of the visible minority population was born outside Canada. According to the 2001 Census, 1,029,000 identified themselves as Chinese (26% of the visible minority), and 917,000 as South Asian (23% of the visible minority). The median age of the visible minority population will be an estimated 35.7 in 2017. In contrast, the median age of the rest of the population will be 43.4 years in 2017. Almost 75% of the visible minority persons in 2017 will be living in one of Canada's three largest metropolitan areas: Toronto will have 45% of all visible minorities, Vancouver 18%, and Montreal 11%. The 2006 census reported 289,400 mixed unions ('between one visible minority group member and one non-member'), a hike of 33.1% from 2001, which is more than five times the 6% increase for all couples.[22]

---

[18] www.census.gov/popest/data/counties/totals/2012/index.html (accessed 26.2.14).

[19] www.pewsocialtrends.org/2012/06/19/the-rise-of-asian-americans/ (accessed 26.2.14).

[20] Reports of net international migration in the US can be found in www.census.gov/population/www/documentation/twps0090/twps0090.pdf (accessed 26.2.14).

[21] www.statcan.gc.ca/daily-quotidien/130508/dq130508b-eng.htm (accessed 9.5.13).

[22] Statistics Canada, www.statcan.gc.ca/daily-quotidien/050322/dq050322b-eng.htm (accessed 29.1.13).

In terms of percentage among international migrants living in foreign countries and territories, the UN report identifies seven of the top ten countries with a predominantly Muslim population, including the Palestinian Territory in the Middle East. Table 4 shows the distribution of international migrants in these *receiving* nations and territories.

Table 4: Countries and Territories with the Highest Percentage of International Migrants[23]

Country	Percentage in National Population
Qatar	87%
United Arab Emirates	70%
Kuwait	69%
Jordan	46%
Occupied Palestinian Territory	44%
Singapore	41%
Israel	40%
Hong Kong, China	39%
Oman	28%
Saudi Arabia	28%
Australia	27%

Source: United Nations, Department of Economic and Social Affairs, Population Division (2009). International Migration, 2009 Wallchart (United Nations publication, Sales No. E.09.XIII.8).

An overview of international migration in the Middle East shows the strategic presence of and contribution by foreigners in the region.[24] In the United Arab Emirates, nationals account for only 19% of the total population of 5,314,317 (2012 estimate). Other Arabs and Iranians comprise 23%, South Asians 50%, and other westerners and East Asians 8%. In Bahrain, 46% are local citizens, while foreigners account for 54% of the total population of 1,248,380 (2010 estimate). In Kuwait, with a total population of 2,646,314 (2012 estimate), 45% are Kuwaiti nationals; the diaspora community comprises 35% Arabs, 9% South Asians, 4% Iranians, and 7% other nationalities.

In neighboring Qatar, out of the population of 1,951,591 (2012 estimate), Arabs comprise 40%. The diaspora communities include 18% Indians, 18% Pakistanis, 10% Iranians, and 14% other nationalities. In Oman, out of the total population of 3,090,150 (2012 estimate), the expatriates may have passed the half million mark (477,294; 2008 estimate). The Kingdom of Saudi Arabia has a total population of

---

[23] The statistics shows only the top ten countries with at least 1 million inhabitants.

[24] Statistics in this particular section comes from the CIA World Factbook: www.cia.gov/library/publications/the-world-factbook/ (accessed 26.2.14).

26,534,504 (2012 estimate), with 5,576,076 international migrants (July 2009 estimate).

An Overview of Literature on Diaspora vis-à-vis Christian Mission[25]

Publications on this emerging study of diaspora vis-à-vis Christian mission are still limited. The following section discusses the emergence of the study of diaspora missiology and presents an overview of literature on diaspora, particularly in relation to Christian mission.

In June 2002, the American Society of Missiology (ASM) held its annual meeting on the theme of 'Migration Challenge and Avenue for Christian Mission'. Subsequently, the ASM published in *Missiology* XXXI (January 2003) a compilation of papers contributed by missiologists and practitioners ministering to diaspora populations. For example, Christine Pohl discussed the biblical themes of 'offering hospitality to strangers' and 'the identity of people of God as resident aliens'. Samuel Escobar and Daniel Rodriguez focused on the Hispanic diaspora and how they had been received by churches in the USA and Spain.

In April 2004 in Seoul, the Filipino International Network (FIN) convened a consultation in which missiologists, theologians, and practitioners discussed the topic of diaspora mission in general, and the phenomenon of the Filipino diaspora's growing role in global mission in particular. These presentations and papers were compiled in a volume entitled *Scattered: the Global Filipino Presence.*[26]

The Lausanne movement has hosted a series of consultations on diaspora and produced important documents.[27] In 2004 in Pattaya, Thailand, the Lausanne Congress of World Evangelization (LCWE) included diaspora as an issue for the first time in the Lausanne Forum. A diverse group was assembled to formulate the firstever Lausanne Occasional Paper (LOP) on diaspora. This Lausanne Occasional Paper 55, *Diasporas and International*

---

[25] Most of the sources compiled in this literature review section are derived from two previously published materials: M. Daniel Carroll, Leiton Chinn, Chandler H. Im, and Sadiri Joy Tira, *Bibliographic Resources for The Cape Town Commitment, Diaspora (Scattered Peoples)* (n.p.: The Lausanne Movement, 2012), 75-76, available at www.lausanne.org/docs/Bibliographic-Resources-for-CTC.pdf (accessed 1.2.13); Enoch Wan (ed), *Diaspora Missiology: Theory, Methodology, and Practice* (Portland, OR: Institute of Diaspora Studies, Western Seminary, 2011), 102-05. These are reprinted here with permission directly from the authors/editors (Carroll, Im, Wan et al.). Several contributors of the present volume made other suggestions for inclusion as well.

[26] Luis L. Pantoja, Jr, Sadiri Joy Tira, Enoch Wan (eds), *Scattered: The Global Filipino Presence* (Manila: LifeChange Publishing, Inc., 2004).

[27] www.lausanne.org/en/gatherings/issue-based/diasporas-2009.html (accessed 26.2.14).

Students: The New People Next Door,[28] dealt with the biblical and theological basis for carrying missions among scattered people. Case studies on Chinese, Filipino, South Asian, Persian, and international students were presented.

The LOP 55 is historic in that it officially placed the topic of diaspora missiology on the global agenda for the church, at least in Protestant circles. Recognizing the limitations of this document, LCWE endorsed the first Global Diaspora Missiology Consultation, which was held in Edmonton, Alberta, in November 2006. At the meeting, case studies were shared by leaders from major diaspora groups – e.g., Chinese, Filipino, Hispanic, Jewish, Kenyan, Korean, Nepalese, Nigerian, North African, South Asian, Tibetan, and Vietnamese. One of the presenters, Tuvya Zaretsky of Jews for Jesus, depicted Jewish diaspora experience as a key to the study of diaspora missiology. He pointed out that the Jewish diaspora was used by God to spread the gospel initially, starting in the Jewish homeland among both Jews and Gentiles after the persecution of Stephen.

At the Lausanne Diaspora Strategy Consultation in Manila in 2009, Leiton Chinn presented a paper entitled 'International Student Ministry: From Blind-Spot to Vision'.[29] It contains a comprehensive overview of the International Student Ministry movement's biblical-missiological perspectives, strategic nature, and global growth. Because this is a burgeoning field in missiological circles, articles on migration, diaspora communities, and diaspora missiology appear in scholarly missiological journals such as *Global Missiology*, *Transformation, Mission Studies*, *Missiology*, *International Review of Mission*, and even in more general mission journals such as *Evangelical Missions Quarterly*.

In a 2007 article, 'Diaspora Missiology', Enoch Wan attempted to define 'diaspora missiology' and delineate its contents, distinctive, and methodology.[30] In July 2007, *Global Missiology*, a multi-lingual free online journal, devoted the entire issue to the study of diaspora missiology. In 2010, *Torch Trinity Journal*, a bi-annual publication of Torch Trinity Graduate School of Theology in Seoul allocated two volumes to the issue of diaspora. Several academic journals that promote diaspora and migration studies include *Diaspora: A Journal of Transnational Studies*, *Journal of Ethnic and Migration Studies*, and *International Migration Review*. Some journals focus on certain regions or populations such as *Asian and Pacific*

---

[28] Lausanne Occasional Paper 55, *Diasporas and International Students: The New People Next Door,* www.lausanne.org/en/documents/lops/871-lop-55.html (accessed 1.2.13).

[29] Leiton Chinn, 'International Student Ministry: From Blind Spot to Vision", a paper presented at the Lausanne Diaspora Strategy Consultation, Manila, Philippines, 4-9 May 2009.

[30] Enoch Wan, 'Diaspora Missiology', *EMS Occasional Bulletin* 20:2 (Spring 2007), 3-7.

Migration Journal and *Notes and Records: An International Journal of African and African Diaspora Studies*.[31]

Insofar as general books on the topic of migration/diaspora are concerned, Stéphane Dufoix's *Diasporas*,[32] Stephen Castles and Mark J. Miller's *The Age of Migration: International Population Movements in the Modern World*,[33] Robin Cohen's *Global Diasporas: An Introduction*,[34] Doug Saunders's *Arrival City: How the Largest Migration in History is Shaping the World*,[35] and Kavita R. Khory's edited *Global Migration: Challenges for the 21st Century*[36] are excellent primers to the study of migration/diaspora. Such first-rate works would orient the reader to basic definitions, the history of sociological and anthropological research, regional trends, and the diverse realities faced and created by global diaspora populations.

For books on diaspora vis-à-vis Christian mission, Philip Jenkins' *The Next Christendom: The Coming of Global Christianity*,[37] now in its third edition, is a significant work about the shift of the center of the Christian faith to the global south. Jenkins raises awareness of the changing face of the church, with theological emphases and religious practices different from what is usually seen in the West. This book can serve as an outstanding resource for those interested in discovering the kind of Christianity that is impacting and reshaping the global church in unexpected ways.

In *Beyond Christendom: Globalization, African Migration, and the Transformation of the West*,[38] Jehu J. Hanciles argues that the demise of the Christendom model worldwide, economic globalization, the changes in the profile of global Christianity, and the South-North migration of millions

---

[31] In addition, there are multiple Internet sites tracking migration and diaspora movements and communities. Many are group- or geographical-specific; others offer a more general view. Note, for example, www.migrationinformation.org/GlobalData/ and the United Nations website on International Migration: www.un.org/esa/population/migration/.

[32] Stéphane Dufoix, *Diasporas* (trans. W. Rodarmor; Berkeley, CA: University of California Press, 2008).

[33] Stephen Castles and Mark J. Miller, *The Age of Migration: International Population Movements in the Modern World* (4th ed.; New York: The Guilford Press, 2009).

[34] Robin Cohen, *Global Diasporas: An Introduction* (2nd ed.; New York: Routledge, 2008).

[35] Doug Saunders, *Arrival City: How the Largest Migration in History is Reshaping Our World* (New York: Pantheon Books, 2010).

[36] Kavita R. Khory (ed), *Global Migration: Challenges for the 21st Century* (New York: Palgrave Macmillan, 2012).

[37] Philip Jenkins, *The Next Christendom: The Coming of Global Christianity* (3rd ed.; New York: Oxford University Press, 2011).

[38] Jehu J. Hanciles, *Beyond Christendom: Globalization, African Migration, and the Transformation of the West* (Maryknoll, NY: Orbis, 2008).

together have triggered an unprecedented missionary reality. Newly-arrived Christian communities from the African continent visualize themselves in America as the vanguard of a fresh missionary movement of God in the world. This volume combines excellent historical research and missiological analysis with impressive case studies.

On African diasporas in European contexts, two key authors need to be mentioned. Gerrie ter Haar's *Halfway to Paradise: African Christians in Europe* has been considered seminal and led to a special edition for Africa in 2001 entitled *African Christians in Europe.*[39] Afe Adogame has also produced prolific and collaborative works with others in the field. He has edited volumes of pertinent studies on and research methodologies for the new African diasporas, especially in Europe.[40]

In October 2010, the Global Diaspora Network distributed *Scattered to Gather: Embracing the Global Trend of Diaspora*[41] to participants of Lausanne III, which was held in Cape Town, South Africa. The monograph is an excellent resource for those who want to understand and evaluate diaspora mission studies in light of theological, biblical, and missiological frameworks.

Diaspora Missiology: Theory, Methodology, and Practice,[42] edited by Enoch Wan, is an introductory volume on the theory, methodology, and practice of diaspora missiology and its sub-fields. It describes the new global demographic realities that have given rise to this new multi-discipline paradigm in missiology, which is different from traditional missiology.

Three ethnic diaspora-specific volumes are worth mentioning here as well. *Korean Diaspora and Christian Mission,*[43] edited by S. Hun Kim and Wonsuk Ma, is an important work on the global diasporas in general and Korean diaspora in particular. *Malalayi Diaspora: From Kerala to the*

---

[39] Gerrie ter Haar, *Halfway to Paradise: African Christians in Europe* (Cardiff, UK: Cardiff Academic Press, 1998); *African Christians in Europe* (Nairobi: Action Publishers, 2001). She also edited *Strangers and Sojourners: Religious Communities in the Diaspora* (Leuven: Peeters, 1998).

[40] Afe Adogame and Jim Spickard (eds), *Religion Crossing Boundaries: Transnational Religious and Social Dynamics in Africa and the New African Diaspora* (Leiden: Brill, 2010); Afe Adogame, Roswith Gerloff and Klaus Hock (eds), *Christianity in Africa and the Africa Diaspora: The Appropriation of a Scattered Heritage* (London: Continuum, 2008); Adogame Afe and Cordula Weisskoeppel (eds), *Religion in the Context of African Migration* (Bayreuth: Eckhard Breitinger, 2005).

[41] LDLT, *Scattered to Gather*.

[42] Enoch Wan (ed), *Diaspora Missiology: Theory, Methodology, and Practice* (Portland, OR: Institute of Diaspora Studies, Western Seminary, 2011).

[43] S. Hun Kim and Wonsuk Ma (eds), *Korean Diaspora and Christian Mission* (Eugene, OR: Wipf & Stock, 2011).

Ends of the World,[44] edited by Sam George and T.V. Thomas, is another ethnic diaspora-specific, multi-author volume of significance. The International Forum for Migrant Mission in South Korea published the book *21C New Nomad Era and Migrant Mission*,[45] edited by Chan-Sin Park and Noah Jung. This volume offers biblical and sociological perspectives and case studies on various ethnolinguistic communities in South Korea and neighboring countries.

The past few years have seen the release of significant publications on migration/diaspora vis-à-vis immigration. In evangelical circles, M. Daniel Carroll's *Christians at the Border: Immigration, the Church, and the Bible*[46] facilitates biblical, theological, and ethical discussions from the Old and New Testaments on the topic of immigration, especially among the Hispanic/Latino community in the USA. *Welcoming the Stranger: Justice, Compassion and Truth in Immigration Debate*,[47] edited by Matthew Soerens and Jenny Hwang (now Yang), deals with issues and questions of US immigration laws and systems while offering concrete ways to welcome and minister to immigrant neighbors. J. D. Payne's *Stranger Next Door: Immigration, Migration and Mission*[48] introduces the phenomenon of peoples' migrations to Western nations and explores how the global church should respond in light of the mission of God.

Daniel Groody and Stephen Bevans are two of the leading Catholic missiologists on diaspora and migration. *Promised Land, A Perilous Journey: Theological Perspectives on Migration*,[49] edited by Groody and Gioacchino Campese, is a compilation of essays on the issue of the US-Mexico border and migration. In his contribution to the book, 'Mission among Migrants, Mission of Migrants; and Mission of the Church', Bevans argues that 'strangers' in our midst actually contribute to transformation of the body of Christ while Christians strive to see the 'face of God' in the 'faces of migrants'.[50]

---

[44] Sam George and T.V. Thomas (eds), *Malalayi Diaspora: From Kerala to the Ends of the World* (New Delhi: Serials Publications, 2013).

[45] Chan-Sik Park and Noah Jung (eds), *21C New Nomad Era and Migrant Mission* (Seoul: Christianity and Industrial Society Research Institute, 2010).

[46] M. Daniel Carroll, *Christians at the Border: Immigration, the Church, and the Bible* (Grand Rapids, MI: Baker Academic, 2008).

[47] Matthew Soerens and Jenny Hwang, *Welcoming the Stranger: Justice, Compassion and Truth in Immigration Debate* (Downers Grove, IL: InterVarsity Press, 2009).

[48] J.D. Payne, *Stranger Next Door: Immigration, Migration and Mission* (Downers Grove, IL: InterVarsity Press, 2012).

[49] Daniel Groody and Gioachhino Campese (eds), *Promised Land, A Perilous Journey: Theological Perspectives on Migration* (Notre Dame, IN: University of Notre Dame Press, 2008).

[50] Stephen Bevans, 'Mission among Migrants, Mission of Migrants: and Mission of the Church', in Daniel Groody and Gioachhino Campese (eds) *Promised Land, A Perilous Journey: Theological Perspectives on Migration*, 90-94. Also, The

In summary, the reality of the dispersion of individuals, families, and people groups on every corner of the globe is an irreversible phenomenon. It is our hope that this volume, *Global Diasporas and Mission,* will encourage the whole church to decisively engage the strategic frontier for world evangelization caused by the movements of people through the centuries. Migration flows around the globe will continue to change the landscape of world missions in dramatic ways. As more people move into cities, new urban centers will continue to arise to accommodate the influx of new population. Evangelicals believe that waves of both immigration and migration triggered by diverse factors, reasons, and circumstances will create new opportunities for gospel advancement. In the midst of all these population shifts, people on the move can be potential *beneficiaries* of grace as *objects of missions*. Likewise, people in dispersion can serve as *channels* of grace as they come to realize their roles as *partners of missions*. Moreover, people in diasporic environments can act as active *agents of missions*, striving to reach their host nations and cities beyond their own ethnolinguistic perimeters.[51] Population shifts facilitate the mission of God and help execute the mission of God's covenant people. Whenever people move, the cause of the gospel advances.

Vatican's Pontifical Council for the Pastoral Care of Migrants and Itinerant People has resources at www.vatican.va/roman_curia/pontifical_ councils/migrants/ index.htm.

[51] This thrust echoes the North America Diaspora Educators' Forum (Global Diaspora Network) document known as The Chicago Resolutions (September 2012), calling 'upon the whole church to engage peoples on the move as *recipients* of grace, *participants* in mission, and *catalysts* to bring the whole gospel to both North American communities and the whole world'.

PART ONE
HISTORICAL AND BIBLICAL PERSPECTIVES

Mission and Migration: The Diaspora Factor in Christian History[1]

Andrew F. Walls

Migration as a Biblical Motif

The first recorded migration, according to the book of Genesis, took Adam and Eve out of Paradise. Genesis is all about archetypes, archetypes basic to the human condition. Migration seems to be basic to the human condition, for it has been repeated endlessly in human history, and has often been determinative in its effects on the life of peoples. But the expulsion from Eden (Gen. 3:23) is not the only migration described in the Genesis narrative, for it moves on swiftly to the wanderings of Cain (Gen. 4:12-16), and soon after that to the mass diffusion of peoples from Babel (Gen. 11:8-9), and thereafter to the saga of Abraham's migration from Mesopotamia (Gen. 12:1-9). In this last instance, we meet characteristic accompaniments of migration, such as the disputes over limited grazing land which lead to a division in Abraham's clan, so that Lot goes his own way (Gen. 13:5-12). Further migrations follow. A family dispute over inheritance causes Jacob to flee back to the old country (Gen. 27), and then to return to the new one (Gen. 31). The sons of Jacob migrate to Egypt – Joseph by *force majeure* (Gen. 38:12-36), the others by economic necessity (Gen. 47). The first book of the Bible might almost as readily have been called 'Migrations' as Genesis.

The great theme of the second book, Exodus, is the migration that created Israel by taking the twelve tribes out of Egypt and on the way to a land of their own. The history that follows describes how divine judgment brought upon Israel successive and forced migrations to Assyria (2 Kings 17:5-23) and Babylon (2 Kings 25), and how divine mercy brought successive re-migrations to the homeland (Ezra and Nehemiah).

If we take all the stories together, we have examples of almost every known form of migration, voluntary and involuntary. There are fugitives (Jacob), transported slaves (Joseph), famine victims (Joseph's brothers), migrant workers, even one with an unresolved claim for residence (Ruth), refugees, traders, invaders, prisoners of war, deportees, and returnees. The categories interweave: Jacob's sons came to Egypt as economic migrants, and they and their descendants became in turn prosperous settlers, slaves,

---

[1] This chapter has been edited and revised from a previously published article: Andrew F. Walls, 'Mission and Migration: The Diaspora Factor in Christian History', *Journal of African Christian Thought* 5.2 (2002), 3-11. Reprinted with permission.

migrants again, and settlers again. The stories highlight how migrations determine the future: the Babel story depicts migration as the source of language differentiation and the prophets attribute the movements, and thus the destinies, of the nations to the actions of Yahweh. It is he who brought Syrians and Philistines from their ancestral homes to places from which they could harass Israel.

Migration often stands for dispossession, loss of patrimony, or habitat. Adam loses Eden; Cain loses the security of the group. Israel loses the land, kingdom, and temple. In all these cases, migration is *punitive*, the result of wrongdoing, leading to dislocation and deprivation.

But there is another style of migration that is *redemptive* rather than punitive. Abraham is not expelled from his Mesopotamian city: he is divinely called out of it, with the promise of another land for his descendants. All he actually receives himself is a burial plot for his wife, and he carefully pays for that, though his Hittite neighbors are willing to give it to him. The settled city dweller becomes a nomadic pastoralist – in other words, a perennial migrant. It is as a nomadic pastoralist that he experiences those divine encounters that become the basis of Israel's religion. Maybe he could never have heard the voice of the God of heaven so clearly in Ur or in Haran; the noisy presence of the gods of the land would have obtruded too much. Once settled in the promised land as regular cultivators or city dwellers, Abraham's descendants readily make terms with the gods of the land, the Baalim, the territorial spirits.

In the beginning, it was to the nomads, the permanent migrants, that God revealed himself.[2] Abraham, the nomadic pastoralist with a promise of land he never settles in, is the archetype of redemptive migration. Centuries later, settled cultivators in Canaan acknowledged, as they made their harvest offerings, that their father was a wandering Aramean (Deut. 26:5), while the prophets pointed to the nomadic period as the happiest era of Israel's history (Hos. 2:14-15).

And in the New Testament it is still Abraham, the perennial migrant, who becomes the exemplar of the Christian faith and the pointer to Christian identity (Rom. 4). In the Epistle to the Hebrews, Abraham heads the list of those who died in faith without attaining the well-founded city prepared for them (Heb. 11:8-10). Christians in that letter are described in terms applicable to migrant workers, seeking that better future that migrants typically desire for their children. Other New Testament writers use the figure of the diaspora, that institutionalized migration whereby so many Jews lived outside the promised land, to portray normal Christian experience in the world (Phil. 3:20). One even describes Christians as 'refugees' (I Pet. 1:1; 2:11, GNB).

---

[2] Historians of religion, from Wilhelm Schmidt and the Anthropos School to Ake Hultkrantz and the ecological interpreters, have commented on the place of the God of heaven in the religions of hunter-gatherers and nomadic pastoralists.

In the biblical record, there is the dual character of migration. There is a paradigm of migration for which we may adopt the description 'Adamic' as convenient shorthand. Adamic migration means disaster, deprivation and loss. But there is another model, which we may call 'Abrahamic', where migration stands for escape to a superlatively better future. The two models overlap, of course, because within the divine economy, disaster itself may have a redemptive purpose. Both models represent the significance of migration for the migrant. For the host community to which migrants go, migration may represent blessing or bane, depending on the community's own numbers and social cohesion, and the numbers and activity of those who come to its area.

Migrants may bring with them the memory of their ancestors (Israel never forgot Abraham, Isaac, and Jacob), and maintain a strong sense of historic identity. But, typically, the connection with localized divinities, the gods of the land, is loosened. And in Abrahamic migration, the promised better future is linked with the knowledge of God. Again we recall that New Testament writers saw the nomadic herdsman or the migrant worker as a fair indicator of the position of Christians in the world.

Migration and Mission

Since migration stands for both disaster and high promise, it is not surprising that there is not a single clear answer to the question whether it favors or hinders Christian mission. It is easy enough to point to historical situations where migration forwarded the spread of the faith. It is clear, for instance, that the earliest spread of the faith beyond Jewish Palestine owed much to prior Jewish migration across the Mediterranean world, as well as into Mesopotamia and beyond. The Jewish communities of the diaspora provided the networks by which the message about Jesus spread. The book of Acts shows how the Antiochene missionaries, Barnabas and Paul, regularly began their mission activity in the synagogues or other Jewish communal places, which often had a fringe of interested Gentiles (Acts 13:14-41; 14:1-7). It is clear from the same source that such Gentiles, who had already been attracted to the worship of the God of Israel by means of diaspora Judaism, were particularly fertile soil for the early Christian preaching – more fertile, indeed, than diaspora Jews themselves. There are signs that something similar happened with the large Jewish communities of the Euphrates Valley, where Christian preaching spread eastward, and in Egypt, where it spread southward. First-century Christianity in its fullness was rooted in the great Jewish migration out of Palestine.

However, it would be equally easy to produce examples where migration inhibited or reversed Christian expansion. It would be difficult to determine whether the overflowing boiling pot of migration among the peoples of the north and west in the period of the conversion of Europe from the fourth century onwards did more to help or to hinder the process of conversion.

There are dramatic examples of migration leading pagan peoples to the faith. The Franks who invaded the region of Tours, for instance, came to acknowledge the superior power of the God of their Romanized Celtic subjects. But for every such example, one could recognize another where migration crushed, overwhelmed, or expelled a well-established Christian community. Teutonic pagan peoples, newly arrived in Britain, often brought the eclipse of a pre-existing Celtic Christianity. Their conversion, in turn, produced Christian settlements which were themselves devastated by the last wave of raiders from Scandinavia. That it took so many centuries for Europe to become Christian was due, at least in part, to the repeated need for re-evangelization of new migrants in areas that had already undergone a process of conversion. Migration both furthered the conversion of Europe and obstructed that conversion. Migration determined the future in both directions. The complex interaction of the migration patterns of the peoples beyond the old Roman frontiers who came to make up the population of Europe, together with that other migration that brought the Arabs with their new faith out of Arabia, form the grid on which centuries of Christian history were worked out.

The history of Christianity within the Roman Empire clearly shows the importance of migrant communities who retained ties to their home locality, while traveling from one part of the empire to another, for trade, or work, or some other reason. Sometimes the reason was persecution. For many years, believers in Jesus, centered in Jerusalem, were eager to declare the good news of the Messiahship of Jesus to the whole of Israel, but made little effort to share it with anyone else, and then only under special circumstances. They themselves were Jewish by birth and inheritance, and the good news for them was the coming of the Savior of Israel. They had not changed their religion by responding to the gospel; the gospel had enabled them to understand more thoroughly now the religion they had always believed in. Everything about Jesus made sense in Jewish terms. The Cornelius incident (Acts 10-11) opened up for Peter and others some new ideas, but there is nothing to suggest that it led to a change of mission policy. Only persecution did that. It was the migration of Jerusalem Christians following the attack on Stephen, that brought cross-cultural mission into being (Acts 8:1-4), first to the people of Samaria, then to the Ethiopian eunuch, and eventually, with momentous consequences, to Greek-speaking pagans at Antioch.

Even so, it was only a section of the Jerusalem migrants who followed this practice. Most, at least at first, seem to have followed the regular church policy of proclaiming Jesus as the Messiah in the diaspora Jewish communities to which they had fled (Acts 11:19- 20). The step of sharing Messiah Jesus with those outside Israel was so unusual that the Jerusalem church sent inspectors to examine what had happened at Samaria and Antioch. The church was transformed, not only in its ethnic composition and its attitude to sharing the gospel, but also in the way it understood and presented that gospel, a way that took seriously the mission of Christ to save the nations, not only the nation of Israel. The mission to the wider world began with Antioch, rather than Jerusalem, as the prime sending church. All this arose from a migration forced by persecution of a group of believers who realized that the Messiah of Israel, in whom all the nations would be blessed, also had something to say to the Greek pagans who had now become their neighbors.

It was not the last time that persecution-driven migration spread the gospel. Recurrent Roman state persecution of Christians produced recurrent small-scale migrations that brought the Christian faith to peoples who had not known it before. There is the instance of Dionysius, Bishop of Alexandria in the middle of the third century, who was exiled from his city and sent to a remote oasis, of which he had scarcely heard before. At first, he was distressed by being parted from his people; but in fact, he was soon busy, and the experience turned out to be an evangelistic and pastoral opportunity.

There is a wider significance in this story of Dionysius. Technically, all other Egyptian bishops were suffragans of the Bishop of Alexandria. However, a cultural fissure ran through the Egyptian church. Alexandria, a huge urban center, belonged to the Greek world and looked to the Mediterranean. But much of Egyptian Christianity was rural, Coptic-speaking, coping every day with the realities of African village life, and looking to the Nile and to the desert. For centuries, this culturally and linguistically diverse church held together. Such incidents as the exile of Dionysius, which drove a metropolitan church leader into a rural backwater where he had to preach to peasant cultivators, use their language and accept village hospitality, can only have strengthened the bonds. Significantly, under the Christian empire, when pagan state persecution was a thing of the past, the Egyptian church broke apart. Official pressure for ecclesiastical and doctrinal conformity simply hardened diversity into division.

We also get illustrations also of how the voluntary migration that was such a feature of the Roman Empire affected the patterns of church life. The major target of intra-Roman Empire migration was, of course, Rome itself. It is clear that the early Roman church included diverse communities, principally Greek-speaking, from different parts of the empire. The second-century fracas over the date of Easter shows some of the effect of this. Victor, a Latin-speaking migrant from Africa, the first bishop of Rome we know of who wrote in Latin, insists on the 'Western' date for celebrating Easter, and finds himself deeply embroiled with the Ephesian and other Asian churches, who insist that the Apostle John, who lived long in their area, had always celebrated the resurrection on 'their' date.

The issue has been obscured by later and irrelevant controversies about the primacy of the Roman Church. We may doubt whether Victor was greatly worried about the date that Christians celebrated Easter in Ephesus. His concern, as leader of a church consisting of diverse ethnic communities, was that Christians in Rome should share the main event of the church year on the same date. Different congregations with roots in different parts of the empire were insisting on retaining the traditions of their home localities. Moreover, they maintained the networks of communication with their places of origin. This explains the vigorous intervention on their behalf by the church authorities of places far away. Victor is aware of the strains migrant solidarity could place on the unity of a multi-centric church. One can visualize also how these migration-based communities would have acted as evangelistic and support agencies for their compatriots, and especially new migrants, in the capital.

We perhaps catch a glimpse of another migration-based Christian community of the second century in the letter of the churches of Lyon and Vienne in the Rhone Valley, describing their appalling sufferings. The letter is written in Greek, the names of the Christians mentioned are Greek, and the letter is addressed to 'the brethren in Asia and Phrygia'. It would appear that the group belonged to an Asian and Phrygian migration to the area. Is the mob fury that seems to have preceded the official action of the authorities, an indication of local dislike of migrant traders who were also a religious and cultural minority?

The migrations most feared within the Roman Empire were those of the peoples living on or beyond the imperial frontiers, the peoples whom the Romans called 'barbarians'. They were land-hungry, turbulent, and restive, and were themselves frequently under pressure from other migrant peoples, as the great population cauldron in Central Asia bubbled over. Christians shared the fears of barbarian migration. When Tertullian explains that Christians are not disloyal because they pray for the emperor, the security of the frontiers and the delay of the End, it is clear that he identifies the anticipated barbarian invasion with the Great Tribulation. Augustine, living to see the Vandals at the gates of his city, would have sympathized.

So would the people of Pontus who were at the receiving end of raids from the Eastern Goths in the third century. One such raid took Christians as slaves to Gothic lands on the Black Sea coast and led to an important accession to the Christian faith. The Pontic church in exile had an impact on the Gothic community who had taken them as captives. In the following century, Wulfila, probably of mixed race, grew up speaking Gothic and became an outstanding evangelist and Bible translator – the Scriptures are the sole known Gothic literature – and leader of a Gothic church. In later years, Wulfila led a Gothic migration of his people from a war zone across the frontier: a new Christian nation arising from a small-scale and quite involuntary migration.

Wulfila's Goths ultimately moved under the pressure of other peoples behind them. European migration frequently followed this pattern, and the imperial frontiers bent, buckled and sometimes collapsed under the pressure. The Romans left Britain, for instance, at a time when it had a small and somewhat scattered Christian population. Irish raiders could take slaves freely, and in one such raid, a young man called Patrick was captured and brought to Ireland. By his own account, his community had been Christian, though not zealously so; in Ireland, Patrick became fervent. Dreams, visions, and acts of power led to his escape and return to Britain; dreams, visions, and acts of power took him back to Ireland as its leading evangelist.

Enforced migration, escape from harsh persecution, capture of prisoners of war, seizure of slaves by raiding, and the peaceful quest for work or for trade seem to have played a part in the spread of the Christian gospel within the Roman Empire, and in the ways in which it was appropriated and became transformative there. And this happened against the background of a wider, more complex pattern of population movement that finally ensured the breakup of the Roman Empire and the permanent eclipse of its Western half. The fact that Christianity also spread so far beyond the Roman borders helped to ensure that Tertullian's vision was not fulfilled. The 'barbarian' destruction of the Western Roman Empire was not the Great Tribulation, though it was violent, bloody, and disruptive. It was the end of the earthly empire but not the end of the Christian church.

Migration and Early Christianity Outside the Roman Empire

The same factors operated in many areas outside the Roman Empire. The persecution is as notable in the church of the East as in the Roman Empire; and the Persian Empire, within which most Eastern Christians lived in the earliest centuries, never had a Constantine. In one 40-year period within the fourth century, no less than 16,000 Christians were put to death under Persian rule, and this happened at the time when conditions for Christians in the Roman Empire were becoming favorable. Severe persecution in what is now Iraq, the area of the strongest concentration of Christians in the East, led to migrations which strengthened the churches in Iran and in India, where Christians were fewer.

There were also forced movements of Christians by deportation, on a larger scale than ever happened in the Roman Empire. One Persian invasion of Roman territory had striking consequences. Large numbers of Christian captives were taken, including the Bishop of Antioch, and were set to work on the new imperial building schemes. They never went home. They established an effective church in the heart of the emperor's ambitious urban developments. It did not long remain a church of expatriates. In a short time, most of the names of people associated with it were no longer Greek but Syriac or Iranian. This migrant church had crossed the cultural frontier and even affected its overlords.

We hear also of remote rural populations turning to Christianity because of what they had seen in the sufferings of Christian deportees being marched across their territory. And the slavery factor also enters the story of the church of the East. A section of the Hun people living in the Central

Asian region of Bactria bought Syriac-speaking Christian slaves from sources in the Persian Empire. They made such an impression that the whole Bactrian Hun community decided to become Christians and, in an ironic twist, applied to the Zoroastrian emperor for a bishop to lead and teach them. They might not be experienced in ecclesiastical matters, but they knew that the faith they desired to embrace had come from within the emperor's dominions.

Other forms of migration played their part. A trading diaspora brought Christian families from the heartlands of the church of the East, such as Mesopotamia, to a vast network of trade routes by land and sea. China silk was the great prize of the land route, the transit of which placed Christian families across the whole Asian land mass. The sea route placed Christian communities in India and in Sri Lanka, and a writer in 600 AD already thought it possible that at this date there were some in South East Asia, too. Both land and sea routes led to South Arabia, and to the Yemen in particular. In all these areas, the Christian trading diaspora brought an already organized church.

There was another form of migration characteristic of the church of the East – more characteristic, indeed, of that church than of the church of the Roman Empire. This was the missionary migration. It is important to recognize that the missionary is a form of migrant. The spirituality of the church of the East was designed to produce spiritual athletes. It produced a corps of devoted people able and willing to travel immense distances, and live under the harshest conditions. By the time of Catholicos Timothy, the end of the eighth and the beginning of the ninth centuries, there were organized churches throughout the former Persian dominions, into what is now Afghanistan, and right along the Silk Road of Central Asia.

To a greater or lesser extent, the faith was present in the majority of the nomadic Turkic peoples surrounding the Chinese empire, and it had been preached in China itself for more than a century and a half. In South India, there was a substantial church that could already be called ancient, and there was a church structure established in Tibet. All this came from the dual migration of traders and missionaries, and the two migrations intersected. It is surely no accident that the T'ang Emperor of China, wishing to open relations with the lands to the west of his expanding territories, in 635 AD welcomed both the representatives of what he called the 'Shining Syrian religion' and a prince from the kingdom of Khotan. Developing good foreign relations meant taking seriously both the commerce and the religions of his neighbors.

We have already noted that migration has often been a crucial factor both in Christian advance and in Christian decline. Migration took the church of the East to its greatest extent; migration also brought it near to destruction. This is not the place to consider the complex movements of population among the nomadic peoples that made the Mongols into a great nation, or the formation and trajectory of the Horde, or the presence of

Christians within it (indeed, within the very family of Genghis Khan); or how Mongol rule gave old Russian Christianity a breathing space to recover after near-disaster; or the period when Western Christendom pondered whether the Mongols were a possible ally against the Muslims or a still more dangerous foe. It suffices to say that the eventual decision of the principal body of the Mongols to embrace Islam remains a turning point in the history of religion, and in the decline of the older Asian Christianity. Small-scale migration had been the engine that drove the church of the East. Large-scale migration brought it into eclipse.

South Arabian migration brought about one of Ethiopia's distinctive features: the Ethiopic writing system, introduced into Africa long before Christian times, but becoming a crucial feature of African Christian expansion after the kingdom of Aksum became Christian in the fourth century. The story that Rufinus tells of how that came about offers another example of involuntary migration aiding Christian mission. Frumentius and Aedesius, the key figures in his account of the evangelization of Aksum, had no intention of going there when circumstances made them both royal slaves and evangelists of the nation.

Migration continued to be vital to the spread of Christianity as Ethiopia developed. Christian migrants moved from the region of Tigre, where Aksum is situated, on to the high plateau of Ethiopia. They settled, as fellow tillers of the soil, among people following the ways of traditional Africa. As Christians, they were vastly outnumbered. There was nothing to be gained by antagonizing their neighbors unnecessarily. In any case, the territorial spirits, the gods of the land, seemed to be powerful. The Christian migrants, far from converting their hosts, seemed set to assimilate to their ways, and their Christianity to be absorbed into the traditional religious systems of the people of the land.

Then came the revival associated with such figures as Takla Haymanot, who often came from migrant families themselves (Takla Haymanot certainly did). They preached first to the immigrants, sharpening their Christian consciousness, as well as developing Christian prayer and devotion among them. From these 're-Christianized' families, they took young men and trained them in a spiritual athleticism not unlike that of the church of the East in the time of its glory. They transmitted scholarship as well as devotion: that special sort of eschatologically conditioned scholarship that is acquired by copying a gospel while sitting on a narrow ledge above a gaping precipice.

These young people became the spearhead of a movement that proclaimed the faith to the indigenous people of the land. They did this by demonstration: in Ethiopia the evangelists constantly confronted the territorial spirits, provoking them in power encounters that proved the gods of the land to be powerless before the God of heaven whom Christians worshipped. Takla Haymanot originally planted his Christian cells, the nucleus of the great monasteries of a later time, in the areas where Christian settlers were fewest, and led preaching tours from these centers. As the indigenous people responded, Christian worship was established, backed by the Christian scriptures and the peculiar writing system that had come with the migration from Tigre.

Migration and Western Christianity

Until some time in the second millennium, Europe was only one of the regions of the world where Christians were to be found in substantial numbers, and the West European tradition of Christianity was only one expression of a faith that was to be found from the Atlantic to East Asia, and from Siberia to East Africa. By 1500, however, the situation was different. European Christendom was still expanding: the Baltic lands had recently been brought forcibly within it, and still more significantly, the Muslims had been driven from Spain after six centuries of Islamic presence there. On the other hand, for a variety of reasons, most of the Christian communities elsewhere had gone into eclipse, and many had disappeared altogether. There were isolated communities, such as those in Ethiopia and South India, and there were other communities in states now under Muslim rule that were undergoing gradual but prolonged attrition. Otherwise, Christianity was now confined to the western end of the Eurasian land mass. And the form of Christianity now dominant was the product of several centuries of interaction with the languages and cultures of European peoples.

It is at this point that the great European migration began. It was an ocean-based migration that lasted for four and a half centuries, during which millions of people left Europe by sea for the worlds beyond, lands unknown or barely known to Europe in 1500. They were a diverse crowd: adventurers and destitute or unwanted people, religious and political refugees, younger sons frustrated by European inheritance laws, discharged soldiers, convicted felons, and solid people looking for a better life or a fairer society than Europe afforded.

The Americas were the first, and always the most favored, target area, but the temperate parts of Africa and the Pacific also received large numbers, with smaller numbers going to other parts of the world. Europeans sometimes even changed the habitations of non-Western peoples, populating previously uninhabited areas such as Mauritius, taking people from India and China and transplanting them in places as far away as Guyana, Trinidad, and Fiji, and, in the biggest transplantation of all, breaking off a huge portion of Africa and setting it down in the Americas.

Generally speaking, the migrants from Europe sought to maintain their ethnic and cultural identity. Interracial unions occurred, and in large numbers, but they were rarely regarded as ideal. The cultural norms most desired by those of European descent continued to be those that had originated in Europe. The European migrants also sought to establish political control of the areas to which they moved.[3] Where political control was not possible, they sought exemption from indigenous political structures.

By the early twentieth century, the migration process had produced a series of new nations, several of them vast in extent or population, or both. In most of these, what was left of the indigenous population was driven to the margins of a society controlled by descendants of the migrants. By the same period, huge maritime empires had fallen to Britain and France, a huge land-based one to Russia, and smaller acquisitions to other Western powers. Western economies were re-oriented to incorporate the human and material resources available to them in the non-Western world.

The engendered competition among the Western powers helped to destroy the world order they had established, and in the second half of the twentieth century, the maritime empires dissolved. This left two large nations to compete for hegemony. One of these, the USA, was as a nation essentially a product of migration; the other, the Soviet Union, took its shape from Russian migration across Asia.

When the great migration began, Europe was more Christian than it had ever been before, and Christianity more European than it had ever been before. Europe was 'Christendom', contiguous Christian territory notionally subject to the law of Christ, its population baptized, its laws forbidding blasphemy, idolatry, or heresy. Such a situation, reinforced by centuries of often violent contact with neighboring Muslim powers, led readily to the concept of crusade, where military action becomes the means to bring territory under the rule of Christ. The final restoration of southern Spain to Christian rule in the fifteenth century was both the most recent and the most successful of the crusades.

The natural instinct of Europeans at the beginning of the great migration was therefore to seek the extension of Christendom by bringing the lands now becoming known to them into the territorial complex where the rule of Christ was acknowledged, and blasphemy, heresy, and idolatry proscribed. The instrument to effect this was at hand, and had been successfully employed in the recent cleansing of Spain. The Spanish migration to the Americas was, in its religious aspect, the last crusade. The Spanish American territories were brought into Christendom, their indigenous populations baptized, the traditional worship proscribed. Mexico became New Spain, with the faith and laws of Old Spain.

But the experience of Spanish America could not be replicated in Asia, nor often in Africa. Conquest outside small, well-defined enclaves was usually beyond the power of the little companies of soldiers, traders, and priests that Portugal could supply. Nor did the existing religious systems – Muslim, Hindu, Buddhist – obligingly lie down and die. Only a minuscule

---

[3] Symbolically, at the very beginning of the movement, the Spanish destroyed the indigenous political systems of Mexico and Peru.

extension of Christendom could result from crusade in most of the areas to which the Portuguese were now migrating as the firstfruits of Europe.

But the economic and political advantages arising from continued involvement in Africa and Asia were palpable. Successive European powers – the Dutch still more than the Portuguese, and the British still more than the Dutch – settled for security and profitability. While not abandoning the rhetoric of the extension of Christendom, they decided on doing little or nothing directly about it. As a result, the political and economic interests of the powers of Christendom increasingly diverged from their religious professions. Perhaps colonialism was the first step to the secularization of Europe.

There was an important religious consequence. The power wielders in Christendom, once committed to the worldwide propagation of the Christian faith, now saw the lands beyond Europe in essentially economic and strategic terms. Radical Christians within Christendom, however, could not be satisfied with anything less than the proclamation of the gospel in these lands. They had therefore to find another way of achieving this, and so the missionary movement was born from the frustration of the crusading instinct. A new sort of migrant appeared, already foreshadowed in earlier centuries, not least in Ethiopia and the church of the East. The missionary was sent to persuade, to demonstrate, to offer – but could not compel. The missionary lived within the host society, sought to know its language and its customs, to find a place within it, and in some degree lived on terms set by it.

The relation of the missionary movement to the great migration is complex and much debated. Much of the material used to decide the matter is ambiguous. Outside Latin America and the small Portuguese enclaves, it was rare for the church settlements that had been worked out in sixteenth- and seventeenth-century Europe to be transported painlessly overseas. Colonial governments with tight budgets were happy to hand to missions most of the burdens of colonial education and health care. But they could inhibit or frustrate evangelistic activity, especially where Muslims were involved. Missionaries, children of Christendom themselves, often retained the Christendom ideal, even when it sat ill with their circumstances and the logic of what they were saying. They often felt that Western colonial governments failed to support them, or even actively obstructed their work. Where missionaries worked in the same territories as Western migrants, there were often intractable problems in combining migrant and indigenous Christians in a single functioning ecclesiastical structure without subordinating the interests of the indigenous people to those of the migrants.

Religious Effects of the Great Migration

The religious effects of the great migration were mixed. The most striking result has been a huge accession to the Christian faith among peoples in the non-Western world. The missionary movement, that semi-detached appendix to the great European migration, was a primary detonator of this movement, though other agencies, indigenous to the non-Western world, carried it forward. Some substantial segments of the accession to Christianity occurred without the presence of missionaries, or, as in China and Myanmar, after the missionary presence had ceased.

By the end of the twentieth century, Christians in Africa, Asia, Latin America, and the Pacific were significantly outnumbering those of the old Christendom and North America combined. Christianity, which in 1500 was apparently the European religion, was by 2000 progressively becoming a non-Western religion. The collapse of the imperial structures seems to have been largely irrelevant to the movement; if anything, the process accelerated after the empires declined.

The massive adhesion to the Christian faith already mentioned was furthered by a series of lesser migrations originating outside Europe. The most significant of these originated through that African migration within the great European migration mentioned earlier: that process whereby Europeans, to serve the labor needs of their own migration, broke off a huge piece of Africa to create Afro-America.[4] North American Black Protestantism produced migrations of the utmost significance for mission expansion. To take only the effect of demobilized soldiers from the black regiments of the British Army in the Revolutionary War: these began the evangelization of plantation slaves in Jamaica.[5] They also began the evangelization of the Black population in the Bahamas and furthered it in Trinidad. They contributed to a major revival in Nova Scotia and established in Sierra Leone the first Protestant church in tropical Africa. This church owed nothing to missionaries, because African congregations came from America with their own leaders, preachers and organization.

Afro-America continued to help determine the Christian story in Africa throughout the nineteenth century. The creation of Liberia, the place of Jamaicans in the establishment of inland missions in the Gold Coast, the initiative in the Presbytery of Jamaica that established the mission in Calabar, and the missionary recruits from Jamaica who sustained it when Western sources faltered, the Barbadian mission in the Rio Pongas, the consolidation of the Catholic church in Western Nigeria by Yoruba returnees from Brazil – these are only samples from a long list. The full story of Afro-American Christian initiatives in Africa has yet to be told.

---

[4] It is worth remembering that, for many years, Africans in the North American colonies outnumbered people of European descent.

[5] It was Africans from these regiments who brought the plantation churches into being, and they who invited the British missionaries.

There were internal migrations within Africa that had momentous consequences for mission. Chief among them was the involuntary movement of people to Sierra Leone from slave ships intercepted on the high seas after the trade in slaves had been declared illegal. In Sierra Leone, an active, literate African Christian community emerged among these people, who by successive involuntary migrations had been taken into slavery and out of it, loosening the bonds to the gods of the various lands from which they came. Sierra Leone, a tiny colony before 1896, when its present boundaries were largely fixed, probably produced more missionaries, ministerial and lay, per head of population than any other country in the world in the second half of the nineteenth century and the early years of the twentieth. Not all were of the stature of the greatest of them, Samuel Ajayi Crowther. But their total impact was crucial in the evangelization of West Africa. Sierra Leone in the nineteenth century was West Africa's missionary reservoir and its language laboratory. It was also important for the influence of its Christian migrants – the professionals, technicians, and traders spread out in the region were the first point of contact with the Christian faith for innumerable African communities.

The movements of Ganda Christians within East Africa tell another story, with the powerful symbolism of their great figure, Apolo Kivebulaya, who directed that he be buried, not as the tradition of his people had it, to face his natal home, but to face the direction of his uncompleted evangelistic work in Congo. The mines of South Africa and the Copperbelt, the causes of so many migrations in Southern and Central Africa, are also the source of many African Christian initiatives, and of new models of the church arising from African re-readings of Scripture.

Nor is Africa the only area where migration and mission have been closely intertwined. The story of Pacific Christianity is closely linked with the activity of Polynesian Christians, moving not only between islands of their region, but from Polynesia to Melanesia. And in the second half of the twentieth century, the migration from North Korea to South Korea during the Korean War clearly played a part in the remarkable Christian movement that has made Korea such a potent single addition to the forces of world mission. The recent work of Cindy Perry has shown how important a factor was the migration of Nepali to India and their service abroad in the Gurkha regiments in opening a closed land to the Christian message. The list could be expanded infinitely.

The least happy aspect of this accession to the Christian faith in the wake of the great migration has been the fate of the perennial migrants – hunter-gatherers, nomadic and semi-nomadic pastoralists, and especially those who were the original inhabitants of the lands newly settled by the migrants from Europe. Despite the fact that the perennial migrant is the New Testament symbol of the Christian life, despite the fact that the old church of the East was able to accommodate to the life of the nomads of

Central Asia,[6] there are few recorded modern examples of nomadic people who wholeheartedly responded to the gospel and remained nomadic. Mission goals and methods were usually geared to what early missionaries to the Native Americans often called 'a civil life', with regular hours and regular places for church and school. It was a regime incompatible with an Australian Aboriginal walkabout. Further, the great migration often created conditions that made the life of the perennial migrant difficult or impossible.

The great migration was the indirect cause of substantial Christian growth outside the West. It also produced renewal and expansion among the non-Christian religions. The British Raj in India established the climate that made Hinduism into a coherent, vigorous faith that could operate nationally in a modern scientific society. Equally, it established the climate that called Pakistan into being, and in Africa and Indonesia, colonial rule did more for the spread of Islam than all the jihads.

Finally, and most surprisingly of all, the period of the great migration and its aftermath saw the decline of Christianity in the West. We have already noted that by the end of the twentieth century, Christians in the non-Western world outnumbered Christians in the West. The reason lies not only in the great accession to the faith in the non-Western world, but also in the accelerating recession in the West, the largest recession from Christianity since the first rise of Islam. The recession was already in progress in the nineteenth century, but was not widely seen for what it was. Those migrating often shared in the recession: in Australia and New Zealand, for instance, the rate of de-Christianization has been faster than in the countries of origin of their populations.

The great exception was the USA – the scene of a religious development during the nineteenth century that one can identify as the greatest success of the missionary movement. The USA ended the nineteenth century a more Christian country by most measures than it had been at the century's beginning. As a result, the USA started its Christian decline from a much higher base than Europe did. Nevertheless, it seems to be exhibiting many of the signs that Europe showed when its own recession from the faith set in.

The New Migration

Perhaps we can date the end of the great European migration in the midtwentieth century, with the final dissolution of the Western empires. Over a couple of decades following the Second World War, Vasco da Gama sailed home. Europe, imperial dreams faded, became absorbed in intra-European constructions, or in defining relations with the two new superpowers.

---

[6] In at least one case, the bishop's 'cathedral' was his tent.

And then the empires struck back. First, Britain and France each found that they had acquired a substantial new population from their former or residual colonies as an inescapable legacy of the colonial past. Then other European nations found a steady flow of people from Turkish Kurdistan and other troubled areas drawn into the labor market of their expanding economies. If Germany coined the expression *Gastarbeiter* ('guest worker') to describe the status of such people, it was soon clear that these 'guests' would not readily return home.

Then North America, and the USA in particular, which had been the main target of the great European migration, began to receive numbers of migrants of a new kind. Some came through new international obligations (Korea, Vietnam), some from new specialist labor needs, and from the inescapable relationship with the rest of the Americas. Central and South America, the first focus of the great migration, brought newcomers by the thousand. What is more, this huge new population called into question the once-popular model of the melting pot of immigration. There was no immediate likelihood of the identities of these peoples melting, as those of European migrants of earlier times had done.

The great new fact of our time – and it has momentous consequences for mission – is that the great migration has now gone into reverse. There has been a massive movement, which all indications suggest will continue, from the non-Western to the Western world. There is much food for thought in the report on population compiled for the United Nations in 2001. It projects a rise in the world's population of 1.2% per year, an annual aggregate of 77 million people. Half that increase will come from six countries: India, China, Pakistan, Nigeria, Bangladesh, and Indonesia. The increase in population growth will be concentrated in the areas least able to sustain it, leading to irresistible pressures for migration. By 2050, the population of Africa would be three times that of Europe, even after allowing for the anticipated deaths of 300 million Africans through AIDS.

But the population of most developed countries looks set to fall: in highly industrialized Germany and Japan by 14% by 2050, in Italy by 25%, and in Russia and the Ukraine by anything up to 40%. In other words, the developed countries will need immigration if they are to sustain anything like their present level of economic activity. That will be true, above all, of the USA, which will be the prime target of the new migration, as it was of the old one. It will need a million new migrants a year to sustain itself, and will be one of the few developed countries in the world to increase its population, perhaps to 400 million, by 2050. The increase, the UN report indicates, will be due entirely to immigration.

Thus far goes the UN report, and I stake nothing on the precision of its predictions. But of the general accuracy of the analysis it points to, there seems to be ample evidence. The United Kingdom authorities try to placate public fears about floods of asylum seekers from Afghanistan and Iraq by announcing stronger controls; simultaneously, they scour the Philippines for nurses to maintain the health service. Control of immigration has suddenly become a major issue in European politics. Anti-immigration parties have entered the governments of several European countries, and are powerful political forces in some of the largest European nations. More importantly, they have frightened traditional political parties almost everywhere into making similar noises. The developed world is faced with a paradox: it *needs* immigrants, but does not *want* them. In a public forum where the presence of Christian voices can be less and less taken for granted, Western Christians may find themselves increasingly called to take stances that are unpopular.

The great European migration has left a strange legacy: a post-Christian West and a post-Western Christianity. Christianity was once the religion of confident technological advance and rising affluence, and sometimes saw these things as a mark of God's favor. Christianity now will increasingly be associated (mostly) with rather poor and very poor people, and with some of the poorest countries on earth. And people from the non-Western world will be the principal agents of Christian mission right across the world.

Even in the Western world, they will have a significant place: for it may be that, at least in some areas of the West, Christianity will be associated increasingly with immigrants. The religious aspect of the new reverse migration that first attracted attention was the new visibility of non-Christian religions – the Hindu temples appearing in or beside redundant churches, the statistics that showed that English Muslims outnumbered all English non-Anglican Protestants put together, the realization that arguments long used to justify Catholic and Anglican schools within the British state education system could now be used to justify Islamic schools there.

The importance of the Christian aspect of the new migration is only now being realized. Studies on African and Afro-Caribbean churches in Europe offer insights into their significance. It is clear that these churches are among the few expanding sectors of European Christianity. It is also clear that they are beginning to have an impact on the indigenous Western population, for some of whom, being untouched by traditional culture-Christianity, immigrants from Africa or Asia (and in Spain, from Latin America) provide the first contact with Christianity as a living faith.

The USA has more of this world Christian diaspora than any other country. Recent studies show that new African congregations are proliferating in New York, often across what was once Archie Bunker territory. Now, however, it is the African, Asian, and Hispanic presence that reveals the church in the heart of the city. Teaching in the USA in recent years, I could not but be impressed by the Asian-American students and by the potential contribution of their quality, industry and devotion to mainstream American Christianity. Equally obvious was their consciousness of their Asian roots and their concern for the study of Asian Christian history and Asian religions. In the USA, it is also possible to find congregations and networks of Somali Christians, a very hard task in Somalia.

Thus the immigration legislation of the 1960s has brought about the most important feature of American religious life today. The fact that the USA, more than in any other country of the world, is, and is likely to remain, the principal target of the new migration, and thus of the new Christian diaspora. The rich diversity of that diaspora (alas, all too often unknown in the national traditional, monocultural congregations) has the capacity to advance Christian mission in both the Western and the non-Western worlds. It also opens the dazzling possibility that the fullness of the stature of Christ that, according to the Epistle to the Ephesians, is reached as people of diverse ethnicities and cultures are united in the body of Christ, could be realized in our time.

The new diaspora differs from the great European migration in significant respects. In the old migration, ties with the original homeland faded, and were often broken completely. The new diaspora, like that of the second century, seems to be keeping its ties with its places of origin, and maintaining networks across the world. Everyone in Freetown or Lagos seems to have a relative in London or Chicago. And the economies of African states gain more from the remittances of their former citizens living in the West than they do from Western development aid.

Such factors tie together the issues of mission in the Western and non-Western worlds. They reveal something of the possible networks by which that mission may be carried out as Christians of African, Asian, and Latin American origin and domicile take on the leadership in world mission. The context of that mission includes both the legacies from the great European migration and the factor of the new migration, and especially that of the new Christian diaspora. Their combination presents us with a situation in which we may incarnate the body of Christ in a wholly new way, or fracture it by self-seeking or neglect.

Consulted Bibliography

Brown, Peter. *Augustine of Hippo: A Biography*. London: Faber, 1967.

———. *Authority and the Sacred: Aspects of the Christianization of the Roman World.* New York: Cambridge University Press, 1995.

Davidson, Allan K. *Selwyn's Legacy: The College of St John the Evangelist, Te Waimate and Auckland, 1843-1992: A History*. Auckland: The College, 1993.

Fletcher, Richard A. *The Barbarian Conversion: from Paganism to Christianity 374-1386 AD*. New York: H. Holt and Co., 1997.

Foster, John. *The Church of the T'ang Dynasty*. London, Society for Promoting Christian Knowledge, 1939.

Frend, W.H.C. *Martyrdom and Persecution in the Early Church*. Oxford: Blackwell, 1965.

Gerloff, Roswith. *A Plea for British Black Theologies: The Black Church Movement in Britain*. 2 vols. Frankfurt: Peter Lang, 1992.

Gillman, Ian and H.J. Klimkeit. *Christians in Asia before 1500*. Ann Arbor: University of Michigan Press, 1999.

Hastings, Adrian. *The Church in Africa 1450-1950*. Oxford: Clarendon Press, 1994.

Hitti, P.K. *History of the Arabs*. New York: St. Martin's Press, 1968.

Luck, Anne. *African Saint: The Story of Apolo Kivebulaya*. London: SCM Press, 1963.

Moffett, Samuel H. *History of Christianity in Asia*. Vol 1. San Francisco: HarperSanFrancisco, 1992.

Patrick. *The Works of St Patrick*. Trans. Ludwig Bieler. Westminster, MD: Newman Press, 1953.

Perry, Cindy L. *Nepali around the World: Emphasizing Nepali Christians of the Himalayas*. Kathmandu: Etka Books, 1997.

Pirouet, Louise. *Black Evangelists: The Spread of Christianity in Uganda*. London: Collings, 1978.

Sanneh, Lamin. *Abolitionists Abroad: American Blacks and the Making of Modern West Africa*. Cambridge, MA: Harvard University Press, 1999.

———. *West African Christianity*. Maryknoll, NY: Orbis Books, 1983.

Scott, C.A.A. *Ulfllas: Apostle of the Goths*. Cambridge: Macmillan and Bowes, 1885.

Tamrat, Taddesse. *Church and State in Ethiopia*. Oxford: Clarendon Press, 1972.

Ter Haar, Gerrie. *African Christians in Europe*. Nairobi, Kenya: Acton Publishers, 2001.

Ter Haar, Gerrie (ed). *Strangers and Sojourners: Religious Communities in the Diaspora*. Leuven: Peeters, 1998.

Walls, Andrew F. *The Cross-cultural Process in Christian History*. Maryknoll, NY: Orbis Books, 2002.

———. *The Missionary Movement in Christian History*. Maryknoll, NY: Orbis Books, 1996.

Global Christianity and Global Diasporas

Todd M. Johnson and Gina A. Zurlo

Migration has always been integral to the global human experience.[1] Yet, there is little doubt that increased movement of peoples worldwide was a distinguishing characteristic of the twentieth century.[2] Both technology and transportation developed during this century, affording individuals more than just rudimentary knowledge about places all over the world and allowing them personal access to distant lands with relative ease.

The movement of people has a direct impact on the religious composition of the lands in which they settle. In some cases, migrants bring an entirely new religion into a country or region; in other cases, they import a new form of an existing religion. Such movement creates what can be called 'religionists in diaspora' or 'religious diasporas'.[3] Although some have had a lengthy history, some religious diasporas (such as the increasing growing Muslim populations in western Europe) have grown around the

---

[1] A preliminary version of this chapter was first published as Todd M. Johnson and Gina A. Bellofatto, 'Immigration, Religious Diasporas, and Religious Diversity: A Global Survey', *Mission Studies* 29 (2012), 1–20, and is reprinted with permission from Koninklijke Brill NV. Its findings were also presented as a case study in Todd M. Johnson and Brian J. Grim, *The World's Religions in Figures: An Introduction to International Religious Demography* (Oxford: Wiley-Blackwell, 2013).

[2] The United Nations estimates that the number of international migrants is now over 200 million, having doubled in the past twenty-five years, with twenty-five million added in the first five years of the twenty-first century. See United Nations, 'Report to the Secretary-General, International Migration and Development, UN General Assembly, 60th Session', *UN Doc. A/60/871*, 18 May 2006 (New York: United Nations, 2006).

[3] Robin Cohen, *Global Diasporas: An Introduction* (Seattle: University of Washington Press, 1997), 26. Cohen identifies nine common features of a diaspora which have particular relevance to this study on religious diasporas: (1) dispersal from an original homeland, often traumatically, to two or more foreign regions, (2) alternatively, the expansion from a homeland in search of work, in pursuit of trade or to further colonial ambitions, (3) a collective memory and myth about the homeland, including its location, history, and achievements, (4) an idealization of the putative ancestral home and a collective commitment to its maintenance, restoration, safety, and prosperity, even to its creation, (5) the development of a return movement that gains collective approbation, (6) a strong ethnic group consciousness sustained over a long time and based on a sense of distinctiveness, a common history, and the belief in a common fate, (7) a troubled relationship with host societies, suggesting a lack of acceptance at the least or the possibility that another calamity might befall the group, (8) a sense of empathy and solidarity with co-ethnic members in other countries of settlement, and (9) the possibility of a distinctive creative, enriching life in host countries with a tolerance for pluralism.

world in recent decades. In light of current migration trends, religious diasporas will likely attract attention well into the twenty-first century. Diasporas also have an impact on religious diversity by introducing variety into the religious demographics of countries and regions.

In order to attempt a quantitative study of religious diasporas and religious diversity, three things need to be in place: (1) a taxonomy of the world's peoples, (2) a taxonomy of the world's religions, and (3) a data collection mechanism by which information related to peoples and religions can be assessed. Taxonomies of the world's peoples and religions exist, and vast efforts are put into the collection of statistics relating to religions, languages, and peoples in today's world.[4] Utilizing the taxonomies of religions and peoples from the *World Christian Database* (*WCD*) and *World Religion Database* (*WRD*), a preliminary examination of religious diasporas shows 859 million people (12.5% of the world's population) from 327 peoples in diasporas around the world. Quantitative analysis of migration in the context of demography – births, deaths, conversions in, conversions out, immigration, and emigration – provides a comprehensive view of changes in religious diasporas. The future of international relations will be greatly impacted by how diasporas are treated and understood by their host countries.

This chapter overviews various aspects of religious diasporas, including the host countries of international migrants and their religious affiliations. Following is a brief discussion of some implications of migration and diasporas on Christian mission.

Religious Freedom

The starting point in any analysis of religious adherence is the United Nations' 1948 *Universal Declaration of Human Rights*, Article 18: 'Everyone has the right to freedom of thought, conscience and religion; this right includes freedom to change his religion or belief, and freedom, either alone or in community with others and in public or private, to manifest his religion or belief in teaching, practice, worship and observance'.[5] Since its

---

[4] The Center for the Study of Global Christianity at Gordon-Conwell Theological Seminary (South Hamilton, Massachusetts) collates and analyzes data on church membership and evangelistic activities collected around the world by Christian denominations, as well as demographics on all the world's religions and their various traditions. Combining these with other relevant data, the center provides information on global Christianity and religion available to various constituents (religious and otherwise) for research and strategic planning. These data are updated quarterly in Todd M. Johnson (ed), *World Christian Database* (Leiden, Netherlands: Brill, 2007) and Todd M. Johnson and Brian J. Grim (eds), *World Religion Database* (Leiden, Netherlands: Brill, 2008).

[5] The full text of the UN resolution can be found in Paul M. Taylor, *Freedom of Religion: UN and European Human Rights Law and Practice* (Cambridge:

promulgation, this group of phrases has been incorporated into the state constitutions of a large number of countries, with many of them instructing their census personnel to observe this principle. If a person claims to be a Christian, Muslim, Hindu, Buddhist, Sikh, Jew, or affiliated with any other religious group, then no one has a right to say that he or she is not.[6]

The declaration has since been distributed in more than 330 languages and serves as the basis for numerous other international human rights declarations, including the 1981 *Declaration on the Elimination of All Forms of Intolerance and of Discrimination Based on Religion or Belief.*[7] Such public declaration or profession must be taken seriously to ensure a proper functioning of society on multiple levels, not simply in the sphere of religion. Despite the critical importance of religious freedom, however, until 2009 there was no quantitative study that extensively reviewed the sources reporting on how governmental and other actors infringe on the practice of religion worldwide.[8]

Data Sources

The collection of data on religion is largely uncoordinated between scholars and uneven across religious traditions, although a wealth of information is available for religious statistical analysis. Starting from the third essential item listed above (a data collection mechanism allowing for the updating of information related to peoples and religions), there are two major sources of information on religious diasporas: data collected by religious communities and censuses taken by governments.

Most religious communities keep some type of record of their members, ranging from simple lists to elaborate membership reports. The most detailed data collection and analysis are undertaken each year by some

---

Cambridge University Press, 2005), 368–72.

[6] An interesting development in a postmodern context is the need to introduce the category 'doubly-counted' or 'doubly-professing', becoming popularly known as 'multiple religious belonging'. See Peter Phan, *Being Religious Interreligiously: Asian Perspectives on Interreligious Dialogue* (Maryknoll, NY: Orbis Books, 2004); Catherine Cornille, *Many Mansions? Multiple Religious Belonging and Christian Identity* (Maryknoll, NY: Orbis Books, 2002); and Paul F. Knitter, *Without Buddha I Could Not be a Christian* (Oxford: OneWorld Publications, 2009).

[7] For more information, see Brian J. Grim and Roger Finke, 'Religious Persecution in Cross-National Context: Clashing Civilizations or Regulated Economies?', *American Sociological Review* 72.4 (2007), 633–58; Brian J. Grim and Roger Finke, *The Price of Freedom Denied: Religious Persecution and Violence in the 21st Century* (New York: Cambridge University Press, 2011).

[8] See the Pew Research Center's Forum on Religion and Public Life, *Global Restrictions on Religion*, 16 December 2009, www.pewresearch.org/pubs/1443/global-restrictions-on-religion; and *Rising Restrictions on Religion*, 9 August 2011, www.pewforum.org/Government/Rising-Restrictions-on-Religion.aspx.

41,000 Christian denominations and their 3.6 million constituent churches and congregations of believers. The latter invest over 1.1 billion USD annually for a massive, decentralized, and largely uncoordinated global census of Christians.[9]

This dispersed collection of data provides a year-by-year snapshot of the progress or decline of Christianity's diverse movements, offering an enormous body of data from which researchers can track trends and make projections.[10] In a similar way, other religious communities also record members or adherents.

At the same time, many of the world's governments collect information on religious populations. In the twentieth century, approximately half of the world's countries asked a question related to religion in their official national population censuses.[11] In addition, most censuses include data on languages spoken in the home, country of origin, and ethnic background, providing further clues on the religious profile in a given country. National censuses are the best starting point for the identification of religious adherents because they generally cover the entire population. Governments typically take major population censuses around the end of every decade, and then take three to five years to publish the complete data. Obtaining these data every ten years enables the calculation of relatively accurate growth rates, which includes targeting the large-scale movement of religious and ethnic communities.

Sometimes, the results from these two methods (government censuses and data collection by religious entities) can be strikingly different. In Egypt, for example, where the vast majority of the population is Muslim, elaborate government censuses taken every ten years for the last 100 years indicate that some 6% of the population declare themselves or profess to be

---

[9] In sum, they send out around ten million questionnaires in 3,000 different languages, covering 180 major religious subjects and reporting on 2,000 socio-religious variables.

[10] The Roman Catholic Church performs the most extensive of these inquiries, wherein each year all Roman Catholic bishops are required to answer a twenty-one-page schedule in Latin and one other culturally relevant language asking 140 statistical questions concerning their work in the previous twelve months. The results are published every January in *Annuario Pontificio* (Citta del Vaticano: Tipografia Poliglotta Vaticana).

[11] This number gradually declined during the second half of the twentieth century, as developed countries increasingly dropped questions on religion as either too controverisal or expensive (in many countries each census costs over one million USD per question). As a result, some countries that historically included a religion question have not included the question in their censuses since 1990. This trend appears to be reversing, however. For example, Britain, which produced the world's first national census of religious affiliation (the Compton Census in 1676) – and later a religion question in the national census of 1851 (though none thereafter) – reintroduced the question in their 2000 census as the best way to receive reliable data on non-Christian minorities.

Christians. However, church censuses reveal the number of individuals affiliated to churches to be as high as 15% of the population. The reason for the discrepancy appears to be that due to Muslim pressure on the Christian minority, many Christians are recorded in government censuses by enumerators, or record themselves, as Muslims. Both of these sources – religious bodies and governments – must be employed together to understand fully the entire context of religious diasporas.[12]

Taxonomies of Religions and Peoples

To enumerate religious diasporas, one must first build two taxonomies, one for religions and one for peoples. The *WCD* and *WRD* include 18 standard categories for religion.[13] These categories can be applied directly to any people in the world. For example, Mandarin-speaking Han Chinese in China, numbering 841 million in 2010, are estimated to be 49% non-religious (agnostic and atheist), 22% Chinese folk-religionist, 18% Buddhist, and 10% Christian.[14]

A 'peoples' taxonomy must take into account both ethnicity and language. The approach taken in 'Ethnosphere' in Part 8 of the *World Christian Encyclopedia* was to match 432 ethnic codes with 13,500 different language codes to produce 12,600 distinct ethnolinguistic peoples.[15] Not all combinations of ethnicity and language are possible, but nevertheless every person in the world can be categorized as belonging to an (mutually exclusive) ethnolinguistic people. For example, there are ethnic Kazaks who speak Kazak as their mother tongue and ethnic Kazaks

---

[12] In practice, another major source of data is scholarly literature that includes surveys conducted by polling organizations, anthropological studies, and studies on a particular religion within a country.

[13] These 18 categories are agnostics, atheists, Baha'is, Buddhists, Chinese folk-religionists, Christians, Confucianists, Daoists, Ethnoreligionists, Hindus, Jains, Jews, Muslims, New Religionists, Shintoists, Sikhs, Spiritists, and Zoroastrians.

[14] This is by far the largest concentration of agnostics and atheists in the world. On the other hand, all major religious traditions are experiencing resurgence in China.

[15] The construction of the taxonomy is explained in more detail in David B. Barrett and Peter Crossing, *World Christian Trends, AD 30–AD 2200: Interpreting the Annual Christian Megacensus* (Pasadena, CA: William Carey Library Publication, 2003), part 18, 'Ethnolinguistics'. The ethnic or culture codes are outlined in David B. Barrett, George T. Kurian, and Todd M. Johnson (eds), *World Christian Encyclopedia: A Comparative Survey of Churches and Religions in the Modern World*, vol 2*: Religions, Peoples, Languages, Cities, Topics* (New York: Oxford University Press, 2001), table 8-1. The languages are listed in *WCE*, Part 9 'Linguametrics', and are derived from David Dalby, David Barrett, and Michael Mann, *The Linguasphere Register of the World's Languages and Speech Communities*, 2 vols. (Carmarthenshire, Wales: Linguasphere Press, 1999). All are available online at www.worldchristiandatabase.org.

who speak Russian as their mother tongue. These are two separate ethnolinguistic peoples.

The next step was to determine the religious breakdown of these 12,600 ethnolinguistic peoples. This work was begun in the 1970s in Africa, where many Christian churches reported the ethnic breakdown of their congregations. Utilizing data gathered by religions and in government censuses, estimates of religious affiliation for all peoples was completed in the mid-1990s and published in *World Christian Encyclopedia*, 2nd edition. These data continue to be updated and published in the *WCD* and *WRD*. The 2009 *Atlas of Global Christianity* also examined the more populous world religions in terms of their peoples and languages.[16]

Religious Diasporas

In order to locate religious diasporas, three steps were taken. First, the *WCD* and *WRD* taxonomy of peoples was sorted by ethnic and linguistic codes in sequence. Second, a filter was added so that only unique codes that were present in more than three countries were counted. Third, the largest population was designated as being in the home country and all others as diasporas. The results of this method produced the summary statistics found below in Table 1 – the religious affiliation of 859 million people living in diasporas (327 peoples), representing 12.5% of the global population. A more refined method would likely uncover more peoples, but the total number in diaspora would not likely rise substantially (this method captures the largest groupings).[17] Nearly half (47.4%) of these are Christians; Christians also have the greatest proportion of adherents in diaspora (18.0%) of the larger world religions (Christianity, Islam, Hinduism, agnosticism, Chinese folk-religion, and Buddhism). Among smaller religions, Daoists, Jews, Spiritists, Baha'is, and Zoroastrians all have higher percentages in diasporas. One interesting observation is that Christians and Muslims make up 55.3% of the world's population, but represent 72.8% of all people in diaspora.

[16] See Todd M. Johnson and Kenneth R. Ross (eds), *Atlas of Global Christianity* (Edinburgh: Edinburgh University Press, 2009), part IV.

[17] One clear limitation of this method is how it treats Mestizos in Latin America. Because ethnolinguistic codes are not differentiated by dialect, Mestizos all across Latin America are treated as one people, even though they are clearly distinct from country to country. Because Mexico has the largest number of Mestizos, it is treated as the home country and all other Mestizos are considered diasporas. To fix this anomaly, one would have to utilize dialect codes to differentiate peoples. Unfortunately, this would artificially create new peoples where there are no significant differences.

Table 1: Religionists in Diaspora, Mid-2010

Religion	***Global total***	***% of global pop***	***# in diaspora***	***% in diaspora***	***% of all diasporas***
Christians	2,260,440,000	32.8	407,548,000	18.0	47.4
Muslims	1,553,773,000	22.5	218,317,000	14.1	25.4
Hindus	948,575,000	13.8	81,429,000	8.6	9.5
Agnostics	676,944,000	9.8	57,379,000	8.5	6.7
Chinese folk	436,258,000	6.3	24,857,000	5.7	2.9
Buddhists	494,881,000	7.2	25,259,000	5.1	2.9
Ethno-religionists	242,516,000	3.5	13,548,000	5.6	1.6
Atheists	136,652,000	2.0	10,060,000	7.4	1.2
New religionists	63,004,000	0.9	7,431,000	11.8	0.9
Sikhs	23,927,000	0.3	1,642,000	6.9	0.2
Jews	14,761,000	0.2	3,249,000	22.0	0.4
Spiritists	13,700,000	0.2	2,749,000	20.1	0.3
Daoists	8,429,000	0.1	2,946,000	35.0	0.3
Baha'is	7,306,000	0.1	1,405,000	19.2	0.2
Confucianists	6,449,000	0.1	933,000	14.5	0.1
Jains	5,316,000	0.1	198,000	3.7	0.0
Shintoists	2,761,000	0.0	101,000	3.7	0.0
Zoroastrians	197,000	0.0	37,900	19.2	0.0
Global total	**6,895,889,000**	**100.0**	**859,088,900**	**12.5**	**100.0**

Source: World Religion Database, accessed February 2012

In 2012, the Pew Research Center's Forum on Religion and Public Life released a report with similar findings for the religious makeup of migrants around the world.[18] The report states that about 214 million people (3% of the world's population) have migrated across international borders in 2010. Of these migrants, 49% were Christian and 27% Muslim (comparable to percentages above, 47.4% for Christians and 25.4% for Muslims).

Host and Sending Countries

Table 2 examines religious diasporas by the country in which they reside. The United States and India top the list, hosting nearly half of all religious diasporas worldwide (45.6%). Likewise, the Pew study cited the United States as the top destination for all migrants, and especially Christians, Buddhists, agnostics, and atheists.

[18] Pew Research Center Forum on Religion and Public Life, *Faith on the Move: The Religious Affiliation of International Migrants*, 8 March 2012, www.pewresearch.org/pubs/2214/religion-religious-migrants-christians-muslims-jews.

Table 2: Top Ten Host Countries of Diasporas Ranked by Diaspora Population, Mid-2010

Country	*Pop 2010*	*Diaspora #*	*Diaspora %*	*Christians*	*Muslims*	*Hindus*	*Buddhists*
1. United States	310,383,948	118,070,000	38.0	96,272,000	2,487,000	1,426,000	3,775,000
2. India	1,224,614,327	93,047,000	7.6	744,000	23,607,000	66,170,000	377,000
3. Colombia	46,294,841	34,203,000	73.9	33,048,000	22,800	9,300	1,800
4. Venezuela	28,979,857	25,608,000	88.4	24,123,000	95,300	0	35,400
5. North Korea	24,346,229	24,298,000	99.8	388,000	0	0	362,000
6. Taiwan	23,216,236	22,780,000	98.1	1,055,000	80,700	0	6,122,000
7. Mexico	113,423,047	19,885,000	17.5	18,395,000	99,400	3,400	0
8. Pakistan	173,593,383	16,947,000	9.8	126,000	16,200,000	499,000	6,200
9. Chile	17,113,688	15,610,000	91.2	13,958,000	15,200	0	5,600
10. Afghan-istan	31,411,743	15,539,000	49.5	29,500	15,468,000	10,700	0

Source: World Religion Database, accessed February 2012

Table 3 examines the countries that send out the largest diaspora communities. Apart from Mexico (which was cited as the top country of origin in the Pew report) and Argentina (and the Mestizo problem mentioned above), Bangladesh emerges as a leading sending country of both Hindus (61 million) and Muslims (25 million). These are Bengalis found in over 20 countries around the world, although the vast majority are found just across the border in India.

Table 3: Top Ten Sending Countries, Ranked by Size of Diaspora Outside of Host Country, mid-2010

Rank / Source country	Diaspora	Christians	Muslims	Hindus	Buddhists
1. Mexico	137,751,000	132,959,000	2,100	6,500	0
2. Bangladesh	87,873,000	446,000	24,728,000	60,785,000	0
3. Argentina	68,156,000	60,574,000	0	2,800	0
4. China	60,580,000	7,095,000	571,000	0	15,171,000
5. India	41,319,000	2,716,000	22,099,000	14,289,000	5
6. South Korea	30,453,000	3,245,000	310	0	1,867,000
7. Russia	24,063,000	15,646,000	2,618,000	0	0
8. Pakistan	22,055,000	52,200	19,026,000	2,909,000	0
9. United States	18,267,000	14,396,000	216,000	0	0
10. Syria	15,951,000	6,114,000	9,155,000	0	0

Source: World Religion Database, accessed February 2012

Peoples in Diaspora

Table 4 ranks the ethnolinguistic peoples in diaspora by the number of countries in which they are found. The top five peoples include several that reflect colonial and economic realities: English, French, USA White (Anglo-Americans), and German. Han Chinese (Mandarin) and Syrian-Arabian Arab (ranked 4 and 6, respectively), are largely spread out as foreign workers and refugees.

Table 4: Top Ten Peoples, Ranked by Number of Countries in Diaspora, Mid-2010

Rank / People name	Total population 2010	# of countries	Diaspora	% in Diaspora	Majority religionists
1. English	52,486,000	171	8,304,000	15.82	Christians
2. French	32,281,000	138	6,333,000	19.62	Christians
3. USA White	121,096,000	118	3,310,000	2.73	Christians
4. Han Chinese (Mandarin)	857,342,000	116	12,293,000	1.43	Agnostics
5. German	65,125,000	90	14,504,000	22.27	Christians
6. Syrian-Arabian Arab	31,701,000	86	15,874,000	50.07	Muslims
7. Greek	13,721,000	85	4,308,000	31.40	Christians
8. Russian	133,886,000	75	21,064,000	15.73	Christians
9. Hindi	141,470,000	69	4,944,000	3.49	Hindus
10. Italian	33,415,000	64	13,039,000	39.02	Christians

Source: World Religion Database, accessed February 2012

Table 5 ranks ethnolinguistic peoples in diaspora by the percentage in diaspora. This ranking reveals a different phenomenon, with 351,000 Assyrian Christians spread over 21 countries (80% in diasporas) and 2.9 million Kuwaiti Arabs (Muslims) in ten countries (72% in diaspora).

Table 5: Top Ten Peoples, Ranked by Percentage in Diaspora, Mid-2010

Rank / People name	***Total pop 2010***	***# of countries***	***Diaspora #***	***% in Diaspora***	***Majority religion***
1. Assyrian (Aisor, Chaldean)	439,000	21	351,000	79.9	Christians
2. Low German	543,000	11	427,000	78.6	Christians
3. Coloured (Eurasian)	506,000	9	369,000	72.9	Christians
4. Syrian Aramaic (Eastern)	105,000	8	76,500	72.8	Christians
5. Kuwaiti Arab	4,034,000	10	2,906,000	72.0	Muslims
6. Euronesian (English)	65,800	9	47,300	71.9	Christians
7. Latin American Black	10,185,000	11	7,287,000	71.6	Christians
8. Jewish (Yiddish)	1,938,000	25	1,380,000	71.2	Jews
9. Hungarian Gypsy	1,710,000	16	1,191,000	69.7	Christians
10. Latin American White	97,528,000	37	67,598,000	69.3	Christians

Source: World Religion Database, accessed February 2012

Religionists in Diaspora

Table 6 presents the largest ethnolinguistic diasporas for each of the four largest religious communities: Christians, Muslims, Hindus, and Buddhists. One can quickly see the origins of peoples representing the largest religious diasporas – Christians (Latin Americans and Europeans), Muslims (Asians and Africans), Hindus (South Asians), and Buddhists (East Asians). This is not surprising: the largest diaspora peoples come from the 'traditional homelands' of each religion.

The Pew study[19] highlighted Jews (not listed in table 6 below) as having the highest level of international migration, with 25% of all Jews worldwide as migrants (currently living in another country than their birth country). This is significant for a religion that, on a global scale, is rather small (14 million adherents). Not surprisingly, the majority of Jewish migrants originate from Europe (56%, most notably Russia) and migrate primarily to the Middle East (76%, almost entirely to Israel).

Table 6: Top Ten Diaspora Peoples by Religions, Mid-2010

Christians		***Muslims***		***Hindus***		***Buddhists***	
People name	*# in diaspora*	*People name*	*# in diaspora*	*People name*	*# in diaspora*	*People name*	*# in diaspora*

[19] Pew Research Center's Forum on Religion and Public Life, *Faith on the Move.*

L. American Mestizo	132,959,000	Bengali	24,728,000	Bengali	60,785,000	Han Chinese (Min Nan)	6,658,000
L. American White	60,326,000	Urdu	16,176,000	Tamil	5,140,000	Han Chinese (Yue)	3,792,000
Russian	15,395,000	Eastern Pathan	14,223,000	Hindi	3,493,000	Han Chinese (Mandarin)	3,308,000
German	11,496,000	Malay (Melaju, Melayu)	9,238,000	Nepalese	3,209,000	Japanese	2,036,000
Italian	10,826,000	Syrian-Arabian Arab	9,155,000	Sindhi	2,909,000	Vietnamese	1,962,000
L. American Mulatto	9,496,000	Hausa	8,544,000	Bhojpuri Bihari	1,658,000	Korean	1,867,000
English	6,973,000	Tajik	7,339,000	Gujarati	1,561,000	Central Khmer	1,400,000
L. American Black	6,336,000	Somali	7,302,000	Eastern Punjabi	803,000	Burmese	647,000
Filipino	6,335,000	Northern Kurd	6,799,000	Telugu	596,000	Central Thai	606,000
Syrian Arab	6,040,000	Palestinian Arab	6,643,000	Malayali	504,000	Sinhalese	598,000

Source: World Religion Database, accessed February 2012

Migration as One Component of Religious Change

The dynamics of change in religious communities over time can be limited to three sets of empirical population data: (1) births minus deaths, (2) converts in minus converts out (defectors), and (3) immigrants minus emigrants. Figure 1 overleaf shows how the six factors mentioned here can be expressed in a formula.

Figure 1: Calculating Net Religious Change

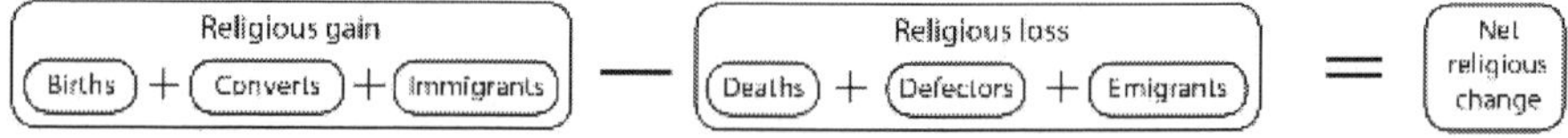

Source: Adapted from Johnson and Ross, Atlas of Global Christianity, *60*

The primary mechanism of religious change globally is births minus deaths. Children are normally considered to have the religion of their parents (this is the law in Norway, for example, and many other countries). This means that a religious population has a close statistical relationship to the number of births into the community and the number of deaths out of it. Many religious communities around the world, in fact, experience little else in the dynamics of their growth or decline.

Nonetheless, individuals (or even whole villages or communities) often change allegiance from one religion to another (or to no religion at all). In the twentieth century, this change has been most pronounced in two general areas: (1) tribal religionists (ethnoreligionists) have converted in large numbers to Christianity, Islam, Hinduism, and Buddhism, and (2) Christians in the Western world have become non-religious (agnostics) or atheists in large numbers. Both of these trends, however, had slowed considerably by the dawn of the twenty-first century. In fact, today's trends point to religious resurgence, with noticeable decreases in the percentages of atheists and non-religious globally.

It is equally important to consider the movement of people across national borders. During the colonial era in the nineteenth century, small groups of Europeans settled in Africa, Asia, and the Americas. In the late twentieth century, natives from these regions immigrated to the Western world. As a result, in the United States religions such as Islam, Hinduism, and Buddhism grew faster than either Christianity or the unaffiliated. This growth has been almost entirely due to the immigration of non-Christian Asians.[20]

In Europe, massive immigration of Muslims has not only been transforming the spiritual landscape but has now become a major political issue, notably in France, Germany, Austria, and Italy, as well as in plans for European Union expansion.[21] In the Central Asian countries of the former Soviet Union, Christianity has declined significantly every year since 1990 due to the emigration of Russians, Germans, and Ukrainians.

The reasons underlying immigration and emigration include economic factors (such as seeking employment), social factors (desire for a better quality of life or family considerations), refugee status (escaping political or religious persecution), and environmental factors (such as natural disasters). These may be described in terms of push and pull factors: push factors are the reasons individuals or groups leave (are pushed out of) their home countries, including denial of needs or rights, while pull factors are the reasons people settle in (are pulled to) particular areas. Pull factors may include better economic opportunities, a preferred climate, lower crime rates, or general stability.[22]

Thus, diasporas comprise both individuals who have chosen to leave and those who were forced to migrate. Such delineations, however, are not always clear-cut. A Syrian Orthodox Christian in the Middle East who loses his job, cannot find work in his Muslim-majority community, and feels there is no hope at home might migrate elsewhere in search of employment. Depending on the perspective, he could be considered either a political or economic migrant.[23]

In the twenty-first century, migration trends are already altering the religious compositions of individual countries. By 2100, it might be

---

[20] In the case of Islam, conversions among African-Americans to Islam also caused increased presence.

[21] Turkey's desire for European Union membership has brought out the interesting contrast of a Union that is mainly 'Christian' with one that could extend to countries not predominantly Christian.

[22] Darrell Jackson and Alessia Passarelli, *Mapping Migration: Mapping Churches' Responses: Europe Study* (Brussels: Churches' Commission for Migrants in Europe, 2008), 5–6.

[23] Jackson and Passarelli, *Mapping Migration*, 9.

difficult to find a country in which 90% or more of the population belong to any single world religion.

Religious Diversity

Underlying the reality of a changing global religious landscape is increasing religious diversity. 'Religious diversity' actually includes two levels: intra- and inter-religious diversity. Intra-religious diversity encompasses the diversity found within a given world religion (for example, traditions such as Roman Catholicism, Orthodoxy, and Protestantism within Christianity), whereas inter-religious diversity describes the degree of overall diversity of distinct religions (Islam, Hinduism, Judaism, and so on) in a given population or area. This article focuses primarily on levels of inter-religious diversity.[24] It is important to note when tracking inter-religious diversity that it can vary greatly from one locale to another, even within a particular country, because religious adherents often cluster in local communities. Such is especially the case for nearly any country receiving significant numbers of immigrants and refugees into major metropolitan areas.[25]

Table 7: Religious Diversity, 1910 and 2010

Continent/region	*Population 1910*	*Pluralism 1910*	*Majority religion 1910*	*Population 2010*	*Pluralism 2010*	*Majority religion 2010*
Africa	**124,541,000**	**0.58**	**Ethno-religionists**	**1,022,234,000**	**0.62**	**Christians**
Eastern Africa	33,012,000	0.49	Ethno-religionists	324,044,000	0.53	Christians
Middle Africa	19,445,000	0.11	Ethno-religionists	126,689,000	0.32	Christians
Northern Africa	31,968,000	0.33	Muslims	209,459,000	0.21	Muslims
Southern Africa	6,819,000	0.52	Ethno-religionists	57,780,000	0.33	Christians
Western Africa	33,296,000	0.43	Ethno-religionists	304,261,000	0.63	Muslims
Asia	**1,026,693,000**	**0.80**	**Chinese folk**	**4,164,252,000**	**0.88**	**Muslims**
Eastern Asia	554,135,000	0.50	Chinese folk	1,573,970,000	0.84	Agnostics
South-central Asia	345,718,000	0.53	Hindus	1,764,872,000	0.62	Hindus
Southeastern Asia	93,859,000	0.81	Buddhists	593,415,000	0.78	Muslims

---

[24] For a complete survey of intra-religious diversity of Christianity, see Johnson and Ross, *Atlas of Global Christianity*, parts II and III.
[25] Johnson and Ross, *Atlas of Global Christianity*, 32.

Western Asia	32,982,000	0.40	Muslims	231,995,000	0.22	Muslims
Europe	**427,044,000**	**0.11**	**Christians**	**738,199,000**	**0.38**	**Christians**
Eastern Europe	178,184,000	0.20	Christians	294,771,000	0.30	Christians
Northern Europe	61,473,000	0.04	Christians	99,205,000	0.43	Christians
Southern Europe	76,828,000	0.07	Christians	155,171,000	0.33	Christians
Western Europe	110,558,000	0.03	Christians	189,052,000	0.51	Christians
Latin America	**78,254,000**	**0.10**	**Christians**	**590,082,000**	**0.15**	**Christians**
Caribbean	8,172,000	0.05	Christians	41,646,000	0.31	Christians
Central America	20,806,000	0.02	Christians	155,881,000	0.09	Christians
South America	49,276,000	0.14	Christians	392,555,000	0.16	Christians
Northern America	**94,689,000**	**0.07**	**Christians**	**344,529,000**	**0.38**	**Christians**
Oceania	**7,192,000**	**0.36**	**Christians**	**36,593,000**	**0.41**	**Christians**
Australia/New Zealand	5,375,000	0.06	Christians	26,637,000	0.48	Christians
Melanesia	1,596,000	0.30	Ethnoreligionists	8,748,000	0.17	Christians
Micronesia	89,400	0.38	Christians	536,000	0.14	Christians
Polynesia	131,000	0.01	Christians	673,000	0.08	Christians
Global total	**1,758,412,000**	**0.83**	**Christians**	**6,895,889,000**	**0.85**	**Christians**

Source: World Religion Database, accessed February 2012

The twentieth century was a transformative time for religion. In general, the world in 2010 was less religious than it was in 1910. In 1910, nearly the entire world claimed adherence to some form of religious belief. By 2010, however, 11.8% of the world's population was either atheist or agnostic. The reasons for this are twofold: the rise of Communism worldwide, and the phenomenon of secularization, particularly in the global north.[27]

Religious Diversity Index (RDI)

The Religious Diversity Index, based on the Herfindahl Index (used by economists studying market competition), describes the inter-religious diversity of a particular country's or region's population using a scale from

[27] Johnson and Ross, *Atlas of Global Christianity*, 6. But note that the percentage of atheists and agnostics has declined since the collapse of Communism in the former Soviet Union. Here, 'global north' is defined in geopolitical terms by five current United Nations regions (comprising 53 countries): Eastern Europe (including Russia), Northern Europe, Southern Europe, Western Europe, and Northern America. The United Nations definition also includes Australia and New Zealand, part of the 'global south' in this survey.

0.0 (no diversity) to 1.0 (most diverse). Calculating measurements on both the country and regional levels provides a 'local' perspective of diversity (country-level) as well as a cross-national view of diversity (regional-level). Table 7 shows that between 1910 and 2010, all but six regions in the world experienced increases in both country and regional RDI levels.[28] Some of the greatest regional increases, primarily due to migration, were found in Western Europe (+0.27 points), Australia/New Zealand (+0.42 points), Eastern Asia (+0.34 points), and Northern America (+0.31 points).[29]

Despite significant changes, since 1910 Asia has remained the most religiously diverse continent in the world. In 1910, over 50% of Asia's population was Chinese folk-religionist or Buddhist; today, these two religions together total only 22%. Ethnoreligions declined from 5.6% of the population in 1910 to 3.7% in 2010. These declines were the result of gains by Muslims (from 16.6% to 26.0%) and Christians (2.4% to 8.5%). However, greater gains were made by agnostics (0.0% to 11.8%) and atheists (0.0% to 2.8%), especially in China.

These religious changes in Asia are not entirely surprising considering the inherently pluralistic nature of Asian culture; in a sense to be Asian is to be inter-religious.[30] It is also common for Asians to cross national boundaries in search of work, such as the large Indian and Filipino migrant worker communities in various Persian Gulf countries. The World Bank estimates that three million Indonesian women work abroad, primarily in Malaysia and Saudi Arabia, and mostly in domestic work.[31] Increases in religious diversity are particularly apparent in the global north, however, where secularization and immigration continue to transform the religious landscape (see below).

Another way of viewing religious diversity is examining the number of religions representing greater than a given percentage (for example, 0.5%, 5%, or 10%) of the population of a country. Eastern and Southeastern Asia in particular claim the most diversity. Only Vietnam has six religions over 5%,[32] while only South Korea has five different religions numbering over

---

[28] The six regions *not* experiencing an increase in religious diversity in this time period were Northern Africa, Southern Africa, South-eastern Asia, Western Asia, Melanesia, and Micronesia. For more on measuring religious pluralism, see Pippa Norris and Ronald Inglehart, *Sacred and Secular: Religion and Politics Worldwide* (Cambridge: Cambridge University Press, 2004), 100.

[29] Johnson and Ross, *Atlas of Global Christianity*, 33.

[30] Phan, *Being Religious Interreligiously*, 117, 127.

[31] Nisha Varia, 'Asia's Migrant Workers Need Better Protection', *Human Rights Watch*, 2 September 2004, www.hrw.org/news/2004/08/31/asias-migrant-workers-need-better-protection.

[32] Vietnam's six religions over 5% of the population are agnostics, atheists, Buddhists, Christians, Ethnoreligionists, and New Religionists.

10% of the population (Buddhism, Christianity, Confucianism, ethnoreligions, and New Religions).[33]

Globalization and Secularization

One factor driving religious diversity in the twenty-first century is a strong trend toward globalization. Globalization involves the development of a certain sector of society (e.g., economic, political, cultural, or technological) to the point where international influence and operation are gained with relative ease. Studies of this phenomenon are multifaceted, complex, and not without criticism.[34] With respect to religion, globalization not only facilitates the presence of multiple religions in a particular geographic area, but it also hastens such a plurality[35] as the movement of peoples, ideas, and cultures across new boundaries becomes the new normal. Religious diversity owes much to globalization, which has made historical religious monopolies (such as Orthodox churches in Europe, the Roman Catholic church in Latin America, and Hinduism in India) more difficult to sustain.[36] One salient feature of pluralistic societies is the benefit of religious choice: an individual is no longer tied to the religion of his or her parents or country of birth if adherents of the world's religions surround him or her in his or her own backyard.

Sociologist Eric Kaufmann has stated that religious diversity is challenged, or even undermined, by secularization.[37] Put most simply, secularization includes an alignment away from religious ideas, attitudes, and activities, either on an individual or societal scale. Many sociologists in the twentieth century assumed that by the twenty-first century most of the

---

[33] Johnson and Ross, *Atlas of Global Christianity,* 32. See also Barrett, Kurian, and Johnson, *World Christian Encycopedia,* I.682-85.

[34] This is expressed by Stanley Fischer in 'Globalization and Its Challenges', conference lecture presented at the American Economic Association meetings in Washington, DC, on 3 January 2003.

[35] Ole Riis, 'Modes of Religious Pluralism under Conditions of Globalization', in Matthias Koenig and Paul de Guchteneire (eds), *Democracy and Human Rights in Multicultural Societies* (Aldershot: Ashgate Publishing Limited, 2007), 251.

[36] Scott M. Thomas, 'A Globalized God: Religion's Growing Influence in International Politics', *Foreign Affairs* 89.6 (2010), 98.

[37] 'Religious diversity, extending to non-religion, leads people to question their faith's claim to exclusive possession of the truth, fostering religious doubt and, eventually, decline...Pluralism also results in an increased rate of inter-faith marriage. Parents who follow different religions often fail to agree on which faith to raise the children in, so the default option becomes the secular culture. Pluralism leads, once again, to an erosion of faith. *Ipso facto*, equality breeds a toleration that corrodes religion'. See Eric Kaufmann, *Shall the Religious Inherit the Earth? Demography and Politics in the Twenty-First Century* (London: Profile Books Ltd, 2010), 17.

world would have released its reliance on religious thought in favor of reason, rationalism, and science.[38]

If 'secularization' had meant only the deinstitutionalization of religion, then such dismal prognostications for religion would have been correct based on the political disestablishment of European churches throughout the twentieth century. However, a broader (and arguably more accurate) definition of the term involves measuring levels of personal piety, not political institutions. Theorists have always been more interested in personal faith than trends at the political or governmental level.[39] Significantly, no Western European or North American country has undergone dramatic *individual* secularization, as opposed to societal or political secularization.[40]

The data seem to support the idea that allowing people to choose faith or no faith does not kill religion. The world has become *more* religious since 1970, not less: throughout the twentieth century, and continuing today, the vast majority of the world's population, never less than 75%, have been religious. The high point for the world's non-religious was around 1970 with 23.5% of the global population; today the figure is about 11.8%. The collapse of European Communism was accompanied by the resurgence of religion, and currently the numbers of both agnostics and atheists are growing much more slowly than the world's population. From a global demographic perspective, these trends cast serious doubt on the premise that secularization, and thus religious diversity, subverts religion. The strongest evidence predicts that the global trend of religious resurgence is likely to continue into the near and, perhaps, distant future, even as globalization and religious diversity increase worldwide.

---

[38] See, for example, Bryan R. Wilson, *Religion in Secular Society: A Sociological Comment* (London: C. A. Watts & Co. Ltd, 1966), and Harvey G. Cox, *The Secular City: Secularization and Urbanization in Theological Perspective* (New York: Macmillan, 1965).

[39] As Starke and Finke have stated, 'At issue is not a narrow prediction concerning a growing separation of church and state. Instead, as we have seen, from the start, the prophets of secularization have stressed personal piety, and to the extent that they have expressed macro interests, it has been to claim that they are so linked that a decline in one necessitates a decline in the other. Thus, if the churches lose power, personal piety will fade; if personal piety fades, the churches will lose power'. See Rodney Starke and Roger Finke, *Acts of Faith: Explaining the Human Side of Religion* (Berkeley: University of California Press, 2000), 60.

[40] K.R. Dark, 'Large-Scale Religious Change and World Politics', in K.R. Dark (ed), *Religion and International Relations* (Hampshire: Palgrave, 2000), 53–5. Individual secularization is defined as *individuals* being less religious than they once were.

Implications for Christian Mission

The implications of increasing religious diasporas and religious diversity are clearly profound. However, these implications reach beyond the social sciences and into the religious communities themselves. From a Christian perspective, the data illustrates a need for a new outlook on the global mission movement. No longer does presenting a Buddhist with the gospel necessarily mean taking a life-threatening trip across the sea to an unknown land. Buddhists, Hindus, and Muslims are now the neighbors, coworkers, and friends of Christians around the world. The increase of religious diversity via migration means Christians in the West are increasingly likely to have friends, and even family members, who are members of the world's religions. This calls for a new, deeper level of engagement with these world faiths.

The church faces a monumental task in practicing mission strengthened by both knowledge of and civility toward other religionists. In sheer quantity, there is enough evangelism in the world today for every person to hear a one-hour presentation of the gospel every other day all year long. This amounts to over one billion hours of evangelism generated by Christians every year, ranging from personal witnessing to television and radio broadcasting.[41] When broken down by United Nations regions, Asia and northern Africa have the lowest amount of evangelism but the largest non-Christian populations.

Another unsettling statistic is that over 85% of all Christian evangelism is directed toward Christians and never reaches other religionists.[42] Much missionary deployment is trying to keep up the growth of the numerous churches founded during the twentieth century in Africa, Asia, and Latin America. Missionaries from the global south have also been drawn into conducting mission among other Christians as well, though movements in areas such as Nigeria and India seem to indicate that there is a shift toward work among other religionists.

The reality is that most Christians in the world are out of contact with Muslims, Buddhists, and Hindus. In fact, recent research has shown that 86% of these religionists do not personally know a Christian.[43] In the twenty-first century it is important to realize that the responsibility for engaging these religionists is too large for the missionary enterprise. While missionaries will always be at the forefront of innovative strategies, the whole church needs to participate in inviting people of other faiths to consider Jesus Christ. The data on religious diasporas illustrate that

---

[41] Todd M. Johnson and Kenneth R. Ross, www.edinburgh2010.org/en/resources/papersdocumentsd4bd.pdf?no_cache=1&cid=33877&did=22382&sechash=801bf75d (accessed 8.8.13).

[42] Johnson and Ross, *Atlas of Global Christianity*, 318.

[43] Johnson and Ross, *Atlas of Global Christianity*, 316–7.

Muslims, Hindus, and Buddhists are increasingly found living in traditionally 'Christian' lands.

An important step for Christian mission (and more generally, cultivating societies of civility) is more thorough education in a variety of areas.[44] The first is world religions, including their histories, texts, theologies, and practices. It is difficult to live compassionately toward one's neighbors if little is known about their worldviews, traditions, and beliefs. A 2010 survey by the Pew Research Center's Forum on Religion and Public Life found that American evangelicals are less knowledgeable about world religions than are atheists, Jews, and Mormons. Evangelicals answered an average of 18 out of 32 questions about world religions accurately while on average atheists/agnostics, Jews, and Mormons answered more than 20 of 32 correctly.[45]

Another important area requiring more education is the situation of the world outside of one's personal context. Many of the world's most pressing problems are out of sight from mainstream evangelicalism – urban poverty, slum settlements, addiction, slavery – and often issues such as these are the daily reality for those in religious diasporas worldwide.

A final area requiring a new focus among many engaged in Christian mission is a renewed spirit for hospitality and friendship with adherents of other religions. Christians are called to know and love their neighbors, and the whole church needs to participate in these acts of service.

---

[44] For more on Christian civility, see Richard J. Mouw, *Uncommon Decency: Christian Civility in an Uncivil World* (Downers Grove, IL: InterVarsity Press, 2010).

[45] Pew Research Center's Forum on Religion and Public Life, 'U.S. Religious Knowledge Survey'. http://www.pewforum.org/2010/09/28/u-s-religious-knowledge-survey/ (accessed 19.6.14).

My Father Was a Migrant Aramean: Old Testament Motifs for a Theology of Migration

Knut Holter

Archaeological and historical sources attest to human migration as a common phenomenon, detectable through time and space. Migration is not a new development in the history of humankind, created by recent colonial structures of political power or modern means of swift travelling; in various forms, it has always been there. This chapter addresses a small, but important aspect of this common phenomenon as seen from a Christian perspective: the historical and theological experiences of the migrants with texts and motifs from the Old Testament (OT), the first part of the Christian Bible. The discussion on the topic falls into three parts: (1) examples of migrant experiences with the OT from two recent historical epochs, (2) a survey of some major OT migration motifs, and (3) a brief discussion of the relationship between the two previous parts as an attempt to bridge the perspective of OT studies to the development of a more general theology of migration.

Migrant Experiences with the Old Testament

Migrant experiences with the OT actually start within the OT itself, such as when Isaiah portrays Judah's return from the Babylonian exile in terminology and concepts echoing Pentateuchal narratives about Israel's exodus from Egypt (cf. Isa. 52:11-12), or when Amos portrays the migration of the Philistines from Caphtor and the Arameans from Kir as parallels to that of the Israelites from Egypt (Amos 9:7). Still, the following discussion is delimited due to space limits. For pragmatic reasons, we focus on interpretive interactions with the OT during the last few centuries in light of two major waves of migration: (1) the European migration of the colonial period and the chronologically (and ideologically, economically, and politically) parallel slave traffic from West Africa to North America, and (2) the reverse migration of the postcolonial period, from previously colonized areas to the West.

The European migrants of the colonial period (e.g., from the early nineteenth century to the midtwentieth century) came from sociocultural contexts that were well acquainted with the Bible, and presumably with the idea that the Bible might serve as a source for reflection about personal and corporate identity and destiny. Consequently, the European migrants allowed biblical (and not least OT) texts and motifs to interact with their own migrant experiences, and they did so in at least two ways.

First, biblical texts and motifs were used to interpret *the other*. The 'peoples' that the migrants encountered wherever they went were related to biblical attempts at constructing demographic world maps. Hence, texts such as the Table of Nations in Genesis 10 were used as grids through which the kind of demographic maps Europeans themselves constructed were interpreted. Although it had been acknowledged that there were peoples on earth that hardly fit into the pattern of Genesis 10, biblical texts nevertheless continued to provide European migrants with resonance as far as 'the other' was concerned. For example, nineteenth-century Europeans in Southern Africa could identify the ethnic groups they encountered as Jews, Egyptians, and Arabs.[1]

Second, and more important in the present context, European migrants also used biblical texts and motifs to interpret *themselves*, even their own experiences as migrants. Again, it should be remembered that they came from sociocultural contexts that were well acquainted with the Bible, and that it was probably taken for granted that their migrant experiences (like all other experiences of life) should be interpreted in relation to the Bible. A biblical motif that seems to have proved particularly useful, as it is frequently referred to in migrant sources, is that of the exodus and conquest. The OT narrative of how God rescued his people from the oppression in Egypt, led them through the wilderness, and eventually let them conquer the promised land and oppress the Canaanite population provided an interpretive paradigm for European migrants to various parts of the world.

One example of migrants making use of the exodus/conquest motif is the various groups of religious non-conformists fleeing persecution by majority churches in Europe and finding themselves a 'promised land' in North America. The OT narrative became their narrative, not only with regard to their newly-discovered promised land, but also with regard to what to do with the 'Canaanites' they encountered there.[2]

Another example of European migrants making use of the OT exodus/conquest motif to interpret their migration experiences is the Boers of Southern Africa. In an attempt to escape British colonization of the Cape, groups of Boers trekked into the interior of Southern Africa in the first half of the nineteenth century, and this 'great trek' was soon to be interpreted from OT perspectives of a chosen people searching for and

---

[1] See M. LeRoux, *The Lemba: A Lost Tribe of Israel in Southern Africa?* (Pretoria: University of South Africa, 2003), 18-27.

[2] See R.A. Warrior, 'A Native American Perspective: Canaanites, Cowboys, and Indians', in R.S. Sugirtharajah (ed), *Voices from the Margin: Interpreting the Bible in the Third World* (rev. and exp. 3rd ed.; Maryknoll: Orbis, 2006), 235-41.

finding its 'promised land' and at the same time having to fight with local 'Canaanites' to achieve it.[3]

What these various European migrant waves of the colonial era have in common is that they were hope-driven and self-initiated, and as such – in relation to recent migrant theory – they can be labeled 'voluntary'. However, the term 'voluntary' should not in this context be identified with the term 'adventurous' – a term with positive connotations. Many from Europe who migrated 'voluntarily' did so to escape rather miserable lives of political, social, and religious marginalization or oppression in Europe, and the OT exodus/conquest motif proved fit to express the hopes they had for a better life on the other side of an ocean.

However, other waves of migration in the same colonial era were indeed 'involuntary' or 'forced'. These terms tend to have connotations of punishment and exploitation, and they reflect the fact that geographical replacement was used by political and economic power structures to rearrange various demographic patterns. In such cases, too, the OT provided texts and motifs that could be meaningful to the experiences of the migrants. One illustrative example concerns the convicts – and others – who were sent to the 'ends of the earth' (e.g., to Australia, which was used as a kind of 'prison' by the British from 1787 to 1868). Such a destination could hardly be conceptualized as that of a promised land, but another OT motif – that of the expulsion from Paradise – gave this biblical sanction.[4]

Nevertheless, the most obvious example of involuntary or 'forced' migration is the massive and disastrous slave trade from Africa – from East Africa to Muslim contexts in Zanzibar and Arabia, and from West Africa to Christian contexts in the West Indies and North America – migrations that impoverished Africa to an extent from which it has thus far not managed to recover. Many of the latter (the West Africans who ended up in the so-called New World) eventually embraced not only the religion of their slave owners, but also their holy book.[5] More than any other community of biblical readers, African Americans have managed to capture OT texts and motifs, and use them to interpret their own experiences, hopes, and gradual liberation. Through their songs and narratives they have also managed to share their interpretations with a more global interpretive community.[6]

---

[3] See M. Prior, *The Bible and Colonialism: A Moral Critique* (The Biblical Seminar 48; Sheffield: Sheffield Academic Press, 1997), 71-105.

[4] For a discussion of postcolonial Australian biblical interpretation, see R. Boer, *Last Stop before Antarctica: The Bible and Postcolonialism in Australia* (The Bible and Postcolonialism 6; Sheffield: Sheffield Academic Press, 2001).

[5] See W.L. Wimbush, 'The Bible and African Americans: An Outline of an Interpretive History', in C.H. Felder (ed), *Stony the Road We Trod: African American Biblical Interpretation* (Minneapolis: Fortress, 1991), 84-5, who argues that the African slaves first embraced the Christian book and then the Christian faith.

[6] See C.H. Felder, *Stony the Road We Trod*; C.H. Felder, *Troubling Biblical*

Turning from the first wave of modern migration (that of the colonial period), to the second wave (the postcolonial, reverse migration since the 1960s), we encounter a multifaceted phenomenon that is difficult to capture thematically and terminologically. The interpretive grid used above, distinguishing between 'voluntary' and 'involuntary' migration, might prove helpful here. Numerically speaking, 'voluntary' migration (i.e., individuals and groups seeking to improve their economic and political conditions by moving to another country or continent) is the most important aspect of contemporary migration. Still, examples of 'involuntary' migration are not difficult to detect. War is a major cause. Today, substantial numbers of minority communities, from as different parts of the globe as Vietnam and Somalia, can be found in their respective neighboring countries as well as in Europe and North America. Ethnic cleansing is another cause, with refugees from Rwanda, former Yugoslavia, and other places. Human trafficking (mainly for commercial sexual exploitation or forced labor) is a third cause, bringing people not only from the global south, but also from Eastern Europe to Western Europe and North America. However, the dichotomy between the two interpretive categories – 'voluntary' versus 'involuntary' migration – does not necessarily fit the complexity of contemporary migration patterns, and an interpretive acknowledgement of simultaneous 'pull' and 'push' factors is probably better (the former referring to factors that are attractive in the destination area, and the latter referring to factors that are unfavorable in the home area).[7]

It is stated above that the European migrants of the colonial period came from sociocultural contexts that were well acquainted with the OT, presumably also with the idea that the OT might serve as a source for reflection about personal identity and destiny. Today – and this might be seen as an irony of fate – the same is the case for many of those being part of the reverse migration of the postcolonial period; in fact, many, not least those coming from sub-Saharan Africa, come from societies likely more acquainted with the OT than those of the receptor societies in Europe. As a result, many 'reverse' migrants to Europe and North America, with Christian backgrounds from Africa, South America, or Southeastern Asia, are shocked when they encounter a secularized society in the West, where the average inhabitant seems to live pretty well without God, and where even those who attend church on a regular basis seem to have accepted that society at large strengthens its secularized profile, for example, by

---

Waters: Race, Class, and Family (Maryknoll: Orbis, 1989); V.L. Wimbush (ed), *African Americans and the Bible: Sacred Texts and Social Textures* (New York: Continuum, 2000); R. C. Bailey (ed), *Yet With a Steady Beat: Contemporary U.S. Afrocentric Biblical Interpretation* (Semeia Studies 42; Atlanta: Society of Biblical Literature, 2003); and A.D. Callahan, *The Talking Book: African Americans and the Bible* (New Haven: Yale University Press, 2006).

[7] See E.S. Lee, 'A Theory of Migration', *Demography* 3 (1966), 47-57.

establishing laws that are seen to be contrary to the Bible. The questions are then: (1) how do the migrants relate to this new interpretive context when they approach the Bible? and (2) to what extent do their interpretations of the Old Testament become 'pull' and/or 'push' factors in their total experience of life as migrants to the West?

Several recent case studies may illustrate this point. One is Frieder Ludwig's analysis of the Liberian Christian presence in Minnesota (USA), being interpreted from the perspective of Joseph, who according to Genesis 37-50 was captured and sold as a slave to Egypt.[8] Ludwig's point of departure is the observation that the Joseph narrative in Genesis plays important roles in early nineteenth-century African American desires to 'return' to Liberia and in late twentieth-century Liberian circles of migration to the USA. The former identified with Joseph, who was sold as a slave, but thereby was able to save his family later. In the same way, African Americans argued that they have been brought here for a purpose, to help people back home, hence their focus on Liberia. The latter, too, identified with Joseph, here not as a slave, but rather with the wealth and insight he was able to gain. In the same way, contemporary Liberian migrants to the USA would argue that they have been led here with the purpose of being able to transfer something back home, not only financial support, but also intellectual and ethical support for the current peace and reconciliation process in Liberia.

In other words, the OT Joseph narrative provides an interpretive framework for both cases of migration to and from Liberia, an interpretive framework that in particular is focused on the two sets of migration experiences as reflecting a divine purpose. As far as the question of 'pull' and/or 'push' factors is concerned, the latter is emphasized in both cases. Early nineteenth-century African Americans wanting to 'return' to Liberia saw a divine purpose in their ability to help – like Joseph saving his brothers – and the late twentieth-century Liberians settling in Minnesota saw a corresponding possibility to help their families back home.

Another recent case study with regard to the interpretive role of the OT vis-à-vis contemporary migration experiences is Kenneth Mtata's study of African diaspora Christianity in the West as space and place of imagination.[9] Mtata proceeds from the oft-quoted question in Psalm 137:4, 'How shall we sing the Lord's song in a foreign land?' to point out the differences between African and Western Christianity and to discuss the frustration African Christians in the West experience due to this

---

[8] See F. Ludwig, '"Just Like Joseph in the Bible": The Liberian Christian Presence in Minnesota', in F. Ludwig and J.K. Asamoah-Gyadu (eds), *African Christian Presence in the West: New Immigrant Congregations and Transnational Networks in North America and Europe* (Trenton: Africa World Press, 2011), 357-80.

[9] See K. Mtata, '"How Shall We Sing the Lord's Song in a Foreign Land?": African Diaspora Christianity as Space and Place of Imagination', in Ludwig and Asamoah-Gyadu (eds), *African Christian Presence in the West*, 335-55.

dissonance. Traditional religious life in Africa – also continuing into various forms of Christianity – tends to be bound by particular locations, such as sacred shrines, rivers, mountains, graves of ancestors, and so on. This spatial focus creates difficulties when the religion is to be expressed and interpreted in a Western context, and new spaces must be found that are not similarly demarcated in traditional Western churches. Mtata's description of how an African Christian migrant to Europe experiences an average European church service – and therefore, eventually, feels forced to establish his or her own church – may have some ironic connotations, but it still points to some key cultural differences:

> The fact that one person is praying invalidates the whole enterprise for this African to come to church. Communal prayer for her or him means each person praying at the top of her or his voice (if she or he still has a voice!), for as long as possible. The hour-long service in the European church does not even serve as an 'appetizer' for the African who is anticipating a four or five hour normal service. The six-minute sermon in a strange language, in addition to strange looks coming from an all-white membership does not help matters. The African observes how her or his European hosts conduct themselves after the church service. The preacher lights up his cigarette just after the service and shares it with the only singing old lady. The keyboard player goes with his friends to a public house next door to the church to drink beer.[10]

Still, the real differences are actually found on a deeper level, according to Mtata. On the one hand, one would expect that African diaspora Christians would feel at home in the traditionally Christian context of the West, as they pray intensively, have regular fellowship meetings, and offer holistic ministry to meet the existential needs of the church members. But then, on the other hand, the kind of church life the African Christians actually encounter in the West tends to lack these characteristics. The Western churches do not function as sources of health and sustenance, as they do in Africa. So when Western Christians feel depressed, in general they do not go to church to ask for prayer ministry, but go to the pharmacy to get antidepressants.

Even more crucial is the role of the Bible. On the one hand, African Christians use it extensively and tend to consider a literal interpretation as binding for the individual, whereas the Western counterparts tend to see the biblical texts as dangerous and conservative, uninformed and unacquainted with the cultural shifts that have taken place in recent centuries. It is indeed difficult to sing the Lord's song in a foreign land, especially when the supposed co-members of the choir sing so differently. Whether these difficulties are interpreted as 'pull' or 'push' factors is difficult to say, but what is not difficult to see is the need for diaspora churches to reflect the experiences of the migrants both with life and with the Bible.

---

[10] Mtata, 'How Shall We Sing the Lord's Song in a Foreign Land?', 348.

Summing up, we have looked for uses of the OT in relation to the two major waves of migration in the last few centuries: the European migration of the colonial period, with the chronologically parallel slave traffic from West Africa to North America; and, the reverse migration of the postcolonial period, from previously colonized areas to the West. It seems that the OT in both cases is capable of providing texts and motifs that make sense vis-à-vis the migrants' need for an understanding of their experiences.

Old Testament Migration Motifs

Migration is in many ways a key motif in the Old Testament, with Abraham's journey from Ur of the Chaldeans, Israel's sojourn in Egypt, and Judah's exile in Babylon as major examples. The current literature analyzing the historical background and theological interpretations of this key motif is able to fill up any library focusing on biblical studies. However, in recent years we have also seen research that relates the OT migration motif to modern migration experiences. One example is provided by Andrew Walls, who states that the theological significance of migration proceeds from what he calls the 'archetypal' figures and narratives in Genesis, making a contrast between a voluntary, hope-driven migration (key figure: Abraham on the way to the promised land) and an involuntary, punitive migration (key figures: Adam and Eve expelled from Paradise). These two categories are then used to discuss current migration patterns and to develop trajectories for a Christian theology of migration.[11]

Another example is John J. Ahn's monograph on Judah's exile in Babylon, interpreted as a case of forced migration.[12] Ahn discusses various twentieth-century experiences and sociological interpretations of forced migration, displacement, and resettlement. He then uses this perspective as an interpretive entry into OT texts that are assumed to reflect the experiences of the 'first' generation (Ps. 137), 'first one and a half' generation (Jer. 29), 'second' generation (Isa. 43), and 'third' generation (Num. 32) of exiled Judeans.

Our search for migration motifs in the OT, for practical and pragmatic reasons, proceeds from one particular text, the so-called Historical Credo in Deuteronomy 26:5-9: practical, in the sense that the present format has obvious space restrictions (as compared to Ahn); and pragmatic, in the sense that this text allows us to relate the migration motifs to key

---

[11] A.F. Walls, 'Towards a Theology of Migration', in Ludwig and Asamoah-Gyadu (eds), *African Christian Presence in the West*, 407-17.

[12] J.J. Ahn, *Exile as Forced Migrations: A Sociological, Literary, and Theological Approach on the Displacement and Resettlement of the Southern Kingdom of Judah* (Beihefte zur Zeitschrift für die alttestamentliche Wissenschaft 417; Berlin: Walter de Gruyter, 2011).

theological lines in the OT (like Walls, but here condensed into one, brief text). The Credo in Deuteronomy 26:5-9 says (NIV):

> Then you shall declare before the Lord your God: 'My father was a wandering Aramean, and he went down into Egypt with a few people and lived there and became a great nation, powerful and numerous. But the Egyptians mistreated us and made us suffer, subjecting us to harsh labor. Then we cried out to the Lord, the God of our ancestors, and the Lord heard our voice and saw our misery, toil and oppression. So the Lord brought us out of Egypt with a mighty hand and an outstretched arm, with great terror and with signs and wonders. He brought us to this place and gave us this land, a land flowing with milk and honey'.

The Credo in Deuteronomy 26:5-9 is a text that on the one hand summarizes some of Israel's major narratives about its way through history and geography, and then on the other hand relates these historical experiences to its faith in Yahweh. Therefore, one needs to take a closer look at the Credo – with some forays into its Old Testament context – from the same perspective (i.e., migration as a narrative and theological motif).

Two or three aspects of Israel's experience and understanding of migration – as reflected in the Credo in Deuteronomy 26:5-9 – should be pointed out here. The first concerns the migration of the ancestors. The Credo starts with a reference to Jacob, one of the three patriarchal ancestors, the two others being Abraham and Isaac. 'My father was a wandering Aramean', it says (or, 'my father was a migrant Aramean', as the title of this essay renders, in an attempt to pinpoint some of its contemporary relevance). The main narratives about the three patriarchs are found in Genesis 12-50, where they are depicted as constantly being on the move, from Syria through Canaan to Egypt, back and forth. They are not settling permanently, in spite of divine promises about the land (Gen. 12:1-3). Actually, the only example of a piece of land that is purchased for more permanent purposes is the Machpelah cave, which Abraham bought – and he really had to struggle to buy it properly – from Ephron the Hittite to be the burial site for him and his family (Gen. 23).

Nevertheless, the informed reader of Genesis will soon notice that the landscape which the patriarchs pass through, and the peoples, kings, and cities they encounter, are not just accidentally mentioned. If one reads Genesis together with the historical books (Samuel, Kings, and Chronicles) of the OT, one can see that there is an intertextual connection between the patriarchal narratives of the former and the narratives about different phases in the history of the chosen people in the latter. That is, when one reads about Abraham (Gen. 20) and Isaac (Gen. 26) interacting with the Philistines, one cannot avoid seeing it in relation to the role of the Philistines in the history of Israel.

Likewise, when one reads about Abraham coming to Canaanite cities like Shechem and Bethel (Gen. 12), or meeting Melchizedek, king of Salem (Gen. 14), one is invited to read the Genesis and historical texts as being in dialogue with each other about key geographical and political structures of the land. In other words, although the patriarchs had no permanent residency in Canaan, the texts are part of a larger narrative structure, where the question of a permanent residency is a key problem.

The Credo in Deuteronomy 26 depicts Jacob as going down to Egypt and 'living' there. The biblical Hebrew verb used here to express 'living', *gur*, has connotations of staying somewhere away from home, and it is often translated 'to sojourn'. Its nominal form, *ger*, 'a sojourner', is used in biblical Hebrew about the 'protected foreigner', that is, someone in a societal position somewhere between the native (*ezrach*) and foreigner (*nokhri*).[13] Here in Deuteronomy, it is repeatedly emphasized that the *ger* is under God's protection. The foreigner is to be treated righteously in judgment (Deut. 1:16; 24:17), and is frequently mentioned alongside others in a vulnerable position such as orphans and widows (14:29; 27:19). It therefore comes as no surprise that the immediate continuation of the Credo in Deuteronomy 26 mentions the *ger* amongst those to rejoice together with Israel for the gifts of the land (v. 11), and to receive from what is set aside of these gifts for God (v. 12).

Deuteronomy 10:18-19 goes one step further, arguing that God loves the *ger*, and that Israel should also love the *ger*, because they themselves have experienced being a *ger* in Egypt. Being a *ger* – a sojourner or protected foreigner – is accordingly a central aspect of the identity of the Israelites. It is an aspect that reflects their double experience with regard to the promised land. It is partly an eternal gift, with promises linked to Yahweh's presence in a permanent temple built of stone. But it is partly also a hope in the desert (diaspora), with promises linked to Yahweh's presence in a transportable tabernacle built of cloth. The ultimate expression of Israel's identity as a *ger* is then found in Jeremiah (a book closely related to Deuteronomy) which portrays God as a *ger*:

> O Hope of Israel, its Savior in times of distress, why are you like a *ger* in the land, like a traveler who stays only one night? (Jer. 14:8 NIV)

A second aspect of Israel's experience and understanding of migration – as reflected in the Credo in Deuteronomy 26:5-9 – is the exodus/conquest motif. In spite of Jacob's descendants becoming a great nation in Egypt, the Credo argues that they were mistreated by the Egyptians. Then they cried out to Yahweh, who heard them and brought them out of Egypt 'with a mighty hand and an outstretched arm, with great terror and with signs and wonders', and eventually he gave them 'a land flowing with milk and honey'.

---

[13] See D. Kellermann, '*gur*', in G. J. Botterweck and H. Ringgren (eds), *Theological Dictionary of the Old Testament,* Vol. 2 (Grand Rapids: Eerdmans, 1975), 439-49. For a more detailed discussion, see M. Zehnder, *Umgang mit Fremden in Israel und Assyrien: Ein Beitrag zur Anthropologie des 'Fremden' im Licht antiker Quellen* (Beiträge zur Wissenschaft vom Alten und Neuen Testament 8; Stuttgart: W. Kohlhammer, 2005).

There is a double concept of Egypt in the OT. On the one hand, the dominant view (it should be admitted) is a negative portrayal of Egypt, keeping alive Israel's memories of her sojourn in what is called 'the land of slavery' (Ex. 13:3) or 'the iron-smelting furnace' (Deut. 4:20). Still, on the other hand (and not to be neglected) is a much more positive portrayal, not only remembering the 'pots of meat' (Ex. 16:2) and other delicatessen (Num. 11:5) in Egypt, but even more the tradition of Egypt as an asylum for refugees that had to flee Israel due to famine or political problems (Gen. 12:10; 26:2; 41:41-57).[14]

Nevertheless, the exodus and subsequent conquest of Canaan motifs are the dominating ones, and the Credo in Deuteronomy 26:5-9 is but one example of the different OT genres – such as narrative (Ex. 1-14), hymn (Ex. 15), and formula (Ex. 20:2) – that express this motif. Of particular interest are the references to migration in a key text like the Decalogue. Both versions of the Decalogue let the exodus motif introduce Yahweh the speaker: 'I am the Lord your God, who brought you out of Egypt, out of the land of slavery' (Ex. 20:2; Deut. 5:6). Both also include the *ger* in the Sabbath commandment, among those who should rest on the seventh day (Ex. 20:10; Deut. 5:14). But the motivation of the commandment is different in the two versions. Whereas Exodus 20:11 legitimizes the Sabbath by referring to six and seven days of creation, Deuteronomy 5:15 instead refers to Israel's own experience of having been slaves – interestingly, not *ger* – in Egypt.

The exodus/conquest motif (with its focus on the chosen people, Israel) is a key motif, not only throughout the Pentateuch, but also in many other parts of the OT. Nevertheless, it is possible to find voices that transcend the particularistic focus of this motif, allowing it to interact with more universalistic ideas. One example is found in Exodus 19:5-6, the core of the Sinai pericope, where the election of Israel (v. 5) is linked to the idea of being a priest among all nations (v. 6). Another example is found in the prophetic corpus, nevertheless echoing – thematically, terminologically, and theologically – the Pentateuch/Joshua and exodus/conquest narrative:

> Are not you Israelites
> the same to me as the Cushites?
> declares the Lord.
> Did I not bring Israel up from Egypt,
> the Philistines from Caphtor,
> and the Arameans from Kir? (Amos 9:7 NIV)

There is a clear, universalistic tone here, comparing Israel with other nations. The tone is set by v. 7a, where the Israelites are compared quite

[14] See M. Cogan, 'The Other Egypt: A Welcome Asylum', in M.V. Fox, et al. (eds), *Texts, Temples and Traditions: A Tribute to Menahem Haran* (Winona Lake: Eisenbrauns, 1996), 65-70.

generally with the African nation of the Cushites.[15] But then, in v. 7b, the comparative approach is narrowed, in the sense that one particular segment of the historical experiences of the Israelites – the exodus/conquest motif – is likened to corresponding migration experiences of the neighboring Philistines and Arameans. The text is unique. It does find some resonance in the universalistic stream of the OT, for example, in the first chapters in the same book of Amos. Still, nowhere else in the OT is the exodus/conquest motif used explicitly about other peoples' migration experiences.

A possible third aspect of Israel's experience and understanding of migration – as reflected in the Credo in Deuteronomy 26:5-9 – is the Babylonian exile in the sixth century BC. When I say a *possible* third aspect, it is because there are no explicit references to the exile on the textual surface of the Credo. However, as much of the literature of the OT found its final form in exilic and early post-exilic times, with the severe experiences of the exile (including the kind of experiences we would here refer to as 'migration') as the immediate interpretive context, it seems reasonable to read also the Credo's focus on the 'wandering Aramean' from an exilic perspective.

The patriarchal migration and exodus/conquest motifs discussed above play key roles in some exilic and early post-exilic literature. Let the exilic/post-exilic parts of the Book of Isaiah provide some examples. First, as far as the patriarchs are concerned, Abraham (cf. Isa. 51:2; 63:16) and not least Jacob (cf. Isa. 49:6; 58:14) are referred to in several places. A most illustrating example is found in Isaiah 41:8-9 (NIV):

> But you, O Israel, my servant,
> Jacob, whom I have chosen,
> you descendants of Abraham my friend,
> I took you from the ends of the earth,
> from its farthest corners I called you.
> I said, 'You are my servant';
> I have chosen you and have not rejected you.

The reference to Abraham makes particular sense in connection with the Babylonian exile, as he, too (according to the OT tradition) was led by God along more or less the same route as the exiled, from Ur of the Chaldeans to Canaan (Gen. 11:31). The exilic and early post-exilic readers, accordingly, are called to see their experiences as a parallel to what the ancestor Abraham had already experienced. The same is the case with the exodus/conquest motif. Several texts in the exilic parts of Isaiah seem to make use of the exodus (and to some extent conquest) motif (cf. Isa. 43:16-21). A most illustrating example is found in Isaiah 52:11-12 (NIV):

[15] See K. Holter, *Yahweh in Africa: Essays on Africa and the Old Testament* (Bible and Theology in Africa 1; New York: Peter Lang, 2000), 115-25.

Depart, depart, go out from there!
Touch no unclean thing!
Come out from it and be pure,
you who carry the articles of the Lord's house.
But you will not leave in haste or go in flight;
for the Lord will go before you,
the God of Israel will be your rear guard.

The Isaiah text interprets the exodus from Egypt antithetically. What the exiled in Babylon will experience is far more than what those leaving Egypt experienced, as they, unlike their predecessors, will not have to leave in haste (Ex. 12:11). Still, like their predecessors, they will experience that Yahweh goes before them and stands behind them (Ex. 14:19).

In other words, when the Credo is read in the light of the Babylonian exile (such as by the exiled themselves or their children, or by the first- or second-generation returnees) it becomes more than a text about a remote past, it is a text about 'us' and 'our' experiences. The interpretive 'we' becomes the Abraham who was called from Babylon, and the Israel that experienced the exodus.

Summing up, it has been argued that migration is a key motif in the OT. Proceeding from the so-called Historical Credo in Deuteronomy 26:5-9, three aspects of the OT experience with migration were discussed: the migration of the patriarchs, the sojourn of Israel in Egypt, leading up to exodus and the conquest of Canaan, and the exile in Babylon.

The Old Testament and a Theology of Migration

The increasing missiological focus on migration is (or, at least, should be) looking for biblical material for its emerging discourses. This last part of the chapter, therefore, highlights some interpretative perspectives on the encounter between the phenomenon of migration and Old Testament texts and motifs. I hope this can serve as a contribution from OT studies to the development of a more general theology of migration. The term 'theology' is not used to denote a mere repetition of texts, nor to refer to a kind of objective distillation from foundational sources (Bible, denominational confessions). In order to have a 'theology', there must be an encounter between 'text' and 'experience', or, in this case, the OT migration motifs have to be seen together with migration experiences with the OT. The following perspectives on the encounter between OT texts and motifs and the phenomenon of migration are included to demonstrate the potential of OT interpretation vis-à-vis the development of a twenty-first-century theology of migration.

From a *textual* perspective: A twenty-first-century interpretation of the Old Testament will acknowledge that the relevance of the texts goes beyond that of the historical context to which they explicitly refer. Israel is portrayed in the OT as having gone through a series of what we today would call migrant experiences, but they are all read through the interpretive experiences of the Babylonian exile. As such, when later readers of the OT – through 2,500 years of interpretive history – perceive their own experiences of migration in light of OT texts and motifs, they follow an interpretive strategy that is developed within the OT itself. Old Testament Israel can testify about a whole spectrum of migration experiences, and more modern interpretive perspectives (such as 'voluntary' versus 'involuntary' migration, or 'push' versus 'pull' factors) can easily find texts with which to interact.

From an *anthropological* perspective: A twenty-first-century interpretation of the Old Testament will notice the particular role of the *ger* – the protected foreigner – as an identity marker of the people of Israel. The experience of being without a permanent residency, which is an existential challenge to most migrants, is in the OT conceptualized both as a rule and as an exception. Truly, staying permanently in the land is an ideal. Still, being in exile is the interpretive frame of many texts, and the *ger* is therefore portrayed both as a subject (you are a *ger*) and an object (you should treat the *ger* well).

From a *theological* perspective: A twenty-first-century interpretation of the Old Testament will see the importance of the universalistic understanding of God in relation to migration. On the one hand, Yahweh follows his migrating people; he is not forever linked to a particular geographical position (the temple in Jerusalem), but follows his migrant people – in front and behind (Ex. 14:19; Isa. 52:12) – and can be worshipped in a transportable tabernacle. On the other, Yahweh is portrayed as the God of all migrants, being credited for not only Israel's migration from Egypt, but also for those of the Philistines from Caphtor and the Arameans from Kir (Amos 9:7).

From an *ethical* perspective: A twenty-first-century interpretation of the Old Testament will admit that migrants (especially in colonial times) have often misused the OT to legitimize their own political and economic interests, at severe costs to others (e.g., the suffering and cruelty experienced by the native inhabitants of the land in North America). Throughout the twentieth century, biblical scholars gradually realized that there is no innocent, public interpretation of the Bible,[16] and that all interpreters have therefore an ethical responsibility vis-à-vis the consequences of their interpretations.

The Old Testament contains a broad spectrum of texts and motifs that reflect experiences with migration, and these texts and motifs continue to engage new generations that have similar experiences. As we Christians increasingly realize the key role played by migration in the past and present mission of the church, we should therefore acknowledge the potential of the

[16] See E.S. Fiorenza, *Rhetoric and Ethic: The Politics of Biblical Studies* (Minneapolis: Fortress Press, 1999).

Old Testament towards contributing to a contemporary emancipatory theology of migration.

Migrants as Instruments of Evangelization: In Early Christianity and in Contemporary Christianity

Werner Kahl

Christianity as a Cross-Cultural Phenomenon

With more than two billion adherents, Christianity is today's largest religion. For more than a century, roughly one-third of the world's population has been counted as Christians. This reality stands in stark contrast to the beginning of the Christian faith in the first century CE. Faith in Jesus of Nazareth as the Christ, the divinely-appointed and anointed savior of the world, originated at the margins of the powerful Roman Empire among Jews in the conquered regions of Galilee and Judea. From there, this belief spread into all directions in unpredictable and uncontrollable ways.

The dissemination of the Christian faith did not unfold in a systematic and organized manner. It was rather due to the forced and impromptu migration of some of the Jews who shared this belief, and who wanted to escape persecution and a possible premature death. On their journeys and at their various destinations, some were able to communicate their faith and their interpretations of the meaning of Christ in intelligible ways to audiences of different cultures, languages, and beliefs.

Only later did Christian narratives about the spread of the belief in Christ present an organized and unified scenario (esp. Acts; cf. Matt. 28:16-20). These presentations are an expression of the conviction of Christ believers of the late first century that they were witnessing the unfolding of God's plan for the salvation of humankind.

Within two decades of its origin, 'the Christian faith'[1] had already taken roots in Rome, the center of the Empire. Although this occurred in the Jewish community in Rome, soon non-Jews of various origins residing in Rome also began to believe in Jesus as the Christ.[2] It should be noted that in this process, Jews did not 'convert' to 'Christianity', for those Jews who believed in Christ did not become 'non-Jews'. They believed in Christ *as*

[1] The expression 'Christian faith' should be used with caution. It is not precise since in the first century – as in worldwide Christianity today – there were various and contrasting interpretations of the meaning of Christ, for instance, the conflict between Paul and Peter according to Galatians 2. The expression is being used here for lack of a more appropriate term. It simply refers to any belief in Jesus as the Christ. It does not denote a particular religion.

[2] Around 55 C.E.: Epistle to the Romans.

Jews just as Greeks later began to believe in Christ as Greeks. To presuppose a 'religion of Christianity' for the first century constitutes an anachronism that should be avoided since it results in a distortion of the historical evidence.

It is apparent that the dissemination of the Christian faith in the first century was *not* the result of a conscious decision drawn by believers aiming to evangelize the peoples of the world. It rather was the result of painful developments beyond their control that forced them into migration.

Among these uprooted individuals, those with multicultural backgrounds were better-equipped than others to cross cultures. On their journeys, their belief in the crucified Jesus as the Christ began to make sense in unforeseeable ways, and it gave sense, dignity, and direction to their lives. Some discovered as central to the meaning of Christ his significance as the ultimate savior of all peoples regardless of nation or culture. They aimed at the realization of a unity of all peoples as *one* people with *one* God without negating cultural particularities and while undermining any claims to national, cultural, or religious privilege.[3] As bearers and disseminators of this message, these migrants appeared – to themselves and to others – as instruments of God, chosen for the fulfillment of a divine plan. It is due to the destiny, the efforts, and the abilities of these Jewish migrants from various Hellenistic diasporas that the belief in Christ survived the first century and that it spread all over the ancient world, eventually resulting in the birth of a new religion called Christianity.[4]

In today's world, certain developments in global Christianity show some affinities to those of the first century as described above. In the past two decades, many European countries have experienced a sharp increase in the arrival of migrants hailing from sub-Saharan Africa, where the majority of residents are Christian.

Many of these believers represent versions of Christianity that had not been common in Europe since they belong predominantly to Pentecostal or charismatic churches rooted in African traditions and cultures. Yet, it is these latter churches that have moved from the margins to the center of global power. Pentecostal migrant pastors, evangelists, and apostles from Africa often interpret their relocation or dislocation as a reaction to a call from God 'to win the Germans (the Dutch, the Swiss, etc.) for Christ'.[5]

---

[3] This insight was gained not only by Paul as has been brought out by proponents of the 'new perspective on Paul'; cf. Krister Stendahl, *Final Account: Paul's Letter to the Romans* (Minneapolis: Augsburg, 1995). It was shared independently from Paul also by Christ-believing Hellenistic Jews who preached for the first time to non-Jewish Greeks in Syrian Antiochia (Acts 11:19-21).

[4] It should be noted that in New Testament scholarship it is debated when Christianity as a distinct religion was recognized in antiquity. Daniel Boyarin argues for a late fourth-century date in his *Border Lines: The Partition of Judeo-Christianity* (Philadelphia: University of Pennsylvania Press, 2004).

[5] Cf. Claudia Währisch-Oblau, *The Missionary Self-Perception of Pentecostal/*

Biblical stories of migration and diaspora existence become especially important and real to them. These stories might serve as a means to reinterpret painful migration experiences positively by inscribing personal histories into the overall plan of God for universal salvation. In this scheme, missionaries from the global south appear as God's chosen instruments. Re-reading the Bible under the impression of their own migration experiences, these Christians are often able to uncover biblical reflections of migration and diaspora existence which tend to be neglected or which are completely overlooked in northern Christianity and theology, including biblical scholarship.

The recent processes of global migration, as well as the philosophical and theological discourses on this phenomenon – postcolonialism and the theory of transculturalism – bring into sharp focus the significance of the realities of migration, diaspora existence, translation, identity change, and power structures not only in contemporary times, but also in the early Christian movements of the first century. They present a unique resource in uncovering migration and diaspora existence as necessary conditions for the successful spread of the belief in Christ in the Hellenistic world, moving from a matrix of constructing reality in a Semitic language and in a particular Jewish encyclopedia of Galilee/Judea into other cultures of Greco-Roman antiquity.

The New Testament is the result of – and it reflects – cross-cultural processes, as becomes apparent by the following observations:

- The 27 writings collected in this canon were composed and written in *koinē*, the common language and lingua franca in much of the Hellenized world. Their authors were probably all Jewish, either narrating incidents that happened in Galilee and Judea or interpreting the significance of these events for Greek-speaking Jews and Gentiles.
- These writings witness certain transformations and modifications of Jewish beliefs, redefining the belief in Christ as a way of adapting it to recipients of various cultures in the Greco-Roman world, with early Christianity as a cross-cultural phenomenon.[6]
- Migration and diaspora existence as social phenomena underlie much of the history of early Christianity.

Charismatic Church Leaders from the Global South in Europe: Bringing Back the Gospel (Leiden and Boston: Brill, 2009).

[6] Cf. Werner Kahl, 'Paulus als Kontextualisierender Evangelist beim Areopag', in Eberhard Bons (ed), *Der eine Gott und die Fremden Kulte: Exklusive und Inklusive Tendenzen in den Biblischen Gottesvorstellungen* (Biblisch-Theologische Studien 102; Neukirchen-Vluyn: Neukirchener, 2009), 49-72; Kahl, 'Die Bezeugung und Bedeutung frühchristlicher Wunderheilungen in der Apostelgeschichte angesichts transkultureller Übergänge', in Annette Weissenrieder und Gregor Etzelmüller (eds), *Religion und Krankheit* (Darmstadt: WBG, 2010), 249-64.

Many of these aspects have been observed and discussed in classical exegesis. From the perspective of *intercultural biblical hermeneutics*, however, these aspects are being placed at center stage of critical reflection. This emphasis is indicative in the following two-fold observation: cross-cultural processes represent a central feature of the spread of early Christianity; as such, they correspond to an understanding of the meaning of the gospel among Hellenized Jews as essentially involving the transgression of boundaries.[7]

In what follows I will concentrate on an analysis of Luke's *Book of Acts* from the perspective of experiences of migration and diaspora existence. I will occasionally refer to relevant passages in other New Testament writings. These writings provide ample evidence for the centrality of the social phenomena of migration, displacement, and diaspora existence in early Christianity.

I will conclude with observations concerning rather unsuccessful efforts of migrant pastors from Africa to evangelize Europeans in recent years. The Book of Acts serves, to many of them, as a blueprint for their own missionary endeavors. The narratives of migrant pastors or evangelists representing their own experiences as missionaries in foreign lands at times appear as a continuation or re-enactment of Luke's work.

Experiences of Migration and Diaspora Existence in the Book of Acts

Here, I will discuss a selection of passages in Acts that reflect experiences of migration and diaspora for the first-generation believers in Jesus as Christ. Luke presents a particular construction of the spread of the Christian faith, covering the three decades from the 30s to the 50s of the first century. He remolded and adapted memories concerning this spread as to fit the agenda for the unfolding of his narrative. The main narrative move of Acts is programmatically expressed in the last clause of Acts 1:7-8: 'He said to them: "It is not for you to know the times or dates the Father has set by his own authority. But you will receive power when the Holy Spirit comes on you; and you will be my witnesses in Jerusalem, and in all Judea and Samaria, and to the ends of the earth"'.

Jesus is addressing his disciples before his ascension into heaven. The scene is located close to Jerusalem at Mount Olive. The remaining eleven disciples are identified by name (v. 13). They are not Judeans – they are Galileans (v. 11). In accordance with the proclamation of verse 8, they do not return to Galilee, their country of origin, but to Jerusalem (v. 12). In Judea, however, their particular northern dialect of Aramaic would betray their origin.

---

[7] With respect to Paul, see Hendrikus Boers, *The Justification of the Gentiles: Paul's Letters to the Galatians and Romans* (Peabody: Hendrickson, 1994).

The proclamation of verse 8 should not be taken literally. It only roughly describes the program of the dissemination of the *witness* to Christ. It should be noted that it was *not* the addressees of this proclamation – Jesus' disciples – who traveled 'to the ends of the earth' as witnesses of Christ (the same holds true for Matt. 28:16-20). Those who eventually gave witness to Christ in the wider Greco-Roman world were not among the disciples of Jesus. Most of them were representatives of the Jewish diaspora in various regions.

It is important to Luke, however, to emphasize that the witnessing activity of the disciples would *begin* in *Jerusalem*, and that the core of the disciples of Jesus would *remain* there. By insisting on remaining in Jerusalem, Luke corrects another tradition that was favored by Mark, and followed by Matthew (Mark 16:7, Matt. 28:5). Here, the women at the grave are instructed to inform the disciples that Jesus would go ahead to *Galilee* and that the disciples would see him *there*. This motif occurs in two following narrative moves in Matthew 28. In verse 10, the proclamation of verse 5 is reiterated to the women, this time by Jesus himself. And verse 16 recounts the encounter of the disciples with Jesus at a mountain in Galilee, presupposing that the disciples had left Jerusalem and traveled to the meeting place. Matthew stresses here the discontinuation of the Jesus movement with historical Israel.

Luke, on the other hand, omits the references to Galilee as the meeting point with Jesus (cf. Luke 24:6-7). In Luke's Gospel, the disciples are still in Jerusalem, where Jesus appears to them (Luke 24:33-36). He explains to them that repentance and forgiveness of sins will be preached based upon his name, for all nations, *beginning in Jerusalem* (Luke 24:47). Luke is here in agreement with Paul, who insisted that Israel would continue to be the favored subject of God's dedication (cf. Rom. 9-11). The gospel from the Pauline-Lucan perspective fundamentally means the complete inclusion of 'all nations' into the covenant of God with his beloved people while not losing their cultural identities.

The programmatic announcement in Acts 1:8 provides the structure of the whole narrative. The story begins with events concerning the witnessing activity of the disciples in Jerusalem and Judea (Acts 1-7), moves to incidents occurring in Samaria (Acts 8-9), and from there lays an emphasis on the proclamation of Christ among 'the nations' (Acts 10-28). The narrative describes in particular a move from the margins of the Roman Empire to its center, ending with Paul's house arrest in Rome.

The apostles engaged in giving witness to Christ are subject to the works of the Holy Spirit. According to Acts, it is the divine spirit who, as the main active subject of the process, brings about the worldwide spread of the gospel. The Spirit of God *initiates* the global dissemination of the gospel of the grace of God (20:24; cf. 15:7) and *prepares*, as well as *directs* those involved in giving witness to Christ. The title 'The Acts of the Holy Spirit' for the second book of Luke would be more appropriate than the traditional title 'The Acts of the Apostles' or the one we also use, the 'Book of Acts'.

The 'good news' spread through the apostles is that both Jews and Gentiles 'may be saved by the grace of the Lord Jesus' (15:11). According to the reconstruction presented by Luke in Acts, it was due to divine grace that the former difference between both groups before God with respect to eligibility for salvation has been overcome. The insight into the universality of salvation was made possible by divine revelation, not by human calculation. During the unfolding of the divine plan as presented in the narrative program of Acts, the circle of peoples included in salvation was progressively widened. In the beginning, *Jews and proselytes from the diasporas* were included as potential recipients of the gospel (chs 1-8), then *Samarians* were added (ch. 8), before non-Jewish and uncircumcised people of the 'nations' were regarded as worthy of salvation (chs 9-28). This last group first included so-called *God-fearers*, non-Jews who believed in the God of Israel and who observed certain Jewish laws (ch. 10), and then *Greeks* and other *uncircumcised peoples* of the Greco-Roman world (chs 11-28).

Jewish migrants with a diaspora background played a significant role in spreading the gospel in the Greco-Roman world of the first century. It is historically plausible that those who were raised as Jews in non-Jewish contexts of Mediterranean antiquity were prepared to interpret the meaning of Christ in terms of an inclusion of non-Jews in salvation. And they were able to communicate the gospel across cultures in ways that could be plausible and relevant to non-Jews. Let me trace their vital contribution to the spread of the belief in Christ as instruments of God in the narrative of Acts.

Besides the fact that the disciples of Jesus remained in Jerusalem as migrants from Galilee after the experiences of Jesus' death and reappearance, migrants from regions beyond Palestine first come into play as potential instruments of evangelization in Acts 2:1-13. At the Jewish festival of *Shavuot,* which concludes the *Pesach* celebrations after 50 days (LXX: *pentēkostē*), many diaspora Jews and proselytes witnessed the presence of the Holy Spirit with the apostles in Jerusalem. According to Acts 2:5, these witnesses 'lived' in Jerusalem, meaning they had migrated permanently to Jerusalem and were not just visiting for the festivities. The Holy Spirit manifested itself in the ability of the Galilean disciples 'to speak in other tongues' (2:4), i.e., in languages different from Aramaic, their mother tongue.

The Jews and proselytes from the diaspora witnessing the event were amazed to hear the Galileans praise God in their various languages (2:7-8, 11-12). It seems significant that this event led to the formation of the first transnational and intercultural community of *Jewish* believers in Christ. According to 2:37-47, Jews and proselytes from Galilee, Judea, and the diasporas of various countries began to pray and eat together, and they shared their belongings.

Intercultural communities with people representing various origins and languages tend to be fragile compositions. Disruptive and disintegrative forces constantly threaten these communities. To regard one another as brother or sister with equal dignity and rights across cultures was not the rule even within ancient Judaism, and what is today referred to as early Christianity was initially a complete Jewish phenomenon.

One intercultural conflict involving migrants in the formation of the first community of Christ believers is reflected in Acts 6:1-6. According to this passage 'Hellenists', Jews who had migrated to Jerusalem from the Hellenistic world, complained that the 'Hebrews', Jews from Judea and Galilee, did not take good care of the Jewish widows with a migration background. Seven Hellenistic migrants from among the community were chosen to organize the daily feeding of the widows, among them one Nicolas, a proselyte from Antioch in Syria. Two of these seven men, Stephen and Philip, are presented as the first migrant witnesses of the gospel in Acts. Both were instrumental in communicating the gospel to non-Hebrews.

In Acts 7, Stephen is challenged by other diaspora Jews, 'some of the so-called synagogue of the Libertines, Cyreneans and Alexandrians, and by those from Cilicia and Asia' (v. 9). The witness of Stephen eventually led to his becoming the first martyr, a 'blood witness' of the Jewish-Christian movement. Ironically, Saul/Paul, himself born and raised in the diaspora and responsible for the killing of Stephen (v. 58), later becomes the prime example of a migrant evangelist among non-Jews. The first persecution of the Christ believers in Jerusalem, which was also led by Saul/Paul (8:1-4), caused a *forced migration* of most members of the Christ-believing community in Jerusalem. They were dispersed not only in Judea, but also in Samaria, where Philip began to preach (vv. 5-25), causing Samarians – whom Hebrews despised as a mixed people and regarded as neither Jews nor gentiles – to accept the gospel (vv. 12-14) and to receive the Holy Spirit (vv. 15-17).

The same Philip was led by divine revelation to the road to Gaza, where he encountered an Ethiopian eunuch who served as a high-ranking official of the Ethiopian kingdom. This person was on his way back home from Jerusalem where he went to pray. Most likely, this Ethiopian was a Jewish proselyte, and as an Ethiopian he would have been circumcised. He accepted the teaching of Philip about Jesus and allowed himself to be baptized. We are not informed about his further development, but the message about Christ might have traveled with this proselyte to Ethiopia shortly after 30 CE.

Acts 9 does not narrate a 'conversion' of Paul. Before and after his dramatic encounter with the risen Christ, he remained a Jew. He was also not 'called' into his particular ministry, but *forced* by divine intervention to serve as a 'chosen instrument to carry the name of Christ before nations, kings and the children of Israel' (9:15). So also in the case of Paul we have an example of – spiritually – *forced migration*. As someone who was born and raised in the diaspora, in Tarsus of Asia Minor, Paul initially tried to convince other diaspora Jews of his belief in Christ, first in Damascus (9:20) and then among Hellenistic Jews in Jerusalem (9:28-29). These first attempts by Paul were apparently not successful.

According to the narrative of Acts, Cornelius, who had migrated to Caesarea as a Roman centurion, became the first non-Jew in the strict sense who accepted faith in Christ (10:1-11:18). He was not a proselyte, but a so-called *God-fearer* (10:2), a *non-circumcised* (11:3) Roman who believed in the God of the Jews. Because of his acceptance of the message about Christ as preached to him by Simon/Peter, his 'whole household' received the Holy Spirit and was saved (11:14-15).

The narrative of Acts communicates a gradual process leading eventually to the preaching of the gospel to uncircumcised non-Jews living outside of Palestine who did not have any relationship to the Jewish tradition. The first such instance is reflected in Acts 11:19-26. Of those Christ believers who had been forced by persecution to leave Jerusalem, some migrated to Phoenicia, Cypress, and Antioch in Syria 'proclaiming the word to Jews exclusively' (v. 19). Some of the Jewish migrants who had been originally from Cyprus and from Cyrenaica in Northern Africa were the first to address also non-Jewish 'Greeks' (*hellēnistes*) with their preaching, and the addressees responded in accepting the message about Christ. This happened in Antioch. Barnabas and Saul/Paul also lived and taught in this city for about one year (v. 26), and it was in Antioch that 'the disciples were first called Christians', followers or adherents of Christ (*christianoi*).

The first transcultural and trans-ethnic community of Christ-believers consisting of both Jews of various origins *and uncircumcised non-Jews* was created in Antioch by migrant diaspora Jews. Acts does not inform us about the motivation or situation behind the decision to include non-Jews into the community. It was obvious to people in Antioch that here a new social phenomenon of a mixed community took shape which transcended Jewish experiences and concepts: the non-Jewish believers neither had to be circumcised nor did they have to follow Jewish dietary laws as the preconditions to be counted among the community of the divinely-chosen ones. They only had to adopt the belief in the one God as he had been witnessed in the Jewish tradition and they had to accept that Jesus was the Christ (cf. Acts 20:21).

This was not a Jewish synagogue community, but a new kind of *ecclesia* community whose adherents were called by others 'Christians'. It is not clear if Jewish Christ believers were included in that term; even if this were the case, this would not have put them in a position of contradiction to Judaism.

The Jews Barnabas and Paul were sent out from Antioch into further migration at the instigation of the Holy Spirit with the objective to evangelize the Gentiles (13:1-3). These two apostles served together with three others as prophets and teachers in Antioch. Two of those colleagues were diaspora Jews with an *African* origin: Symeon who was also called *Niger* (from Latin: 'black man') and Lucius from Cyrene in Northern Africa. The Holy Spirit instructed them together with Manaen to single out Paul and Barnabas for their particular responsibility of preaching to the Gentiles. It is significant that two of the three pairs of hands that were laid onto Barnabas and Paul as a way of blessing them for their journey belonged to Jewish migrants from Africa.

In the narrative of Acts, political and spiritual factors forced Paul and his companions into migration toward the West, resulting finally in Paul's arrest by the Romans and in his transfer to Rome, where he awaited trial. On his journeys in the Hellenized Roman Empire, Paul increasingly, but by no means exclusively, preached about Christ before non-Jews, i.e., members of various ethnic groups who believed in a multitude of gods. As a diaspora Jew born and raised in Minor Asia, Paul shared with these addressees of his sermons a common language, *Koinē-Greek* as the lingua franca of the Roman Empire.

Cross-cultural communication in general and interreligious encounters in particular cause misunderstandings. Acts reflects the challenges of cross-cultural communication that Paul encountered while preaching as a Jewish migrant and cultural outsider in various regions of Asia Minor and Greece.

One such incident is represented in Acts 14:8-18. According to the passage, on his visit of Lystra in the Roman province Galatia, Paul (who was accompanied by Barnabas) commanded a man lame from birth to stand on his feet. Polytheistic witnesses of the event concluded that some of their gods were involved in the miracle. This comes to expression by a comment passed in their mother tongue: 'The gods have taken on human shape and have come down to us' (14:11). To them, Zeus appeared as Barnabas and Hermes as Paul. As was demanded by tradition, the local priest of Zeus was getting prepared to sacrifice offerings to 'these gods'. In a dramatic attempt to dissuade the people from so doing, Paul insisted that he and Barnabas were 'merely human beings', and by referring to the one and only god of his Jewish tradition, he pointed to the numinous subject who had brought about the miraculous restoration.

Paul himself, however, had caused the misunderstanding. In commanding the lame man to rise and walk, Paul appeared as an *immanent bearer of numinous power*, i.e., as a god in human shape. As the agent of a transcendent god, Paul would have been expected to *refer* to a god during the healing performance. Paul, however, did not do so. The polytheistic inhabitants of Lystra had no choice but to make sense of the miracle within their traditional frame of reference, so they had to conclude that gods had appeared before them. From their cultural perspective, this interpretation was evident, and it took Paul great efforts to convince the inhabitants of his human nature (v. 18).

Luke was keenly aware of this danger of misunderstanding among polytheistic audiences, especially with respect to miracles. Therefore, Luke regularly presents Peter and Paul as *agents* of God in miracle-healing stories, and as petitioners and/or mediators of numinous power. In the miracle healing stories of Acts, the apostles typically appeal to God through *prayer*, command healing in the *name of Jesus*, and/or lay on their hands on a person in need signalling that divine healing power was transferred *through* the apostles in a particular case.[8] Immediately preceding our passage, Luke has the polytheistic readers of his work understand that *only God* is the miracle worker: '... the Lord causing signs and miracles to happen through their hands' (14:3; cf. 5:12; 19:11; and even with respect to Jesus of Nazareth: 2:22).[9]

In general, however, Luke presents Paul as a person who tried to avoid or at least minimize resistance to his message in order to maximize the positive reception of the gospel among various groups of addressees. As far as possible, Paul would adjust to the culture and to the expectations of respective listeners. He did so as a Jew who had come, by means of a miraculous event (9:1-19; cf. 22:3-21; 26:9-20), to believe that Jesus of Nazareth was the Christ. Following this strategy, he could have his assistant Timothy – an uncircumcised Jew: his mother was a Jew and his father a non-Jewish Greek – circumcised 'because of the Jews in those regions' (16:1-3). Paul did *not* reject Jewish customs for Jews, including himself (cf. 21:20-26). To him, circumcision *for Jews* still remained important as an identity marker deeply rooted in Jewish tradition, but *not* as a means and sign of salvation.

The letters of Paul are in agreement with this Lucan presentation of Paul's strategy to evangelize peoples with a variety of cultural traditions on his journeys. Of course, he did not 'preach [*kēryssō*] circumcision' (Gal. 5:11) since circumcision was not part of the *kerygma*, the salvation message. Paul himself clearly brings to expression his strategy to communicate the gospel in his multicultural encounters, in 1 Corinthians 9:19-23:

> Though I am free and belong to no one, I have made myself a slave to everyone, to win as many as possible. I approached the Jews as a Jew, to win the Jews; those under the law as someone under the law (though I myself am

---

[8] The only other passage where a similar misunderstanding is narrated is Acts 28:2-6.

[9] For a detailed analysis of Luke's attempts to preempt a common polyteistic misunderstanding of the role of the apostles and of Jesus in miracle healing performances, cf. Werner Kahl, *New Testament Miracle Stories in Their Religious Historical Setting: A Religionsgeschichtliche Comparison from a Structural Perspective* (Forschungen zur Religion und Literatur des Alten und Neuen Testaments 163; Göttingen: Vandenhoeck & Ruprecht, 1994), 111-20, 226-28.

> not under the law), so as to win those under the law; those not having the law as someone not having the law (though I am not without the law of God but in the law of Christ), so as to win those not having the law. I approached the weak as a weak person, to win the weak. I have approached all people in all various ways so that by all possible means I might save some. I do all this for the sake of the gospel, that I may serve as its co-worker.[10]

It is in line with this strategy that Paul had Timothy circumcised and that Paul underwent the Nazarite vow in Jerusalem (21:17-26). At the same time, this strategy necessitated Paul's refusal of the Jewish demand of circumcising Titus, his Greek companion (Gal. 2:3). According to Paul's understanding of the gospel, it was a question not of ethnic belonging, gender, or societal status that decided one's inclusion in God's family, but of belonging to Christ (Gal. 3:26-29). This interpretation allowed for a high degree of flexibility in preaching the gospel to different audiences, which resulted in the successful translation of the gospel among various cultural groups of peoples in the Mediterranean world.

One remarkable example of Paul's ability to adjust his message with great freedom and flexibility to audiences of polytheistic cultures is the report of his speech before philosophers in Athens (Acts 17:16-34). Here, Paul is able to connect positively to traditional customs and philosophical insights shared by his listeners. He skilfully focuses his speech on the common ground of Jews and polytheistic philosophers, for instance, the notion that ultimately the God who created the world and who sustains life is *one,* and that he cannot be captured in human creations. Paul carefully avoids any references about Christ that might be misunderstood as suggesting that Christ was another god. Instead, Paul consequently introduces Christ in passing as a 'certain man' appointed by God (17:31).

Paul was a diaspora Jew who was born and raised in the multicultural metropolis of Tarsus, a rich Asian Minor city well-known for its philosophical schools and large Jewish community. His mother tongue was Greek. His upbringing prepared him sufficiently for his later engagement as a sensible cross-cultural evangelist in migration. In Acts this multifaceted translation ability is not presented as a divinely-bestowed gift. Spiritual revelation with respect to Paul had the foremost function to direct his travels at particular turning points, beginning with his encounter with the risen Christ in chapter 9, via his call to migrate to Macedonia (16:6-10), and ending with his final return to Jerusalem (20:21-23), which led to his capture. In addition, it is the Holy Spirit that enables the apostles to preach freely and boldly (4:31; cf. 28:31).

But in Acts, the Holy Spirit is not featured as the subject who enables apostles and believers to miraculously speak other languages spontaneously for the sake of evangelizing other peoples. Acts 2 describes a unique event

---

[10] My own translation. In this passage Paul does not specially qualify his being a Jew or being weak. The reason is that he regards himself as a Jew and a weak or ill person.

which took place among the Galilean followers of Jesus and which was witnessed by Jews from various diasporas present in Jerusalem. These Galileans did not evangelize among people speaking other languages, and they did not migrate into the surrounding Greco-Roman world as evangelists. The disciples and earliest followers of Jesus were largely representatives of the uneducated strata of Jewish society in Galilee (cf. 4:13). It is not a coincidence that these Galileans are not featured in Acts as evangelists beyond the traditional Jewish territories. Historically speaking, they were not able to do so. It rather was the human resources – language ability, cross-cultural experiences, and sensitivities – of *migrant diaspora Jews from Hellenized Mediterranean cities* of the Roman Empire that provided the backbone for a successful communication of the gospel to various peoples. In this regard, the narrative presentation of Acts is historically plausible.

Louis H. Feldman has pointed out 'deep Hellenization of Judaism in Asia Minor and hence the existence of a common language of discourse with non-Jews' as one of the most important preconditions for successful missionary endeavors by Jews among non-Jews, attracting quite a number of non-Jews 'as proselytes or as sympathizers' to the Jewish faith.[11] The same holds true for the Christ-believing Jewish evangelists of the first century. The turn of these evangelists toward non-Jews was part of general Jewish missionary endeavors in the first century. Their interpretation of Christ's death and resurrection as the salvific event that *alone* grants access of non-Jews to the chosen community of God made it much easier for non-Jews to identify with the Christologically reconstructed Jewish tradition.

Luke, with his focus on Paul, only represents a cross-section of the phenomenon of the spread of the belief in Jesus as the Christ in the first century. This limitation is most likely due not to an extraordinary importance of Paul in and for early Christianity, but to Luke's personal acquaintance with Paul.[12] Many other Jewish migrants from the diasporas were involved in the spread of the belief in Christ, some of whom are mentioned in passing in Acts. The memories of their efforts have not survived.

From Reverse Mission to Mission Impossible: The Experience of African Migrant Evangelists in Europe

Up to the 1980s European countries, apart from England, France, and the Netherlands, had only a minimal presence of migrants from Africa. This

[11] Louis H. Feldman, *Jew and Gentile in the Ancient World: Attitudes and Interactions from Alexander to Justinian* (Princeton: Princeton University Press 1993), 440-42.

[12] Of all the Gospel writers, Luke betrays the closest affinities to Pauline theological thought, both in his Gospel of Luke and in Acts.

situation has changed with the arrival of tens of thousands of Africans, the majority mostly hailed from West Africa, especially from Ghana and Nigeria. Most of the immigrants were Christians representing versions of Christianity markedly different from the mainline Christian traditions on European soil. They had brought along not only their particular languages and cultures, but also their distinct confessions, beliefs, and forms of worship.

In the 1980s and 1990s, a remarkable shift within Christianity took place in Nigeria and in Ghana. Pastors, evangelists, and prophets engaged in extensive missionary work, which resulted in the foundation of thousands of neo-Pentecostal ministries, and the historic churches of European origin became more or less charismatic. At the same time, the number of Christians in the sub-Sahara region increased. Due to the efforts of charismatic leaders and their followers, Christianity in the sub-Sahara region has become an indigenous religion, a version of the Christian faith in tune with traditional understandings of life. In West Africa, the majority of people, Christians included, acknowledge the reality of a variety of spirits that are believed to pervade all spheres of life at potentially any time. From a neo-Pentecostal/charismatic perspective, all spirits apart from the Holy Spirit, like ancestral spirits, bush spirits, local gods, and water spirits (like *Mami Wata*) are regarded as demonic.[13] In this context, Christ as 'super power' is expected to ward off these spirits, which are feared for their life-destroying potency.[14] With respect to this general West African spiritualistic construction of the world, there is a great contrast to the interpretation of reality in Northern and Western Europe, where people tend to reject the notion of any reality of spirits, at times including God.

When West Africans migrated to Europe, the vast majority felt neither comfortable nor at home, and often not even welcomed, in the churches of the Europeans. Soon upon their arrival in Europe, Christian congregations were created by and among West Africans, often around a charismatic figure who functioned as pastor. In these congregations, people could conduct services and celebrate according to their own traditions, which met their needs on various levels.

In the first phase in the 1980s-90s, the majority of the leadership personnel in these churches were not sent as pastors or evangelists from mother churches in West Africa. Many, however, felt chosen and sent by God to fulfill evangelistic functions in Europe. In her groundbreaking study, Claudia Währisch-Oblau explains that many pastors from Africa and

---

[13] For an analysis of this demonization of traditional culture, cf. Birgit Meyer, *Translating the Devil: Religion and Modernity Among the Ewe in Ghana* (Edinburgh and London: Edinburgh University Press, 1999).

[14] For this function of Christ and the construction of reality, cf. Werner Kahl, *Jesus als Lebensretter: westafrikanische Bibelinterpretationen und ihre Relevanz für die neutestamentliche Wissenschaft* (New Testament Studies in Contextual Exegesis 2; Frankfurt am Main and New York: Peter Lang, 2007), 153-83, 272-307.

Asia construct their migrant biographies in terms of a response to a particular call from God to serve as instruments of evangelization in Europe.[15] According to their narratives, some intentionally decided to come to Europe as chosen evangelists after a revelation, and others felt called to do missionary work after they had arrived in Europe. The common denominator is the conviction to be following a call from God, and to fulfill an important function in the salvific plan of God for the world. Easily the migrant evangelists can identify with early Christian figures engaged in missionary activities: 'It's just the call of God; it's nothing else but the call of God. You know when God call[s] you, just like Paul, to come out of darkness into his marvellous light, then you have to obey the call [...] and sacrifice'.[16]

Below, I will concentrate on the experiences of migrant evangelists from Africa in Germany. Initially, a number of African migrant pastors tried to reach out to the indigenous population, often employing techniques they used in West Africa, especially street evangelism. Generally, these attempts did not result in winning numbers of converts, be it from mainline churches to charismatic ministries, or from among the non-Christian population. The African evangelists were not able to communicate their message across the divides in language, semantic universe, culture, and belief. There are exceptions, but the vast majority of the migrant evangelists had no skills in cross-cultural communication.

The contents of their message, which would be translated at times, and the very performance of the preacher, would not only fail to attract German audiences, but it would put people off, especially when they were confronted with topics that sounded offensive, simplistic or just beyond their listeners' frames of reference. Such examples include references to witches, demons, the devil, the end times, subordination of women to men, Jews as murderers of Christ, evangelistic programs as crusades, hell, divine punishment, ancestral curses, etc. Due to their failure in winning converts among the European people, most evangelists and preachers then focused on the growing African population in Germany. Today, there are about 1,000 congregations with an African leadership and an almost exclusive African membership[17] in Germany, the largest concentration of which is found in Hamburg, with more than 80 of these congregations, which are commonly called 'ministries' by their leaders.

The initial hope of many African migrant pastors and evangelists in a divine program of 'reverse mission' did not materialize due to a widespread inability to overcome cross-cultural communication barriers. The attempt to evangelize among indigenous Germans by migrant preachers from West African of the first generation has turned out to be a 'mission impossible',

---

[15] Währisch-Oblau, *Missionary Self-Perception*, 133-303.

[16] Währisch-Oblau, *Missionary Self-Perception*, 159.

[17] There are exceptions like the international New Life Church in Düsseldorf, which was founded and which is being led by the Ghanaian-born pastor Richard Aidoo.

as African pastors in Germany have begun to realize. Analyzed from the perspective of sociolinguistics or the sociology of knowledge, this development is not surprising: The overlap of encyclopedias between African evangelists and their European audiences was not sufficient to allow for a transfer of signals that could be both plausible and relevant to the recipients. And miracles like xenolalia that were experienced by the apostles according to Acts 2 have not occurred in the recent history of the presence of neo-Pentecostal African migrant pastors in Europe.

Lessons from Mission History and Prospects

As could be learned from the New Testament accounts of the dissemination of the gospel by Jews among non-Jews, these efforts proved successful due to a personal transcultural background and sensitivity of these evangelists that prepared them for the cross-cultural communication of the gospel on their missionary journeys as migrants in foreign lands.

During the first half of the eighteenth century, when young missionaries from Denmark, Germany, and Switzerland were sent out to the former Gold Coast by the Reformed Mission agencies in Basel and Bremen, they failed in their attempts to convert the indigenous people.[18] They were unable to connect to the populations on the Gulf of Guinea in meaningful ways – they needed people who were wellversed in both encyclopedias, both that of the missionaries and that of the local populations, not only for a successful communication of the gospel, but for their very survival in those regions. After all, the first missionaries sent by the Basel Mission to the Gold Coast had died – with the sole exception of the Dane Andreas Riis, who had seen a traditional healer when he fell seriously ill[19] – and no convert had been gained.

The Mission Board then decided to invite 24 Christian Africans from the diaspora in the West Indies to assist with the mission work in the Aquapim Mountains north of Accra, Ghana. They arrived in 1843.[20] With their presence and help, and due to their abilities to intermingle and communicate easily with the local population, missionary efforts began to bear desired fruits.

The first European migrant evangelists in West Africa could not become instrumental in communicating the gospel. They did not even survive. They

---

[18] See Werner Ustorf, *Bremen Missionaries in Togo and Ghana: 1847-1900* (trans. James C.G. Greig; Legon, Ghana: Legon Theological Studies Series, 2002), 267-75; and Werner Kahl, 'Geh in ein Land, das ich dir zeigen werde: Biblische und theologische Aspekte der Identität von Migranten', *Interkulturelle Theologie: Zeitschrift für Missionswissenschaft* 37.2-3 (2011), 204-22, esp. 217-19.

[19] Cf. the report in *Magazin für die neueste Geschichte der evangelischen Missions- und Bibel-Gesellschaften* (Basel, 1833), 344-55.

[20] Cf. the report in *Magazin für die neueste Geschichte der Evangelischen Missions- und Bibel-Gesellschaften* (Basel, 1844), 173-97.

needed people who could cross the cultural divide. Today in Europe, most migrants from Africa of the first generation are also not able to engage in a successful cross-cultural communication of the gospel.

In the past 20 years, however, their children have grown up in Europe. Most have gained the nationality of their country of residence/birth. The second generation in Germany *are* Germans, not migrants. As such, they speak the German language fluently and share to a large extent the value system of the society of which they are a part. At the same time, many grow up in families in which a particular neo-Pentecostal or charismatic belief is celebrated. A good number of these teenagers and young adults, however, do not feel completely at home spiritually and culturally in the congregations of their parents. At the same time, the church life and the services of the mainline churches in Germany do not appear attractive to them. Still, a deep belief in God, the quest for a meaningful Christian life, and joyful church services are of essential importance to these members of the second generation.

In order to meet their particular spiritual needs, teenagers and young adults with an African migrant background have founded two parachurch organizations recently in Hamburg: His Kingdom United and GADED ('God all day every day'). These organizations aim at the creation of new ways of celebrating and communicating the gospel, which could become meaningful also for the wider population, at least among their respective age groups.

Part Two
Ethnic and Regional Developments

THE CHINESE DIASPORA

Allen Yeh

China and the Chinese are a land and people of longevity and extremes. It is well known that China has the largest population of any nation on earth (1.3 billion). It has the fourth largest land mass of the countries of the world, after Russia, Canada, and the USA. It has one of the longest extant civilizations and cultures of any nation with a continuous unbroken history, along with India and Egypt. Samuel Huntington successfully predicted the rise of China in his 1996 book *The Clash of Civilizations*, listing China as one of the three contending 'superpower' civilizations of the twenty-first century, along with the West and the Islamic world. Today, China is quickly becoming *the* global economic powerhouse.[1]

What has often gone unnoticed, however, is the Chinese diaspora, which is the largest diaspora in the history of the world. The Jewish diaspora gets the most attention (as does the Jewish Holocaust),[2] but the Chinese have numbers on their side. When people typically think about the Chinese, they only consider those on the mainland, or perhaps including Taiwan and Hong Kong. But the population, influence, and economic clout of the overseas Chinese should not be underestimated. Collectively, they:

- are at least 36 million in population,[3]
- may have more economic muscle than mainland China itself,

---

[1] Samuel P. Huntington, *The Clash of Civilizations and the Remaking of World Order* (New York: Simon & Schuster, 1996), 102: 'Asia and Islam stand alone, and at times together, in their increasingly confident assertiveness with respect to the West. Related but different causes lie behind these challenges. Asian assertiveness is rooted in economic growth; Muslim assertiveness stems in considerable measure from social mobilization and population growth. Each of these challenges is having and will continue to have into the twenty-first century a highly destabilizing impact on global politics. The nature of those impacts, however, differs significantly. The economic development of China and other Asian societies provides their governments with both the incentives and the resources to become more demanding in their dealing with other countries. Population growth in Muslim countries, and particularly the expansion of the 15- to 24-year-old age cohort, provides recruits for fundamentalism, terrorism, insurgency, and migration. Economic growth strengthens Asian governments; demographic growth threatens Muslim governments and non-Muslim societies'.

[2] There were estimates of up to 20 million Chinese killed by the Japanese during World War II, which is now dubbed the 'Forgotten Holocaust'. Compare this to six million Jews killed by the Nazis. See Iris Chang, *The Rape of Nanking* (New York: Penguin, 1997).

[3] Of which three million are in the USA. Statistics provided by Iris Chang, *The Chinese in America: A Narrative History* (New York: Penguin, 2003).

- are often Christians, and
- may have more influence worldwide than their compatriots on the mainland due to their leadership roles and comparative freedoms.

Current State of the Chinese Diaspora

Let us not make the opposite mistake of thinking that the overseas Chinese are only those who reside in the West. Most of the diaspora Chinese are actually in Southeast Asia: for example, Indonesia, Malaysia, Thailand, Vietnam, and the Philippines.[4] There is also a sizeable population in Latin America. And the Chinese are now making inroads in Africa. In the 1990s, the four resurgent economies were dubbed the 'Little Tigers' of Asia: Singapore, Hong Kong, Taiwan, and South Korea. Three of the four are diaspora Chinese states, and their climbing economic success is a pattern echoed throughout the world. In fact, the Central American nations[5] tried to model their economic policies off the Little Tigers and allied themselves politically with Taiwan over China.[6] It has been noted that:

> the Chinese, who account for only 2 percent of the population of Indonesia, own three-quarters of its private domestic capital...Chinese in the Philippines are only 2 percent of the population, but they probably control half the capital. In Thailand they are 10 percent of the population, with 80 percent of the private wealth. In Malaysia they constitute almost 30 percent of the population, but control over half of private wealth.[7]

The success of the overseas Chinese has not just been economic. Some notable diaspora Chinese who have made their mark recently include Gao Xingjian, who won the Nobel Prize for Literature in 2000. Although born on Chinese soil, he became a French citizen in 1997, thus he was not considered the 'first' mainland Chinese to receive that prize (that distinction would go to Mo Yan, who won the Nobel Prize for Literature in 2012). Another prominent person is Dr Patrick Soon-Shiong, the wealthiest man in Los Angeles. He was born in South Africa, but moved to Canada and then to the USA after medical school and is responsible for numerous medical breakthroughs. Successful Hong Kong movie directors who have made inroads in American cinema include Ang Lee (*Crouching Tiger, Hidden Dragon*; *Brokeback Mountain*) and John Woo (*Face/Off*; *Mission*

---

[4] For official statistics and numbers, see: Patrick Johnstone, *The Future of the Global Church: History, Trends, and Possibilities* (Downers Grove: InterVarsity Press, 2011), 187. For a fuller description of what Christianity looks like in these other Asian countries, see: Peter C. Phan (ed), *Christianities in Asia* (Chichester: Wiley-Blackwell, 2011).

[5] Belize, Guatemala, Honduras, El Salvador, Nicaragua, Costa Rica, Panama.

[6] The notable exception is Costa Rica, which recently switched its allegiance to China. In return, China just constructed their brand-new soccer arena for them.

[7] Dick Wilson, *China the Big Tiger: A Nation Awakes* (London: Abacus, 2000).

Impossible 2). The Hong Kong film industry is rivaled only by Hollywood and Bollywood.

Iris Chang, a product of California's Bay Area and a rising star among historians before her untimely death in 2004, garnered two honorary doctorates and won the John D. and Catherine T. MacArthur Foundation's Program on Peace and International Cooperation Award. There is now a museum dedicated to her and her research on the Rape of Nanking located in Nanjing, China. Classical musicians such as Yo-Yo Ma (French-born cellist who resides in Boston) and Lang Lang (Chinese-born pianist who now lives in New York) are well known.

Chinese American author Sheryl WuDunn, along with her husband, Nicholas Kristof, earned critical praise for their *New York Times* bestselling book *Half the Sky: Turning Oppression into Opportunity for Women Worldwide*, whose title is derived from a Chinese proverb: 'Women hold up half the sky'. Jeremy Lin, the phenom basketball star out of Harvard, has even outstripped Yao Ming in terms of his marketability and changing the face of the NBA, being claimed by both mainland China *and* Taiwan in the so-called 'Linsanity' of his popularity. Even more notably, he has become a representative of evangelical Christianity among the Asian American community, but garnering far less criticism than his parallel in American football, Tim Tebow.

Alberto Fujimori, though of Japanese and not Chinese ancestry, was the President of Peru from 1990-2000, and ran for office under the banner of 'El Chino' ('The Chinaman') due to the fact that Peru has the oldest (since 1849) and largest Chinese community in Latin America.[8] Fujimori beat out Nobel Prize laureate Mario Vargas Llosa for the presidency. His presidency was historic in that it was the first time someone of an ethnic minority group within a nation was elected to the top political post of that country,[9] but certainly he could not have been elected without the sizeable Chinese vote in Peru.

Historical Patterns of Chinese Immigration

How did we get to where we currently are, however? There have been four waves of Chinese immigration around the world, as detailed by Wang Gungwu,[10] an ethnic Chinese academic who was Indonesia-born and Malaysia-raised.

---

[8] There are so many Chinese restaurants in Lima that they have coined a name for that fusion style of cooking: *chifas*.

[9] The second (and only other) time in history that happened was the 2008 election of President Barack Obama in the USA.

[10] Wang Gungwu, 'Patterns of Chinese Migration in Historical Perspective', in Hong Liu (ed), *The Chinese Overseas* (Milton Park: Routledge, 2006), 34-41.

The first, *huashang* (lit. 'Chinese trader'), was when Chinese voluntarily expanded throughout Asia as artisans and merchants. This explains the plethora of Chinese scattered throughout Southeast Asia as detailed above.

The second is known as *huagong* (translated as 'Chinese coolie') and refers to the system of indentured servitude where peasant Chinese moved to the Americas and Australia in the late nineteenth and early twentieth centuries, drawn by the gold rushes, but more often in order to work the railroads, sugar cane plantations, and other manual labor tasks. They planted the majority of the Chinatowns around the world.[11] The Chinese who emigrated to Peru[12] are indicative of this type.

The third, *huaqiao* ('Chinese sojourner'), includes what has been known as the 'brain drain' of highly-educated Chinese to the West. They not only brought a high skill set and intellectual expertise, but were promoters of quality Chinese culture worldwide since they tended to be more upper-middle class. Gao Xingjian and Ang Lee are examples *par excellence* of this type.

Finally, there is *huayi* ('Chinese descent or re-migrant'), which refers to ethnic Chinese who started off as being foreign-born and have emigrated from one non-Chinese nation to another. Dr Patrick Soong-Shiong and Yo-Yo Ma are two representatives of this burgeoning phenomenon.

This explains the wide diversity of Chinese socioeconomic statuses, as well as settlement patterns. Chinese usually seem drawn to cities, but the Cantonese-speaking ones who tended to be more lower-class and ghettoized themselves in Chinatowns[13] are vastly different from the newer waves of immigrants who either voluntarily came over or were the only ones allowed in the USA due to policies such as the Chinese Exclusion Act of 1882, which forbade blue-collar workers from entering the USA. This explains why many cities have several Chinese enclaves: Los Angeles has Chinatown but also Monterey Park and Rowland Heights; New York has Chinatown but also Queens; Vancouver has Chinatown but also Richmond. And in all of these communities, it is the latter which are more prosperous, are more recent in immigration, and largely speak Mandarin rather than Cantonese.

---

[11] Chinatowns have much in common with the historical Jewish ghettoes, of which the one in Venice was the first in the world, as chronicled in Shakespeare's *The Merchant of Venice*.

[12] Also included are the Chinese who moved to San Francisco for the gold rush and to build the railroads, and to Hawaii to work the sugar cane plantations.

[13] For examples of how Christianity plays out in Chinatowns, see James Chuck (ed), *Chinatown: Stories of Life and Faith* (San Francisco: First Chinese Baptist Church, 2002).

Implications of Chinese Immigration for Mission

It is often assumed that globalization means the westernization of the rest of the world. With Commodore Matthew Perry's opening of Japan in the mid-nineteenth century, and with the Chinese capitulation before the British in the Opium Wars, historically this is the way it seems to be with Asia as well.

Nevertheless, the Silk Road, which was the main artery of trade between East and West, brought more than just noodles from China (via Marco Polo) to Italy! Chinese engineering contributions to the West include printing, the crossbow, gunpowder, lock-gates and drive-belts, the mechanical clock, the spinning wheel, iron-chain suspension bridges, equine harnesses, deep-drilling techniques, and more. The influence was not just limited to technology: Chinese art and architecture was all the rage in Europe, especially France, as seen in the *chinoiserie* ('Chinese-esque') movement of the seventeenth and eighteenth centuries in vases, rugs, and Impressionist art.

Financially, the Chinese have also been dominant not just in the stock market[14] but with their general business acumen and economic resources. For example, because much of the wealth of Las Vegas casinos comes from overseas Chinese, most casinos have placed twin Chinese stone lions in front of their main doors to signify good fortune to lure in potential gamblers.[15] But it could be said that the greatest Chinese export – more than its science or aesthetic beauty or economic clout – is its people.

The following is a non-exhaustive list of ten implications the Chinese diaspora may have for mission:

1) *Business as mission.* Because of the entrepreneurial nature of Chinese, they tend to be found in 'gateway' places of immigration and crossroads of the world like the Panama Canal, New York, Hawaii, San Francisco, Vancouver, Hong Kong, and Singapore (the Straits of Malacca). Thus, they are often in places of economic significance and where trade happens. The Chinese can either be a mission field or the missionaries themselves.
2) *Urbanization.* This point is related to the one above. More so than other Asian groups or even the US population in general, Chinese are drawn particularly to large cities,[16] which often contain the richest of the rich and the poorest of the poor. From the Chinese

[14] Hong Kong's *Hang Seng* index is as prestigious as the *Nikkei* in Japan or the Dow Jones in the USA.

[15] For example, one of the premiere hotels in Las Vegas, the Bellagio, has the twin Chinese lions in front of their doors despite their Italian theming. And the MGM hotel, which previously had as their main entrance an open lion's mouth which customers walked into, completely redesigned their front door when they were informed that the Chinese consider it bad luck to walk *into* a lion's mouth.

[16] Ronald Takaki, *Strangers from a Different Shore: A History of Asian Americans* (New York: Penguin, 1989), 239.

ghettoes to the upper echelons of influence, Chinese tend to influence and infiltrate all economic strata. The focus on cities is especially important since the world experienced a 'tipping point' in 2008, when it shifted to becoming more than 50% city dwellers, an increasing trend for the future. This is the real estate idea of 'location, location, location'.

3) *Mobilize the* huaqiao *and* huayi. These are the third and fourth types of Chinese immigration, representing the most influential people in society: not only the wealthy, hence business as mission, but the culture-makers, as seen in film, politics, and sports. Influence and power are tenuous things to hold onto, but if wielded rightly they can be used effectively for the Kingdom of God. This top-down approach often works better in Asian societies, where a corporate mentality dominates, more so than in the individualistic West, where a democratic model works better.

4) *Universities.* Chinese have a disproportionate representation in the top institutions of higher learning around the world. Despite being only 5% of the US population, for example, Asians represent about 40% of the enrollment of the University of California system. Not only do Asians (Chinese in particular) make up a large portion of the students, but increasingly the faculty, and especially the membership of on-campus Christian groups such as Campus Crusade for Christ, InterVarsity Christian Fellowship, and other parachurch organizations. Their evangelistic influence, combined with the rarified intellectual air of such top institutions, provides a marked contrast to the typical leaning toward secularism of most other demographics of university campuses. One trend which must be mentioned, however, is that mainland Chinese who go to prestigious Western universities to study tend to focus on the sciences and not the humanities. Yet, Chinese who study overseas are often, like their counterparts who remain on the mainland, open to the gospel. As Asia becomes increasingly pragmatic (driven by only those things which can produce concrete verifiable results and which generate substantial money), the potential for either a faith/science divide, or an integration of the two, is possible and must be handled with care. It is among the Chinese where these two realities often meet.

5) *Ethnicity.* No matter how acculturated to a foreign land an ethnic Chinese person becomes, there will always be some ties to the motherland because of genetics and physiology. Overseas Chinese can relate to mainland Chinese and be ambassadors of, and build bridges with, their ethnic land of origin. The best example might be sports figures like Jeremy Lin, who is claimed by both China and Taiwan, despite having been born and raised in the USA. Hall-of-Fame tennis player Michael Chang likewise was born and raised in

the USA, but represented mainland China as an ambassador for their 2008 Olympic Games. Both athletes are devout Christians and evangelistic in their public personas and thus have a powerful platform on which to witness to ethnic Chinese everywhere, and much of this has to do with ethnic ties and strong ideas of community, not just individualism.[17]

6) *Religion.* Asia is the most religious continent in the world, and is the birthplace of every major extant world religion: Judaism, Christianity, Islam, Hinduism, Buddhism, Jainism, Sikhism, etc. Samuel Huntington observed:

> As Lee Kuan Yew explained for East Asia: ...If you look at the fast-growing countries – Korea, Thailand, Hong Kong, and Singapore – there's been one remarkable phenomenon: the rise of religion...The old customs and religions – ancestor worship, shamanism – no longer completely satisfy. There is a quest for some higher explanations about man's purpose, about why we are here. [18]

This vacuum, a spiritual hunger, is a real opportunity and a crucial difference from the Islamic world, which already has a competing religion. Not only are Chinese often the ones with much of the economic power in foreign countries, but they are often Christians as well. In multiethnic Singapore, where the Malays, Indians, and Chinese live harmoniously, the reality is that the Chinese not only control most of the wealth and occupy the powerful political positions, but tend to be Christian, as opposed to the Muslim Malays and Hindu Indians. Indonesia, the largest Muslim nation on earth, not only has the largest Chinese population outside of China at over nine million, but also has the largest Protestant Christian percentage among them at 43%.[19]

7) *Neglected populations.* Because the Chinese diaspora can be found everywhere, our typical way of categorizing the world by political nations tends to be limiting. When we ask 'Is Mexico reached with the gospel?', we do not think about the significant minority of Chinese who reside and work in Mexico City and are largely unreached. The same is true of Chinese populations in unexpected places such as Africa, and forgotten places such as Southeast or Central Asia, where the Chinese tend to blend in more with the indigenous population like in Malaysia. If those Chinese are Christian, they can be the 'salt and light' that infuses every part of

---

[17] Helene Lee, 'Hospitable Households: Evangelism', in Peter Cha, S. Steve Kang, and Helene Lee (eds), *Growing Healthy Asian American Churches: Ministry Insights from Groundbreaking Congregations* (Downers Grove: InterVarsity Press, 2006), 124-25.

[18] Huntington, *Clash of Civilizations*, 97.

[19] Johnstone, *Future of the Global Church*, 187.

the world. If they are not Christian, they are an untapped mission field.

8) *A missionary force.* The relatively large and influential Christian population of Chinese within Indonesia can be an inside force to evangelize the largest Muslim nation on earth. Another example is the 'Back to Jerusalem' movement,[20] in which the Chinese are traveling westward along the old Silk Road to bring the gospel to everywhere in between China and Israel, which shows prominently how the most populous country in the world can mobilize its people for worldwide missions. This is sometimes called 'reverse mission' when the Majority World is now evangelizing the West. Reverse mission can also be seen another way: the diaspora Chinese can bring the gospel back to mainland China!
9) *Chinese theologizing.* The potential for overseas Chinese to contribute much to world Christianity is great, especially given their relative freedom of speech compared to their compatriots on the mainland.[21] As theology and praxis go together, any missionary force can be theologizing 'on the road'. This was exemplified by the Apostle Paul, who was the greatest theologian (after Jesus) precisely because he was the greatest missionary (after Jesus). Or, perhaps it is the other way around – his mission work was great because his theology was great. This shows the integral connection between the two. However, the danger with the diaspora Chinese is their tendency to assimilate to the home culture.[22] This has been both a strength and a weakness. It has allowed Chinese to blend in well and succeed in places like the USA, but has also caused overseas Chinese to lose their unique voice.[23] But a unique voice, speaking out of culture, is absolutely necessary in contributing to an authentic global theology.
10) *World Christianity.* The most populous country in the world is already estimated to be between 5-10% Christian.[24] If it is the

---

[20] Paul Hattaway, et al., *Back to Jerusalem* (Atlanta: Piquant, 2003).

[21] For a good example comparing indigenous Chinese theology vs diaspora Chinese theology, see Khiok-Khng Yeo, 'Christian Chinese Theology: Theological Ethics of Becoming Human and Holy', 102-15, and Amos Yong, 'Asian American Evangelical Theology', 195-209, both in Jeffrey P. Greenman and Gene L. Green (eds), *Global Theology in Evangelical Perspective: Exploring the Contextual Nature of Theology and Mission* (Downers Grove: InterVarsity Press, 2012).

[22] Greer Anne Wenh-In Ng, 'The Asian North American Community at Worship: Issues of Indigenization and Contextualization', in David Ng (ed), *People on the Way: Asian North Americans Discovering Christ, Culture, and Community* (Valley Forge: Judson Press, 1996), 147-48.

[23] Fumitaka Matsuoka, *Out of Silence: Emerging Themes in Asian American Churches* (Cleveland: United Church Press, 1995), 50-52.

[24] The official statistic is 7.92% Christian, according to Jason Mandryk, *Operation World* (7th ed; Colorado Springs: Biblica, 2010), 215.

greater number, that is 130 million Christians, then it is the second-largest Christian nation on earth (in terms of absolute numbers) after the USA. Even if this number is lower, 65 million Christians, this is still larger than the population of most countries in this world. As the center of gravity of Christianity has shifted to the Majority World, the thesis that Philip Jenkins outlines in his *The Next Christendom*, China is playing an increasingly prominent role in the world's Christianity.[25] But Soong-Chan Rah points out in *The Next Evangelicalism* that while Jenkins' thesis is correct, another dimension must be added: the domestic and not just the international.[26] The center of gravity of Christianity in the West has shifted to the ethnic minorities and immigrants.[27] This is one of the main reasons the USA continues to be one of the only majority-Protestant Christian nations in the West.[28] And this is why the Chinese diaspora is so important to study. Mark Noll makes the argument that while many have postulated that Majority World Christianity has patterned itself off of American Christianity, it is not an *influence* but a *parallel*,[29] and thus we should soon see Chinese Christianity (both in the mainland, as well as overseas) experience much of the same growth, influence, and 'success' that the USA has enjoyed over the course of the last couple hundred years.

Conclusion

The Chinese diaspora cannot be ignored. Not only is it the largest diaspora in the world's history, but it is a complement, parallel, and influence (both

---

[25] David Aikman, *Jesus in Beijing: How Christianity Is Transforming China and Changing the Global Balance of Power* (Washington, DC: Regnery, 2003), 293.

[26] Soong-Chan Rah, *The Next Evangelicalism: Freeing the Church from Western Cultural Captivity* (Downers Grove: InterVarsity Press, 2009), 12-14. Certainly Canada, Australia, Great Britain, are post-Christian. Roman Catholic nations such as Italy, and Orthodox nations such as Greece, can continue to claim a Christian majority if only by birth, but actual devotion to Christianity is a different story.

[27] Another interesting dimension of ethnic minorities are those within mainland China itself. Though the Han Chinese constitute over 90% of the population, there are more than 450 minority groups of over 100 million people as outlined in Paul Hattaway, *Operation China: Introducing All the Peoples of China* (Pasadena: Piquant, 2000), xi. These groups ought not to be ignored as they are among the least-reached peoples on earth. And they can have a vibrant faith, even more than the Han Chinese, as described in Ralph R. Covell, *The Liberating Gospel in China: The Christian Faith among China's Minority Peoples* (Grand Rapids: Baker, 1995), 10-11.

[28] Rah, *The Next Evangelicalism*, 14.

[29] Mark A. Noll, *The New Shape of World Christianity: How American Experience Reflects Global Faith* (Downers Grove: InterVarsity Press, 2009), 11-12.

on and by) mainland China. With so many Chinese becoming Christian, this diaspora has profound implications for world Christianity and mission. Unfortunately, the attention paid to overseas Chinese is far less, proportionally, than is its importance. Hence the call to action and attention on the diaspora Chinese, who not only are an inviting mission field, but also have the potential to be one of the major mission-sending forces on earth.

Understanding Filipino International Migration

Andrew G. Recepcion

A Snapshot of Filipino International Migration

The experience of migration in the Philippines cannot be captured in a few pages. One can only give a snapshot of the different experiences of Filipino migration.

There are Filipino migrants in almost all the nations of the earth. The Philippines has a population of 101,833,938, with the median age of 22.4 for males and 23.4 for females.[1] Since the majority of the population is made up of young professionals at the peak of their productive lives, it has become difficult for the government to provide jobs for these people. Unable to find well-paying work in the Philippines that can support their families, many Filipinos leave the country (including their spouses and children) in search of better opportunities. There are push and pull factors that cause migration – that is, the state of the economy at home pushes Filipinos to look for better opportunities in other countries and the attraction of well-paying jobs overseas pulls them to stay in the host countries. The data and categories of migration flows in the Philippines indicate that:

> ...[an] estimated 8.23 million overseas Filipinos were working in more than 190 countries, categorized under three distinct flows: permanent or settler immigrants numbering about 3.5 million, found mostly in the United States, Canada, Australia, Japan, United Kingdom and Germany; temporary migrants commonly known as 'overseas Filipino workers' (OFWs), numbering approximately 3.8 million employed in Saudi Arabia, the United Arab Emirates, Kuwait, Hong Kong, Japan and, in recent years, Italy and Spain; and the undocumented workers or unauthorized migrants, estimated at more than 800,000.[2]

Due to the difficulty in securing work permits in the first category of migration, many Filipino migrants end up as 'contract workers in the Asian tiger nations, the Middle East and Western Europe',[3] and they take on domestic jobs commonly referred to as 'dirty, difficult, and dangerous' ('3-D'). However, many stay in their jobs in spite of the nature of their work

---

[1] Pio Estepa, 'The Asian Mission Landscape of the 21st Century', *SEDOS* 43.5-6 (May-June 2011), 122.

[2] Dante Ang, 'Improving Governance in Migration: Lessons from the Philippine Experience', 3-4; available at www.policydialogue.org/files/events/Ang_Improving_Governance_in_Migration_Speech.pdf (accessed 12.9.12).

[3] Estepa, 'Asian Mission Landscape', 123.

since 'the laws in their host countries allow them to come and go as long as their work contracts last, but not to settle or bring their families to reside with them'.[4]

The majority of Filipino migrant contract workers are women with '3-D' jobs, and they are often labeled 'housemaids' or 'nannies' (by people in Hong Kong and in the Middle East) or as *domestica* (by Italians) – that is, 'domestic helpers'. A report on the situation of Filipinos in Italy indicates that:

> Filipinos were among the first migrant groups to come to seek work in Italy, starting in the late 1970s and 1980s. They are mainly employed in the domestic or family care sector as caregivers and domestic helpers. Given the employment opportunities in this sector and the fact that women take up these jobs, it is not surprising that close to 60 percent of the Filipinos in the country are women.[5]

The impression created by these labels resulted in a controversy in 1987 'when it was revealed that the new edition of the *Oxford English Dictionary* would include the word 'Filipino', and one of the associated usages of the word would refer to 'domestic help'. A few years later, a Greek dictionary similarly defined the word as a generic term for a maid or nanny…'.[6] Filipino migrant workers, however, cannot be confined to domestic work and '3-D' jobs. Filipino migration 'is as colorful and interesting as our history'.[7]

There are three waves of Filipino international migration. The first wave has been described as follows:

> In 1417, a trade mission to China headed by Zulu royalty Padua Bazaar marked the first recorded migration of the Filipino. During the Hispanic period, in 1763, Filipino seafarers who jumped one of the galleons plying the Manila-Acapulco Galleon route eventually settled in the bayous of Louisiana. Our first venture into organized migration, however, was in the 1906 travel of agricultural labor to Hawaii, both being colonies of the United States, in the case of the Philippines after more than 300 years of Spanish colonization. During the first wave, Filipinos also arrived in the United States as scholars or *pensionado,* a privilege granted by the U.S. colonial government to woo

---

[4] Estepa, 'Asian Mission Landscape', 123

[5] Dr. Cristina Liamzon, 'Accompanying and Journeying with Overseas Filipinos in Italy', *SEDOS* 43.5-6 (May-June 2011), 153.

[6] Philip F. Kelly, 'Filipino Migration and the Spatialities of Labour Market Subordination', in Susan McGrath-Champ, Andrew Herod, and Al Rainnie (eds), *Handbook of Employment and Society: Working Space* (Cheltenham, UK, and Northampton, Mass.: Edward Elgar, 2010), 159-76, quotation from 159.

[7] Dante A. Ang, 'Philippine International Migration: Causes and Consequences', lecture, Dalhousie University, Canada, 16 April 2008, 2; available at www.philippinesintheworld.org/sites/default/files/Philippine%20Intl%20Migration_Causes%20and%20Consequences.pdf (accessed 12.9.12).

> the Philippine elite as it sought to establish a Commonwealth run by Filipinos.[8]

Further, as Dante Ang describes it, the second wave:

> ...of organized migration came in the aftermath of the Second World War, when Filipino veterans who served in the U.S. armed forces were given a chance to migrate to the United States along with their dependents, including Filipino war brides of U.S. servicemen. The 1960s also saw the unprecedented reforms in the immigration laws of Canada (1962), the United States (1965) and Australia (1966), reducing restrictions to Asian immigration. Europe also introduced a guest worker program which many Filipino professionals took advantage of.[9]

The migration after the Second World War was the beginning of what has been referred to as the *American Dream.* The American Dream continues with Filipino nurses and other professionals migrating to the USA. In recent years, new waves of migration to the USA are made up of those who are hired to teach English as a second language to children of Spanish-speaking immigrants.

The third wave:

> ...came in the form of contract labor in the 1970s, a time when the country was gripped by severe unemployment, especially in the ranks of the professionals. Coincidentally, the Middle East oil boom in the same period provided impetus for skilled and semi-skilled labor to migrate to other countries. The third wave persists to this day with much of the flow in recent years directed toward East and Southeast Asia as Japan, South Korea, Taiwan and Singapore became economic powerhouses in the [19]80s and the [19]90s. As overseas employment grew, the type of occupations shifted from construction work and engineering services to domestic work, tourism, and service jobs, healthcare, communications technology and host of other expertise.[10]

Many documents and articles on Filipino international migration, however, do not include missionary congregations that send priests, religious men and women, and missionary families that belong to new ecclesial movements and communities. Recent statistics show that 86% of religious sisters in the Catholic church are from Asia, with Filipinos, second in number to India.[11] The annual statistics of the Catholic church also indicate that in Asia there is an increase in the number of religious

---

[8] Ang, 'Philippine International Migration', 2; see also Veltisezar B. Bautista, *The Filipino Americans, from 1763 to the Present: Their History, Culture and Traditions* (Farmington Hill, MI: Bookhaus, 2002).

[9] Ang, 'Philippine International Migration', 3. This is the case of my hometown in the Philippines where almost all the families have a son in the US Navy.

[10] Ang, 'Philippine International Migration', 3-4.

[11] James H. Kroeger, MM, 'Asia's Rich Diversity: Pathway into Mission', *SEDOS* 43.5-6 (May-June, 2011), 101.

sisters and priests.[12] Filipino missionaries stay for more than three years in their countries of destination according to the mandate of their institute.[13]

Filipinos who marry those of other nationalities is another population of migrants that has not been given much attention in research and study. In fact, there are stories of Filipino women who are happily married to non-Filipino Americans, Germans, and Italians, just to name a few. Just as in any marriage, however, some fail, resulting in separation, and in some tragic cases the death of a Filipino wife.[14]

Migration and Filipino Core Values

The migration of Filipinos is often interpreted from the labor market point of view and from the financial benefits that the migrant families receive. Analysis of the Filipino migration also focuses on the social costs with particular attention to the negative consequences of migration to families. There are couples that experience strained relationships due to years of physical separation and infidelity. Failed marriages are common, and cause the fragmentation of families and psychological problems for children. Social analysis, although necessary, is not enough to adequately understand Filipino migration. Thus, it is important to understand migration axiologically.

There is a perception that migration has become an integral part of culture in the Philippines.[15] It is important, however, to ask whether the Filipino value system supports the conclusion that migration has become a constitutive part of Filipino identity and meaning-making.

More than the run-of-the-mill description of Filipino values as *hiya* (shame), *bayanihan* (solidarity with the community), *salo-salo* (family meal), *pagtanggap* (hospitality), and so on, it is necessary to go to the heart of the Filipino *loob* (core identity) expressed in five core values,[16] namely:

1. *kabutihang loob* (KBL) (innate goodness)
2. *kalinisang loob* (KLL) (purity of intention, honesty, transparency)
3. *kagandahang loob* (KGL) (generosity, selflessness, kindness)

---

[12] See 'Presentazione Dell'Annuario Pontificio 2012', available at www.news.va/en/news/60795 (accessed 12.9.12).

[13] See also Sister Victoria Joson, RGS, 'Filipino Missionaries in Europe: Witnesses of Re-Evangelization', undated; available at www.babaylan-europe.org/index.php/2007/03/07/filipino-missionaries-in-europe-witnesses-for-re-evangelization/ (accessed 12.9.12).

[14] I vividly remember a visit that I made to one of the Filipino chaplaincies in Europe. The Filipino chaplain narrated a story of a Filipino who was shot dead by her non-Filipino husband due to serious differences and jealousy.

[15] See Maruja M.B. Asis, 'The Philippines' Culture of Migration', *Migration Information Service* (January 2006), available at www.migrationinformation.org/feature/display.cfm?ID=364 (accessed 12.9.12).

[16] See Dionisio Miranda, SVD, *Buting Pinoy* (Manila: Logos Publication, 1998).

4. *kapangyarihan* (KPR) (power, authority, skill, capacity, talents, resources)
5. *katahimikan* (KTH) (peace, harmony, success, comfort, stability)

These five core values are related to one another as expressed through decisions and actions *(labas)* that articulate the Filipino identity in daily life.

The Filipino notion of innate goodness (KBL) refers to what is common to all humanity and that is typically manifested as kindness, generosity, and selflessness (KGL) to the point of involving great personal sacrifice for the sake of the beloved, even if it would mean pain, separation, and ordeal. The test of purity of intention, honesty, and transparency (KLL) comes from the proof of *kagandahang loob,* that is, from consistent action and not from an empty promise. The quality of good action, however, can only be realized when a Filipino is able to use all ways and means (KPR) to demonstrate his or her honest intention (KLL). It is only when one's resources and capacity have been optimized that one can truly achieve success, comfort, stability, and true harmony of relationships (KTH).

Filipinos who leave the country are in search of a better life for their families and of a means to provide for the needs of their children. Many migrants are highly motivated to earn money overseas, hoping that by sending their children to reputable schools they can look forward to a successful career and a comfortable life. Others are equally motivated to find a 'right job' abroad in order to have a nice house, start up a business, invest in real estate, and have enough savings in the bank. It is necessary to note that *Katahimikan* (KTH) is a primary value that pushes Filipinos to take up the challenge to improve the lot of their families. Thus, KTH is not only the dream of a better life for their families, but also the resilience amidst difficulties in order to have stability in life.

The overarching influence of KTH in the consciousness of a Filipino leads one to use all the available means and resources at his or her disposal (KPR) in order to attain his or her goals. Let me illustrate this point through a personal account.

I was invited to a friend's housewarming party. My friend's mother had been working in Milan, Italy, for more than 30 years. It was through her hard work and strength of will that she was able to send all her children to good schools. She saved enough money to buy a car and build a beautiful house for her family. Behind her success story was her unforgettable experience of when she first entered Italy illegally through an agency that brought her to Russia and transported her to Europe by delivery trucks. She was often hidden underneath goods. She was placed inside the trunk of a car by a driver who was high on drugs and took her to a place near an Italian border. She had to walk at night with a few others ready to hide any time from border police. She almost gave up due to exhaustion and fear. But what kept her going was the thought of her family. When she arrived at the central station of Milan, she could only be grateful to God for keeping her alive.

Filipinos are ready to show people that they are hardworking and generous (KGL) while they struggle to make others know what they truly feel (KLL). Thus, they end up justifying what they do for the sake of a higher reason. A letter from a migrant worker illustrates this point:

> When that girl I take care calls her mother 'Mama,' my heart jumps all the time because my children also call me 'Mama.' I feel the gap caused by our physical separation especially in the morning, when I pack her lunch, because that's what I used to do with my children… I used to do that very same thing for them. I begin thinking that at this hour I should be taking care of my very own children and not someone else's, someone who is not related to me in any way, shape and form. Don't we think about that often? Oh, you don't, but we – the Filipino women over here – feel that all the time. The work that I do here is done for my family, but the problem is they are not close to me but are far away in the Philippines. Sometimes, you feel the separation and you start to cry. Some days, I just start crying, while I am sweeping the floor because I am thinking about my children… my family in the Philippines. Sometimes, when I receive a letter from my children telling they are sick. I look up out of the window and ask the Lord to look after them and make sure they get better even without me around to care after them. If I had wings, I would fly home to my family. Just for a moment, I want to see my children, take care of their needs, help them, and then fly back over here to continue my work.[17]

What truly matters for Filipino migrants is to be recognized by their family members. They want to be acknowledged that all their sacrifices have paid off, and in spite of their limitations and shortcomings, they exemplify selfless love for their family (KBL).

Filipino Migration and Mission

Our cursory exploration of Filipino core values offers a better perspective on the experience of Filipino migrants. The core values, however, are not complete without the dimension of faith that gives deeper meaning to all circumstances of life. It is the faith of Filipino migrants that prompted the Catholic church to call them 'missionaries'.

Pope Paul VI encouraged Filipinos to share their faith when he visited the country in 1970:

> At this moment one cannot but think of the important calling for the people of the Philippine islands. This land has a special vocation to be the city set on the hill, the lamp standing on high (Matt. 5:14-16) giving shining witness

[17] This letter from a migrant worker in Rome, Italy is cited by Gilbert A. Garcera, 'Filipino Migrants as New Evangelizers', available at www.familiam.org/pcpf/allegati/1593/4_Garcera_ENG.pdf (accessed 12.9.12).

> amid the ancient and noble cultures of Asia. Both as individuals and as a nation you are to show forth the light of Christ by the quality of our lives.[18]

During his apostolic visit to the Philippines in 1981, John Paul II said, 'There is no doubt about it: the Philippines has a special missionary vocation to proclaim the Good News, to carry the light of Christ to the nations'.[19] How do we understand the relationship between migration and faith from the perspective of mission?

One has to point out that unlike priests and nuns who have a specific missionary mandate, migrant Filipinos, the majority of whom are Catholics, leave the country mainly for economic reasons and not for missionary work. Many Filipinos are nominal Catholics, and when they leave the country to work overseas, their faith experience is limited to going to Sunday masses. On some occasions, they participate in the Holy Week services and in the yearly *Aguinaldo masses* or *Misa de Gallo*, a Christmas tradition in the Philippines used by Spanish missionaries to catechize the faithful about the meaning of Christmas. Since the majority of Filipinos are Catholics, migrants do not feel strongly the difference between their Catholic faith and other faiths when they are in their home country.

The situation becomes different when they work outside the country. The experience of being away from home reinforces the need to entrust their lives and family to God. Thus, there is a re-awakening of faith that seeks out a community that can edify a life away from home. It is not surprising to find many Catholic Filipino migrants to be actively involved in religious activities organized by Filipino chaplaincies all over the world. The mission of Filipino migrants begins with a more personal encounter with the Lord Jesus Christ in their lives as they try to find the meaning behind their struggles being away from home. By finding a deeper relationship with the Lord, they start to appreciate the value of the sacraments, prayer, and the Bible in their work and in dealing with all the challenges that come their way as migrant workers. It is from this fundamental conversion experience that they start to give witness to their faith to fellow Filipinos, people they work with/for, and even the community in their host country. Benedict XVI has rightly indicated that the world is in need of 'living signs of the presence of the Risen Lord; it seeks for credible witness of people enlightened in mind and heart by the

---

[18] Cf. Paul VI, 'Address to the Members of Various Communities, Manila, Philippines', 29 November 1970, available at www.vatican.va/holy_father/paul_vi/speeches/1970/documents/hf_p-vi_spe_19701129_enti-sodalizi_en.html (accessed 12.9.12)

[19] Cf. John Paul II, 'Address of His Holiness to the Philippine Episcopate and Asian Bishops, Villa San Miguel (Manila)', 17 February 1981, §6, available at www.vatican.va/holy_father/john_paul_ii/speeches/1981/february/documents/hf_jp-ii_spe_19810217_manila-episcopato_en.html (accessed 12.9.12).

word of the Lord, and capable of opening the hearts and minds of many to the desire for God and for true life, life without end'.[20]

[20] Benedict XVI, Apostolic Letter *Porta Fidei*, §15; available at www.vatican.va/holy_father/benedict_xvi/motu_proprio/documents/hf_ben-xvi_motu-proprio_20111011_porta-fidei_en.html (accessed 12.9.12).

THE JAPANESE DIASPORA IN BRAZIL

Key Yuasa

'The Japanese emigration to the land of Brazil has been one of the greatest and well succeeded Japanese-Brazilian undertakings in the twentieth century in spite of the difficulties and sufferings of each one of the participants'[1] tells a sympathetic observer. A large phenomenon of transference of hundreds of thousands people has taken place in South America: from an old, overpopulated Far Eastern country (Japan) with a rather ethnocentric outlook on history, society, and culture to this young, large, and multi-racial country (Brazil).[2]

Historical Background

In 1895, Japan and Brazil subscribed to a treaty of friendship, commerce, and navigation. From then on, there have been several initiatives to bring in Japanese immigrants to Brazil. Yet, it was only in 1908 that the first Japanese ship with 781 immigrants arrived in Santos port after a favorable report on coffee plantation farms in São Paulo state by Fukashi Sugimura, the third Japanese Plenipotentiary Minister in Brazil. The majority of them on the ship were contract workers for coffee plantations in São Paulo state.[3] Since then, 250,000 Japanese people have immigrated to Brazil: 190,000 between 1908 and 1941, and about 60,000 after World War II, in the 1950s and 1960s.

---

[1] Elias Antunes, 'Notas do Tradutor', in T. Tokunaga, *História da Emigração Japonesa para as Américas* [*History of Japanese Emigration to Americas*] (Sao Paulo: The Province of Miyazaki Association, 2009), 24.

[2] Prof. Roger Bastide, a famous French Sorbonne Brazilianist (sociologist, cultural anthropologist), referred to 'Brazil, communion table of almost all the peoples of the Earth', in his personal, handwritten dedication to the present writer of his magnum opus, *Les Religions Africaines au Brésil: Vers une Sociologie des Interpenetrations de Civilisations* [*African Religions in Brazil: Towards a Sociology of the Interpenetration of Civilizations*] (Paris: Presses universitaires de France, 1960).

[3] Hiroshi Saito, *O Japonês no Brasil-Estudo de Mobilidade e Fixação* [*Japanese People in Brazil: A Study on Mobility and Settlement*] (S. Paulo: Editora Sociologia e Política, 1961), 27-29; Tadashi e Ishii, *Cem Anos da Imigração Japonesa no Brasil, através de Fotografias* [*One Hundred Years of Japanese Immigration to Brazil in Pictures*] (Fukyosha, Tokyo: Museu Histórico da Imigração Japonesa no Brasil 2008), 13-4.

Japanese Population among Other Immigrant Populations in Brazil

Table 1 indicates that the majority (75%) of immigrants to Brazil have been from Southern (Mediterranean, Latin) Europe. The column 'Middle Easterners' include Turks, Syrians, Egyptians, Lebanese, and Arab peoples from several countries in addition to Jews, while the column 'Others' includes smaller numbers of other Northern Europeans (Austrians, Dutch, Belgians, etc.), Eastern Europeans (Russians, Ukraines, Poles, etc.), and people from the Far East (e.g., Chinese, Taiwanese, and Koreans).

Table 1: Japanese Population among Other Immigrant Populations in Brazil[4]

Period	Portuguese	Italian	Spanish	German	Japanese	Middle Easterners	Others
1880-89	104,690	277,124	30,066	18,901			17,841
1890-99	219,353	690,365	164,293	17,084		4,125	103,017
1900-09	195,586	221,394	113,232	13,848	861	26,846	50,640
1910-19	318,481	138,168	181,651	25,902	27,432	38,407	85,412
1920-29	301,915	106,835	81,931	75,801	58,284	40,695	181,186
1930-39	102,743	22,170	12,746	27,497	99,222	5,549	62,841
1940-49	45,604	15,819	4,702	6,807	2,828	3,351	34,974
1950-59	241,579	91,931	94,639	16,643	33,593	16,996	87,633
1960-69	74,129	12,414	28,397	5,659	25,092	4,405	47,491
Totals	**1,604,080**	**1,576,220**	**711,711**	**208,142**	**247,312**	**140,464**	**671,035**
	31%	30%	14%	4%	5%	3%	13%

Brazilian population was formed originally as a result of an early encounter of three different groups: Portuguese; Brazilian aborigines ('Indians') with several languages and ethnicities; and African populations, slaves of several racial, linguistic, and cultural backgrounds. These groups of peoples met, lived together, and mixed in different proportions for at least 300 years since the 'discovery' of the land in 1500, before the arrival of other immigrants.

The Japanese immigrants and their descendants in Brazil learned to speak an European language akin to other Mediterranean, Latin, or Romance languages. They also began learning to live and interact with peoples of diverse national origins, as well as with 'prehistoric' indigenous populations. Many who have become Christians see this opportunity to rethink cultural, racial, and above all human identity as a very rich and unique blessing from God.

Indeed, the Amazon area is the region with the strongest Indian (ethnic, cultural, linguistic) influence. Bahia is the state with the strongest African influence in terms of language, religion, music, and food culture. The northeastern states would be where the blend among the three groups was the most thorough, according to Brazilian anthropologist Gilberto Freire.[5]

[4] Gilberto Freyre, *Casa Grande e Senzala* [*Mansions and Shanties*] (34th ed.; Rio de Janeiro: Editora Record, 1998).

[5] See also Freyre, *Casa Grande e Senzala*.

São Paulo is the state where most immigrants have settled, and has become the richest, most populous, and most cosmopolitan.[6] Meanwhile, Santa Catarina and Rio Grande do Sul have received more German and Italian immigrants than other states, and these southern states have been more European in a number of ways – especially ethnically and culturally.

But these stereotypes are gradually being modified in Brazil by internal migration, and not only of rural peoples. There is a widespread movement of both workers and qualified professional and technical people that is triggered by new agricultural frontiers, the establishment of new urban projects, the growth of universities and beginning of new learning centers, and the widespread growth of the government machinery. There is a considerable growth of all urban centers. There are new oil prospects, establishment of alcohol refineries, new electricity plants, and new automotive industries. The expansion of bank branches can be seen everywhere. The overall demographic and economic growth of this country is demanding a shuffling of populations and movement of qualified people and workers.

This helps to explain the presence of Japanese immigrants and their descendants in every state of the country, even those north of the Amazon region (e.g., Roraima and Amapá), to the extreme northwest such as Acre. On the other hand, besides the embassy in the Federal District (Brasilia), the Japanese government has established seven General Consulates: two in the northern region (Manaus and Belem), one in the northeastern region (Recife), two in the southeast region (São Paulo and Rio de Janeiro), and two in the southern region (Curitiba and Porto Alegre). Consular services thus are available not only to the Japanese people and descendants, but also to corporations, state and city governments,[7] universities, and individuals in order to facilitate the cultural, scientific, technological, and economical exchanges between the two countries.

The Japanese Diaspora in Brazil as a Mission Field

The stories of different churches which have worked in the Japanese diaspora in Brazil since the 1920s are examined by John Mizuki,[8] who gives the big picture of all the denominations he was aware of in the 1970s.

---

[6] A recent report indicates that 47.2% of all foreign workers to Brazil nowadays come to Sao Paulo State; Ana Paula Boni and Guilherme Genestreti, 'Outros Trópicos' [Other Tropics], in *S. Paulo* 18-24 March 2012, 24-32, http://www1.folha.uol.com.br/revista/saopaulo/sp1803201210.htmv (accessed 7.3.14)

[7] Several cities and states in Brazil maintain sister relationships to cities and provinces in Japan.

[8] John Mizuki, *The Growth of Japanese Churches in Brazil* (Pasadena, CA: William Carey Library, 1978); this is the edited PhD thesis presented by the author to the Fuller School of World Missions and Evangelism in Pasadena, in 1976.

Denominational stories have also been written by Shimekiti Tanaami,[9] Nagafumi Yamazaki,[10] and Chieko Nampo and Liana Goya[11] for the Brazil Evangelical Holiness Church. Carmen Kawano[12] has written with better historiographic tools about the Anglican Episcopal Church among the Japanese people in Brazil, and Midori Oshima[13] has written about the beginnings of the Free Methodist Church in Brazil. Ziel Machado has done an excellent study of a local church of that denomination in São Paulo.[14]

Today, there are perhaps 25 Japanese(-Brazilian) denominations (some with only one local church), and about 150 Nikkei[15] churches in Brazil.[16] There are now first-, second-, and third-generation Japanese Brazilian pastors.[17] These churches are located mostly in São Paulo state, especially

---

[9] Shimekiti Tanaami, *Burajiru Fukuin Horinessu Kyodan: Senkyo Godjushunen Kinen* [*Brazil Evangelical Holiness Church: Fiftieth Anniversary*] (S. Paulo: Igreja Evangélica Holiness do Brasil, 1980).

[10] N. Yamazaki, *A História dos 65 anos de Evangelização da Igreja Evangélica Holiness do Brasi* [*65 Years History of the Brazil Evangelical Holiness Church*] (Sao Paulo: IEHB, 1998).

[11] Chieko Nampo and Liana Tatsumi Goya, *Monobe: Da Morte para a Vida – Um Missionário Japonês no Brasil na Década de 20* [*From Death to Life: A Japanese Missionary to Brazil in 1920s*] (Sao Paulo: IEHB, 2006).

[12] Carmen Kawano, *Seikokai: A História da Primeira Construção Religiosa dos Japoneses no Brasil* [*Seikokai: The Story of the First Religious Building by Japanese People in Brasil*] (S. Paulo: Maluhy & Co., 2008), and *João Yasoji Ito: A vida e a obra do missionário* [*João Yasoji Ito: The Life and Work of a Missionary*] (S. Paulo: Maluhy & Co. and Igreja Episcopal Anglicana do Brasil, 2010).

[13] MidoriOshima, *Vitória: Relatos dos Primeiros Anos do Povo Metodista Livre no Brasil* [*Victory: Reports on Early Years of Free Methodist People in Brazil*] (Sao Paulo: Igreja Metodista Livre, Concílio Nikkei, 2011).

[14] Machado, Ziel, 'Pequenas Iniciativas Podem Gerar Transformação' ['Small Initiatives May Generate Transformation'], in René Padilla and Péricles Couto (eds), *Igreja: Agente de Transformação* [*Church: Agent of Transformation*] (Curitiba, Missão: Aliança & Kairos, 2011). Machado analyzes the paradigm shift which has been occurring in recent years from 'Church in the City' toward 'Church for the City', as paralleling the shift that occurred with the expansion from the church in Jerusalem to Antioch in the New Testament.

[15] '*Nikkei*' or '*Nikkey*' means 'related to Japanese people', and refers to Japanese people and descendants who have acquired other languages, culture, and customs. So while related to Japanese people and culture, they have been somewhat changed by foreign influences. They are thus not merely Japanese, but have become *Nikkei*, i.e., related to Japanese.

[16] There are 110 churches affiliated with *Federação Evangélica Nikkei do Brasil* [Nikkey Evangelical Federation of Brazil], but there are also churches with no such affiliation. For instance, the Assemblies of God '*Nipo Brasileira*' led by a second-generation pastor has 100 branch churches. Information from Rev. Luis Sato, president of the '*Federação Evangélica*'.

[17] The information circulated in Cape Town at the Lausanne III Conference (2010) that the Japanese immigrant population in Brazil is one of the unreached populations of the world was mistaken.

in the greater São Paulo City area, but also in neighboring states such as Paraná, Mato Grosso do Sul, Minas Gerais, and Rio de Janeiro. They are also found farther from São Paulo states: Mato Grosso, Bahia, Rio Grande do Sul, Pará, Amazonas, etc. Although not having specific evangelistic works aimed at the Japanese, several denominations, churches, and communities also have converts from that group of people.

However, it is clear that evangelization among the Japanese diaspora has not been accomplished. There is still much to be done. There are new fields and untouched fields, geographically speaking and otherwise. The Japanese and Nikkei population in Brazil are working and studying in all arenas of human activity. New spaces, including the middle class and above, are being reached. However, there is still a need for missionaries to partner with Nikkei pastors to reach them with the gospel.

The Racial, Cultural, and Linguistic Shift within the Evangelical Holiness Church in Brazil

The Evangelical Holiness Church in Brazil (EHCB) was started by a missionary pastor, the son of a Buddhist priest, who came to Brazil in 1925 following the steps of believers who departed Japan in 1924, as many other people did after the 1923 earthquake in Tokyo. During the 60-day journey across the oceans and continents, Takeo Monobe conducted services almost every day on a ship filled with immigrants, inviting and encouraging people with gospel hymns, exhortations, and prayers. Many non-Christian emigrants did come to the services and once they were placed on coffee plantations in São Paulo state, this contact became the link for visiting them.

The racial shift, accompanied by the language and culture shift, is illustrated by the composition of the executive board of the Brazil Evangelical Holiness Church, to which I belong. In Table 2, 'Japanese' means people who were born in Japan; '2nd Gen.' means people born in Brazil of Japanese parents; '2nd1/2' means that one of the parents was born in Japan, and the other is of the '2nd Gen.'; and '3rd Gen.' means that his or her parents are of the '2nd Gen.' In Table 2, all that are not listed below 'Japanese' are Brazilian citizens. 'Brazilian,' in the last column, refers to those without Japanese ancestry.

Table 2: Brazil Evangelical Holiness Church's Executive Board Composition

	Japanese	2nd Gen.	2nd1/2	3rd Gen.	Brazilian
1925	1				
1946	7				
1968	6	1			
1990	1	4	2		
2012		1	1	4	1

Since the 1980s, Portuguese has become the language for denominational business and communications, and as of 2012 there is nobody on the executive board who was born in Japan. This natural shift has been occurring in local churches, too, in varied degrees of speed and proportions. This shift is more than a change from one language to another and from a set of cultural values, customs, and habits to another set. It is a shift from an ethnocentric outlook to a multiracial, pluralistic reality.

There are churches where the Nikkei membership is the majority. There are others where non-Nikkei (i.e., the Brazilian population of all origins) is the majority. Larger churches with Japanese-speaking members may have two or more pastors, one of whom speaks Japanese. There are churches where the pastor is Brazilian and the majority of the members are Brazilian, while a number of Nikkei people hold leadership positions.

Evangelical Holiness Church in Brazil's Missionary Endeavors

Missionaries from Brazil to Japan

In the late 1980s a missionary challenge was put before the denomination. It did not have surplus pastors or evangelists. However, believing that it was a calling for the church, a young couple, Rev. Shinji and Raquel Kanno, were prepared and sent to Japan in 1992. The arrangement that lasted for three years was as follows: the sending board in Brazil was interdenominational, and the work would be overseen in Japan by an interdenominational board chaired by Rev. Koji Honda, president of the Ocha no Mizu Christian Center in Tokyo. Another representative on this board was Rev. Hiroshi Sakakibara, pastor of the Nakayoshi Kyokai (Japan Holiness Church) and radio and TV evangelist with the Pacific Broadcasting Association.[18]

The EHCB missionaries lived in an apartment for married students at the Tokyo Biblical Seminary. Shinji was fluent in Japanese and Portuguese and Raquel could follow a course in the seminary in the Japanese language. After three years, it was decided that it would be better to do denominational work building church communities.[19]

This pioneer missionary couple has been replaced by a number of others. Until that happened, all the pastors who served in Japan had plans to return to Brazil and continue their ministry in Brazil. Three young people who chose to study at the Tokyo Biblical Seminary graduated and are now

---

[18] Since the church in Brazil had no prior experience of sending a missionary to Japan, and since the need was to do an interdenominational work, there was a desire to have a board in Japan which would be respected by different groups and effective.

[19] There were more denominational communities being formed, and more *Nikkey* pastors were working in Japan.

serving in Japan. Two of them married Japanese women and intend to remain in Japan.

The diaspora of Brazilian Nikkeis in Japan currently comprises about 300,000 people. Due to the hardships at work and the loneliness they may experience in a foreign society, many have been very open to the gospel. There has been a feeling of God's '*kairos*' for evangelization among that diaspora.

Since the 1990s, the number of trips to Japan by Nikkei pastors from Brazil and vice versa has increased. The number of pastors from Brazil appointed to churches in Japan has increased also. Once a year, a member of EHCB's executive board visits the country. Besides the official visitation, less formal visits have been made by other pastors and relatives of those working in Japan. EHCB's former church members in the diaspora in Japan have gathered together and regular Portuguese services occur in eight places. Annual retreats and business sessions are also taking place in Japan in the Portuguese language. Many other churches and denominations in Brazil are doing similar things.

Missionary to China

There was an adolescent in the Campo Grande Holiness Church who felt a calling to be a missionary to China.[20] She went to a theological school and had the opportunity to be trained in Latin America (Bolivia for a month, Peru for a year), and at YWAM bases in São Paulo and in the USA before going with a Brazilian YWAM team to Macao.

After a number of years on the mission field, she met a Brazilian pastor from Minas Gerais and they married. Their support became a joint venture between EHCB and Peniel Church. They have been doing denominational (Holiness) work in Macao, maintaining an administrative relationship solely with the Holiness Church.

Portuguese-speaking Holiness churches in Japan have been visiting the EHCB's Macao mission station. This was not formally planned by the directors of the denomination. Instead, it has occurred naturally.

Missionary to India

An EHCB's missionary to India has served as a youth leader, and by profession was a civil engineer. He received YWAM training in Belém, where he met his wife. The couple departed to India about 18 years ago. This man was fluent in English; however, in India he improved it, and studied Konkani and Hindustani. Their three children are fluent in Portuguese, English, and Hindustani. This man began as a team member,

---

[20] To protect the identity of missionaries in countries such as China and India, no names will be given.

became the leader of the Brazilian team, and eventually became leader of one of the provinces. He is now responsible for more than 400 full-time YWAM workers in India and has become one of the international regional leaders.

Missionary to Northeastern Brazil

Another missionary couple, Marcio and Elivaine Sato, is based in João Pessôa, the capital city of Paraíba state. They work with an interdenominational mission agency which helps denominations start new churches in regions that are less evangelized.

After graduating from business and administration school, Marcio completed a four-year bachelor of theology program, and a number of other related courses. He has since continued his missionary work. He helps the JUVEP Mission[21] organize a one-month saturation evangelism in communities with no evangelizing work. After that period, an evangelist or a pastor is sent to organize a church with those who have been converted. This has occurred every year for more than a decade.

A Contribution to Contemporary Theology of Mission from Brazil?

During the Third Lausanne Conference in Cape Town in October 2010, the Brazilian delegation produced a letter of apology for almost 400 years of slave trade and slavery as a system of economy. That letter (Appendix I) was read before the African regional meeting in Cape Town. There were about 500 leaders in the regional meeting chaired by the Anglican Archbishop Henry Luke Orombi of Uganda. After I read the letter (I was accompanied by five other Brazilians), the Archbishop asked Rev Dr Judy Mbugua from Kenya to represent the mothers of Africa who lost their husbands and children to slavery and pray for the Brazilian visitors who kneeled.

During her prayer, many Africans stood up and prayed together. Some wept, some sang. After the prayer, Mbugua asked all present to declare in one voice with her: 'You are forgiven!' Everyone repeated it a number of times. We were embraced by the seven men and one woman on the platform. We then went back to the Brazilian regional gathering and five delegates from the African regional meeting, including Mbugua, came to the Brazilian meeting. They introduced themselves as being representatives

---

[21] JUVEP (www.juvep.com.br) stands originally for *Juventude Evangélica Paraibana* [Evangelical Youth of Paraiba (state)] but is a church planting mission focused on one of the least evangelized regions of Brazil. It has also a theological school for the formation of evangelists, pastors, and missionaries. It is a missionary sending agency as well. JUVEP also invites and works with missionaries from abroad for short- or long-term assignments.

from West Africa, East Africa, Southern Africa, and as representing the mothers of Africa. They shared how the letter and words of the apology from the Brazilian delegation had touched them as 'from the Holy Spirit and from God' and repeated the declaration of forgiveness. This was followed by general embraces. I would hope that the event in Cape Town, reiterating the importance of our unity in the body of Christ, might serve as a contribution to the missionary ethos when Brazilians go to Africa.

Appendix I

A Letter of Apology from the Brazilian delegation to the African Christian leaders, South of Sahara, written by Key Yuasa, during Lausanne III, in Cape Town, approved by Brazilian leaders, and signed by 59 Brazilian delegates. It was not signed by more, because we could not find them in time, in the midst of the Lausanne Congress.

Dear Brothers and Sisters in the Great Continent of Africa:

We the Brazilian participants of Lausanne III are being blessed abundantly in this Congress and we are very happy to be in this part of the world. The Portuguese navigators in the XVth century overcame the fears and the real difficulties of the Cape of Torments and opened the trade way to Mozambique and to India. That feat had as a result its renaming as the Cape of Good Hope. Here they got inspiration, boldness and courage to explore the Atlantic Ocean westward, 'through seas never before navigated' and Pedro Alvares Cabral was able, years after Columbus to 'discover' the Island of Vera Cruz, which was renamed as the Land of Holy Cross when they realized that it was not an island, and later, as the land of Brazil.

As we remember these historical facts related to the birth of our land and nation, we cannot help but remember our historical, moral and physical debt to the great continent of Africa, its peoples, and nations. After the discovery, and for almost 400 years Brazil Colony and Independent Brazil relied on slave labor for the formation of plantations, for digging our mines, for building our houses, our cities and our nation. So we have committed the sin of kidnapping people, destroying families and villages. We have left behind plenty of orphans, destroyed homes and villages, and harmed deeply your nations.

We have committed the sin of assassination, of treating human beings made in the image of God, as beasts imposing on your people moral, psychological and physical violence, abuse and suppression – and sub-human conditions of life. We have committed the sin of destroying whenever possible their national, ethnic and familiar identity.

The moral debt we have in relation to your nations and peoples, therefore, is so vast, deep, and high, that we have not started to measure it. We deem it, of course, un-payable.

If we wanted to show that we are really sorry and repentant about this historical sin of our nation towards your nations, we would have to come to you and say: Please, give us the privilege of being your slaves. Please be our lords and bosses; give us the opportunity to serve you. Let us help you to build your plantations, your mines, your houses and cities, with our sweat and blood as your kinsmen did for us. Let our bodies be buried anonymously under your roads and your cities, as did your people for us.

Then we would perhaps realize that you are truly our blood brothers and sisters and we are your blood brothers and sisters, because your people shed their blood and blessed us, and you will have given us the privilege and opportunity of shedding our blood and of blessing you.

Then perhaps we shall together discover the width, the length, the height and the depth of the love of Christ, who shed his precious blood for us both, so that the wall of partition might be put down, and that we might realize that we are together, one family in Him!

But today, we need your forgiveness for the unforgivable. Please forgive us. Please forgive the sins of our people against yours. Please do forgive the sins of our nation against yours.

Your people have been building our country not only with sweat, toil and blood. Your people and their descendants have been building with hands, heads and legs (Pelé, Ronaldo, Robinho, etc. etc.), with heart, mind, faith, hope and love as many musicians, novelists, artists, or with technical skills as doctors, engineers, jurists, politicians, etc. in all walks of life. Many are church members, pastors, bishops, saints, professors and leaders. Your people and descendants are a blessing in our country. Instead of hitting us back, they have blessed us, with the richness of their music, their food culture, and above all by their peculiar, rich and beautiful way of being human, neighbors and soul brothers, as all of us are experiencing here this week with you. Your people have become an integral part of our country, and of our families. Very many of us take pride in being descendants in certain measure of African peoples.

Please accept us as your servants and your slaves in the name of our Lord Jesus Christ. With love and fraternal tenderness.

Brazilian participants in Cape Town 2010
Cape Town, October 24, 2010

South Asian Diaspora Christianity in the Persian Gulf

T.V. Thomas

Introduction

A vibrant church life is not what one thinks about when focusing on the Persian Gulf region, which is primarily Muslim.[1] Very few know about the state of Christianity in this vast region. There is a colossal degree of ignorance because very little study has been undertaken and very little of what is studied is published. Whatever is published does not receive the wide circulation it deserves. Some of the reluctance to disperse collected information is caused by self-imposed restrictions to ensure the security of the followers of Jesus and to protect their worship sites.

Although there are South Asians[2] and expressions of South Asian Christianity throughout the Middle East, this study is restricted to the South Asian Christianity in the five small countries that line the Persian Gulf – Kuwait, Qatar, Bahrain, the United Arab Emirates, and Oman. In undertaking this study, I realize there are very few printed resources and negligible statistical records. The only pragmatic approach was to conduct one-on-one interviews with Western and non-Western Christian leaders, lay pastors, and lay people. For this reason, I traveled to Kuwait and the United Arab Emirates to conduct 51 face-to-face interviews over a two-week period. I also conducted similar interviews with 28 South Asian Christians in the USA and Canada who had recently migrated from Persian Gulf countries. In addition, I conducted telephone interviews with another 23 South Asian Christians from Bahrain, Qatar, and Oman. For the security of the interviewees and by mutual agreement, most of the interviewee names are being withheld while the remainder are pseudonymously identified. This study is an overview of South Asian diaspora Christianity in the Persian Gulf and is far from being exhaustive.

The Coming of Christianity to the Persian Gulf

According to tradition, the gospel was preached in south Arabia by the Apostle Bartholomew.[3] Christianity began flourishing in the first century

---

[1] Annegret Kapp, 'In Dubai Christians Pray Side by Side but Not Always Together', *Earned Media*, 19 May 2008, 1.

[2] South Asians are people living in and originating from Bangladesh, Bhutan, India, Maldive Islands, Nepal, Pakistan, and Sri Lanka.

[3] John Holzmann (ed), *The Church of the East* (Littleton, CO: Sonlight Curriculum

and was introduced in the southern part of Arabia, which then spread to the Gulf region. Historical records indicate that Qatar was a Bishopric as early as 225 AD[4] and three churches existed in Yemen by 356 AD. Bishops from Arabia were participants at the Council of Nicea in 325 AD. By the fourth century Nestorian Christianity dominated the southern shores of the Persian Gulf. Tiny ancient Christian communities existed in pre-Islamic times, but they almost disappeared when Islam became a dominant presence. For over 1,200 years Christian influence was virtually absent in the region.

With the arrival of the Portuguese in the Persian Gulf in 1506, the region's inhabitants began to renew their acquaintance with Christianity.[5] However, the indiscriminate killing of women, children, and the aged, and the destruction of property at Khor Fakkan under the direction of Portuguese sea Captain Alphonso de Alburquerque left a bitter legacy with Portuguese Christians. The Portuguese soon dominated the eastern coast of Arabia and exercised their power over the locals by building forts.

In contrast, Captain Thomas Perronet Thompson of Britain, with deep Christian convictions, was a bridge-builder.[6] Upon arrival in Ra'sal-Khaimah in 1819, Thompson learned Arabic. This acquisition proved to be a great asset in relationship building with the local Arabs. In 1820, he crafted the General Treaty of Peace for the Cessation of Plunder and Piracy, which was signed by Britain and the Gulf states.[7] With this initiative, formal relationships were established which were mutually beneficial.

With the influence of William Carey, the English Baptist Missionary Society was launched in 1792. This was catalytic in the formation of numerous missionary societies, including the London Missionary Society in 1794, the Church Missionary Society in 1799, and the American Board of Commissioners for Foreign Mission (ABCFM) in 1810.

The initial effort to spread the gospel in the Persian Gulf was by Henry Martyn, a chaplain of the English East India Company. Martyn translated the New Testament into Arabic and distributed copies of it.[8] Then in 1843, John Wilson, a Church of Scotland missionary based in Bombay sent some Bible teachers to the Persian Gulf. In 1848, a new Arabic translation of the Bible was initiated by the ABCFM. Thomas Valpy French, an Englishman

---

Ltd, 2001), 17.

[4] K.P. Koshy, 'Christianity in the Arabian Gulf and Kuwait: The Role of Kuwait Town Malayalee Christian Congregation', in *The Kuwait Town Malayalee Christian Congregation Golden Jubilee Souvenir* (Safat, Kuwait: published privately, 2003), 37.

[5] Andrew Thompson, *Christianity in the UAE: Culture and Heritage* (Dubai, UAE: Motivate Publishing 2011), 25-26.

[6] Thompson, *Christianity in the UAE,* 27.

[7] Thompson, *Christianity in the UAE,* 30-31.

[8] Raymond F. Skinner, 'Christians in Oman: Ibadism in Oman and Development in the Field of Christian-Muslim Relationships', unpublished paper (1992), 46.

and a retired Anglican Bishop from Lahore, Pakistan, arrived in Muscat, Oman, in February 1891 to open a new mission.[9]

Samuel M. Zwemer, James Cantine, Philip T. Phelps, and John G. Lansing from the USA organized the Arabian Mission in 1889. They soon set sail for the Persian Gulf region for evangelism, education, and medical care. They set up hospitals, schools, Bible shops, and organized tours. Zwemer, with the help of the Reformed Church in America, co-operated with Bishop French from the Church Missionary Society to expand the Christian witness in the region.[10] The medical ministry of the Gulf-wide work of the American Arabian Mission was what won the favor and gratitude of the local people.[11] First Protestant church services were held as early as the 1900s in Kuwait and Bahrain. Construction of church buildings followed only much later. The first resident Roman Catholic priest only arrived in Kuwait in 1948.[12] The establishment in 1960 of the hospital and church in Al-Ain, a desert oasis in the UAE, by The Evangelical Alliance Mission opened doors for Christian witness and outreach home visits.[13]

The marked Christian presence in the Persian Gulf is a very recent phenomenon related to the large economic migration of people into the region. The rulers of the Gulf region have been very tolerant and have granted freedom for expatriates to gather for Christian worship and have even donated land for the construction of church edifices.[14] Every Friday, thousands of Christians gather to worship the God of the Bible, often at the same time as Muslims have their Friday prayers in their mosques.

The majority of Christians belong to several denominations and nationalities. These include the Anglican Church, Reformed Church, Roman Catholic Church, Coptic Orthodox Church, Greek Orthodox Church, Armenian Orthodox Church, Mar Thoma Church, Syro-Malabar Church, Malankara Orthodox Syrian Church, Syrian Jacobite Church, Church of South India, St Thomas Evangelical Church of India, Pentecostal Churches, the Brethren Assemblies, and more. In addition, there are hundreds of independent congregations and house groups of various traditions and sizes.

---

9 Skinner, 'Christians in Oman', 50.

10 Michael Nazir-Ali, *From Everywhere to Everywhere: A World View of Christian Mission* (Eugene, OR: Wipf & Stock Publishers, 2009), 144.

11 Thompson, *Christianity in the UAE*, 31.

12 K.M. George, *Development of Christianity through the Centuries: Tradition and Discovery* (Tiruvalla, India: Christava Sahitya Samithi, 2005), 301.

13 Vikram Ebenezer, 'Roots for the Redemption of the Arab Arabians' (PhD Dissertation, Fuller Theological Seminary, 2011).

14 Sacha Robehmed, 'Christianity in the Gulf', *Open Democracy* 13 August 2012, available at www.opendemocracy.net/sacha-robehmed/christianity-in-gulf (accessed 14.8.12).

Figure 1: Estimates of Christians in the Persian Gulf[15]

	Total Population	Christian Population	Percentage of Country
United Arab Emirates	8,260,000	980,000	11.9
Kuwait	3,600,000	550,400	15.3
Oman	3,090,000	320,000	10.4
Qatar	1,840,000	340,000	18.5
Bahrain	1,248,000	147,600	11.0
Grand Total	18,038,000	2,338,000	

South Asian Diaspora to the Persian Gulf

The five Persian Gulf countries have great wealth from oil. But with low populations, they face acute labor shortages. These shortages are met not by open migration, but through the use of temporary import workers.[16] These transient migrants constitute more than two-thirds of the labor force of these nations and the population numbers of import workers are proportionately larger than the local citizens. The spectrum of migrants ranges from highly skilled to non-skilled workers. The major growth in immigration to the Gulf followed the oil boom of 1973-74.[17]South Asians constitute the biggest expatriate community in the Gulf region with Indian migrants being the largest. The remaining hail from Bangladesh, Pakistan, and Sri Lanka. The Nepalis began appearing in large numbers from the early 1990s.[18] The largest single group of South Asian workers in the Gulf are in the construction industry and a sizeable number are employed by the private sector and the Gulf governments. South Asian migrants often come with no baggage of political ideologies and make few demands. Furthermore, temporary migrants are not accorded any political representation.[19] Their wages are often less than their Western or Arab

---

[15] Sources used to arrive at rounded-off estimates: 1) Foreign and Commonwealth Office, United Kingdom – www.fco.gov.uk/en/, 2) Local Government Agencies – www.dubaifaqs.com/population-of-uae.php; www.qsa.gov.qa/eng/index.htm' and 3) BBC: Information on Christian Population – www.bbc.co.uk/news/world-middle-east-15239529.

[16] Myron Weiner, 'International Migration and Development: Indians in the Persian Gulf', in Prakash C. Jain (ed), *Indian Diaspora in West Asia: A Reader* (New Delhi: Manohar Publisher, 2007), 127.

[17] Parvati Raghuram, 'Immigration Dynamics in the Receiving State: Emerging Issues for the Indian Diaspora in the United Kingdom', in Parvati Raghuram, Ajaya Kumar Sahoo, Brij Maharaj, and Dave Sangha (eds), *Tracing an Indian Diaspora: Contexts, Memories, Representations* (New Delhi: Sage Publications, 2008), 173.

[18] Cindy L. Perry, *Nepali around the World: Emphasizing Nepali Christians of the Himalayas* (Kathmandu: Etka Books, 1997), 173.

[19] Margaret Walton-Roberts, 'Globalization, National Autonomy and Non-Resident Indians', in Laxmi Narayan Kadeker, Ajaya Kumar Sahoo, and Gauri Bhattacharya

counterparts.[20] They are generally paid about half the salary of locals, but do twice the amount of work.[21] The number of South Asians who are merchants, shop owners, and traders are also significant in light of the law that requires each foreigner to have a local Arab partner to obtain a business license outside the free zones.

Figure 2: Estimates of Indian and Pakistani Populations in the Persian Gulf[22]

	Total Population	Indians	Percentage of Country	Pakistanis	Percentage of Country
United Arab Emirates	8,260,000	1,900,000	23.0%	1,250,000	15.6%
Kuwait	3,600,000	650,000	18.1%	230,000	6.4%
Oman	3,090,000	500,000	16.1%	70,000	2.3%
Qatar	1,840,000	450,000	24.4%	120,000	6.5%
Bahrain	1,248,000	240,000	19.2%	80,000	6.4%
Grand Total	18,038,000	3,740,000		1,750,000	

South Asian Christian Presence in the Persian Gulf

The first South Asian Christian congregation in the Gulf region was believed to be the 'Ahmadi Christian Congregation' in Ahmadi, Kuwait. It was non-denominational and primarily consisted of Malayalee Christians from Kerala, India, who worked at the Kuwait Oil Company. More Malayalees arrived in Kuwait City from Kerala and the Kuwait Town Malayalee Christian Congregation was formed in 1953.[23]

With oil exploration and drilling expanding to the other Gulf States beginning in the 1960s and exploding in the 1970s, the need for migrant workers escalated. Waves of migration from various South Asian countries took place to tap into the economic boom. Among the thousands of South Asians were also Christians who brought their languages, cultures, Christian traditions, and worship styles. Multiple congregations were established primarily in larger urban centers or in areas where there were

---

(eds), *The Indian Diaspora: Historical and Contemporary Context* (Jaipur, India: Rawat Publications, 2009), 210.

[20] Weiner, 'International Migration and Development', 127.

[21] *INF Diaspora Digest No. 10 of INF Diaspora Initiative* (Kathmandu, Nepal: International Nepal Fellowship, August 2012), 4.

[22] Sources used to arrive at rounded-off estimates: 1) CIA, The World Factbook – www.cia.gov/index.html, 2) Foreign and Commonwealth Office, United Kingdom – www.fco.gov.uk/en, 3) The World Bank –www.data.worldbank.org/country/united-arab-emirates, 4) Indexmundi – www.indexmundi.com, 5) Local Government Agencies – www.dubaifaqs.com/population-of-uae.php and www.qsa.gov.qa/eng/index.htm.

[23] Koshy, 'Christianity in the Arabian Gulf and Kuwait', 39.

significant enclaves of South Asian Christians. The largest group of Christians in the Gulf States are South Asians, with the predominance being Indian Christians.

Categories of South Asian Diaspora Congregations

South Asian congregations can be categorized by language, location, or liturgy. Seven types are presented.

Mother-tongue congregations. Most South Asians worship in their own mother-tongue congregations: Malayalam, Tamil, Telegu, Urdu, Hindi, Punjabi, Nepali, etc. These groups are transplanted congregations of denominations in their respective country or state. The established denominations like the Anglican Church, Church of South India, Mar Thoma Church, Malankara Church, Syro-Malabar Church, Malankara Orthodox Syrian Church, Syrian Jacobite Church, St Thomas Evangelical Church of India, Pentecostal churches, and Brethren Assemblies have one or more congregations in each of the five Gulf nations. Using the mother tongue has been crucial to impact unreached peoples globally and to develop disciples and churches.[24] To ensure transmittance of cultural values and pride in their heritage and identity, some congregations offer weekly mother-tongue language instruction for Gulf-born children of their families.

English language congregations. South Asians who prefer English-medium worship services choose to go to congregations which are often Western-based, Western-led, and trans-denominational. More often than not, these are multinational, multicultural, and multiethnic in composition. Therefore, diversity is highly valued, passionately pursued, and embraced. In recent years, a few mother-tongue congregations have offered English worship services for their second-generation youth.[25]

Church compound-based congregations. Most of the denominational mother-tongue and English-language congregations are registered with the governments. With diverse worship styles and practices, they gather weekly at the state-designated church compounds in major cities. These huge compounds, like the National Evangelical Church of Kuwait (NECK) compound in Kuwait City, have multiple buildings which facilitate the weekly worship services of 85 congregations of all Christian traditions and languages with a combined attendance of 20,000.[26] The facilities are also used for various gatherings like congregational leadership meetings, discipleship classes, training, membership classes, and baptisms. NECK is a beehive of kingdom activity every day and most evenings. Since the early 1970s, a similar broad scope of ministries has occurred in Dubai at the

---

[24] Barbara F. Grimes, 'From Every Language', in Ralph D. Winter and Steven C. Hawthorne (eds), *Perspectives on the World Christian Movement: A Reader* (4th ed.; Pasadena, CA: William Carey Library, 2009), 565.

[25] Interview with a South Asian media specialist, UAE, 6 April 2012.

[26] Warren Reeve, email message to author, 6 September 2012.

Holy Trinity Church compound at Bur Dubai. Likewise at the Dubai Evangelical Church Centre at Jebel Ali since 2002, and at the Religious Complex in Doha, Qatar, since 2008.

Non-church compound-based congregations. The numbers of Christian groups throughout the region not registered with the governments are mushrooming.[27] They are often independent groups who meet for worship and prayer in large villa-type homes or hotel meeting rooms. Most operate with uncertainty and run the risk of being discovered and shut down by the governments.[28]

Labor camp congregations. Thousands of South Asian male, blue-collar workers live in labor camps some distance from the urban centers. Transporting them to churches in the cities can be a challenge. As they come to Christ, they are organized into small 'house churches' which are male-dominated. Pastors and Christian workers from the cities provide the leadership, co-ordination, and spiritual nurture of these groups.[29]

Liturgical congregations. Most of the historical congregations use prescribed, standardized, and printed liturgy during their worship services.[30] The liturgy could be in English, but often it is in the peoples' mother tongues. Some larger denominations have worship books containing not only their liturgy in the mother tongue, but also a Romanized version to encourage the second generation to participate in corporate worship. Some traditions use icons and incense in their worship ritual and liturgy.[31]

Non-liturgical congregations. The Baptists, Brethren, Pentecostals, and other independent churches are non-liturgical. Therefore, their worship is more informal, extemporaneous, and contemporary. Their singing may range from solemnity to joyous hand clapping and sometimes are accompanied by sacred rhythmic movements.[32]

Leadership in South Asian Christian Congregations

The criteria, structures, and roles of congregational leadership differ widely and depend upon their respective Christian heritage and tradition. Pastors, women, and lay leader roles are discussed.

Role of Pastors

The congregations of established denominations have duly-appointed priests and pastors who are granted time-sensitive clergy visas to serve the

---

27 Interview with a Filipino health care worker, UAE, 7 April 2012.
28 Interview with a South Asian tentmaker #1, UAE, 5 April 2012.
29 Interview with a South Asian youth worker, UAE, 9 April 2012.
30 Interview with a South Asian pastor, UAE, 8 April 2012.
31 Interview with a South Asian lay elder, Bahrain, 9 May 2012.
32 Interview with a Charismatic South Asian pastor, Kuwait, 31 March 2012.

Gulf congregations for three to five years.[33] These theologically-trained clergy with proven ministry track records in their homelands are often appointed to specific parishes by the hierarchy of respective ecclesiastical headquarters overseas. Volunteer lay people are elected to serve as officers on church boards or councils under the leadership of the clergy. Together, they fulfill their governance functions according to well-established constitutions and by-laws and agreed-upon policies. Dialogue, discussion, and even debate on issues are welcomed in the decision-making process.

Most of the independent congregations are led by bi-vocational or lay pastors. A vast majority of such leaders have not undergone much formal theological training.[34] Most have had no opportunity. Only a few see the need for extra training because the majority believe that the success in leading and sustaining their group legitimizes their call and effectiveness.[35] This is obviously a subjective evaluation and conclusion. A tiny percentage is seeking to upgrade and enhance their ministry competence by enrolling in distance learning avenues like theological education by extension courses offered modularly onsite or through the Internet.[36] Some Asian seminaries are even offering their courses in Malayalam and Telegu. One frequent observation by interviewees was that there was a greater tendency of pastors of independent and/or charismatic congregations or fellowship groups to be autocratic and dictatorial in their leadership style.

Role of Women

The traditional roles of South Asian men and women are demarcated. These roles are maintained in the Gulf as well, even if a congregation is constituted by a women majority in membership and attendance. Women are seldom in pastoral roles or serve any major leadership role that involves key decision-making for the congregations. In general, the women's role is the traditional one. Women serve in the kitchen, prepare meals for their community fellowships or special functions, and clean up. Women also serve in some lesser leadership roles in ministries related to women, children, and youth.[37]

There is generally neither friction between men and women in regards to their roles nor do women voice dissent about lack of authority. South Asian Christian women do not define themselves as being in an inferior and powerless position. Rather, they see their role as different (not necessarily less important) than that of men. Women value their traditional family structure because of the power it gives them over their children.[38]

---

[33] C.M. Kurien, interview by author, Kuwait, 2 April 2012.

[34] Interview with a South Asian tentmaker #1, UAE, 5 April 2012.

[35] Interview with a South Asian tentmaker #2, UAE, 8 April 2012.

[36] Interview with a South Asian tentmaker #2, UAE, 8 April 2012.

[37] Interview with a South Asian homemaker, Qatar, 3 May 2012.

[38] Interview with a South Asian social worker, Bahrain, 8 May 2012.

Emergence of Lay Leaders

The adage 'Necessity is the mother of invention' is a daily reality in Gulf congregations. The dearth of competent clergy to lead congregations and fellowship groups provides the appropriate context for the lay person to step into leading roles.[39] Many of them incrementally learn about the joys and pains of leadership through experimentation with hardly any mentoring. They often polish up their leadership skills through the 'school of hard knocks'.

In the last two decades, lay people in major centers have had access to excellent ministry leadership training. These one- to two-day or multi-evening seminars are often parachuted into the region from the West, but increasing options are originating from South Asia as well.[40] This explains why there are proportionately higher numbers of competent lay leaders in the Gulf congregations than their sister congregations back home or elsewhere. Several lay leaders sensing God's call have entered into full-time or bi-vocational ministry.

South Asian Diaspora Christians in the Persian Gulf and the Great Commission

The Great Commission is Christ's command to 'make disciples of all nations' (Matt. 28:19-20). One of the primary emphases of the late Donald McGavran was: 'The purpose of missiology is to carry out the Great Commission. Anything other than that may be a good thing to do, but it is not missiology'.[41] Diaspora missiology is a new strategy for missions and can be defined as the 'Christian response to the diaspora phenomenon in the twenty-first century'.[42] This strategy can be viewed in three ways as one focuses on South Asian diaspora in the Persian Gulf: missions *to* the South Asian diaspora, missions *by* the South Asian diaspora, and missions *by and beyond* the South Asian diaspora.[43]

Missions to the South Asian Diaspora

South Asian diaspora populations in the Persian Gulf countries are relatively unreached. There is little evidence of attention being drawn to

---

[39] Interview with a South Asian lay pastor, Oman, 4 May 2012.

[40] Interview with a South Asian tentmaker #1, UAE, 5 April 2012.

[41] David Hesselgrave is quoting from a personal letter he received from the late Donald McGavran on 7 April 1988. See also Hesselgrave, *Paradigms in Conflict: 10 Key Questions in Christian Missions Today* (Grand Rapids: Kregel Publications, 2006), 316.

[42] Enoch Wan, *Diaspora Missiology: Theory, Methodology, and Practice* (Portland, OR: Institute of Diaspora Studies at Western Seminary, 2011), 105.

[43] Wan, *Diaspora Missiology*, 115.

highlight the need for a missional emphasis among them or any orchestrated mobilization being undertaken to reach them. The estimated total number of South Asians in the Gulf ranges from 6.5 to 7 million.[44] The majority of the South Asians are Hindus, Muslims, Buddhists, and Sikhs. Despite the lack of a concerted and comprehensive vision or strategy to reach South Asians, many are turning to the Christian faith. Among several people groups, the rate of conversion is significantly higher than among their own people back in their homeland.[45] The following are various outreach methods among South Asians in the Gulf.

Relational evangelism. God has used diaspora South Asian Christians to reach out to their fellow South Asians with the gospel using the relational paradigm.[46] Authentic relationships have proved to be key for much of the spiritual harvest.[47] Since South Asian society is highly relational, the pain of loneliness is especially intense for migrants away from family and friends. Such displacement of people from their familiar surroundings causes them to 'seek God, if perhaps they might grope for him and find him' (Acts 17:27). This is an important aspect of diaspora mission. Through relocation, unsaved South Asians like the Roman centurion Cornelius (Acts 10:1-11, 18) come into proximity with gospel and are being saved.[48]

Christian television. Christian television plays a major role in pre-evangelism and evangelism. Channels like God TV, Powervision, and Holy God TV offer popular Western Christian television shows sub-titled in South Asian languages. In addition, a plethora of South Asian-produced Christian programs cater to the major mother tongues. Hundreds of non-Christians who respond to the Christian message in the privacy of their residences often rely upon these television programs and other messages on DVDs to nurture them spiritually.[49] Frequently, it is months before they are part of a regular prayer fellowship group or congregation.

Visiting ministers. In the last two decades, there have been an increased number of South Asian itinerant mother-tongue pastors, evangelists, and musicians who have been sponsored by Christians for brief periods of time to do focused ministry in the Gulf States.[50] Some conduct large-scale evangelistic crusades within the church compound, while others conduct

---

[44] Indians are the largest component of South Asians with a total of more than 3.79 million followed by 1.75 million Pakistanis. Statistics about other South Asians are not readily available or accessible.

[45] Interview with a South Asian lay elder, UAE, 6 April 2012.

[46] Wan, *Diaspora Missiology*, 145.

[47] Interview with a South Asian pastor, Kuwait, 30 March 2012.

[48] Craig Ott, 'Diaspora and Relocation as Divine Impetus for Witness in the Early Church', in Wan (ed), *Diaspora Missiology*, 84.

[49] Interview with a South Asian business executive and lay elder, UAE, 5 April 2012.

[50] Gabrial Khan, interview with author, Kuwait, 31 March 2012.

multiple small home meetings or provide leadership training or counseling seminars. The net result is that non-Christian South Asians are becoming followers of Jesus while nominal and relapsed Christians are revived and the Kingdom of God is expanding.

Distribution of gospel materials. Careful and strategic distribution of gospel booklets and JESUS DVDs in respective mother-tongue languages have stimulated numeric growth.[51] The periodic coming of Operation Mobilization ships to Gulf ports with their grand book exhibitions has galvanized evangelism.[52] Curiosity attracts hundreds to go on board to tour the vessel, visit the book displays, purchase books and Bibles, pick up gospel literature, and even hear the gospel preached. Bible Society bookstores operating in the region also serve as invaluable sources for appropriate literature and media resources for churches to use in evangelism, discipleship, and spiritual growth.[53]

Labor camp outreach. Labor camps are very fertile for gospel outreach. With high levels of functional illiteracy among labor camp residents, the interactive chronological Bible story evangelism is proving effective.[54] Furthermore, Christmas and Easter seasons are especially conducive for concentrated evangelistic thrusts which also seem relatively fruitful. Some city congregations and various ministry agencies have organized weekly visits to labor camps to provide counseling, conduct gospel studies, and even lead worship services.[55]

Youth outreach. Younger South Asians are highly responsive to the gospel. Retreats, camps, and Christian groups on university campuses are proving effective in presenting the truth claims of Christ and in discipleship.[56]

An analysis of the evangelistic results indicate many South Asians from unreached and unreachable people groups in their home countries are being saved in their host countries.

Missions through the South Asian Diaspora

Most of the first generation of South Asian diaspora Christians and congregations in the Gulf demonstrate little mission interest beyond their own mother-tongue people.[57] On the other hand, there is an encouraging, emerging trend among the second-generation South Asians. Although

---

[51] Interview with a South Asian Christian volunteer at labor camps, UAE, 7 April 2012.

[52] Interview with a South Asian lay man, UAE, 8 April 2012.

[53] Interview with a Western pastor, UAE, 9 April 2012.

[54] Interview with a South Asian Christian volunteer at labor camps, UAE, 7 April 2012.

[55] Interview with South Asian a lay pastor, Kuwait, 2 April 2012.

[56] Samson George, interview with author, UAE, 6 April 2012.

[57] Interview with a retired South Asian pastor, Qatar, 9 May 2012.

second-generation South Asians are in a state of flux because they cannot call the Gulf region their home, some of these believers are growing in vision and passion to reach out interculturally with the gospel.[58] Some have taken advantage of small-group training in evangelism and have been exposed to world-class mission events like the Urbana Student Missions Convention.

Missions by and beyond the South Asian Diaspora

One of the commendable traits of South Asian Christianity in the Gulf is its engagement with missions beyond their immediate region. The Gulf South Asian Christians and churches have become a funding source for many ministries, primarily in South Asia: evangelistic thrusts, church planting, orphanages, church-building projects, etc. Their generosity is widely known. It is not uncommon to find a prayer fellowship committed to raising funds to support an evangelist or a church planter back in his or her home country. Representatives of multiple ministry agencies from South Asia make repeated visits, sometimes annually, to secure financial resources.[59] They often chart an itinerary of several weeks in all five Gulf States. Seldom are they disappointed with the gracious and bountiful response to their appeal.

Numerous new South Asian Christians have returned to their homelands and witnessed to their family and friends. As a result, many house churches and church plants have been established.[60] Several South Asian diaspora congregations in Australia, Canada, the United Kingdom, and the USA have been blessed by the visionary leadership of some South Asian Christians who have migrated from the Gulf.[61]

Concerns and Challenges

The following are ten major concerns and challenges South Asian Christianity faces in the Persian Gulf:[62]

- There is an acute lack of theologically equipped leaders who can serve as pastors, teachers, and leaders of congregations and prayer fellowship groups. Many current leaders are untrained and untested. The result is that spiritually-impoverished congregations are surviving without balanced, sound doctrinal teaching.

---

[58] Interview with a Western tentmaker, Kuwait, 7 April 2012.
[59] Interview with a South Asian lay person, Oman, 8 May 2012.
[60] Dinesh Maharaj, interview by the author, Kuwait, 9 April 2012.
[61] Interview with a retired South Asian lay pastor, Bahrain, 19 August 2012.
[62] These are the ten most common concerns and challenges that were raised by multiple interviewees from all five Gulf nations.

- The gospel preached is sometimes watered down and people embrace an easy believism. The result is that believers do not receive solid biblical instruction or pursue serious discipleship or training.
- Much of the evangelism approaches are less than holistic. The result is that maximum potential gospel impact for the kingdom is not attained.
- About 30-40% of South Asians are functionally illiterate. The result is that evangelizing and discipling them is a challenge which needs to be addressed sensitively and creatively.
- Frequent splits in congregations occur for non-biblical reasons, including egotism or regionalism. The result is that suspicion and mistrust among leaders and members of various congregations are sustained.
- Some churches are fiercely independent and tend to be insulated and isolated. The result is that non-collaboration with the rest of the body of Christ robs every believer of corporate witness and partnership.
- Some visiting ministers manipulate their audiences and raise obscene amounts of money for personal and family use, while others teach spurious doctrine. The result is that there is a loss of credible witness by tarnishing the gospel and confusing believers.
- Many of the established denominational congregations employ traditional and formal styles of worship. The result is that second-generation Christians feel disconnected from the service and neglected in the meeting of their needs or preferences.
- Most congregations are monocultural and/or monolingual. The result is that an ethnocentric worldview and attitude which discourages intentional cross-cultural evangelism is developed.
- Most Christians and congregations have neither a burden nor a strategy to reach the local Muslim populations. The result is that there are missed opportunities to communicate the good news of Jesus even within the restrictions imposed by the Islamic rulers.

Few could conclude that South Asian diaspora Christianity in the Persian Gulf is dormant or dull. Spiritual passion and church attendance are commendably high. Congregational life is generally meaningful and vibrant. With strong, godly, collaborative leadership coupled with kingdom-minded visionary strategy, the region can be a powerhouse for *glocal* (global and local) missions in the future.

THE KOREAN DIASPORA CHURCHES IN THE USA: THEIR CONCERNS AND STRENGTHS

Chandler H. Im

'The new *immigrants* represent *not* the *de-Christianization* of *American* society *but* the *de-Europeanization* of *American Christianity*'.[1]

R. Stephen Warner, Professor of Sociology at the University of Illinois at Chicago

This paper focuses on the Korean diaspora communities and churches[2] across the USA. A brief history of the influx of Korean immigration, along with an overview of the Korean diaspora churches, is given. Six areas of concern and challenge, and four areas of strength and opportunity pertaining to Korean diaspora churches (hereinafter abbreviated as KDCs) vis-à-vis Korean diaspora communities in the USA are also elucidated. The final section contains missiological implications.

The Korean diaspora has been contributing to the 'browning' of the face of America. To illustrate this point, though not in scientific terms, I will briefly share a segment of my diaspora journey. My family emigrated from South Korea to the USA in June 1980 when I was a teenager. The student makeup of the high school I attended in northern Virginia in the early 1980s was about 97% white. In its 2,000-member student body, the non-white population was probably fewer than 60, including about 20 Korean/Korean-American students. In almost every class I attended, I was the only non-white, limited-English-speaking student. A few years ago I revisited my high school[3] alma mater, located 25 miles west of Washington DC. I was stunned to see signs in five languages above bathroom doors, from the top: English (Restroom), Spanish (Banos), Korean (화장실), Vietnamese, and Cambodian. In March 2010, I revisited my high school again, this time with my family. When I asked an African America counselor at the school about the Korean students' enrollment status, he told me there were about 400 Korean/Korean American students out of its 2,000-member student body. That's an increase of 20 times in 30 years! This is an isolated, but dramatic example that demonstrates how the

[1] R. Stephen Warner, '"Coming to America: Immigrants and the Faith They Bring', *Christian Century* 121 (10 February 2004), 20-23.

[2] One limitation of this article is that only Protestant churches are discussed; Catholic and other non-Protestant churches are not discussed unless specified.

[3] W.T. Woodson High School, located at 9525 Main St. Fairfax, Virginia.

multicultural tapestry of the USA population has gradually widened over the last 30 years.

The Demographic Shift in the USA and Asian Americans

In 1900, according to the US Census Bureau, 86% of the immigrants living in the USA came from Europe. During the same period, only 1.2% of the immigrants were from Asia and 1.3% from Latin America.[4] In 2000, 26.4% of the immigrants living in the USA came from Asia, and 51.7% from Latin America. During the same period, those who emigrated from Europe declined to 15.8%.[5] After the Immigration and Nationality Act of 1965 (Hart-Celler Act) abolished the National Origins Formula, which had been in place in the USA since the Immigration Act of 1924, the demographical landscape across the USA has been rapidly changing.

As reported by the Pew Research Center, in a comprehensive survey released in June 2012 in the USA, 'Asian Americans are the highest-income, best-educated and fastest-growing racial group'.[6] First, Asians as a whole have a median household income of $66,000, compared with the US median income of $49,800.[7] Second, 'Recent Asian arrivals are the most highly educated...immigrants in U.S. history', stated Paul Taylor, executive vice president of the Pew Research Center.[8] The educational credentials of these recent arrivals are striking. More than six in ten (61%) adults ages 26 to 64 who have come from Asia in recent years have at least a bachelor's degree. Third, Asians have surpassed Hispanics as the largest group of new immigrants, making up 6% of the US population. They appear to be more satisfied than the general public with their lives, finances, and the direction of the country than Americans as a whole, and they place more value on marriage, parenthood, hard work, and career success than other Americans do.

---

[4] US Census Bureau, Historical Census Statistics on the Foreign-Born Population of the United States: 1850-2000. www.census.gov/population/www/documentation/twps0081/twps0081.html (accessed 25.6.12).

[5] US Census Bureau, Historical Census Statistics on the Foreign-Born Population of the United States: 1850-2000.

[6] www.pewsocialtrends.org/2012/06/19/the-rise-of-asian-americans/ (accessed 21.6.12).

[7] Pew Research Center analysis of 2010 American Community Survey, Integrated Public Use Microdata Sample (IPUMS) files. Median 2010 US household incomes: Indians ($88,000), Filipinos ($75,000), Chinese ($65,050), Whites ($54,000), Vietnamese ($53,400), Koreans ($50,000), Hispanics ($40,000), and Blacks ($33,300).

[8] www.usatoday.com/news/nation/story/2012-06-18/asian-american-study/55677050/1 (accessed 17.6.12).

Table 1: The Six Largest Asian Groups in the USA (US Asian population in 2010: 17,320,856)

US Asian Groups	Numbers	Percentage Among Asians
Chinese	4,010,114	23.2%
Filipino	3,416,840	19.7%
Indian	3,183,063	18.4%
Vietnamese	1,737,433	10.0%
Korean	1,706,822	9.9%
Japanese	1,304,286	7.5%

Source: Pew Research Center and analysis based on Elizabeth M. Hoeffel et al., The Asian Population: 2010, US Census Bureau, March 2012.

A History of Korean Immigration to the USA

According to Enoch Wan, a leading diaspora missiologist, many factors that contribute to global diasporas, including the Korean diaspora in the USA, can be summarized in two main categories of 'the push and pull factors':

> The push factors for the Korean diaspora are: the threat of the communist regime in the North, the political instability and economic hardship in South Korea in the last century, etc.; whereas the pull factors are: the political stability and economic opportunities overseas, the strong desire for their children to enjoy educational and economic opportunities abroad, etc.[9]

The history of the influx of Korean immigrants to the USA can be divided into four major periods or 'waves' based on the US government's immigration policies and situations in the Korean peninsula: the first wave: 1903-45; the second wave: 1945-65; the third wave: 1965-89; and the fourth wave: 1989-present. There is no consensus among Korean (Korean American) scholars and historians as to how to clearly divide these immigration waves from Korea to the USA. The four periods listed here are my own arbitrary categories, adapted from other various views of Korean immigrant waves.

The first wave of Koreans hit a US shore on 13 January 1903, as 121 Koreans landed in Honolulu, Hawaii, after a 22-day voyage across the Pacific Ocean from the Korean port of Busan. Within three years, 7,226 Koreans – 6,048 men, 637 women, and 541 children – came to Hawaii mainly for economic reasons.[10] Many came in pursuit of the American Dream and worked on sugar plantations on Hawaii's islands, sometimes in

---

[9] Enoch Wan, 'Korean Diaspora: From Hermit Kingdom to Kingdom Ministry', in S. Hun Kim and Wonsuk Ma (eds), *Korean Diaspora and Christian Mission* (Oxford: Regnum, 2011), 104-5.

[10] Roberta Chang and Wayne Patterson, *The Koreans in Hawaii: A Pictorial History, 1903-2003* (Honolulu: University of Hawaii Press, 2003), iv-ix.

horrible conditions. To resolve the high male-and-female ratio discrepancy, 1,066 'picture brides' from Korea also arrived in Hawaii during this period.

Koreans call 22 August 1910 the national day of humiliation, the day on which the Japan-Korea Annexation Treaty was signed. The Imperial Japanese regime ruled the Korean peninsula for 35 years, 1910-45. Besides Honolulu, small Korean communities began to form on the mainland: Los Angeles, San Francisco, New York, Chicago, etc.

In the meantime, the Immigration Act of 1924, or Johnson-Reed Act, established a national origins quota system, which was devised to restrict immigrants from 'undesirable' parts of the world, including immigrants from eastern and southern European nations.[11] In the same vein, the Oriental Exclusion Act, a special provision of the 1924 act, specifically barred immigrants from Asian countries, which included China, Japan, and Korea. The 1924 act effectively stalled the first Korean wave.

As the Emperor of Japan unconditionally surrendered to the Allies on 15 August 1945, World War II abruptly ended, and Korea became an independent nation again. During the 1945-65 period, the second 'wave' of Koreans to the USA comprised of international students, 6,000 wives of American soldiers who were stationed in Korea,[12] about 5,000 war orphans after the Korean War (1950-53) who arrived in the USA as adoptees,[13] and others.

The third wave (1965-89) of Korean immigration began when the USA opened her gates wide open once again to immigrants from all over the world. The Immigration and Nationality Act of 1965 (Hart-Celler Act) abolished the national origins quota system and replaced it with a system that preferred immigrants with skills and/or family ties to US citizens and legal residents.

Based on Table 2's data, legal immigration from South Korea to the USA reached its zenith during the 1980-89 period. Subsequently, there was a whopping 45% drop during the 1990-99 period. After the 1997 International Monetary Fund (financial) crisis in Korea, the numbers of emigrants from Korea picked up again, but at levels far short of the 1980-89 decade. Meanwhile, a few months after the 1988 Seoul Olympics, the South Korean government enacted a historic law that enabled Korean

---

[11] The Immigration Act of 1924 discriminated against those immigrants not from western and northern European countries. Its main purpose was to preserve the USA's white Protestant population as the majority. See Mae M. Ngai's 'The Architecture of Race in American Immigration Law: A Reexamination of the Immigration Act of 1924', *Journal of American History* 86 (June 1999), 67-92.

[12] Injin Yune, 'Korean Diaspora: Immigration, Accommodation, Identity of Overseas Korean' (in Korean), *The Society of Social Study in Korea* 6 (2003), 127. Between 1950 and 2000, Korean women who married American soldiers and went abroad numbered around 100,000.

[13] Doug K. Oh, 'History of the Korean Diaspora Movement', in Kim and Ma (eds), *Korean Diaspora and Christian Mission*, 189.

nationals to freely travel overseas for tourism and other personal purposes.[14] As a direct result, the numbers of I-94 forms (US arrival-and-departure records for non-immigrant visitors) that Korean citizens filled out skyrocketed: under 100,000 in 1985; 250,000 in 1990; 700,000 in 1995; 1,000,000 in 2007; and 1,300,000 in 2010.[15] Thus, over the past two decades, the number of non-immigrant visitors such as tourists, business travelers, and international students and workers from Korea has enormously surpassed the numbers of legal immigrants from Korea. This is the fourth and current wave (1989-present). The fourth wave's implications in relation to KDCs in terms of church attendance in the USA are explained later.

Table 2: Korean Immigration to the USA, 1940-2009

Period	Korean Immigrants to the USA
1940-49	83
1950-59	4,845
1960-69	27,048
1970-79	241,192
1980-89	322,708
1990-99	179,770
2000-09	209,758

Source: www.dhs.gov/files/statistics/publications/LPR11.shtm Table 2.[16] *(accessed 29.6.12)*

The Korean Diaspora Churches' Functions vis-à-vis the Korean Communities in the USA

Beginning with the early Korean pioneer immigrants to Hawaii, KDCs have functioned as the epicenter of a Korean diaspora community in the USA. Based on interviews with 131 Korean pastors serving at KDCs in the New York City area, Korean sociologist Pyong Gap Min identified 'four major social functions of Korean immigrant churches': (1) providing fellowship for Korean immigrants, (2) offering social status and positions for Korean adult immigrants, (3) maintaining the Korean cultural heritage,

[14] Before this law took effect in 1 January 1989, the Korean government's excessive and rigid regulations severely restricted Korean citizens' international travels.

[15] John Oh, 'Korean Diaspora Churches for the Mission of God' (in Korean), Presentation at the 8th Korean Diaspora Forum in Johannesburg, South Africa, 16 February 2012.

[16] These numbers include both South and North Koreans. However, the numbers of North Koreans' influx to the USA have been extremely insignificant, e.g., about 140 refugees and asylees from North Korea over the last few years.

and (4) providing social services for church members and the Korean community as a whole.[17]

First, the KDCs have served the first-generation Korean immigrants as safe and comfortable havens in which they can converse in their native tongue while enjoying (Christian) fellowship with other church members from the same motherland. Away from their homeland, working hard to make a living and support the family in a foreign country, the adult immigrants have found solace and encouragement in relationships developed at KDCs, while their minds and hearts continually travel back and forth like a pendulum that swings between the USA and Korea (e.g., between Los Angeles Koreatown and Seoul).

Second, the KDCs have offered adult immigrants who were born and raised in a highly hierarchical culture (Korea) titles and positions of importance which the newly-settled society (USA) did/does not grant to the newly arrived. Involvement in the KDCs as decision makers in leadership roles such as elders and deacons has given them a sense of empowerment and significance.

Third, the KDCs in the USA have consistently served Korean communities as educational centers, in which the Korean language, culture, and history, in addition to Christian faith, are taught to US-born Korean Americans. The KDCs have played (and continue to play) an indispensable role in preserving and permeating Korean traditional values and practices in Korean homes and communities. For instance, as of June 2012, there were 37 Korean language and culture schools in the Greater Chicago area, offering classes mostly on Saturdays. Of those, 28 (75.7%) of the schools met at Korean Protestant churches; three at Korean Catholic churches, and two at Korean Buddhist temples.[18]

Fourth, since the inceptions, many KDCs have served the Korean communities in general and KDCs members' needs in particular as social service centers. The KDCs and their members offer various social services, ranging from employment tips and leads for the unemployed to Korean-English interpretation/translation needs for their children's schools. Based on a 2011-12 nationwide survey of over 4,000 Korean Christians, their responses to the question 'How helpful was a KDC in your early immigrant years in the USA?' were as follows: very helpful (29%), somewhat helpful (23%), little helpful (23%), and no help received (26%).[19] In other words, the majority of Korean Christians received some sort of assistance from their churches' members to cope with new realities and laws of the New World.

---

[17] Pyong Gap Min, 'The Structure and Social Functions of Korean Immigrant Churches in the United States', *International Migration Review* 26.4 (Winter 1992), 1370-94.

[18] www.ksamusa.org/bbs/board.php?bo_table=school_list&page=2&page=1 (accessed 29.6.12).

[19] www.koreatimes.com/article/737225 (accessed 27.6.12).

One distinct function of KDCs and Korean Christians in the USA that Min does not mention is their contributions to political and human rights causes for Korea's independence movement. It is estimated that about 40% of the early immigrants to Hawaii were either Christians or were exposed to Christianity before or right after their arrival in Hawaii.[20] During the 1910-45 Japanese forced occupation period, for example, the Korean communities and KDCs in the USA (e.g., in Honolulu, Los Angeles, and San Francisco) became international hubs for raising funds for Korean freedom fighters and their independence movement.

The Korean Diaspora Churches' Growth and Expansion

Among the people of the worldwide Korean diaspora, there is a tongue-in-cheek saying: *Wherever the Chinese go (around the world), they open Chinese restaurants; wherever Koreans go, they plant churches.*[21] Although it is said in an overly generalized fashion, almost as a joke, the statement carries a lot of weight. Ever since the first wave of Korean immigrants hit the Hawaiian shore in the 1900s, KDCs have been planted and growing in numbers steadily, especially after the Immigration and Nationality Act of 1965, which opened the floodgate for the third Korean immigration wave. Consequently, the numbers of the KDCs in the USA have increased exponentially over the last five decades: 30 KDCs (1967); 150 (1972); 300 (1975); 600 (1980); 1,700 (1989); 2,617 (1991); 3,334 (1997).[22]

Table 3: Korean Populations and Korean Diaspora Churches in Top Nine US States in 2010

	US State	Korean Population	Korean Diaspora Churches	Korean Population vs KDC Ratio
1	California	505,225	1,313	385: 1KDC
2	New York	153,609	443	347: 1KDC
3	New Jersey	100,334	239	420: 1KDC
4	Texas	85,332	191	447: 1KDC
5	Virginia	82,006	201	408: 1KDC
6	Washington	80,049	199	402: 1KDC
7	Illinois	70,263	196	358: 1KDC
8	Georgia	60,836	189	322: 1KDC
9	Maryland	55,051	150	367: 1KDC

Sources: Adapted from 2010 U.S. Census Summary File 1 PCT 7 and Mijoo Christian Today's 2010 Overseas Korean Church Directory.

---

[20] Chang and Patterson, *The Koreans in Hawaii*, 1-10.

[21] See the Appendix Table 1 for the top nine countries around the world with the most KDCs.

[22] *Mijoo Christian Today*, 5 January 2011.

As of 2010, there were 4,144 KDCs in all 50 states; over 1,000 KDCs were present in southern California alone. Some Korean experts estimate that there are as many as 5,000 KDCs in the USA if all the 'house churches'[23] are counted. The largest KDC in the USA, and around the world, is Sarang Community Church (in the Presbyterian Church of America denomination), with 8,000 members, located in Anaheim, California.

Table 4: The Korean Diaspora Churches' Top Six Denominations in the USA

	1	2	3	4	5	6
Denomination	Presbyterian	Baptist	Methodist	Independent	Pentecostal	Holiness
Churches	1,698	710	620	294	281	273
Percentage	41.0%	17.1%	15.0%	7.1%	6.8%	6.5%

Source: Mijoo Christian Today, 6 January 2010

Among the Protestant KDCs' denominations, the Methodist churches were the fastest growing: a 11.9% increase in 2009 and a 11.3% increase in 2010.[24] The number (228 KDCs or 5.5%) of other Protestant deniminations such as Lutheran and the Seventh Day Adventist are not specified in Table 4 above. It is intersting to note that the percentages of the Protestant denominations in the USA loosely resembled the statistics of the denominations in Korea: Presbyterian (63.7%), Pentecostal (23.2%), Methodist (17.7%), Baptist (9.3%), and Holiness (8.7%).[25] Those percentage numbers, except for the Baptist group, can be seen as a strong indication of Korea's denominational interest in and leadership influence over KDCs in the USA (e.g., in the areas of church planting and missionary endeavors). The US Korean Baptists (17.1% in the USA vs 9.3% in Korea) were the only group in a higher number category compared with the resepctive Korean denominations' numbers. I would surmise that the increase was caused in part by the church-planting partnership and assistance contributed from the Southern Baptist Convention, the biggest Protestant denomination in the USA.

[23] The 'house churches' here refer to small churches that meet in a home of a church member (or pastor).

[24] *Mijoo Christian Today*, 6 January 2010.

[25] (Korean) Ministry of Culture, Sports and Tourism, 'Religious Realities of Korea' (in Korean) (2012), 42-47. www.kmctimes.com/news/articleView.html? idxno=25035 (accessed 30.6.12).

Areas of Concern and Challenge for the Korean Diaspora Churches in the USA

I have identified and listed only six items in this section. There are several other issues, but I will leave those to later discussions and to others to explore.

'Islandization' of the Korean Diaspora Communities and KDCs[26]

The Korean diaspora communities in general, and the KDCs in particular, still look like scattered islands in an ocean called the USA. The biggest 'Korean islands' in the USA are located in the metropolitan areas of Los Angeles, New York, Chicago, Washington, DC, Atlanta, San Francisco, and Seattle. Providing Korean diaspora people with cultural comfort and safety zones, these Korean communities have evolved in relative isolation, somewhat distanced from other neighboring ethnic communities and mainstream America. This cultural tendency to stick with 'my own people' seems to be common in other Korean diasporas around the world. In addition, this phenomenon actually can be seen to some extent among other ethnic diaspora communities and churches in the USA and around the globe.

In a similar manner, a majority of KDCs and Korean Christians in the USA do not seem to have meaningful relationships with neighboring churches and non-Korean neighbors, including Christians, in large part due to language (English) barriers and cultural differences. However, coming from a homogeneous culture, certain Korean ethnocentric tendencies might have played a major role in this isolationalistic behavior.

Culturally, the KDCs in the USA often identify neither with the church in Korea nor with the church in America.[27] They possess a distinct 'third culture' milieu as churches in diasporic mode. Biblically and theologically, however, many KDC traits of being aloof and too Korean-community-centric – separated from or not interfacing much with other non-Korean communities, denominations, and churches – are unhealthy, for all the KDCs, too, belong to the universal church as well.

Tensions Within the Korean Diaspora Churches

As in many (diaspora) churches, various dimensions of internal tension and conflict exist in KDCs in the USA: between pastors and laity,

---

[26] Chandler H. Im, 'Beyond the Korean Line: Toward the Multi-Ethnic Ministry in North America', Presentation at Korean Diaspora Forum in Fullerton, California, 5 May 2011.

[27] There are some exceptions to this. For instance, certain KDCs in the USA and around the world still belong to and are governed by their mother denominations based in Korea.

between/among church members, between generations, etc. According to a 4,109-member survey, which included 864 Korean pastors from 600 Korean churches in the USA, conducted in 2011-12, a majority of the Korean pastors (51.9%) selected 'financial matters' as the most prevalent cause of conflict within KDCs. The pastors also identified these as causes of tension within the KDCs in the USA: conflict between senior pastors and elders/church leaders (46.7%), disharmony among laypeople (43.1%), and cultural differences between generations (31.1%).[28]

On the other hand, first-generation Korean laypeople saw 'pastors' lack of quality or pastors' lack of gifts and talents' (63%) as the leading cause of tension, 'internal discord and disorder' (47%) as the second, and Christian education issues for the second-generation (29%) as the third most prevalent concerns within KDCs.[29]

Interestingly, lay Korean Christians in the USA placed a major emphasis on pastors' preaching abilities. An overwhelming number of the laity (78%) chose the pastor's preaching as the number one criterion when selecting a church in which to settle down, whereas 28% considered leaving the church if unsatisfied with their pastor's sermons.[30] Unfortunately, it is difficult to admit as a 1.5-generation[31] Korean American leader that internal tensions among KDCs' leaders have resulted in church splits and church plants, although several other reasons[32] have contributed to the KDCs' phenomenal growth and expansion in the USA.

The 'Silent Exodus' of the English-speaking Generations from KDCs

Korean American, English-speaking generations have been leaving KDCs by droves, which is commonly referred to as 'the silent exodus'.[33] In a recent survey of second-generation Korean Americans, 54.2% left KDCs after high school, 26.1% during college years, and 10.7% after college. Of

---

[28] Sang Cheol Oh, 'North American Korean Immigrant Churches' Issues', Presentation at the 4th (Korean) Immigration Forum (in Korean) (Korean) Immigration Theology Center, Youngrak Presbyterian Church in Los Angeles, 18 June 2012.

[29] Oh, 'North American Korean Immigrant Churches' Issues'.

[30] http://www.koreatimes.com/article/737225 (accessed 27.6.12; already cited in full).

[31] There are many views as to how to define the 1.5-generation. I define a 1.5-generation immigrant as a bilingual/bicultural person who left his or her homeland between ages 5 and 17.

[32] Other reasons may include fervent prayer life (early morning and midweek services, etc.), passion for mission, sacrificial giving (tithing, special offerings, etc.) toward building projects and missions.

[33] See also Peter Cha, Paul Kim, and Dihan Lee, 'Multigenerational Households', in Viji Nakka-Cammauf and Timothy Tseng (eds), *Asian American Christianity Reader* (Castro Valley, CA: The Institute for the Study of Asian American Christianity, 2009), 127-38.

those who left KDCs, 45.7% did not attend any church.[34] The top five reasons for the 'silent exodus' of the English-speaking members were: not seeing 'vision/hope' in KDCs (40.9%), having language barrier issues (35.8%), lacking a sense of ownership in KDCs (32.7%), becoming atheists (31.9%), and switching to mainstream ('American') churches (30.7%).[35] And 55% of the second-generation perceived the silent exodus to be a 'dire situation'.[36] However, it is also necessary to point out the fact that this phenomenon of the silent exodus from (any) church is not exclusive to US-born Korean Americans; it appears that this church-leaving trend generally applies to all the postmodern young generations in the country, regardless of their ethnic/cultural backgrounds.

Lack of Korean-American Pastors at KDCs

Closely related to and a contributing factor to the silent exodus explained above is lack of US-born Korean-America pastors at KDCs, or a silent exodus of Korean American (English-speaking) pastors themselves from KDCs. One Korean American pioneer pastor in his sixties declared that 'This is a national crisis!' within the KDCs in the USA, and that first-generation senior pastors have to pay more attention to this crucial issue.[37] I unreservedly concur with his assessment.

The top six reasons for Korean American English ministry (EM) pastors' departure from KDCs were: (1) cultural conflict or differences with first-generation Korean senior pastor (59%), (2) leadership conflict with first-generation Korean senior pastors (40%), (3) lack of clear sense of calling to (English) ministry (32%), (4) call from another church (29%), (5) lack of ministry experience (24%), and (6) low compensation (22%).[38] On average, Korean American EM pastors served KDCs for 3-5 years (51%), 1-2 years (25%), and under one year (9%).[39]

Another disturbing reality is that enrollment levels of Korean American students at mainstream seminaries in the USA have been very low and seemingly in decline compared with Korean-speaking and international students from Korea. According to a 2007 survey conducted by a 1.5-generation mission leader, the difference between Korean-speaking seminarians and English-speaking (or bilingual) Korean American seminarians at these seminaries were too wide to ignore: Southwestern (370

---

[34] www.koreatimes.com/article/737519 (accessed 28.6.12).

[35] www.koreatimes.com/article/737519 (accessed 28.6.12). For this question/ category, multiple answers were allowed.

[36] www.koreatimes.com/article/737519 (accessed 28.6.12).

[37] I. Henry Koh, Korean Ministry Co-ordinator at Presbyterian Church in America, personal conversation, 30 July 2008.

[38] www.koreatimes.com/article/737519 (accessed 28.6.12; already cited in full). Multiple answers were allowed for this question.

[39] www.koreatimes.com/article/737519 (accessed 28.6.12).

vs 20), Golden Gate (100 vs 20), Trinity in Illinois (100 vs 25), Gordon-Conwell (140 vs 60), Talbot (200 vs 50), and Fuller (1,700 vs 200).[40] The numbers of US-born Korean Americans have been increasing in Korean diaspora communities since 1903. Accordingly, there were, are, and will be dire needs for KDCs to hire and retain more EM pastors. However, low enrollments of Korean Americans at seminaries, coupled with Korean American pastors' silent exodus from the KDCs themselves, is a huge issue for KDCs in the twenty-first century. Therefore, there are and will likely be vast shortages of Korean American pastors in the USA.

Generation transition and Leadership Issues at KDCs

In the 1990s, several prominent and highly-respected Korean senior pastors[41] at KDCs publically proclaimed that in the twenty-first century, Korean ministries (KMs) would meet in small sanctuaries and (bigger) EMs would meet in the main sanctuaries. In reality, in part due to the silent exodus, as explained above, this transition from the KM-strong mode to the EM-strong has not happened in KDCs. Also, the tsunami of non-immigrant visitors – international students and workers, long-term visitors, etc. – since the 1990s has more than made up for the declining numbers of immigrants from Korea, thereby perpetuating the needs for Korean-language worship services at KDCs.

Second, generational leadership transitions from first-generation senior pastors and leaders to 1.5-generation senior pastors and leaders that all expected to take place at large and mid-sized KDCs in the twenty-first century have happened on a very small scale, partially because of a high supply of capable pastors who came from Korea as international students to pursue advanced degrees at American seminaries. If this trend of no or little leadership transition to the next generation persists, many bilingual and bicultural 1.5-generation pastors and leaders (most in their thirties and forties now) will continue to feel powerless in and disheartened with KDCs.

The Undocumented

According to US Citizenship and Immigration Services' (USCIS) data, as of January 2011, approximately 230,000 Koreans resided in the USA unlawfully.[42] Surprisingly, the undocumented Korean residents' number in

---

[40] John Oh, 'Korean Diaspora Churches for the Mission of God'.

[41] Dong Sun Lim of Oriental Mission Church (LA); Hee Min Park of Youngrak Presbyterian Church (LA); Kwang Shin Kim of Grace Church (Fullerton, CA), et al.

[42] US Citizenship and Immigration Services. Estimates of the Unauthorized Immigrant Population Residing in the US www.dhs.gov/xlibrary/assets/statistics/publications/ois_ill_pe_2011.pdf (accessed 17.6.12).

2011 shot up from 2010's 170,000, a stunning increase of 35.3% in one year, according to USCIS. That would be about 13.5% of the entire Korean diaspora population, and 2% of the entire undocumented population[43] in the USA. This is a cause for concern for the Korean diaspora communities and churches, for the undocumented often live with a fear of getting arrested and deported back to Korea while they and their family members, including English-speaking children, face other hardships and challenges such as obtaining and retaining (well-paying) jobs, with benefits like health insurance coverage and pension programs.

To these 'paperless' people, receiving the permanent residency card, commonly referred to as 'the green card', is like getting a lifeline. In my opinion, KDCs in the USA have not adequately addressed this immigration-related question: *How can we effectively serve and help these 'document-less' (i.e., very vulnerable) brothers and sisters in Christ?*[44]

Areas of Strength and Opportunity for the Korean Diaspora Churches

I have identified and listed only four items in this section. While KDCs are losing their second generation, much of the optimism discussed in this section pertains to first-generation immigrants, particularly since Korean immigration trends are expected to continue unabated going forward.

High Church Attendance

According to US Census' data, 1,423,784 Koreans/Korean Americans lived in the USA in 2010. It is estimated that the number of the Korean population in the USA in 2010 would increase to be about 1.73 million when the undocumented, international students and workers, et al. who did not partcipate in the 2010 Census are added. If that's the case, as of 2010, on average, one Korean American Protestant church existed for 417

---

[43] US Citizenship and Immigration Services. Estimates of the Unauthorized Immigrant Population Residing in the US httpwww.dhs.gov/xlibrary/assets/statistics/publications/ois_ill_pe_2011.pdf (accessed 17.6.12). As of January 2011, of the 11.6 million unauthorized immigrants estimated, top eight nations of their origin were: Mexico (6.8 million; 58.6%), El Salvador (660,000; 5.7%), Guatemala (520,000; 4.5%), Honduras (380,000; 3.3%), China (280,000; 2.4%), Philippines (270,000; 2.3%), India (240,000; 2.1%), and Korea (230,000; 2.0%). Of the eight nations, Korea was the only nation in 2011 which had a 90-day no-visa treaty with the US government.

[44] This very question can be addressed with respect to other vulnerable groups in the Korean diaspora communities and KDCs in the USA: the low-income, people with disabilities, shut-ins, victims of human trafficking, the 140-plus North Korean refugees, et al.

Korean(-American) residents in the USA.[45] In that regard, Koreans could possibly be the most evangelized or most church-attending (-affiliated) ethnic/diaspora group in the USA.

Fervent Prayer Life

The KDCs in the USA have experienced phenomenal growth and expansion in the last few decades for several reasons. One key component of this success can be contributed to the fervent prayer life of KDCs' members. As mission historian Tetsunao Yamamori correctly claims, 'Every significant movement begins with prayer, and is sustained by prayer'.[46] As in churches in Korea, most KDCs in the USA have an early morning prayer service that usually begins between 5:30 a.m. and 6:00 a.m., five to six times a week. This early morning ('dawn prayer' in Korean) service or tradition applies to those KDCs without their own buildings, too; they normally use their host churches' buildings for the morning services. Generally, the KDCs also have a weeknight, usually Wednesday or Friday, service, in which corporate prayer time is often incorporated.

Evangelism Outreach to non-Christians

Another by-product of the Korean diaspora in the USA is the immigrants' contact with and openness to the gospel. An exceedingly high percentage at that time, about 40% of the early immigrants to Hawaii were Christians, and many more were exposed to Christianity before or right after their arrival in Hawaii.[47] In 2002, it was estimated that up to 70% of the Korean diaspora in the USA attended churches,[48] and 61% and 10% of Koreans/ Korean Americans in the USA are Protestants and Catholics respectively, according to a 2012 survey done by Pew Forum on Religion and Public Life,[49] whereas the corresponding number in Korea indicated less than one-

---

[45] As of 2011, the US state for the highest ratio between the KDCs and its Korean population was Arkansas (175: 1 KDC), and the lowest ratio was Minnesota (1,249: 1 KDC). *Korean Churches Yellowpages* (Los Angeles: Christian Today, 2012), 93 and 202.

[46] Tetsunao Yamamori, personal conversation, 6 May 2011.

[47] Chang and Patterson, *The Koreans in Hawaii*, 1-10. American Methodist pastors, among others, began to minister to these immigrants in Hawaii.

[48] www.articles.latimes.com/2002/oct/26/local/me-religkorean26 (accessed 15.6. 12). It is my interpretation from the article that the 70% figure mentioned is believed to include Protestants and Catholics.

[49] www.pewsocialtrends.org/2012/06/19/the-rise-of-asian-americans (accessed 19.7. 12) (already cited in full).

third of the South Korean population in 2005 were Christians, both Protestants and Catholics combined.[50]

Arrival and living in the USA has enticed many non-Christians, often lonely and homesick, to step into KDCs' buildings. As a direct result of their church-going activity either voluntarily or through a friend's invitation, many who had no previous religious affiliation (23%)[51] or followed other religions (5%) such as Buddhism[52] in Korea have become Christians for the first time in their new adopted land.[53]

Passion for Global Mission

Besides fervent prayer life and evangelism enthusiasm, the church in Korea's passion for global mission is well known. As of January 2012, 23,331 Korean missionaries were serving in 169 countries around the world,[54] whereas in 1955 there were only two Korean missionaries serving in one country.[55]

As the table below substantiates, the numbers of Korean missionaries serving on foreign mission fields have skyrocketed. There are several factors/causes for this exponential expansion both geographically and numerically. One factor is the US-based Korean World Mission Conferences (KWMCs) held every four years at Wheaton College (Illinois) since 1988.[56] Initially organized by US-based Korean mission leaders and pastors, these five-day KWMCs mobilize and stimulate overseas KDCs, especially in the USA, and the church in Korea to engage in missionary ventures globally.

Along the same line, the KDCs in the USA have participated in global missionary endeavors by supporting missionaries, mostly Korean, with

---

[50] 2005 South Korea Census: Among the Korean population, 18.3% were Protestants and 10.9% Catholics. The Korean census is taken every 10 years (…1995, 2005, 2015, etc.). www.pewresearch.org/pubs/657/south-koreas-coming-election-highlights-christian-community (accessed 17.7.12).

[51] 2005 South Korea Census: Among the Korean population, 46.9% indicated they had no religious affiliation. www.pewresearch.org/pubs/657/south-koreas-coming-election-highlights-christian-community (accessed 17.7.12) (already cited in full).

[52] 2005 South Korea Census: Among the Korean population, 23.1% were Buddhists. www.pewresearch.org/pubs/657/south-koreas-coming-election-highlights-christian-community (accessed 17.7.12) (already cited in full).

[53] www. Koreatimes.com/article/737510 (accessed 28.6.12; already cited in full).

[54] Korean Research Institute for Mission, www.krim.org/2010/english.html (accessed 19.7.12).

[55] Korean Research Institute for Mission, www.krim.org/2010/english.html (accessed 19.7.12) (already cited in full).

[56] John Koh (KWMC General Secretary), 'An invitation letter to the 2012 KWMC' (June 2012). The attendance numbers of the previous KWMCs were: year 1988 (1,500); 1992 (2,500); 1996 (3,300); 2000 (3,500); 2004 (4,000); 2008 (4,500).

finances and prayers, and by sending short-term and long-term missionaries overseas, among other means of partnership.

Table 5: Korean Missionaries Serving Around the World: 23,331 in 169 Countries in 2012

	1955	1973	1979	1986	1992	1996	2000	2002	2012
Countries	1	9	26	47	80	138	162	164	169
Missionaries	2	24	93	511	2,576	4,402	8,103	10,422	23,331

Source; Korean Mission Handbook 2007-2008[57] *and Korean World Misison Association's data*[58]

Another interesting dimension to this area of global mission is the aspect of reciprocol mission. As of 2010, 1,468 Korean missionaries were in the USA.[59] What are these Korean missionaries doing on US soil? Many are in seminaries getting advanced degrees. But many are also church planting for Koreans, and serving at KDCs. However, there are many who also serve in many other specialized capacities such as multiethnic church planting, homeless ministries, campus ministries (e.g., University Bible Fellowship and Korean Campus Crusade for Christ), etc. I have personally met with several missionaries from Korea who were/are working with Native Americans on reservations in the USA and with First Nations peoples in Canada.

Missiological Implications

Over the last few decades, Korean-dominant pockets or enclaves have popped up and been expanding in major cities across the USA. However, it seems the Korean diaspora communities and KDCs have not had significant interaction with other neighboring communities and their churches. This process of growth in cultural isolation is not exclusive to the Korean diaspora communities and churches in the USA.[60]

---

[57] Steve Sang-Cheol Moon, 'The Protestant Missionary Movement in Korea: Current Growth and Development' (2007), http://krim.org/files/moon_on_korean_mission.pdf (accessed 19.7.2012).

[58] www.christiantoday.co.kr/view.htm?id=252905 (accessed 20.7.12).

[59] See the Appendix Table 1 for more details.

[60] Simply put, it feels safe and comfortable to mingle with people from one's own culture who speak the same language. However, the Los Angeles Riots of 1992, in which Koreans suffered tremendous losses as an ethnic group, was a historic turning point, which shook up this kind of complacent mentality among Koreans in the USA. After the 1992 riots, Los Angeles' Korean leaders, including Christian pastors, saw the need to connect more meaningfully with leaders from African-American and other non-Korean communities.

Against this backdrop of the fast-transforming multiethnic/multicultural/ multireligious realities of the USA, what would be some mission implications for the Korean diaspora churches, leaders, and mission agencies in the USA? I have identified at least four:

1. *Korean churches, Christian leaders, and mission agencies in the USA have heavily focused on overseas missions.* As a result, many have overlooked or underemphasized the need to reach out to the nations (ethnic people groups) within the US borders. It is of monumental importance that the KDCs and Korean Christian leaders in the USA recognize the USA as an important and strategic mission field, and then actively engage in cross-cultural ministries and missions here.[61]

In other words, Korean churches, Christian leaders, and mission agencies in North America have overemphasized the Great Commission mandate (Go to the ends of the earth!), and underemphasized the Great Commandment's second mandate (Love your neighbor as yourself!). They need to challenge and teach Christians how our unbelieving neighbors (i.e., people from all over the world, which include non-Christian Anglos) need Jesus Christ as well, not only those on the mission fields 'out there' (overseas).

2. *The numbers of 1.5-generation and 2nd-generation Korean American seminarians have been low and declining in the USA.* Korean diaspora churches, Christian leaders, and mission agencies in the USA need to encourage, challenge, support (with prayers and finances), and mentor the next generation of Korean American Christian leaders, as many of them are and will be involved in multiethnic ministries and cross-cultural missions in their communities.

3. Korean churches, Christian leaders, and mission agencies in the USA need to intentionally invest their time, resources, and efforts into racial reconciliation, unity, and collaboration among the diverse people groups (e.g., with Japanese American, African American, Latino American, and Anglo Christians) in the body of Christ in the USA.

4. In reaching out more to other ethnic churches/leaders (see above), Korean churches, Christian leaders, and mission agencies in the USA need to deliberately and passionately join hands with other non-Korean ministry/mission networks, especially connecting with influential mainstream networks such as Mission America Coalition (US Lausanne) and Ethnic America Network, to collaborate with and maximize efforts and resources.[62]

---

[61] One positive example of this would be: SEED International, a US-based Korean mission agency, at its annual board meeting in November 2010, recognized the USA as a strategic mission field and made intentional efforts to encourage multiethnic church planting and cross-cultural missions here.

[62] A good example of this kind of joint effort with the mainstream would be the First and Second 4/14 Movement Summits, hosted by The Promise Church (senior pastor: Rev. Dr Nam Soo Kim) in New York in 2009 and 2010.

By and large, Korean diaspora churches (and communities) still exist like 'islands' on the face of the US church and mission landscape. It is imperative that the KDCs and their leaders make more intentional efforts to reach out to create meaningful 'bridges' within their respective communities and with other communities (e.g., with other non-Korean churches and their leaders), serving together their neighbors, both Korean and non-Korean, with the message and love of Jesus Christ. If not, the KDCs' spheres of Christian and mission influence may not extend much beyond the 'Koreatown' boundaries.

Appendix

Table 1. Top Nine Worldwide Korean Diaspora Nations' Churches: 5,404 Churches in 78 Countries

	1	2	3	4	5	6	7	8	9
Country	USA	Canada	Japan	Austrailia	Germany	Argentina	Brazil	UK	Mexico
Churches	4,144	254	206	177	104	61	56	53	21

Source: Mijoo Korean Christian Today 2010 Overseas Korean Church Directory.[63]

Table 2. Top Nine Countries in which Most Korean Missionaries are Serving

	1	2	3	4	5	6	7	8	9
Country	China	USA	Japan	Philippines	India	Russia	Thailand	Indonesia	Germany
Missionaries	3,775	2,697	1,347	1,290	847	659	641	612	502

Source: Korean World Mission Association (January, 2012).[64]

[63] *2010 Overseas Korean Church Directory* (LA: Mijoo Korean Christian Today, 2010). See also its 2012 Internet version: www.webpublished.com/fileRoot/en/c/t/ctoday/DigitalAlbumRoot/120131075010/appendix/guide.htm.
[64] http://www.christianitydaily.com/echurch/view.htm?id=216464&code=mw (accessed 19.7.12).

IMMIGRANTS IN THE USA: A MISSIONAL OPPORTUNITY

Jenny Hwang Yang

The USA is undergoing what may prove to be the greatest demographic shift in its history, and the church is facing a pivotal decision in how it will respond to this change. Will it respond in fear and view the change as a threat, or will it recognize the incredible missional and transformational opportunity this change provides in the expansion of Christ's kingdom?

For Christians who participate in God's redemptive purposes, the migration of people, whether forced or voluntary, should be viewed not as accidental, but part of God's sovereign plan. God determines the exact times and places where people live 'so that they would seek him and perhaps reach out for him and find him' (Acts 17:27). We are called to 'make disciples of all nations' (Matt. 28:19); with immigration, the nations show up on our doorstep. The mission field has crossed our borders and settled into our communities as our coworkers and neighbors.

Missiologists around the world recognize that God is drawing people to himself using ministry to, through, and beyond diaspora communities. Immigrants coming to the USA are not just open to hearing the gospel, but are *themselves* transforming the Christian landscape in America. This chapter will explore current realities of immigrants in the USA, theological reflections of the movement of people and the church's response, and the multifaceted opportunities that immigration provides in expanding God's kingdom.

USA Immigration Background

Over the past ten years, the USA has seen an unprecedented number of immigrants coming to its shores. Out of a total population of 309.3 million people, an estimated 39.9 million are immigrants (13%) (17.4 million of whom are naturalized USA citizens).[1] In 2011, 1,062,040 persons were granted legal permanent resident status; 481,948 of them (45.4%) were new arrivals.[2] Although the USA ranks 26th in the percentage of residents who

---

[1] US Census Bureau, '2010 American Community Survey 1-Year Estimates, Selected Social Characteristics in the United States', www.factfinder2.census.gov/faces/tableservices/jsf/pages/productview.xhtml?pid=ACS_10_1YR_DP02&prodType=table> (accessed 25.4.12).

[2] The other 54.6% who were granted permanent residency were already residing in the USA, often under temporary legal status. Department of Homeland Security Office of Immigration Statistics, 'Annual Flow Report: US Legal Permanent

were born abroad compared to 159 countries (with populations of one million or more), in terms of sheer numbers, the USA receives more immigrants than any other country.[3]

This is resulting in more dramatic demographic and cultural shifts than the USA has experienced in past generations. Beyond European, Latino, and Asian immigrants, recent immigration demographics include large numbers of immigrants from 'non-traditional' linguistic, ethnic, and cultural backgrounds. Cities like Detroit (Michigan) and Minneapolis (Minnesota) boast significant numbers of Iraqis and Somalis, respectively, outside their countries of origin. At the Times Square Church in New York City, there are over 100 nationalities represented.[4] In 2010, the University of Southern California had 6,944 international students from 116 different places of origin.[5] The USA is now the home of immigrants from nearly every country in the world.[6]

This shift is no longer just happening in traditional 'Gateway Cities' like New York, Los Angeles (California), and Chicago (Illinois), but also in rural areas of South Carolina, Idaho, and Ohio. In the last decade, for example, Stafford County (Virginia) saw its immigrant population nearly triple, and the foreign-born population in Newton County, in central Georgia outside Atlanta, quadrupled.[7] From 1990 to 2009 the foreign-born population of the small Midwestern meatpacking town Beardstown (Illinois) grew from 0.7% to 17.3%.[8]

In July 2011, for the first time in USA history, minority births represented the majority of births in the USA. This is a 'tipping point,' according to William H. Frey, senior demographer of the Brookings Institution, a 'transformation from a mostly white baby boomer culture to the more globalized multiethnic country that we are becoming.'[9]

Residents: 2011' (April 2012), 2, www.dhs. gov/xlibrary/assets/statistics/ publications/ lpr_fr_2011.pdf (accessed 21.6.12) .

[3] The Pew Forum on Religion and Public Life, 'Faith on the Move: The Religious Affiliation of International Migrants' (8 March 2012), www.pewforum. org/Geography/ Religious-Migration-united-states.aspx#_ftn10 (accessed 25.4.12).

[4] The Times Square Church, 'The People: Over 100 Nationalities', www.tscnyc.org/the_people.php (accessed 29.5.12).

[5] University of Southern California, 'International Student Enrollment Report Fall 2010', www.sait.usc.edu/ois/Upload/Publications/EnrollmentReport/2010-2011%20 ER.pdf (accessed 1.7.12).

[6] The Pew Forum on Religion and Public Life, 'Faith on the Move'.

[7] Sabrina Tavernise and Robert Gebeloff, 'Immigrants Make Paths to Suburbia, Not Cities', *New York Times* 14 December 2010, www.nytimes.com/2010/12/15/ us/15census.html> (accessed 29.5.12).

[8] Cristina Costantini, 'Beardstown, Small Midwestern Meatpacking Town, Wrestles with Immigration Issues', *The Huffington Post* 8 December 2011, www. huffingtonpost.com/2011/12/07/beardstown-illinois-small-town-wrestles-with-immigration-issues_n_1134797.html (accessed 25.4.12).

[9] Sabrina Tavernise, 'Whites Account for Under Half of Births in U.S.', *New York*

Since 1965, the USA immigration system has been founded on the idea that those who wished to work or be reunited with family would be allowed to enter on a visa. These immigrants are coming to the USA for a variety of reasons:

A. Most of the immigrants who enter the USA come to work (either permanently or temporarily) or to be with family.
B. Many people come to the USA to study. There were 723,277 international students at USA colleges and universities during the 2010-11 academic year, many of whom will go back to their homelands to pursue a career.[10]
C. The USA also admits humanitarian migrants, and refugees fleeing persecution are resettled through an annual refugee admissions program managed by the USA Department of State. In fiscal year 2011, the USA admitted 56,424 refugees.[11]

It is also estimated that 17,500 people are trafficked across USA borders every year.[12]

Evangelicals' Attitudes Toward Immigrants

Many white Americans lament the fact that the face of America is becoming non-European. In fact, according to a study by the Pew Research Center, faith groups (including white evangelicals, white mainline Protestants, and white Catholics), more than secular groups, view immigrants as a threat and a burden to traditional American customs and values, with white evangelicals at 63% the most inclined among the faith groups to think of immigrants as a menace.[13] In the USA, immigration is often debated in terms of the impact immigrants have on the economy, and there are limited discussions on the spiritual, social, and missional impact

---

Times 17 May 2012, www.nytimes.com/ 2012/05/17/us/whites-account-for-under-half-of-births-in-us.html# (accessed 18.5.12).

[10] The Institute of International Education (IIE), 'International Student Enrollment Increased by 5 Percent in 2010/11, Led by Strong Increase in Students from China', *Open Doors* 14 November 2011, www.iie.org/en/Who-We-Are/News-and-Events/Press-Center/Press-Releases/2011/2011-11-14-Open-Doors-International-Students (accessed 25.6.12).

[11] Department of State, 'Protecting the Persecuted: The Successes and Challenges of Safeguarding Refugees', Testimony of David M. Robinson, Acting Assistant Secretary of State, Bureau of Population, Refugees, and Migration, Washington, DC, 26 October 2011, www.state.gov/ j/prm/releases/remarks/2011/181081.htm (accessed 1.7.12).

[12] Department of State, 'Trafficking in Persons: US Policy and Issues for Congress' (18 February 2010), 2, www.fpc.state.gov/documents/organization/139278.pdf (accessed 25.4.12)

[13] Greg Smith, 'Attitudes Toward Immigration: In the Pulpit and the Pew', Pew Research Center, 26 April 2006, www.pewresearch.org/pubs/20/attitudes-toward-immigration-in-the-pulpit-and-the-pew (accessed 25.4.12).

of immigrants. A survey of faith groups found that almost all white evangelicals – 88% – say that their views on immigration are *primarily* influenced by concerns (political, economic, personal experience, etc.) other than their Christian faith.[14]

The fact that Christians are seeing immigration from secular worldviews is troubling because Christians are missing an enormous missional opportunity. In order to view immigrants not as a threat but as part of God's greater missional purposes, the Christian community in the USA must consider biblical principles and divine providence in the movement of people. 'Whenever there is an opportunity for the church to reach out to people in our communities, we must consider what it will take to further the Kingdom. If this means putting down the American flag and raising the Kingdom flag, that is what we should do,' says Bill Nelson, an InterVarsity Fellowship pastor who works with and has seen many conversions among international students.[15]

Symptomatic of the need for changes in attitude and heart among Christians in the USA, many churches have been slow to extend welcome, in part because the evangelical church in the USA is still largely segregated at 92.5%.[16] By not having and actively building relationships within and across ethnic lines in the USA, the American church is missing out on an enormous blessing, as we never know which of the strangers we welcome might be angels in disguise (Heb. 13:2). Our attitudes and actions toward immigrants has an enormous impact on how immigrants hear the message of the gospel, for the Great Commission – Christ's command to make disciples of all the nations (Matt. 28:19) – is 'not just to be assumed or to be taken for granted. It has to be explicitly and constantly reminded'.[17]

Towards a Biblical Understanding of Immigrants

It is clear throughout scripture that God cares for the immigrant. In the Old Testament, the word for stranger is *ger*, which is often mentioned alongside the widow and orphan as people who were particularly vulnerable because they often did not have family members to take care of them, or property in

[14] The Pew Forum on Religion and Public Life, 'Few Say Religion Shapes Immigration, Environment Views' (17 September 2010), www.pewforum.org/Politics-and-Elections/Few-Say-Religion-Shapes-Immigration-Environment-Views.aspx (accessed 25.4.12).

[15] Matthew Soerens and Jenny Hwang, *Welcoming the Stranger: Justice, Compassion and Truth in the Immigration Debate* (Downers Grove, IL: InterVarsity Press, 2009), 175.

[16] Michael Emerson and Christian Smith, *Divided by Faith* (New York: Oxford University Press, 2001).

[17] Lausanne Committee for World Evangelization (LCWE), *Scattered to Gather: Embracing the Global Trend of Diaspora* (Manila: LifeChange Publishing, 2010), 22.

order to become self-sufficient. Thus, the assistance of the community to which they migrated was critically important.

God loves immigrants and provides for them, and calls his followers to do the same (cf. Deut. 10:18; Ps. 146:9; Zech. 7:10; Ezek. 22:7; Mal. 3:5; Jer. 7:6; Deut. 24:21). In Matthew 25, God commands us to extend hospitality (literally, the love of strangers) – with the suggestion that they may bless us more than we assist them (cf. Rom. 12:13; Matt. 25:35-45; Heb. 13:2).

Migration indeed is not a new phenomenon. Scripture is a story of people in exile and on the move, and many of the prominent characters in the Bible had a migration experience which was fundamental to their experience of God. Abraham, who was called to leave his homeland; Ruth, who followed her mother-in-law into Moab; Joseph, who was sold into slavery in Egypt; and even Jesus was a refugee who had to flee with his parents into Egypt. What is unique about the current migration of people is that churches that had traditionally sent missionaries in order to fulfill the Great Commission find that through diaspora communities, the mission field can be accessed without one having to cross borders.

Religious Makeup of Immigrant Populations in the USA and Missional Implications

An understanding of the religious makeup of immigrants in the USA is important to seeing how immigrants have and will impact the Christian landscape. The USA is the world's number one destination for Christian migrants, who make up nearly three-quarters (74%) of all foreign-born people living in the USA.[18] With its huge population of immigrants, the USA has been a leading destination for many, though not all, religious groups. The USA is the top destination for Buddhist migrants (including many from Vietnam) and for people with no particular religious affiliation (including many from China). It is the world's second-leading destination for Hindu migrants, after India, and for Jewish migrants, after Israel. Among the other leading countries of origin for USA immigrants have been the Philippines (1.8 million), India (1.7 million), China (1.4 million), and Germany (1.2 million).

Recent immigrant groups to the USA are coming from countries where missionaries have not been allowed access or where access has been extremely difficult. China, Saudi Arabia, and Iran are all countries in which missionary activity has been extremely limited, but there are thousands of immigrants coming from these countries into the USA. When immigrants come to the USA, they experience a freedom they often did not have in their countries of origin, allowing them to find Christ and worship freely.

---

[18] Information in this paragraph is derived from the previously referred to Pew Forum on Religion and Public Life, 'Faith on the Move' website.

However, many Christians in the USA have concerns in particular about the arrival of Muslim migrants, viewing their arrival as a threat to the idea of the USA as a 'Christian nation', even though the USA ranks seventh as a destination for Muslim migrants, behind many Arab nations and Europe. This kind of fear is paralyzing and undermines God's missional purposes. 'Only by living out of love and compassion for immigrants in the USA will followers of Christ be able to move out of their comfort zones and into the mission of God', says a local Pastor Daniel Darling.[19]

The fact that a majority of immigrants coming to the USA adhere to Christianity also suggests that immigrants will not just be a mission field, but will actually be agents of mission. Immigrant congregations are growing more quickly than any other segment of American evangelicalism.[20] Many of the nation's evangelical denominations are growing increasingly diverse. Two decades ago, the Southern Baptist Convention had only 1-in-20 non-Anglo churches; by 2010, it had 1-in-5 non-Anglo churches.[21] The Foursquare Church also has 20-25% of its churches in the USA that are distinctly ethnic, while ethnic church planting is among the fastest-growing segments in the denomination.[22] Similarly, the Assemblies of God and the Church of the Nazarene are growing more diverse. Much of this growth can be attributed to the increase in Hispanic immigration to the USA. One in six Foursquare churches are Hispanic and more than 20% of weekly attendees at Assemblies of God churches are Hispanic.[23]

The church has a great missional opportunity to minister to, through, and beyond diaspora communities. Biblically, there is just one church – one Body, with many diverse members, interdependent upon one another, sharing in suffering (1 Cor. 12:12-26).

Missions to the Diasporas[24]

When God moves diasporas, making them accessible to believers, the church should reach them with the gospel. Many churches are experiencing

---

[19] Daniel Darling, 'When Fear Fuels Our Worldview', UnDocumented.TV blog (8 June 2012), www.undocumented.tv/2012/blog/when-fear-fuels-our-worldview/ (accessed 8.6.12).

[20] Todd Johnson, 'USA Evangelicals/evangelicals in a World Context', *Lausanne World Pulse* (January 2006), 34, www.lausanneworldpulse.com/research.php/196/01-2006 (accessed 25.4.12).

[21] Ed Stetzer, 'The Changing Ethnic and Racial Landscape of Denominations in America', *Christian Post* (19 June 2012), www.christianpost.com/news/the-changing-ethinic-and-racial-landscape-of-denomoninations-in-america-76873/ (accessed 20.6.12).

[22] Ed Stetzer, 'The Changing Ethnic and Racial Landscape'.

[23] Ed Stetzer, 'The Changing Ethnic and Racial Landscape'.

[24] LCWE, *Scattered to Gather*, 24.

tremendous growth through intentionally choosing to welcome and integrate immigrants into their faith communities. In doing so, pastors and lay members are personally seeing God's providential workings in the migration of people.

The welcome comes most often through authentic relationships with Christians and the development of church-based programs that serve immigrants and help them in their integration process. Willow Creek Community Church, for example, is a large church in South Barrington, outside of Chicago (Illinois), which serves 5,000 people at their Care Center that provides food, English as Second Language (ESL) classes, and legal services. They have a Spanish-speaking ministry, Casa de Luz, which has grown from a small ministry to one with several hundred members and their own Spanish-speaking pastor.

Vineyard Columbus in Columbus (Ohio) has a congregational makeup of 30% minorities, with 20% African Americans and 10% who are foreign born.[25] Of the foreign born, 110 nations are represented. They have 20 intentional programs serving the foreign born in their community, including English as Second Language (ESL) programs, refugee resettlement co-sponsorship, and home-stay hospitality for hundreds of international students arriving in Central Ohio. This expansive list of services has provided an opportunity for the church to reach many people in the community. 'The growth of immigrants (along with the African American population) has changed our church forever', said Bill Christensen, Associate Pastor at Vineyard Columbus. 'We are expressing more fully what the Kingdom of God looks like. This is all wonderful… at times challenging…but extraordinarily rewarding!'[26] Indeed, churches that have cross-cultural ministries are not only testifying to the gospel in their relationships with the foreign born, but are themselves being transformed through the process.

While the experiences of many churches in the USA speak to God's hand in ministering to the diaspora, this is not the case across the evangelical community. According to a survey by Harford Seminary, only 10% of evangelical churches in the USA have any sort of ministry or ministry partnership focused on immigrants.[27] This is an unfortunate reality because God's hand is moving in diasporas communities to come to know him in a real way, and he has called his body to welcome and bless the nations of the world arriving to our neighborhoods.

---

[25] Email conversation with Pastor Bill Christensen of Vineyard Church of Columbus, 27 June 2012.

[26] Email conversation with Pastor Bill Christensen of Vineyard Church of Columbus, 27 June 2012.

[27] '2010 National Survey of Congregations: Evangelical Protestant', Harford Seminary Faith Communities Today Survey, 3, www.faithcommunitiestoday.org/sites/faithcommunitiestoday.org/files/2010EvangelicalFrequenciesV1.pdf (accessed 20.6.10).

Missions Through the Diasporas

Diaspora communities are not just a mission field, but are themselves evangelizing their own people groups, whether in their newfound communities or back in their homeland.[28] About 38.5 million (37%) USA immigrants come from Latin America.[29] While the majority of these Latinos are Catholic, approximately 24% are Protestant or 'other Christian'. This means that at 9.5 million, there are more Latino Protestants than American Jews, Muslims, Episcopalians, or Presbyterians.[30] Orlando Quintana is a Latino youth who was brought to New Life Covenant Church in Chicago by a friend. 'I think the key is family. Hispanics are really big on extended family, and people that are not family, bringing them in as family'.[31] This church used to have only a few dozen members, but now has a membership of around 12,000 people.

Many other immigrant groups are reaching out to their own people groups. Among the refugee populations that have been resettled in the USA, many are coming from previously unreached areas. The Bhutanese, for example, are a group of refugees who were confined to live in camps in Nepal for decades. Many of the young Bhutanese children have only known camp life with no hope of a better future. Despite this difficult existence, it was in these camps where many first encountered Jesus. Approximately 72% of the Bhutanese are Buddhist and the country was closed to Christian witness until 1965.[32] Having fled persecution and war, these refugees often experience a newfound freedom in the USA. Many started their own churches soon after arrival and are very evangelistic in nature. Several baptisms have happened among new arrivals in Nashville (Tennessee); at one event, 180 Bhutanese came to Christ through a Nepali Jesus video. They often gather in small house churches, and in Memphis (Tennessee) they have a second-generation Bhutanese church. Nathan Kinser, World Relief Nashville's Office Director, said, 'When Bhutanese arrive, they have a vibrant faith and generic knowledge of the Bible but discipleship is a great need in this community'.[33]

---

[28] LCWE, *Scattered to Gather*, 25.

[29] Kate Brick, A.E. Challinor, and Marc R. Rosenblum, 'Mexican and Central American Immigrants in the United States', Migration Policy Institute 2011, www.migrationpolicy.org/pubs/MexCent Amimmigrants.pdf (accessed 1.7.12).

[30] Bruce Murray, 'Latino Religion in the U.S.: Demographic Shifts and Trend', National Hispanic Christian Leadership Council, www.nhclc.org/news/latino-religion-us-demographic-shifts-and-trend (accessed 28.6.12).

[31] Barbara Bradley Hagerty, 'U.S. Hispanics Choose Churches Outside Catholicism', National Public Radio, 19 October 2011, www.npr.org/2011/10/19/141275979/u-s-hispanics-choose-churches-outside-catholicism (accessed 25.6.12).

[32] Historymakers, 'The World's Only Buddhist Kingdom', www.historymakers.info/missions/bhutan.html (accessed 4.3.14).

[33] Interview conversation with Nathan Kinser, 28 August 2012.

Because of their previous persecution, other refugee groups, including many of the Burmese refugees and Iraqis, have a depth of theology and a fire for evangelism when they arrive to the USA. Chin refugees, an ethnic minority in Burma, are estimated to be 90% Christian, while the Karen and Karenni are similar in their religious makeup. The Chin Baptist Churches USA has growing churches in Indianapolis (Indiana), Dallas (Texas), Minneapolis (Minnesota), and Baltimore (Maryland). Many of these refugees are more evangelical in nature than American evangelicals. They hold regular outreach events and are well-connected throughout the USA.

Missions Beyond the Diasporas

The USA is becoming a significant destination target for missionaries sent from nations in the global south. This is one powerful expression of the vibrancy of faith and evangelistic zeal found among many newly arriving believers to the USA. Missionaries, pastors, and leaders from immigrant communities must be invited as equal co-laborers in existing missional efforts. The sharing of vision, resources, gifts, and callings will serve to impact all peoples residing in the USA. Where needed, evangelical educational institutions can play a powerful role in providing theological training and teaching alongside diaspora communities.

Providing discipleship training and developing partnerships between immigrant churches and non-immigrant churches will also be critical for developing a diverse church community in which segregation does not persist. Among the activities necessary are:[34]

- Building intentional relationships between immigrant and non-immigrant leaders.
- Equipping and mentoring non-immigrant churches and immigrant churches for relationship with one another.
- Mediating church-to-church relationships and 'host-church' partnerships.
- Providing or networking the resources of organizations and churches for immigrant churches' (1) logistics, (2) vision, (3) leadership, and (4) second generation issues.
- Providing or networking the expertise of organizations and churches skilled in contextual (1) church planting, (2) discipleship, and (3) leadership development.

Conclusion

Scripture, history, and contemporary missiologists recognize and celebrate God's sovereign work of moving diaspora peoples across the earth as a

[34] World Relief USA Strategic Directions, October 2009.

central part of his mission and redemptive purposes for the world. This God-ordained movement is impacting the USA in at least four ways:

A. Cities, towns, and rural communities are demographically diversifying in unprecedented numbers.
B. Christian immigrants to the USA are transforming the landscape of American Christianity through rapid growth and vibrancy.
C. Non-Christian immigrants are among the most receptive groups of people to the gospel.
D. American Christians are being required to adjust both to the new diversity in our churches and denominations as well as the missional opportunity on our doorsteps.

In making these important adjustments, not only will Christians in the USA honor their own rich heritage as a nation of immigrants, but will usher in a diversity in which people from every tribe, nation, and language worship Jesus (Rev. 7:9).

Evangelical churches that are ministering to, through, and beyond diaspora communities have born tremendous fruit in the USA. However, much more can be done. First, discipleship that works to biblically align the attitude of Christians in the USA towards immigrants, where only 16% of white evangelicals have heard about immigration from their pastor or other clergy, will be essential to seeing a more widespread desire in the Christian community to minister to diaspora communities.[35]

Second, more concrete outreach and ministries to the foreign born in the USA will be needed. Many of these ministries must ensure that cross-cultural relationships are built and there is diversity not just within the USA Christian landscape but within specific churches as well. Third, the equipping and empowering of diaspora community leaders themselves will be crucial to ensuring that a new diverse leadership is ready and able to lead.

Diasporas have been and will continue to be an indispensable means by which God accomplishes his redemptive purposes through Jesus Christ.[36] The choice that the church faces in its response to immigrants will determine its future. The church can respond in fear and view the change as a threat, or recognize the missional and transformational opportunity presented by diaspora peoples.

---

[35] The Pew Forum on Religion and Public Life, 'Few Say Religion Shapes Immigration, Environment Views'.

[36] LCWE, *Scattered to Gather,* 17.

A New Paradigm of the Parish as a Result of the Pastoral Openness of the Missionary Oblates of Mary Immaculate to the Phenomenon of Polish Immigrants in Canada

Wojciech Kluj

The great emigration of people of Polish origin to Canada began in the late nineteenth century,[1] and later intensified in the years following both world wars and the Solidarity movement in the 1980s. The pastoral activity of Catholic priests among them led to a very specific form of work with the Polish communities: the Polish Parishes, both ethnic and personal. The latter notion of the parish as personal refers to affiliation on the basis of the personal choice of those who wish to belong to the community of faith. Because the vast majority of Poles living abroad associate themselves with the Roman Catholic church, this presentation is confined to the Roman Catholic parishes.

The Polish Parishes in Canada are now a very peculiar phenomenon in comparison with other structures for pastoral care of migrants. The basic form of pastoral work with Poles in other countries in Europe is the so-called *Polish Catholic mission,* which is under the dual authority of local bishops, but in co-operation with the Polish Episcopal Conference. The institution of the Polish Parishes in Canada, which was developed earlier than in Europe, is only under the local bishops. Polish bishops tend to be honorably invited for some special ceremonies, but they have no authority over them.[2]

The Beginning of Polish Immigration to Canada

Even if the issue of the First Nations in Canada is set aside, ever since the arrival of the English settlers, Canada has never been a mono-ethnic society. In Canadian history, the English and French communities played a key role, but during this time many came from other nations and ethnic groups as well.

---

[1] At that time, Poland did not exist on the political map of Europe. The country was under the triple occupation of Russia, Prussia, and Austria. Polish traditions, language, and faith were kept alive in families and in the Catholic parishes. It was only in 1918 that Poland regained independence.

[2] They have certain indirect authority when it comes to language because these communities use liturgical books approved for Polish dioceses.

The Canadian government's decision in the late nineteenth century to open the borders to immigrants from Central Europe was prompted by the shortage of manpower on farms out west. In addition, a gold rush in the Yukon and the construction of new railway lines caused more than three million immigrants to arrive in Canada between 1896 and 1914. The reality of present-day Western European countries ill-prepared to deal with the increasing pluralization of their societies, caused by the influx of Turkish and North African migrants, is not unlike what Canada experienced in the beginning of the twentieth century.

The Canadian government invited immigrants from Central and Eastern Europe knowing next to nothing about their histories and specific cultural and religious needs. The arrival of the new immigrants was characterized by astonishment, caused by the arrival of such a 'weird' people, aversion toward them, and finally strong criticism by the local society. This was due in great part to the ignorance of the history of these people.

As for the Poles in Canada, there were examples of exceptional immigrants such as Sir Casimir Gzowski and the Globensky family, who integrated well into their new society, which represented a small, well-educated group. But the wave of immigrants that interests us, from the late nineteenth and early twentieth century, had different sociocultural origins and their process of integration into Canadian society proceeded very differently. Most of the immigrants were poor, landless farmers from villages or small trade merchants.

For all immigrants, the first challenge was survival. Some lost their lives. One group settled on farms (homesteads); others worked in the building of railways and in the construction industry, as well as in the lumber and mine industries. At that time, the largest group of Polish immigrants in Canada settled in Winnipeg and to the west.

The Missionary Oblates of Mary Immaculate (OMI), the Catholic missionary congregation, was the main group of Catholic clergy there. They had worked on the Canadian prairies, originally among the First Nations people, since the mid-nineteenth century. Since the beginning of the immigration, they supported the rights of French-speaking immigrants to preserve their language and culture. This was to help them preserve their faith, which was generally Catholic. Such efforts became a kind of religious umbrella for other immigrants, including Poles.

Demographic changes in Western Canada forced the creation of new church structures. Catholics of Central European descent were not able to pray together with local Catholics. It was both a matter of language and traditions in living out their faith. Bishops were aware of the changes taking place on the prairies. The parish structures in these dioceses could not simply be a replica of the ecclesial structures of Quebec or Europe, where people grew up in the same culture and spoke the same language. The largest group of Catholics at the time were Ukrainians, Germans, and Poles and many immigrants did not trust 'foreign' priests.

Searching for suitable workers, Archbishop Adelard Langevin OMI from St Boniface found two brothers, Jan Wilhelm (John William) and Wojciech (Adalbert) Kulawy, who were graduating from the Oblate seminary in Ottawa. They were the perfect people for such work because, apart from their native Polish, they also knew German (spoken in their region) as well as French and English, in addition to Ukrainian, Czech, and Slovak.

New Paradigm: Holy Ghost Parish in Winnipeg

The first community of this kind, Holy Ghost parish, provides an interesting example for detailed study both ecclesially and sociologically. However, for the history of the beginning of this parish, here I will simply highlight a few conclusions which characterize the functioning of this parish.[3]

In April 1898, Archbishop Langevin named Wojciech Kulawy OMI a missionary for the Poles, Germans, Slovaks, Ukrainians, and other European settlers in and around Winnipeg. Wojciech Kulawy began visiting the scattered settlers in the prairies, and Jan Wilhelm began working on the creation of a parish in the city. At first, Archbishop Langevin thought of creating a cosmopolitan parish for all immigrants – thus the name of the parish, Holy Ghost, for the many languages.

It seemed logical that in addition to two normal parishes in the city, there would also be a mixed one. The two largest groups of Roman Rite Catholics were the Poles and Germans. However, gradually tensions began to rise between these groups. Archbishop Langevin, hoping to resolve these problems, had even commanded that there be two main Masses celebrated: one for the German group and one for the Polish group. Yet the problem intensified and in 1905 the German group created their own parish which was run by the Oblates of purely German origin. Another large group, the Ukrainians, wanted to have their liturgy not only in their own language, but also in their own Eastern rite.

To better appreciate the magnitude and clarity of Archbishop Langevin's idea and that of the first priests in the Holy Ghost parish, it is worth recalling the tensions that emerged among Polish immigrants in the United

---

[3] For more bibliography about this parish, see my article: 'Początki Pracy Misjonarzy Oblatów M.N. wśród Polskich Emigrantów na Kanadyjskich Preriach – Parafia Ducha Świętego w Winnipeg 1898-1926' [The Beginnings of the work of the Oblates of Mary Immaculate Among the Polish Immigrants on the Prairies of Canada – Holy Ghost Parish in Winnipeg 1898-1926], *Collectanea Theologica* [Warsaw] 70.2 (2000), 127-51. For larger background, see my article: 'Forms of Work of the Oblates of Mary Immaculate Among Polish Immigrants in the Prairies of Canada (1898-1926)', *Vie Oblate Life* [Ottawa] 56.3 (1997), 363-401, and 57.1 (1998), 27-76.

States, which resulted in the creation of the national church.[4] By noting the historical background of this movement, we can appreciate the wise decisions made by Archbishop Langevin and the Oblates working with the Polish immigrants. Despite many misunderstandings and tensions, all attempts to create a Polish Protestant church failed. It is difficult to say why. This could be in itself an issue worth more study: *Why, even to this day, are there not many Polish Protestant communities in Canada?* Even those who disagreed with Catholic authorities remained attached to the Catholic culture.

A major concern was the vision of the pastoral work of these first pastors. They were young, almost all newly-ordained priests, without pastoral experience, and often with little experience of life in Canadian society, but with good will and great openness to the new reality. The only preparation was their lectures on pastoral theology. In general, one can say that they were sent to Winnipeg to do 'something'. Their living conditions were very difficult, but they were young and full of enthusiasm and ideas.

When Archbishop Langevin died in 1915, a new archdiocese was founded on the other side of the river in Winnipeg. The first Archbishop of Winnipeg was Alfred Arthur Sinnott, who was of British origin. He decided to create another Polish Parish in the city – St John Cantius. It was a type of concession to those who were in conflict with the pastors, but

---

[4] The Polish National Church (*Polskokatolicki*) was founded from out of the realities of the US Catholic church. From the beginning, many tensions accumulated among Polish Catholics there. These resulted from the traditional Polish and American ways of determining competence in parish life. In addition to tensions arising from the personalities of some priests, a much more serious conflict arose because of the actions of some bishops. It was mainly a question of church property, especially of the official title. The immigrants who built the churches with their hard-earned money wanted to have a certain control over them. In addition, some bishops created many difficulties in the use of the Polish language during worship and in the parish schools. Moreover, although the Poles were an important group of Catholics in the United States, there was no bishop of Polish descent. It was not a matter of faith or of the Roman Rite, but the supremacy of American bishops. The best-known example of this kind of 'resistance movement' was the National Church (*Polskokatolicki*), founded by Fr Francis Hodur, who had received Episcopal consecration from the Old Catholic (Utrecht Union) bishops. His situation was known in Winnipeg. At the end of 1902, a group of parishioners from Holy Ghost parish wrote to the United States asking for a Polish priest. There were two problems. First, some priests had difficulty with the Polish language, and second, some people simply had a difficult character. Hence, in 1903 a priest came to Winnipeg and began a campaign against the priests and for the creation of a new parish. But it soon became known that he was sought with an arrest warrant in the United States and was soon arrested by the police. Later, between 1909 and 1911, other priests arrived in Winnipeg in order to create a second, 'more Polish' parish. When Bishop Hodur did not name Fr Markiewicz national bishop of Canada, in 1913 he created a new Polish Catholic Apostolic Church. None of these attempts, however, survived long.

wanted to remain Catholic. The parish grew, but nevertheless always remained in the 'shadow' of its older sister parish.

Why was it so important? This ethnic personal parish was not only a place of worship in the church, but something of a 'small Poland' with different social groups and institutions. The Polish community needed its own school and established one in 1902. A Polish newspaper also played an important role in the life of this ethnic community.[5] From the perspective of the new idea of the ethnic parish community, it is interesting to note that the owners of the newspaper were not Poles, but a company belonging to the Oblates.[6] Coming to a new society, a newcomer often needs some help. The first of the Holy Ghost parish organizations was the Fraternal Aid Society.[7] Among the more devotional groups existed the parish choir of St Cecilia and the Holy Rosary Confraternity (created primarily for women, especially mothers). Shortly after his arrival in Winnipeg, Fr Kowalski organized the St Stanislaus Kostka Society for young boys.[8] There was also a theater group, the St Vincent de Paul Society, *Elenteria* Society, and the St Elizabeth Society. Also, some parish matters were partially put under the responsibility of different parish committees that cared for the church building, school, cemetery, and the finances. Since 1902, the parish also had a council and the Third Order of St Francis. In addition, there existed the Gymnastic Association *Sokól* – more athletic than pastoral – in principle, a very patriotic group. In order not to divide the Polish immigrant communities, in 1909 the Polish Federation of Catholic Societies was founded, whose purpose was to unite the various activities and place them under the patronage of St Michael the Archangel.

Development of the Paradigm

Such a 'new' model of community proved to be a good solution. First, this new paradigm was copied in Western Canada. In 1913, Holy Rosary parish

---

[5] Oblates working on the prairies understood this well. West Canada Publishing Company, led by the Oblates, in 1914, printed five weekly newspapers in five different languages: *La Liberté* (in French) *North-West Review* (in English), *West Canada* (in German), *Kanadyskyj Rusyn* (in Ukrainian), and *Gazeta Katolicka* (in Polish).

[6] Without the support of the congregation, the newspaper would have never survived. Only in 1934 did it become a part of the Association of Poles in Canada.

[7] It was a common form of affordable insurance in case of illness or death. It was very popular among immigrants. The Association gave aid especially to new immigrants.

[8] This association, like other similar ones founded by priests in Europe, was organized in a way that interested especially young immigrants from Europe. They were more prone to play sports than to participate in the evening discussion groups or reading clubs.

was founded in Edmonton. In the beginning, the Oblates too were responsible for it, and later diocesan priests (1926-61). But after this time, the Oblates returned once again to staff the parish. In 1931, a native of this parish, Fr Frank Kosakiewicz OMI, was ordained a priest there.[9] After World War II, with the arrival of a new wave of immigrants, it was necessary to enlarge the church. The structure of the parish was similar – to give 'not only heaven, but also bread' to Polish immigrants. Of course, the number of initiatives and groups depended on the size of the parish.

In 1944, the Oblates were entrusted with the creation of a Polish parish in Vancouver, still farther west. A school was also established there, and later, a nursing home.[10] Next, in the 1980s, in view of the great number of new immigrants, a new Polish parish in Edmonton was created under the patronage of Mary, Queen of Poland.[11]

After World War II, during 1946-50, more than 35,000 Poles arrived in Canada. This time, however, they were more educated and often settled in cities, especially in Eastern Canada. Similarly, as in the west, local parishes could not meet all the expectations of the newcomers. In places where there were more Poles, Polish-Canadian parishes were created, but this was only possible in larger centers. In some localities the Polish priests said occasional Masses in Polish, but most of the ministry was done in English.

The first Oblate who worked in the Polish community in what is today the largest Polish community in Canada, the Greater Toronto Area, was Fr Stanislaw Puchniak OMI, who came to St Stanislaus Kostka Church in Toronto in 1935.[12] This parish had existed since 1911 and was at first entrusted to diocesan priests. There were many different associations and groups in this parish. In 1945, the St Stanislaus Credit Union was founded, which later united with the St Casimirs Credit Union, and it still exists to this day. The model here was similar as in Winnipeg, but Toronto quickly surpassed Winnipeg. The second Polish parish in Toronto was St Mary's. It was founded in 1915, and was entrusted to the Oblates in 1940.[13] Seeing the great needs, in 1944 the Oblates began to look for land in order to build a

---

[9] See his article, 'Polish Oblate Ministry and Immigration in Alberta', in Raymond Huel (ed), *Western Oblate Studies 1 / Études Oblates de l'Ouest 1* (Edmonton: Western Canadian Publishers and Institut de recherche de la Faculté Saint-Jean, 1990), 171-79.

[10] See Janusz Blazejak, *A Half of Century: The Missionary Oblates of Mary Immaculate – Assumption Province in Canada* (Toronto: Missionary Oblates of Mary Immaculate – Assumption Province, 2006), 58-60.

[11] See Blazejak, *A Half of Century*, 101-3.

[12] See Blazejak, *A Half of Century*, 25-8, 66-8. Edward Walewander (ed), *Leksykon geograficzno-historyczny parafii i kościołów polskich w Kanadzie* [*Geographic-Historical Lexicon of Polish Parishes and Churches in Canada*], vol. 1 (Lublin: KUL, 1992), 260-74.

[13] See Blazejak, *A Half of Century*, 69-72. Walewander, *Leksykon*, 302-8.

third Polish parish in Toronto. The new church was finished in 1954. St Casimir was for many years the largest Polish community in Toronto.[14]

The big challenge was the creation of St Maximilian Kolbe Parish in Mississauga. This fairly new parish began in late 1979. Today, it has more than 11,000 families.[15] On a regular Sunday about 8,000 people participate in the Masses. To all the regular parish activities, the festival of religious songs was added in 1991. Because St Maximilian had grown to approximately 40,000 people, it was necessary to create a yet another community in Brampton, where St Eugene de Mazenod parish now stands.[16]

Although outside of the Toronto area, but still in the east, since the 1950s the great development of the parish of St Hyacinth in Ottawa has been noted.[17] Similarly, when many Poles arrived in St Catharines,[18] especially in the 1970s, the Polish parish there experienced immense growth.

Since the Greater Toronto Area currently has many Polish parishes, it is possible to create common projects. Such a project is the Catholic Youth Studio, which is a Catholic radio program that has been operating since 1994.[19]

Conclusion

Many other religious congregations have also been working with Poles in Canada. This article does not have the space to fully elaborate on the work of the Oblates, much less on the work of the other religious congregations. Even though the normal form of parish work in the Roman Catholic church remains territorial, the examples given above show that there might be well founded exceptions to this rule. Today, even church law makes provisions for personal, especially ethnic parishes.

Ethnic personal parishes are a very peculiar form of pastoral work. Practice has indicated that the Christian emigrants (in this case, the Poles) feel better and find it easier to pray in a community of their own culture and language. It is especially so when they belong to some kind of social umbrella organizations analogous to what they knew from home. What at first was seen as a kind of exception (in Winnipeg) later became normal.

Of course, this way of working has its difficulties. Sometimes, Polish Catholics know what is happening in a Polish parish a few hundred kilometers away, but do not know what is happening in their neighboring parish. This is, however, a reality of Canada – a country of immigrants. For

---

14 See Blazejak, *A Half of Century*, 79-81. Walewander, *Leksykon*, 275-301.

15 See Blazejak, *A Half of Century*, 97-100. Walewander, *Leksykon*, 164-69.

16 See Blazejak, *A Half of Century*, 109-12.

17 See Blazejak, *A Half of Century*, 85-7. Walewander, *Leksykon*, 185-99.

18 See Blazejak, *A Half of Century*, 82-4. Walewander, *Leksykon*, 208-14.

19 See Blazejak, *A Half of Century*, 104-8.

example, we may recall a situation from the Ottawa diocese. A Polish-Italian couple knowing both official languages may belong to four parishes: territorial English, territorial French, ethnic Polish (after husband), and ethnic Italian (after wife). What would be the ecclesial identity of their children? Similarly, in the great Toronto area today, Sunday Masses are celebrated in over 40 languages. This creates new problems, but also new pastoral possibilities.

In summarizing this paradigm of pastoral ministry, what seemed to be important in creating this new approach was the initiative of Archbishop Langevin. At first, Archbishop Langevin wanted to create a *multicultural* parish; eventually, it appeared to be a question of *language*. Finally, experience led to the creation of *ethnic and personal* parishes. Will this paradigm of ethnic and personal parishes last?

On the one hand, the younger generations now feel more at ease with the local language and culture, and therefore do not connect themselves so closely with the parishes of their parents. On the other hand, there are more mixed marriages, therefore, more services are offered in the local (here English) language. Instead of judging the question of temporality of this paradigm, perhaps it is better to see this development as an example of the process of inculturation on the level of church structures.

From the perspective of missiology, the Catholic church hasn't yet found a perfect form of evangelization of peoples 'in motion'. This applies both to traditional societies of nomads as well as to large groups of contemporary immigrants. In principle, the church structures are based on the criteria of the territory.

It seems, therefore, that although this is not an ideal solution, the idea of personal parishes for certain groups may be a good solution for now. In a sense, this idea was confirmed in two basic documents of the Catholic church on the pastoral care of immigrants (i.e., *Exsul Familia Nazarethana* [The migrant Holy Family of Nazareth][20] and *Erga Migrantes Caritatis Christi* [The love of Christ towards migrants][21]). The paradigm of working with Polish immigrants proposed by the first Oblate missionaries on the Canadian prairies at the beginning of the twentieth century, after certain amendments, was accepted in the universal church as an effective and acceptable form of evangelization.

---

[20] Apostolic Constitution of Pius XII of 1952.

[21] In 2004, the Pontifical Council for the Pastoral Care of Migrants and Itinerant People issued this instruction *Erga Migrantes Caritas Christi*. No. 91 gives an outline of possible pastoral structures, including a personal parish.

Identity and Ecumenical Partnership of Churches of African Origin in Germany

Benjamin Simon

Since the 1970s, there has been an increasing immigration wave of Africans to Germany. Thus, from 22,603 in 1967, the African population in Germany increased more than tenfold in 30 years. By 1999, the official number had already grown to 300,611,[1] which did not include the unrecorded cases, tens of thousands of Africans living there illegally. The diagram below shows statistics over the past decades in terms of increasing numbers of Africans among the population in the Federal Republic of Germany.

Figure 1: *Increase of Africans Living in Germany Since 1967.*

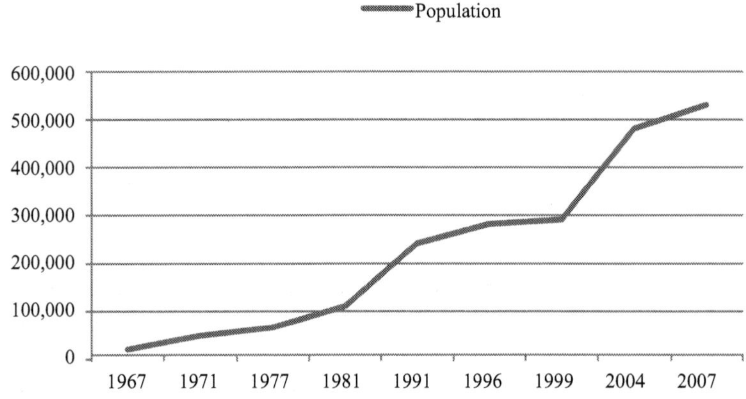

Due to these rapidly increasing numbers, the African community in Germany is gaining more self-confidence. Whereas until the end of the colonial time in the 1960s the 'roots of everyday life and religion were without exception heteronomous',[2] the life of Africans in Germany appears

---

[1] See 'Statistisches Bundesamt', available at www.destatis.de/ EN/Homepage.html (accessed 8.9.12).

[2] Amélé A.A. Ekué, 'An den Ufern von Babylon Saßen wir und Weinten, wenn wir an Zion Dachten…: Wahrnehmungen zur Religösen Reinterpretation von Exil unter Afrikanischen Christen und Christinnen in der Hamburger Diaspora', in Theo Ahrens (ed), *Zwischen Regionalität und Globalisierung: Studien zu Mission,*

in a new light. They organize themselves in sociocultural communities, establish friendship groups[3] and societies for aid projects, and make plans and decisions for their own religious life. The African religious landscape is by no means homogeneous. Besides a small group of Muslim Africans from the Maghreb, the majority of Africans are members of Christian churches. To illustrate this plurality not only with regard to their national and social composition, but also to their religious composition, some figures are given: in Berlin and in the Rhine-Main region, there are about 100 African congregations each; in Hamburg, there are far more than 100; and in the Ruhr region,[4] as many as 98 African-initiated congregations and churches have been registered since 2000.

These congregations see themselves first as congregations *by and for* Africans, while mostly 'maintaining ecumenical and international openness'.[5] Most churches of African origin – whether initiated in Africa or in Germany in diaspora – have made it their task to carry their vision beyond their own sociocultural boundaries and to preach the gospel to all people. It is remarkable that even more than 30 years ago, Harold W. Turner drew attention to the static state of the European churches and the dynamics of African churches in Europe:

> Some of the African churches have a sense of mission towards us [the Europeans]. They see how static and ineffective we are, and how little we share some of their own central convictions about prayer, fasting, healing, the power of the Spirit and the joy of worship. They ride on the crest of a religion that works. They share also in the new-found African convictions of having an important contribution to make to the nations of the world, especially in the realms of human relations and of the spiritual where we are increasingly desiccated and inadequate. One sign of the authenticity of their Christian faith is desire to share their discoveries and open up to us again the dynamic of our mutual heritage...[6]

The international orientation of many of these congregations is demonstrated in their renaming efforts: to their old names they have added

---

Ökumene und Religion (Hamburg: Ammersbek, 1997), 327-45, at 330. All translations from German sources in this chapter are by the author.

[3] See, e.g., the *Deutsch-Nigerianischer Freundeskreis*, eingetragener Verein (e.V.), at www.afrika-nrw.net/index2.php?id=121&aid=502 (accessed 8.9.12).

[4] For the Ruhr region, see the thorough research by Claudia Währisch-Oblau, former representative of the United Evangelical Mission (UEM) for foreign congregations: Claudia Währisch-Oblau, 'From Reverse Mission to Common Mission...We hope', *International Review of Mission* 354 (2000), 467-83. Very helpful for a further understanding is Währisch-Oblau, *The Missionary Self-Perception of Pentecostal/Charismatic Church Leaders from the Global South in Europe: Bringing Back the Gospel* (Leiden: Brill, 2009).

[5] Ekué, 'An den Ufern', 332.

[6] Harold W. Turner, *Religious Innovation in Africa: Collected Essays on New Religious Movements* (Boston: G. K. Hall, 1979), 291.

words such as 'international', 'global', 'world', or 'worldwide'.[7] By this renaming, they want to draw attention to their transnational connections. For example, the Primate of the Church of the Lord (Aladura)-Worldwide stated that his church is open to all nations, and that it acknowledges the globalization of the religious market in which it wants to be present '(in) other parts of Africa and the world in general'.[8] Already during the 1998 workshop talks in Hamburg,[9] the primate reiterated this point:

> The mission of our church is to bring Christ to all nations, particularly outside Africa, so that they too may experience spiritual fulfilment in Christ Jesus. This is revealed to our founding fathers an age of importation of the gospel, or mission-reversed, into the industrialized world from Africa...Our church is making an attempt to restore life into the churches through Spirit-filled worship sessions and in-depth studies of the word of God...Our mission is to bring good news to all people in this land, irrespective of race or color, and to present to them yet another form of worshipping in the beauty of His Holiness in spirit and in truth...[10]

This mission orientation toward the world can be observed in many Christian churches of African origin. In this respect, more African Initiated Churches (AICs) with the qualities already described have become established in Germany and across Europe, along with the Church of the Lord (Aladura)-Worldwide. Among them, there are the Celestial Church of Christ Worldwide, the Aladura Church International, the Rhema Church International, the International Central Gospel Church, the Global Revival Outreach, the World Miracle Church, the Liberty Church International, the Bethel Prayer Ministry International, The All Christian Believers Fellowship, Gospel Light International Church, and the *Eglise de Jésus-Christ sur la terre par son envoyé spécial Simon Kimbangu* (EJCSK).

Some of these congregations and churches boast of a number of daughter congregations founded in Germany and Europe. Others consist of only one congregation and yet have added one of the above designations to their name. That changing does indicate the intention of developing not only regionally, but also internationally[11] and transculturally in the future.[12]

---

[7] According to a personal communication in spring 2005 with Dr Rufus Ositelu, The Church of The Lord (Aladura) has called itself Church of the Lord (Aladura)-Worldwide since 1964.

[8] Rufus Ositelu, *African Indigenous Churches* (Langen: Alexander Verlag, 1984), 44. This statement implies an idea already expressed in the 1950s by the founder of the church, the late Dr J.O. Ositelu.

[9] See Benjamin Simon, *From Migrants to Missionaries: Christians of African Origin in Germany* (Frankfurt: Peter Lang, 2010), 22-8.

[10] Rufus Ositelu, 'The Church of the Lord (Aladura), Hamburg-Altona', unpublished presentation to *Werkstattgespräche zur Bedeutung der afrikanischen religiösen Diaspora in Deutschland* [Workshop Talks on the Significance of the African Religious Diaspora in Germany], Missionsakademie, University of Hamburg, 9-11 September 1998.

[11] In this context, see also Afe Adogame, 'Betwixt Identity and Security: African

Anthropologist Gerrie ter Haar pleads with regard to the abbreviation 'AIC' to no longer speak of 'African Independent Churches' or 'African Indigenous Churches', but of 'African International Churches': 'Most churches in fact label themselves as "international churches"' expressing their aspiration to be part of the international world in which they believe themselves to have a universal task'.[13] I am of the opinion that it would be premature to call all AICs 'international'. Although quite a few AICs have already achieved transnational relationships and intercultural membership, the attribute of internationality can by no means be extended collectively to all Christian congregations and churches of African origin in the diaspora in Europe. For instance, the Kimbanguist Church (EJCSK), which is counted among the largest AICs and represented by many congregations in Europe and North America in the diaspora, cannot be described as an international African church with regard to its membership, since the origin of the members in the German congregations is limited to Lingala-speaking ethnical groups.[14] It might be transcultural by its structure.

If one wants to retain the internationally-recognized abbreviation 'AIC' and use it also as a relevant term in the diaspora situation, it appears to be meaningful to speak of 'African-Initiated Churches'. This would take care of the diverse types of African-Christian churches in Africa, Europe, and, in this case, in Germany. The churches are 'African-initiated' to the degree that they were founded by people of African origin. This terminology gives the possibility of including three types of African-Christian churches: those founded in Africa ('autochthonous ecclesiogenesis'); those founded in the diaspora, viz., in Germany, and only exist there ('diasporal ecclesiogenesis'); or those founded in the diaspora and have their headquarters there and in turn are starting congregations in Africa ('transcultural ecclesiogenesis').[15] This trisection includes churches that are more focused on African people groups and those more internationally orientated.

Religious Movements and the Politics of Religious Networking in Europe', *Nova Religio* 7.2 (2003), 24-41.

[12] See for the concept of transculturality, see Moritz Fischer, *Pfingstbewegung zwischen Fragilität und Empowerment. Beobachtungen zur Pfingstkirche 'Nzambe Malamu ' mit ihren Transnationalen Verflechtungen* (Göttingen: V&R Unipress, 2011).

[13] Gerrie Ter Haar, 'The African Diaspora in the Netherlands', in Peter B. Clarke (ed), *New Trends and Developments in African Religions* (London: Greenwood Press, 1998), 245-62.

[14] The ethnical groups in question are from the present Congo-Brazzaville, from the Democratic Republic of Congo, and from Angola.

[15] See Simon, *From Migrants to Missionaries*, 39-50.

The Three Phases of Finding Identity

On a macro level, it makes sense to talk about the African-Initiated Churches. On a micro level, in a certain diasporic situation I would suggest talking about the Churches of African Origin in the Diaspora (CAOD). This term places an emphasis on the origin of the church by leaving further ethnical and cultural developments open.

When one tries to get an overview of the CAOD in Germany in respect to their individual migratory history, one can show that they move backward and forward within a specific framework of identity-finding.[16] This can be described as a three-phase model:

A. The phase of seclusion
B. The phase of opening
C. The phase of interculturation

Here, it is important to point out that the three phases are not evolutionary. The congregations and churches do not necessarily run consecutively through the three phases. A church congregation can move backward and forward in the identity phase, depending upon its sociological or theological development. CAODs do not persevere in a static condition in their search for identity in the diaspora, but are caught up in an inherent dynamic. Hence, it is suggestive to speak about *phases of alternation.* A church may thus switch forward or backward from one phase to another. Different reasons may cause such developments. For example, the second generation of immigrants growing up and finding its home in the European context may push the church from the phase of seclusion to the phase of opening. Through the increased use of the German language – which would be the first language of proficiency for the second generation – German friends may find access to a CAOD.

On the other hand, there are various factors that may cause a step backward, such as the ongoing fluctuation in membership. In particular, the continuous influx of new church members arriving from Africa may impact concerned congregations as the newcomers are at a different level of 'integration' and identity-building than older members. The church might thus find it difficult to bridge the gaps. If these gaps cannot be bridged, schisms may follow.

Space permits only a brief sketch of each of these three phases.[17] With respect to the phase of seclusion, three main characteristics are evident:

- Members of the church use their African mother tongue in their worship service. There is little missionary activity.

---

[16] Simon, *From Migrants to Missionaries*, 39-50.

[17] For a more in-depth description of the three phases, see Benjamin Simon, 'Christians of African Origin in the German Speaking Diaspora of Germany', *Exchange: A Journal of Missiological and Ecumenical Research* 31.1 (2002), 23-35.

- Members of the church are mostly composed of the same ethnic background. There are few ecumenical contacts and relationships with other churches.
- Special theological teaching may arise (e.g., ancestor worship).[18]

With respect to the phase of opening, these main characteristics are often clear:

- Church members prefer a European language during the worship service.
- There is openness to Christians irrespective of nationality and denominational background.
- There is an active missionary outreach.
- First ecumenical contacts are made.

With respect to the phase of interculturation, these main characteristics are often seen:

- The influence of the German language becomes more important.
- German members of the church affect the life of the congregation.
- There is an active missionary enterprise and evangelization between Germans and Africans.

In 1980, Joseph Blomjous, the Catholic theologian and Bishop of the Dutch White Fathers, introduced the term 'interculturation' instead of 'inculturation'. In the years that followed, the term was rarely used in theology or in mission studies. However, interculturation seems to be of greater importance and more convenience for this topic than the more common term 'inculturation'. Interculturation demonstrates clearly that one does not move between two 'monolithic meaning systems', but 'between multiple cultural orientations'.[19] Both the mutual exchange and joint learning community are clearly stressed by the term 'interculturation'. While I do not want to do away with the more common term 'inculturation', it seems that for the present discussion, the term does not emphasize enough the patterns of exchange between German and African members in the CAOD.

In this third phase, German members and parishioners of African origin in the second generation set the standards. The German members influence the social and interpersonal realm of the church life. Through their mere presence they may foster the use of the German language in prayers, greetings, or even sermons. Moreover, the presence of German members influences and escalates the level of exchange between German and

---

[18] For further information on the Kimbanguist Trinitarian theology and the role of ancestors in it, see Benjamin Simon, 'Leadership and Ministry in the Kimbanguist Church', in Ronilick E.K. Mchami and Benjamin Simon (eds), *Church Ministry in African Christianity* (Nairobi: Acton Publishers 2006), 126-42.

[19] Frans Wijsen, 'Intercultural Theology and the Mission of the Church', *Exchange: A Journal of Missiological and Ecumenical Research* 30.3 (2001), 218-28, at 221.

African-origin members, which is present in every congregation to varying degrees. A more or less open and critical treatment of subjects and problems of everyday life may occur. For instance, German women members who are either unmarried or married to Africans may express their criticism concerning the (mis)treatment of women in society. This could either initiate an improvement of the situation or be the reason for a voluntary or enforced separation of certain members from the church. It could possibly also lead to subordination under the hierarchical structure.

Partnership with Established Churches

The ecumenical co-operation among CAOD and German-established church communities and churches of different denominational backgrounds turns out to be quite diverse. If one analyzes the German context – and if this might be equivalent to other continental European settings – three different models of ecumenical partnership can be identified.

First, a 'parallel model'. The CAOD rents a church hall and meets there Sunday after Sunday without any further contact with the host congregation. A caretaker of a CAOD once said, 'At noon, the Germans go home preparing their Sunday meal, and at 2 p.m. the foreigners come and make noise'. Between the two congregations, not a (single) meaningful contact is made.

The rent the CAOD pays has nothing to do with a partnership between brothers and sisters in Christ. Rather, the rent is used to help reduce the budget deficit of the German church. There are no communal events. The guest congregation's name does not appear in any space in the parish newspaper or in the display case. It is a parallel structure in which it is obvious that a balance of power is not given; it is a non-Christian co-existence of brothers and sisters.[20]

Second, a 'sister-church model'. Both congregations have come closer to each other. There is an exchange – one lives in conviviality[21] and celebrates regularly by having services and feasts together. There is a platform for communal life where one gets known to others and shares with the others. One of the elders of the host congregation has become a visiting elder with the guest congregation and vice versa. Youth groups feast together and do not experience any barriers between the two cultures. Here, the turn to the second generation becomes important. Through the exchange, the two culturally different congregations reduce prejudice and mediate among the cultures and traditions of the different backgrounds.

---

[20] See Jacques Matthey, 'Mission und Macht–damals und heute', *Interkulturelle Theologie* 4 (2009), 346-58.

[21] Theo Sundermeier, 'Konvivenz als Grundstruktur ökumenischer Existenz heute', in Wolfgang Huber, Dietrich Ritschl, und Theo Sundermeier (eds), *Ökumenische Existenz heute I* (Muenchen: Kaiser, 1986), 49-100.

Third, an 'integration model'. In recent times, the Bund Freikirchlicher Pfingstgemeinden (BFP), the German Pentecostal community, has grown by 20% in its membership by integrating CAOD.[22] The outcome of that intercultural step is not yet clear. Due to the high number of CAOD becoming members, it represents a certain challenge. The established German state churches must rework their juridical articles to open up their doors for CAOD to be integrated in the German church system, including the tax system. Based on my estimation, some 20% of the members of CAOD are tax payers already. Here, the German churches should play a mediational role by living out integration in its own rows and not only by claiming integration from the state.

A sub-integration model can be seen in the '*mitenand*-Church' – the 'togetherness-Church' – in the city of Basel, Switzerland. This German-speaking congregation started out of a crisis (as many good developments sometimes do). The congregation should have been closed due to lack of members of Swiss background. Therefore, the Reformed Church of Basel decided to start a new congregation in which Christians of different cultural and traditional backgrounds could worship and celebrate together. Participants come from very different backgrounds: Orthodox Christians from Eritrea, Catholics from Poland, Christians with evangelical background from Basel, etc. The singing and praying in different languages as a community, the confidence in each other, and the meal they share after the service creates a sense of community.[23]

Mediational Role for Ecumenism

The CAOD are moving up and down in the three different phases of identity-finding process. Depending upon the phase they are in, they can play a more or less important role in mediation. Finding themselves in a phase of seclusion, they deal too much with themselves to mediate in an ecumenical sense with other Christian groups or even with the political power. This meditational role for ecumenism takes place mainly in the second and third phases, where CAODs open themselves toward others and where interculturation happens.

Depending upon the three phases of the identity-finding process, possibilities of ecumenical mediation with other churches open up. A CAOD which finds itself in the phase of seclusion will neither be able to start a partnership with another congregation nor be a sister church ready to follow the model of integration. Here, only a parallel model will be adequate. Moving toward identity phases, possibilities of opening up for

---

22 www.geistbewegt.de/pages/posts/geistbewegt-im-november-zukunft-wagen207.php (accessed 11.6.11).

23 www.erk-bs.ch/die-kirche-und-ihre-gemeinden/kleinbasel/diakonische-gemeinde/mitenand-kirche (accessed 25.4.12).

further ecumenical mediational models are given. For ecumenical mediation to be meaningful, the process has to be mutual. Both CAOD and German congregations must participate in order for real transformation to take place. Transformation happens through the social and political influences and propels toward new identity phases. Furthermore, transformation also takes place through the ecumenical mediation when two different background congregations meet in a convivial togetherness and step toward each other in the name of Christ and for his mission to the world.

The Experience of Migrants in a Native British Church: Towards Mission Together

Emma Wild-Wood

Introduction

This chapter presents the findings of a small and continuing research project on the role of migrants in native British churches and locates them within wider research on migrants and Christianity in Europe in order to further debate and widen the scope on mission and migration. It assumes two things: (1) that multiethnic[1] churches have a particular missional role in the UK and (2) that forms of unity across cultural differences are desirable and enriching, a sign of the work of the Spirit, and a fulfillment of the instructions of the Apostle Paul to an ethnically diverse Roman church: 'Live in harmony with one another… so that together you may with *one* voice glorify the God and Father of our Lord Jesus Christ' and 'Welcome one another, therefore, just as Christ has welcomed you' (Rom.15:5-7). It also acknowledges that such harmony is not always easily achieved. While a study on the comprehension of church and mission by *all* members is required to gain an appreciation of expectations and possibilities, this chapter focuses on the perceptions of migrant members of a congregation in order to provide a sociological background for missiology.

Background: Mission by Migrants

From the late 1990s sociologists of religion highlighted a growing phenomenon – the rise of new international churches established by migrants in the cities of Europe.[2] Since then, the religious activities of Christian diaspora, or transnational, communities to Europe and the USA have been researched extensively.[3] These churches, often broadly

---

[1] I use the word 'multiethnic' to suggest a variety of national and cultural origins. The word 'multicultural' could also be used; however, it has been associated with particular UK government policies presently undergoing some scrutiny.

[2] Gerrie ter Haar, *Half Way to Paradise: African Christians in Europe* (Cardiff: Cardiff Academic Press, 1998), and Gerrie ter Haar (ed), *Strangers and Sojourners: Religious Communities in the Diaspora* (Leuven: Peeters, 1998).

[3] See, for example, Afe Adogame and James V. Spickard (eds), *Religion Crossing Boundaries: Transnational Religious and Social Dynamics in Africa and the New African Diaspora* (Leiden, Brill, 2010); Afe Adogame, Roswith Gerloff, and Klaus Hock (eds), *Christianity in Africa and the African Diaspora: The Appropriation of a Scattered Heritage* (London: Continuum, 2008); Jacob K. Olupona and Regina Gemignani (eds), *African Immigrant Religions in America* (New York: New York

Pentecostal and globally connected, follow an historical trajectory of migrant churches that include, in Britain at least, churches established decades earlier by migrants from erstwhile colonies who were often unwelcome or uncomfortable in traditional congregations.[4]

Some research analyzed a social trend; other work attempted to predict implications of migrant Christianity. Philip Jenkins warns of attitudes of mistrust. Apparently unaware that his predictions were already reality, he imagines southern Christians evangelizing the north, 'changing many familiar aspects of belief and practice, and exporting cultural traits presently found only in Africa and Latin America'.[5] He adds bleakly that this form of Christianity will appear so alien to the north that it will be labeled as, 'fanatical, superstitious, demagogic... politically reactionary and sexually repressive...jungle religion...'[6]

Other commentators, in contrast, see in transnational churches a remedy for the spiritual malaise of the West, describing them as 'a remarkable gift of God to a secularized world', and suggest that 'they could contribute to the renewing of the whole church ...when voices from the non-western world are properly heard and understood'.[7] Within mission studies, this second opinion predominates: the growth and vibrancy of transnational churches are missiologically hopeful for Western nations.

Jehu Hanciles' *Beyond Christendom* provides a missiological appreciation of migrant African Christianity in the USA and its contribution to global Christianity.[8] Hanciles critiques Jenkins' 'secularist perspective' and his normative use of the Western Christian experience to reach his negative predictions.[9] He echoes van Laar's aspirations saying, 'An infusion of Christian immigrants has regenerated many a moribund (often long-established) congregation in Western societies'. The focus of his analysis are 'independent churches that have their origin in the initiative of an individual African migrant' and have developed 'through the missionary-sending initiatives of ministries or movements that are African founded (or African led) and African based' (which he calls *Abrahamic* and *Macedonian* types). While he recognizes that migrants worship in other

---

University Press, 2007); Afe Adogame and Cordula Weisskoeppel (eds), *Religion in the Context of African Migration* (Bayreuth: Eckhard Breitinger, 2005).

[4] An early example is the Nigerian, Daniels Ekarte, who established the African Churches Mission in Liverpool in 1931; see Marika Sherwood, *Pastor Daniels Ekarte and the African Churches Mission* (London: Savannah Press, 1994).

[5] Philip Jenkins, *The Next Christendom: The Coming of Global Christianity* (Oxford: Oxford University Press, 2002), 14.

[6] Jenkins, *Next Christendom*, 161-2.

[7] Wout van Laar, 'It's Time to Get to Know Each Other', in André Droogers, Cornelis van der Laan, and Wout van Laar (eds), *Fruitful in this Land: Pluralism, Dialogue and Healing in Migrant Pentecostalism* (Geneva: WCC, 2006), 16.

[8] Jehu Hanciles, *Beyond Christendom: Globalization, African Migration and the Transformation of the West* (Maryknoll, NY: Orbis, 2008).

[9] Hanciles, *Beyond Christendom*, 132-3.

churches, he concentrates his efforts on these types of transnational churches because he understands them as forming 'the vanguard of the African missionary movement'.[10]

Background: Mission to Migrants

Historic, or native, British churches have largely engaged with issues surrounding migration and mission in a different way. Aware of their previous neglect and racism, conscious that immigration has become an emotive political issue in Britain, that border controls have been tightened, and that debate is often infused with zenophobia, individual denominations and ecumenical groups have questioned government policies on migration, challenged suspicion toward migrants in society and the media, and provided pastoral care.[11] They have composed statements, study materials, and service outlines, and in so doing have articulated a 'mission to migrants',[12] which has plumbed nomadic and migratory stories and injunctions of care in the Bible and called for a theology of hospitality and welcome.[13]

In the battle against misconceptions of migrants, the misery of trafficking, ill treatment of asylum seekers, and negative immigration policies, mission *by* migrants is often underemphasized in church reports. There may be recognition of the contribution of migrants, as in the Catholic Bishops' Conference report:

> ...in all our dioceses we have migrants from nearly every continent in the world, adding people and vibrancy to our parishes...We recognise and celebrate their rich cultural and spiritual patrimony and the ways in which they are enriching us as they join us...[14]

This recognition is used to create 'a statement calling for a more visible culture of welcome, hospitality and solidarity with our migrant sisters and brothers in God's family' – a statement which appears to be addressed largely to non-migrant members. Likewise, *Migration Principles,* a booklet sponsored by Churches Together in Britain and Ireland and Churches'

---

[10] Hanciles, *Beyond Christendom,* 326-7.

[11] See for example, Susanna Snyder, 'Hospitality and "Hanging Out": Churches' Engagement with People Seeking Asylum in the UK', and Nicholas Sagovsky, 'Exile, Seeking Asylum in the UK and the *Missio Dei*', both in Stephen Spencer (ed), *Mission and Migration* (Sheffield: Cliff College, 2008), 129-40 and 141-59 respectively.

[12] Catholics Bishops' Conference of England and Wales, *Mission of the Church to Migrants in England and Wales,* www.catholic-ew.org.uk/Catholic-Church/Publications (2008), 5 (accessed 7.12.11).

[13] See as examples, Christine Pohl, 'Biblical Issues in Mission and Migration', *Missiology* 31.1 (2003), 3-15; Tim Naish, 'Mission, Migration and the Stranger in our Midst', in Spencer (ed), *Mission and Migration,*7-30.

[14] Catholics Bishops' Conference, *Mission to Migrants*, 4.

Commission for Racial Justice, asks what it means for the Christian communities to welcome newcomers, strangers, and migrants before it sets out 'measures for Churches to commend' in the area of public policy.[15]

This approach emphasizes a social and political dimension of mission which challenges the non-migrant population about its conduct in church and society. The impact of these church documents in local congregations varies, yet their concerns are to be welcomed. The single emphasis, however, might reinforce the very attitudes the statements are attempting to challenge. An overemphasis on what non-migrant British Christians can do for migrants might inadvertantly encourage a perception that one group is essentially vulnerable and weak while another is strong and influential.[16] While churches *are* shifting their emphasis – many have migrants working in them, most prominently the Anglican Archbishop of York, John Sentamu, and have a forum for clergy from ethnic minorities – further engagement on the role of migrants in native British churches is beneficial.

Although the importance of the role of migrants in changes to Christianity in the West is well documented, it remains partial because previous research has given insufficient attention to migrants who are part of native congregations. An understanding of their contribution and their decision to worship within native churches will provide a balance to the perspective presented so far.

The focus of this chapter is not on congregations with majority migrant membership that operate under the structure and polity of native British churches, a type Hanciles refers to as 'Jerusalem'. Some analysis of their role is being carried out.[17] Rather, I choose to attend to those who would fit into Hanciles' fourth, 'Samuel-Eli' type of migrants who attend mainline denominations and contribute to their life and worship. I have had for some time an interest in commonplace and unpublicized forms of migration and their impact on ordinary Christian identity.[18]

As a white British person who has been a mission-migrant to the African continent and now is a member of a native British congregation whose ethnic mix is becoming increasingly diverse, I wanted to explore why some

---

[15] Paul Weller (ed), *Migration Principles, Statement for Churches Working on Migration Issues* (London, Churches Together in Britain and Ireland and Churches Commission for Racial Justice, 2007), back cover.

[16] Thorsten Prill, *Global Mission on Our Doorstep: Forced Migration and the Future of the Church* (Munster: MV-Wissenschaft, 2008), chapter 8, analyses the implicit messsages of a number of church documents.

[17] Amos Kasibante, 'The Ugandan Diaspora in Britain and Their Quest for Cultural Expression within the Church of England', *Journal of Anglican Studies* 7.1 (2009), 79-86; Dominic Pasura, 'Religious Transnationalism: The Case of Zimbabwean Catholics in Britain', *Journal of Religion in Afrcia* 42:1 (2012), 26-53.

[18] Emma Wild-Wood, *Migration and Christian Identity in Congo, DRC* (Leiden: Brill, 2008); 'Mission and Home-Making: Church Expansion through Migration in DR Congo', in Spencer (ed), *Mission and Migration*, 119-28.

migrants chose to attend that church and how they understood church and mission.[19] This research was, therefore, carried out as a contribution to reflection on local Christian witness. It can also provide background for further exploration of the possibilities of mission together, non-migrants and migrants.

Research Methods, Participants, and Setting

The research[20] which informs this article took place beyond the urban, multicultural settings of city life, which has naturally held the attention of researchers. Its focus was instead on a single congregation in a new town (of about 4,000 houses) being built in a semi-rural area with a white British majority population in the east of England. The church was ten years old and was a Local Ecumenical Partnership (LEP) church.[21] In 2010, the church had a membership of 100 people, with another 50 attending regularly and 70 less frequently. First-generation adult migrants to the UK, all of whom lived in the parish, made up about 15% of each of these groups. White British people completed the rest of the adult members of congregation.[22]

Conscious that its ecumenical unity should be apparent in welcome and participation of all in worship and mission, the church council had already sought feedback from the congregation and had reflected on issues of mission and hospitality. This paper uses qualitative data analysis of semi-structured interviews and group discussion with first-generation adult migrants to the UK (both members and regular attenders) worshipping in this native British church.

A focus on a single congregation permits depth of scrutiny and places particular parameters around the scope of research. A few statistics indicate both the limitations and the variety available: 73%[23] of the migrants interviewed were from Africa, 20% from Asia, and 7% from Europe; 53% were women and 47% men.

It is particularly pertinent that they were confident English speakers and mainly professional people: 33% worked in health professions, two were students, another was an au pair. At the time of interview they had spent

---

[19] As a researcher, I am both an insider and an outsider, a position which demands significant self-scrutiny in order to avoid easy assumptions.

[20] This research is the first part of a wider project that includes interviews with first-generation migrants training for ministry in native British churches.

[21] The LEP was supported by the Baptist Union of Great Britain, the Church of England, the Methodist Church, and the United Reformed Church with the Roman Catholics and Quakers as associated members. The Catholic congregation is of similar cultural diversity.

[22] There were two exceptions: one adult who had migrated as a child and one adult who was a second-generation migrant.

[23] Percentage figures have been rounded to the nearest whole number.

between one and 20 years living in the UK and had attended the church between one and six years. Most had regularized immigration status and some had become British citizens. While some referred obliquely to 'difficulties' with immigration procedures, most preferred to talk as if such things were behind them. Eighty percent were married. Fifty-three percent belonged to Protestant denominations associated with denominations that supported the LEP, 20% were Roman Catholics,[24] 13% came from an Orthodox church, and 13% had a Pentecostal background. Thirteen percent were on the church council of the LEP.

Interviews were carried out individually or in pairs, and 60% of those interviewed were able to participate in further group discussion.[25] The questions posed to migrants started with the micro (the local congregation and wider community, their own life and faith), which form the context in which migrants engage with British church life and in which responses to macro questions (nature of church, of mission, perceptions of British society) were being developed. Below is a summary of opinions given on the main themes followed by an analysis of their usefulness for further reflection.

Church and the Local Congregation

Respondents demonstrated a correlation between their understanding of the function and nature of church and their appreciation of the local congregation. 'Home', 'family', 'belonging', 'community', a 'social' place, and an 'hospitable' place were prominent descriptors of the local congregation and influenced descriptors of church as 'the source of all our relationships, the center of the community'. Within it, relationships with God and others are formed and maintained and as such it was 'becoming the body of Christ'.

Church was understood as forming a body for worship and mutual support, in order that 'blessings flow…to the wider community'. There was some discussion about the relative importance of place and people, and to what extent a building was significant to the meaning of church. There was recognition that provision of sanctity and sanctuary were important – that a place of holiness, awe, and wonder can aid the worship of God and can help a process of cleansing and purifying, bringing humanity closer to God. Furthermore, a church building was perceived to locate and make sense of the acts of Christian worship. The congregation was understood to provide nurture to those in the wider community and therefore the visibility of a building was regarded as an asset.

---

[24] A further 13% were born into Catholic families, but chose to worship in Protestant churches prior to their arrival in the UK.

[25] White British members of the congregation were also interviewed in two groups. The content of these discussion groups is used only indirectly in this article.

Few metaphors were sustained during discussion, but one respondent spoke at length about church as a watering hole. He identified the watering hole as a vital place in his society of origin: people came together to seek an element necessary for life, and when they did so, they shared their lives. Watering holes were the place of stories, news, and contact with others. He connected the communal exchange aspect of the watering hole with Jesus' meeting the Samaritan woman at the well.

Respondents identified a number of reasons for attending the LEP: 'I wanted to get involved', 'I wanted to nurture my faith', I like 'being part of the local community'. The forming of friendships was key: 'You feel that people know you and you end up feeling that you know almost everyone who is here', articulated one person; another said, 'It's more of a family than a church', while another said, 'People feel at home and they are accepted'. One woman noted a cultural difference of moving to a new town:

> Everyone is new...people are friendly, they'll talk to one another. They'll say, 'How long have you lived here?' or 'Where did you come from?' [At] church everybody was, 'How are you? Are you new here?'

The largely white British population had given themselves license to articulate curiosity. It was not perceived to be rude or intrusive to ask immediately about moving or previous location because everyone was a migrant and therefore they appeared friendlier to newcomers. This contrasted starkly with a church one woman had visited in a long established community. She described it this way:

> I went there once and I never went back again. Because when I walked in everyone just looked at me, like who are you? ...after the service people knew each other and were talking to each other and you felt you were just standing there by yourself. No one is [sic] saying a word to you...

Since the communal and relational nature of church was of great importance, migrants were conscious of the way in which they were initially welcomed. One identified a 'casualness' in the approach that felt alien, but added 'people are also genuinely showing interest in you'. Two noted with pleasure that if they missed a Sunday somebody noticed and asked about them. It helped some to realize that other members in the congregation had visited their country of origin. Another was relieved that he was not asked to stand and introduce himself on his first visit – a custom common on the African continent and often part of transnational church services. Yet another felt her welcome was diminished by not being given this opportunity. Personal preference naturally played a role in responses to particular practices.

The informal, contemporary style of worship appealed to most respondents. Some wished the singing was more animated and the repertoire included a greater number of songs from around the world, but they largely expressed contentment at the form and content of the services. Some were pleased that they had been asked to participate in services and considered it a sign that 'everyone's equal, we're all God's children'. One was pleased that 'you are given an opportunity to do what you can in the church without feeling you are being pushed'. Another summed it up with, 'Here you get a group effect, a group worship effect, rather than just keeping silent and just concentrating on God and doing a one-to-one prayer'. Another said, 'You feel you're brothers and sisters in Christ'.

Despite coming from a variety of denominations, respondents did not dwell on the ecumenical nature of the local church. It was considered a helpful attribute, but not essential. One person thought that the focus on denominational unity permitted a 'flexibility' in services and a greater openness to difference, while still allowing an emphasis on the importance of worshipping together.

Another combined ecumenism with the multiethnic nature of the church: 'It's a place where we worship – people from different cultures, different denominations – we get together like we are one, and we feel we are the same. You feel like everybody else, you feel that there is this umbrella bringing you all together'. This aspect of unity was emphasized by a couple who compared the local congregation with a church which had a majority African membership: 'We have felt more at home in a church that seems to be welcoming to everybody regardless of where people are from. In my view, that's completely irrelevant, anyway, which part of the world you're from'. The wide welcome was expressed as close union by one woman, who said, 'You can go and worship as one person'.

For some of the respondents, becoming members of the local church had not been a conscious intention; instead, it happened through a gradual appreciation of what appeared to fit their circumstances. For others, it was a deliberate choice. One respondent stated, 'I hate homogenous churches' and 'I don't like spiritual ghetto-ism'.[26] A conscious desire to participate in British society was frequently articulated, along with a sense that their engagement in British society would be diminished if they sought out a church in which people of their own country or region dominated. The church had a role in 'helping us to integrate more with the wider community. Because we feel easier making friends with the people we have something in common with, these are Christians from your church, people that will introduce you to X B and so on'. Indeed, the local church was seen as a place of acceptance when other areas of society appear less accepting: 'You feel you are in sync with everybody, that these are your friends and they've accepted you'.

Aspirations for children were significant motivators for several respondents. The church's children's and youth activities were seen to

[26] One respondent said: '...if you have come, genuinely, in a country like this and you want to settle and broaden your horizons, you cannot tell me genuinely that you are going to be benefiting from within just your community. You might as well have stayed in from where you are [sic] – unless you have come because you are a refugee or something'.

provide spiritual nourishment and Christian community for children, one that linked with the church school and their friends and simultaneously upheld the values their parents appreciated. One couple explained:

> We know it's very important to integrate and for our children to grow up getting the culture of this place...our long-term plan is to move back to [Africa] but we'd like them to grow up as international...We will bring them up with Christian values...and interacting with other young people at church kind of makes [those Christian values] universal.

Likewise, the parents felt that their own faith was affirmed by worshipping in a multiethnic congregation: 'When you hear people from different places and they are talking about the same message, I think it really reinforces it'.

Transnational Churches

Some questions explored how far the interviewees had contact with churches established by migrants and whether they liked to worship in them.[27] Responses fell into two categories according to continent of origin. The Asians (all Indians from the state of Kerala) talked about their relationship with the Syrian Orthodox church in which some had been brought up. The Africans all had some experience of transnational Pentecostal churches with a predominantly African membership.[28]

For the Indians, marriage to someone of a non-orthodox denomination had begun a detachment from the Orthodox church. They spoke nostalgically of special celebratory services, of the rhythm of prayer and fasting, and of the importance of community rituals as they grew up. They felt, however, that their spiritual needs were met in the LEP and they were content to worship in English, rather than Malayalam.[29] They also expressed relief at the shorter length of services in native British churches. It allowed them time for other activities in a weekly routine which often felt pressurized and hurried.

There was also a sense that they had moved away from the cultural expectations generated in the close connection between the Orthodox church and wider society that they knew in India. One person suggested that her family dynamics would come under greater scrutiny in that environment:

---

[27] This research is not attempting to discover how far the judgments made about these churches may be correct or common, but rather what such perceptions might indicate about the priorities of those who make them.

[28] There were at least five such congregations within a 15-mile radius of the new town.

[29] This was clearly not the same for all Kerelan migrants as there is a thriving Syrian Orthodox church which worships in Malayalam meeting in the same building. Its members are participating in the wider project.

> …in UK churches, you leave the person who believes to go to church every Sunday. Whereas in India it's not like that, they would be asking, 'Where is your husband? Where is your child? Why are you coming on your own?' And all that. Whereas here, it's not like that. You are free to do what you want to do.

She appreciated the greater focus of the faith and practice of the individual. While she did not discount a possible return to worship with the Orthodox, she felt that regular participation in Orthodox services was not essential for her spiritual well-being. Another Indian respondent articulated it this way: 'It's one God we worship. All churches are just facilitating'.

All the African respondents had visited a transnational Pentecostal church or fellowship group with family or friends who were members. Some expressed an unfamiliarity with Pentecostal worship and doctrine and a desire to remain within the denomination in which they had grown up: 'The service was too long. And was so tiring. I didn't feel connected at all… it's different from what I'm [sic] used to when I was growing up'.

They wished to remain faithful to the doctrinal teachings of their tradition and they found that the local LEP was closer to the belief and practice they were accustomed to than the transnational churches they had experienced. Some interviewees were wary about forms of prosperity teaching. One said that the pastor of a church he and his wife visited 'was talking about money, money, money all the time…it felt like a commercial…like a business'. His wife agreed but also mentioned the sense of being at odds with the rest of the congregation:

> Everybody seemed to be really enjoying the sermon and we would get out and wonder…were we in the same sermon with them? I mean how could anyone stand there in front of everybody and start talking about their car and it's completely irrelevant to whatever message is being preached. And everybody seems to be, like, cheering and happy. So anyway, I think it's us who didn't really get the concept of it.

Another concern was the levels of commitment perceived to be expected. One person criticized her sister's church for behaving 'like all they want to get out of people is money', expecting members to spend 60% of their time in church and 'be available when they want'. Failure to comply with these expectations, she said, meant 'you're guilt-tripped'. Another mentioned,

> …they will expect you to go there, to open up, to go to their houses, have lunches, help them get to work. You know, they expect you to do the sort of things you would do back at home.

A nervousness of repeating patterns of socialization from 'home' was mentioned by other respondents. Some believed this was the cause of the conflicts, quarrels, and gossiping that they thought arose among members of Christian groups that came largely from the same country. Others disliked perceived status issues. One, with great indignation, recounted attempts in a large fellowship group to establish hierarchies based on family and work relationships in her country of origin:

> It wasn't 'let's worship'. It was first, 'Where do you come from? What do you do? What are you doing here?' And for some reason it was the older people, so – this was really offending me – they asked me, 'Oh, where did you work?' and 'Who is your Mum?' Like, who is my Mum! My Mum is in [Africa], I'm here… It's like an interrogation and I thought we were here to pray.

Faced with relationships she perceived to be intense, intrusive, and predicated on the priorities of a culture in which she was no longer living, she preferred to join the local church. Worshipping in the LEP was a way of being 'anonymous', a form of 'sanctuary'. Although she and others could recognize the support transnational churches or fellowships might give for significant events, like weddings and funerals, they were resistant to transplanting concerns from 'home'.

Forms of support that could be called 'cultural' were, nevertheless, seen to be important to respondents. At least half the migrants interviewed were part of networks they had developed with friends or local residents who came from, or had links with, their countries of origins. These were small, informal groups. One met fortnightly and had been formed expressly 'to maintain the culture, language and all intact and pass it on to our children'.

The Christians in this group also met for prayer. Another, based on the friendship of the adults, met irregularly because the friends lived some distance from each other. They celebrated childrens' birthdays together, met in memory of deceased relatives, and included a time of prayer in these gatherings. The respondents prefer to establish their own small groups for cultural comprehension and fulfilling of family responsibilities rather than joining a larger and more structured group. They had largely separated their Christian commitment to a worshipping community from cultural solidarity. These friendship and support networks were seen as distinct from participation in a local church.

Perceptions of Mission

All respondents assumed that their Christian commitment would influence their lives and naturally used the language of witness and service: 'I have a responsibility as a Christian to behave in a certain way and to be a good example. I am representing God. I use that as a basis to shape who I am and what I am in society'.

Being a good neighbor, talking about one's faith, praying and using remittances to support relatives, alleviating poverty, and offering education to the disadvantaged in their country of origin were considered important. When asked to define 'mission', one person described it as 'fitting our faith into our specific circumstances'; another as using 'our gifts and talents' as part of the body of Christ. Another explained mission by way of a prayer,

'Show me what you want me to be, Lord. Where do you really want to send me?' Yet another said mission was the act bringing of the powerful word of God into difficult situations and it was an attitude of service at home and at work.

Spreading the gospel through words and deeds, hospitality, spreading 'good neighborliness', visiting sick and prisoners as instructed in Matthew 25, encouraging and supporting others, and moving from familiarity to risk were all suggested as being part of Christian mission.

There was some debate as to whether mission was a particular task, had a specific goal, or was an open-ended attitude. The legacy of the nineteenth-century missionary movement was evoked by the mention of 'mission': the provision of good and subsidized schools and hospitals, heroes like David Livingstone, and evangelistic campaigns were mentioned. This legacy prompted respondents to connect mission to specific projects or gifted individuals working in their countries of origin.

Nevertheless, most acknowledged that their understanding had shifted because they knew of indigenous missionaries operating in India and Africa, of restrictions on Western missionaries, and of missionaries from the global south to the north. Furthermore, they expected mission to be practiced locally and they tried to apply this altered understanding to their present circumstances.

In conversation, there developed a corporate sense of the flow of mission: mission started with church activities, spread into the local community, and then into the world. Included in mission were Bible study, Christian teaching, helping in church, supporting Christian young people, understanding the diversity of church members, acts of practical service for members of church, caring for the local community, providing living examples of Christ, action to help the poor and needy, and supporting international aid projects. Mission discipleship was important for 'outreach' from the church beyond its constituency. Its aim was to interest people in coming to church. The importance of belonging to a Christian community for the development and maintenance of Christian faith, and the corporate act of worship was reiterated in this understanding of mission.

The discussion groups were asked whether migrants have a particular role in God's mission in the UK. Many appeared not to have considered the question before. There was some debate about whether mission was a specific calling or whether since 'we are all saints' we are all equipped for mission. A couple of respondents thought their experience as migrants meant that their practical engagement in mission would most obviously lie in helping other migrants, particularly those they identified as being less fortunate than themselves, namely international students and asylum seekers. They could offer care and advice to others and show that they understood their difficulties. They also suggested that they may be able to facilitate a link between the LEP and immigrant churches in order to develop a partnership with them in mission.

One respondent reported his experience of white British Christians, believing that migrants bring a more 'interesting' way of being church. On one hand, he appreciated this assessment and agreed that the style of worship of many Christian migrants, which included lively singing and dancing, could be more engaging and that using experience from the world church through firsthand stories and illustrations was enriching and might attract the curiosity of white British people and bring them back to church. On the other hand, he considered that white British Christians could be patronizing, 'Sometimes it can almost be like they pat you and say, "It's good to be preached to by someone who really knows poverty and has seen it"'.[30]

Another respondent suggested that travel itself broadens the mind and is 'enlightening', but she queried whether those whose experience is geographically limited were able to appreciate gifts of diversity. These two respondents considered that the role migrants play in mission depended largely upon the response of the native British churches to them. Power and material resources, they said, still lie with indigenous people and their institutions. The influence of migrants depends on their acceptance by the local churches. Migrants and natives, they added, must work together and share resources if migrants are to have a positive influence.

The articulation of powerlessness was also evident in a conversation about verbal witness to Christ. Evangelism was seen as a significant part of mission and all respondents considered that they should share their Christian faith. They suggested that many migrants appear stronger in their faith because they have come from countries where faith is openly discussed. Yet there was uncertainty about how one might witness in the UK because respondents were aware of *causes célèbres* whose expressions of Christian faith in the workplace had resulted in severe sanction.[31]

In this discussion, there was a cultural sensitivity to contextual issues and a concern that inappropriate action could result in the loss of one's employment and possible repatriation. It caused deep unease about the approach one should use: 'I don't share my faith...compared to what I used to do in India, in the UK faith is personal and you don't want to share it in your workplace...you can't go and talk to everybody'. Respondents wondered whether Christians could witness publicly and, if not, whether

---

[30] This respondent was training for ordained ministry. Other migrants in ministrial training are being interviewed as part of the wider project.

[31] The following two cases were mentioned among others, 'Nurse Suspended for Offering to Pray for Elderly Patient's Recovery' (31 January 2009), www.telegraph.co.uk/health/healthnews/4409168/Nurse-suspended-for-offering-to-pray-for-patients-recovery.html (accessed 7.12.11), and, 'Christian British Airways Employee Sent Home for Wearing Cross Loses Appeal over Religious Discrimination' (12 February 2010), http://www.dailymail.co.uk/ news/article-1250459/Christian-British-Airways-employee-sent-home-wearing-cross-loses-appeal-religious-discrimination.html#ixzz1frvktt6M (accessed 7.12.11).

people really knew about Christianity and were able to 'make an informed choice'.

Concern was registered for the spiritual well-being of the white British population; the British showed great generosity to national charitable campaigns, said one, but they lacked a relationship with Jesus. 'They seem well prepared about this life,' said another, 'but what about the next?' There was concern about the level of consumerism in the UK and a belief that a comfortable life made people uninterested in Christianity and made Christians reluctant to share the gospel. In discussing all aspects of mission, respondents appeared attuned to the British context and their place within it. This meant they considered mission in the UK to be particularly complex.

Analysis of Themes: Toward Mission Together

The findings of this research provide more food for thought than can be digested here, but I will highlight a few issues.

First, *mission was understood as rooted in the church, perceived as the source, impetus, and first location for mission.* The research angle implied a missional practice centered on the local congregation, yet this was further emphasised by the respondents. Mission included going beyond a Christian group identity to permeate the wider community, but it was rooted in a corporate and relational understanding of Christian faith. The way in which this was articulated focused on belonging, integration, and inculturation.

Second, *a sense of belonging, inculcated through use of familiar languages, traditional practices, and social hierarchies, is an important part of church communities.* As research on transnational churches has shown, this is a reason to create new congregations which adopt and adapt home cultures when settling in a new location.[32] Belonging to a welcoming Christian community was also important for respondents, but played out differently in the LEP. They had a theology of the universality of the church and its inherent relationality which connected with their self-perception as confident, successful, international people who desired to integrate into British society, to establish good relationships with people of different ethnicities, and to find a place where their children could be nurtured in faith and appreciate British culture.[33]

While respondents used 'family' and 'home' to describe the LEP, they used these metaphors in the sense of making a *new* home, of 'integrating'. They did not necessarily want a church which had social structures similar

---

[32] For example, Dominic Pasura, 'Modes of Incorporation and Transnational Zimbabwean Migration to Britain', *Ethnic and Racial Studies*, 36:1 (2013), 199-218.

[33] Pasura, 'Modes of Incorporation', suggests that the protection of children from the evils of British society is one reason why some Zimbabwean migrants remain within their own fellowships.

to those in the place most still referred to as home – the country from whence they came.

The lower level of involvement acceptable in native British churches, accompanied by attitudes of Western individualism, were identified by some respondents as being positive attributes. Friendships were being formed with white British members of the congregation (who also identified integration and unity as important). They enabled respondents to feel at home and comprehend British society, but they were not seen as making unwelcome demands on stretched time and resources. The choice of church was influenced by the reasons respondents had come to the UK, their professional status, and the way in which they wished to live their lives. They acknowledged similarities and strove for Christian harmony and unity within the congregation.

Third, *the focus on integration and unity led to an inculturated form of Christian adherence.* While respondents could be perceptively critical of aspects of British culture, they were also positive about its benefits for them and their families. They demonstrated a desire to understand British culture and act appropriately within it, rather than openly challenge its values. This perhaps entailed a greater sense of vulnerability about their faith and thus an increased privacy of its expression.

Fourth, *they had few complaints about the worship or the life of the congregation.* They were content to worship in a contemporary British way, which included occasional songs and prayers from other parts of the world and in different languages. Yet their expressions of contentment should not lead to complacency. Few are involved in church life beyond Sunday services and their hesistancy about mission action suggested that they did not immediately see themselves as actors in mission. This may have arisen from an assumption that they are not full participants in UK churches or society. Yet their attentiveness to culture and concerns for British society makes them particularly good partners for thinking through missional issues. Precisely because respondents have attempted to get under the skin of UK church and society yet have recourse to a different set of experiences and values by which to compare them, their concerns and questions may aid the congreation of which they are part. This is largely untapped.

Fifth, *the local congregation considers itself enriched by a growing multiethinic profile which provides a more complete image of the universality of the body of Christ.* Yet the emphasis on intergration by all respondants raises questions for the LEP. How can all the members together demonstrate the diversity of the church for the glory of God and the furtherance of God's mission in the world? A united expression of Christian faith, if it is to be lasting, has to contain recognition of incarnational diversity.

Ignoring difference makes harmony superficial. The variety of migrant experience can be misunderstood by white British members (many of whom have little personal experience of migration) and can lead to an expection of assimilation into its *modus operandi*. Perhaps one way of beginning to learn from migrants is to further explore their comprehensions of church as home and family – a conversation which may enable the majority white British members become more aware of their own cultural and religious peculiarities.

The LEP already has a certain level of 'togetherness'; however, to develop a greater witness to Christ it needs to move from being multiethnic to being inter-ethnic, allowing our variety to inform each other. This is true intergration and unity.

Conclusion

Emerging findings prepare some ground for reflection on mission together, migrants and non-migrants. As a member of the congregation, I look forward to ways in which we can participate in God's mission by belonging together in our differences and providing an inter-ethnic witness to God's love. The research studied a neglected group: migrants who worship in native British congregations where they are the minority. They are not members of transnational churches. Neither do they see themselves in need of the mission of advocacy for and pastoral care to migrants, although they may be able to aid vulnerable migrants.

They change the expectations of migrant patterns of Christianity and are at the vanguard of a change to the demographics of churches in small towns. However, there can be no expectation that this demographic will grow significantly if congregations do not grapple with obvious questions of unity and diversity that their presence raises. Native British churches have often been ethnically (and socially) distinct. Careful internal work on the assumptions and expectations of members is needed, for multiethnic churches to develop an inter-ethnic identity and a mission that models love across difference.

Part Three
Missional Implications

NEW OPPORTUNITIES AND STRATEGIC PRACTICES OF DIASPORA MISSIONS IN SOUTH KOREA

Enoch Wan and Chandler H. Im

Introduction

According to mission data published by the Korea World Missions Association, 23,331 South Korean missionaries were serving in 169 countries as of January 2012.[1] South Korea has one of the fastest growing missionary-sending forces in global mission. Yet, South Korean churches are also engaged in mission to the diaspora in their homeland. The term 'diaspora' refers to 'those people who are on the move, taking up residence away from their places of origin'.[2]

This chapter is written as a response to the call and challenge of 'A Statement of the 9th Korean Mission Leaders Forum' (English translation of Korean title):

> ...to take a careful look at various types of diaspora within Korea in order to develop appropriate training programs for them. Our goals for diaspora mission in South Korea are witnessing, discipleship, and missionary training because the people reached represent potential future missionaries for their own countries...Korean mission societies should provide workers for this ministry. For this migrant mission we also need to have various networks to have more effective ministries.[3]

This chapter shows that while Korean missions are growing globally, Korean churches are seizing the opportunities presented by the growing number of foreigners who come to South Korea from various countries (see also Table 2 below).

---

[1] www.christiantoday.co.kr/view.htm?id=252905 (accessed 20.7.12). See also Timothy Kiho Park, 'Korean Christian World Missions: The Missionary Movement of the Korean Church', in Enoch Wan and Michael Pocock (eds), *Missions from the Majority World: Progress, Challenges, and Case Studies* (EMS Series 17; Pasadena: William Carey Library, 2009), 97-120.

[2] Enoch Wan, *Diaspora Missiology: Theory, Methodology and Practice* (Portland, OR: IDS-USA, 2011), 3.

[3] From the Korean World Missions Association's 9th mission leader forum, cited in David Chul Han Jun, 'World Christian Mission through Migrant Workers in South Korea and through the Korean Diaspora', a presentation at Tokyo 2010 Global Mission Consultation and Celebration, Tokyo, May 2010, published in Yong J. Cho (ed), *Tokyo 2010 Global Mission Consultation Handbook* (Seoul and Pasadena, CA: Tokyo 2010 Global Mission Consultation Planning Committee, 2010), 171-73, quotation from 172; this document is also available online at www. tokyo2010.org/resources/Tokyo2010_NM_David_Jun.pdf.

Here, the 'case study'[4] approach is employed to highlight new opportunities and strategies for contemporary mission to foreigners within the 'Hermit Kingdom', if Korean churches are ready to practice 'mission at our doorstep'[5] to diaspora groups. Eleven case studies are presented to illustrate major points of this study, which intends to fill in the gap in the missiological literature on the subject as not much has been reported or documented on diaspora groups in South Korea from a missiological perspective, especially in the English language.[6]

At the outset, definitions of key terms are offered for the sake of clarity. 'Diaspora ministry' involves ministering *to* the diaspora (i.e., serving the diaspora) and ministering *through* the diaspora (i.e., mobilizing the diaspora to serve others). 'Diaspora missiology' refers to the missiological framework that seeks to comprehend what it means to participate in God's redemptive mission among diaspora groups.[7] 'Diaspora missions' describes Christian evangelization among diaspora communities away from the homeland and, through various initiatives, to natives in the homelands and beyond.[8] Three types of diaspora missions, also shown in Table 1, are:

A. Missions *to* the diaspora – reaching diaspora groups in evangelistic and pre-evangelistic social services, and forming disciples as worshiping communities and congregations.

---

[4] 'Case study' is 'a type of qualitative research in which the researcher explores a single entity or phenomenon (i.e., the case) bounded by time and activity (a program, event, process, institution, or social group) and collects detailed information by using a variety of data collection procedures during a sustained period of time'; see J.W. Creswell, *Research Designs: Qualitative and Quantitative Approaches* (Thousand Oaks, CA: Sage, 1994). For additional reference, see Robert K. Yin, *Case Study Research: Design and Methods* (4th ed; Thousand Oaks, CA: Sage, 2009), and R.E. Stake, *The Art of Case Study Research* (Thousand Oaks, CA: Sage, 1995).

[5] The concept of 'mission at our doorstep' is elaborated further in the rest of this chapter.

[6] There are a few exceptions including the work of David Chul Han Jun, 'A South Korean Case Study of Migrant Ministries', in S. Hun Kim and Wonsuk Ma (eds), *Korean Diaspora and Christian Mission* (Oxford: Regnum, 2011), 207-22, and Myunghee Lee's research on Mongolian migrant workers in Korea: 'Migrant Workers' Churches as Welcoming, Sending and Recruiting Entities: A Case Study of Mongolian Migrant Workers' Churches in Korea', in Wan and Pocock (eds), *Missions from the Majority World*, 371-85.

[7] See 'The Seoul Declaration on Diaspora Missiology', available at www.lausanne.org/documents/seoul-declaration-on-diaspora-missiology.html (accessed 25.3.10).

[8] See Enoch Wan, 'Global People and Diaspora Missiology', a presentation at Tokyo 2010 Global Mission Consultation and Celebration, Tokyo, May 2010, published in Cho, *Tokyo 2010*, 92-100; this document is also available online at www.tokyo2010.org/resources/Handbook.pdf.

B. Missions *through* the diaspora – mobilizing diaspora Christians to reach out to their kins through networks of friendship and kinship in host countries, homelands, and abroad.
C. Missions *by* and *beyond* the diaspora – motivating and mobilizing diaspora Christians for cross-cultural missions to other ethnic groups in their host countries, homelands, and abroad.

Table 1: Diaspora Missiology: Diaspora Ministry and Diaspora Missions[9]

<table>
<tr><td rowspan="8">DIASPORA MISSIOLOGY</td><td colspan="7">DIASPORA MINISTRY</td></tr>
<tr><td>Type</td><td colspan="3">ministering to the diaspora</td><td colspan="3">ministering through the diaspora</td></tr>
<tr><td>Means</td><td colspan="6">the Great Commandment: pre-evangelistically serving others</td></tr>
<tr><td>Target Group</td><td colspan="3">serving the diaspora by attending to their social and spiritual needs</td><td colspan="3">mobilizing diaspora Christians to serve other diaspora people</td></tr>
<tr><td colspan="7">DIASPORA MISSIONS</td></tr>
<tr><td>Type</td><td colspan="2">missions to the diaspora</td><td colspan="2">missions through the diaspora</td><td colspan="2">missions by and beyond the diaspora</td></tr>
<tr><td>Means</td><td colspan="6">motivate and mobilize diaspora individuals and congregations for the Great Commission in evangelistic outreach and missions</td></tr>
<tr><td>Target Group</td><td colspan="2">members of diaspora community</td><td colspan="2">kinsmen in homeland and elsewhere; not cross-culturally</td><td colspan="2">cross-culturally to other ethnic groups in host society and beyond</td></tr>
</table>

Demographic Trends and Selected Diaspora Groups in South Korea

Although historically known to be a relatively homogeneous nation, Korea 'is transforming into a nation with multiple ethnicities, cultures, and languages representing some 40 countries of the world'.[10] According to government statistics, as of August 2012, the foreign population in South Korea, including the undocumented or unregistered with the Korean

[9] Adapted from Enoch Wan, 'Research Methodology for Diaspora Missiology and Diaspora Missions', presentation at North Central Regional EMS Conference, Trinity Evangelical Divinity School, Deerfield, Illinois, 26 February 2011, 5.
[10] Lee, 'Migrant Workers' Churches', 371.

government, was 1,409,577.[11] The entire population of the nation officially exceeded 50 million in June 2012.[12] Thus, the foreign population of South Korea in August 2012 was about 2.8%. The projection of the Korean government is that by '2020 we are expecting it to increase to 5%'.[13]

Tables 2-11 below show the trend and actual number of foreigners residing in South Korea. This number is relatively less than that of the diaspora population due to legal and practical differences in definition. The Korean law simply defines 'foreigner' as a 'person without Korean citizenship'.[14] The Korean government requires that all foreigners register with a Korean government agency if they stay in South Korea for over 90 days. These groups of people would include, but are not limited to, international students, migrant workers, and 'marriage immigrants' from around the world.[15]

Table 2: Trend (2002-2012): Number of Registered Foreigners in South Korea[16]

Year	Number of Registered Foreigners	Legal Residents	Illegal Residents
2002	252,457	168,678	83,779
2003	437,954	365,454	72,500
2004	468,875	379,018	89,857
2005	485,144	378,095	107,049
2006	631,219	524,562	106,657
2007	765,746	658,468	107,278
2008	854,007	760,546	93,461
2009	870,636	786,907	83,729
2010	918,917	840,372	78,545
2011	982,461	899,613	82,848
Feb. 2012	961,775	877,577	84,198

[11] www.article.joinsmsn.com/news/article/article.asp?total_id=9006286&ctg=1202 (accessed 23.8.12).

[12] www.news.hankooki.com/lpage/economy/201206/h2012062218324821500.htm (accessed 23.8.12).

[13] Based on data from Ministry of Justice [in Korean], 31 December, 2009; see also Jun, 'A South Korean Case Study of Migrant Ministries', 209.

[14] Korean Immigration Law Clause 31 (in Korean): www.law.go.kr/LSW/LsiJoLinkP.do?docType=JO&lsNm=%EC%B6%9C%EC%9E%85%EA%B5%AD%EA%B4%80%EB%A6%AC%EB%B2%95&joNo=003100000&languageType=KO¶s=1#J31:0 (accessed 6.9.12).

[15] Korean Immigration Law Clause 31 (already cited in full).

[16] Data compiled from Korea Ministry of Justice: www.moj.go.kr (accessed 29.2.12).

Table 3: Number of Foreigners in South Korea by Country[17]

Category	Total No. of Foreigners as of Feb 2011	February 2012		
		Total No. of Foreigners	No. of Legally Staying Foreigners	No. of Illegally Staying Foreigners
Total	1,260,841	1,367,495	1,197,134	170,361
China	623,006	675,874	609,263	66,611
(Korean-Chinese)	(421,923)	(468,682)	(451,602)	(17,080)
USA	129,372	134,621	126,611	8,010
Vietnam	103,505	114,849	94,856	19,993
Japan	40,161	47,567	46,295	1,272
Philippines	47,500	45,867	32,747	12,393
Thailand	40,447	40,867	26,182	14,685
Indonesia	29,433	31,448	25,713	5,735
Uzbekistan	26,513	31,479	26,544	4,935
Mongolia	30,222	28,521	18,908	9,613
Taiwan	25,160	27,006	26,058	948
Canada	20,057	21,772	21,002	770
Sri Lanka	18,312	21,206	18,440	2,766
Cambodia	18,312	21,206	18,440	2,766
Bangladesh	12,785	13,412	8,412	5,000
Nepal	10,091	13,497	11,714	1,783
Pakistan	10,404	10,259	6,852	3,407
Russia	9,741	9,861	8,812	1,049
India	7,471	7,787	6,621	1,166
Australia	6,097	7,149	6,779	370
UK	5,620	6,601	6,502	99
Myanmar	4,668	6,480	5,289	1,191
Hong Kong	2,303	3,223	2,009	214
Others	43,022	48,173	41,352	6,821

Table 4: Number of the Korean-born or Korean Diaspora with Foreign Citizenship Living in South Korea

Country	Number	Country	Number
China	94,700	Kazakhstan	580
USA	42,934	UK	251
Canada	12,226	France	204
Australia	3,492	Brazil	120
Uzbekistan	2,194	Netherlands	115
Russia	1,610	Argentina	108
New Zealand	1,597	Sweden	96
Germany	843	Others	832
Japan	700	**TOTAL**	**162,602**

[17] Data from Korea Ministry of Justice: www.moj.go.kr (accessed 29.2.12).

The above-mentioned 162,000-strong Korean-born or Korean diaspora people ('*dongpo*' in Korean) holding non-Korean passports and now living in South Korea had intercultural experiences overseas. A majority of this group of 'reverse-immigrated' persons would be culturally Korean to varying degrees, although legally listed as 'foreigners' in Korea.[18]

Table 5: Number of 'Marriage Immigrants' to South Korea[19]

Year	2006	2007	2008	2009	2010	2011
Number	93,786	110,362	122,552	125,087	141,654	144,681

According to the South Korean Ministry of Justice's definition, a 'marriage immigrant' is a non-Korean national who is or was married to a Korean citizen.[20] As can be seen in Table 6, a majority of inter-ethnically married residents in South Korea are from Asia. In terms of the female vs male ratio, of the 144,681 'marriage immigrants' in 2011, 125,031 (86.4%) were women, and 19,650 (13.6%) were men. The numbers in Tables 5 and 6 exclude those marriage immigrants who have become naturalized Korean citizens, for the foreign-born naturalized are now by law Korean citizens.

[18] Data in table 4 derives from www.moj.go.kr/HP/COM/bbs_03/ListShowData.do ?strNbodCd=noti0097&strWrtNo=98&strAnsNo=A&strNbodCd=noti0703&strFile Path=moj/&strRtnURL=MOJ_40402000&strOrgGbnCd=104000&strThisPage=1& strNbodCdGbn (in Korean) (accessed 23.8.12). On 29 August 2012, C. Im had a phone conversation with Hee Chang Woo, a Korean consul at South Korea Consulate in Chicago, located at 455 North City Front Plaza Dr. NBC Tower Suite 2700 Chicago, IL 60611, tel: (312) 822-9485. The term '*dongpo*동포' can be translated into English as Korean-born or Korean-diaspora individuals with foreign citizenship. According to Consul Woo, in Chicago a '*dongpo*' is a person who holds a non-Korean citizenship but who was born in Korea under Korean parent(s)/citizen(s), or who once had a Korean passport, including those who were born outside Korea under Korean parent(s)/citizen(s). To be or to become a Korean citizen, at least one parent must have Koran citizenship. For more detailed information on the legal definition of '*dongpo*' (in Korean), see also: www.hikorea.go.kr/pt/InfoDetailR_kr.pt?categoryId=1&parentId=155&catSeq=&s howMenuId=122 (accessed 29.8.12).

[19] www.index.go.kr/egams/stts/jsp/potal/stts/PO_STTS_IdxMain.jsp?idx_ cd=2819 &bbs=INDX_001 (accessed 29.8.12).

[20] 'Laws regarding Korea-Residing Foreigners' (in Korean), available at www.lawkorea.com/client/asp/lawinfo/law/lawview.asp?type=l&lawcode=a736367 #0000000000 (accessed 23.8.12).

Table 6: Number of Marriage Immigrants in South Korea by Nationality (December 2011)[21]

Country	Vietnam	China	Korean-Chinese	Japan[22]	Philippines	Others	Total
Number	37,516	34,989	29,184	11,162	8,367	23,463	144,681

As of September 2010 in South Korea, the average age difference between foreign-born wives and Korean husbands was nearly ten years. Not surprisingly, there was a direct correlation between the economic power of the foreign wife's nation and the age gap. As Table 7 shows, the age gaps between foreign wives from (1) the Western nations and (2) Japan (all countries with high average incomes) and their Korean husbands were very narrow: (1) 2.0 and (2) 2.3 years respectively. On the contrary, the biggest age gaps existed between Korean husbands and wives from Vietnam (17 years) and Cambodia (17.5 years), countries with relatively low average incomes. Many of these young brides from Vietnam and Cambodia came from poor families in rural areas. According to the same report, 45.4% of the female marriage immigrants age 24 and under were living with Korean husbands over the age of 40.[23] The education levels of the female marriage immigrants were as follows: those who attended or graduated from college (20.6%); high school (42.3%); middle school (27.7%); and elementary school (9.4%).[24]

A significant number of foreigners are migrant workers (approximately 600,000, which includes E-Visa, short-term workers, intern-workers, and work-seekers), temporary residents (approximately 240,000), and international students (approximately 80,000). Table 8 shows the number of migrant workers in South Korea. This data, derived from Withee Mission International, is less than what is said about the total population of migrant workers.

---

[21] 'Laws regarding Korea-Residing Foreigners' (already cited in full).

[22] A more-than-normal number of marriage immigrants came from Japan to Korea in 2011 partially because of the mass international marriages conducted for members of the Unification Church.

[23] Seung Kwon Kim, Ae Jeo Cho, and Hyun Joo Min, *A Strategy Report: Employment Assistance and Development for Female Marriage Immigrants* (in Korean) (Seoul: Korea Institute for Health and Social Affairs, 2010), 59.

[24] Kim, Cho, and Min, *A Strategy Report*, 60.

Table 7: Female Marriage Immigrants' and Their Korean Husbands' Average Ages (2010)[25]

Country/Continent	Female Marriage Immigrants' Average Age (A)	Male Korean Husbands' Average Age (B)	Age Difference between Foreign-Born Wives and Korean Husbands (B-A)
All	33.3	43.2	9.9
N. America, Australia and Western Europe	38.3	40.3	2.0
Japan	40.0	42.3	2.3
China (Korean Chinese)	39.5	46.2	6.7
Thailand	34.5	41.6	7.1
China (non-Korean)	33.9	42.7	8.8
Mongolia	31.3	41.3	10.0
Philippines	31.7	42.6	10.9
Vietnam	24.3	41.3	17.0
Cambodia	23.5	41.0	17.5
Others	32.0	40.9	8.9

Table 8: Migrant Workers in South Korea as of 2008[26]

Country	Number	Country	Number
China	60,300	UK	1,000
Philippines	21,000	Australia	700
Uzbekistan	10,400	New Zealand	600
Canada	4,500	Romania	400
USA	4,300	South Africa	300
India	3,400	Germany	200
Russian Federation	2,500	France	200
Japan	1,200	Others	186,800
Total	**358,167**		

The number of international students in South Korea has been growing rapidly for the past decade. As Tables 9 and 10 illustrate, the number of international students coming to Korea to study or to get trained shows no signs of abating.

[25] Kim, Cho, and Min, *A Strategy Report*, 60.

[26] Data compiled from Withee Mission International: www.withee.or.kr (accessed 7.9.12).

Table 9: Number of International Students in South Korea[27]

Year	2003	2004	2005	2006	2007	2008	2009	2010
Number of International Students	12,314	16,832	22,526	32,557	49,270	63,952	75,850	83,842

The majority of international students came to South Korea from countries across the Asian continent.

Table 10: Number of International Students in South Korea by Country (as of April 2011)[28]

Country	China	Japan	Mongolia	USA	Vietnam	Taiwan	Others	Total
Number of International Students	59,317	4,520	3,699	2,707	2,325	1,574	15,395	89,537
Percentage	66.2	5.0	4.1	3.0	2.6	1.8	17.2	100.0

Table 11: Number of Refugee Applicants in South Korea (1994-2011)[29]

Year(s)	Number of Applicants	Approved	Temporary Stay Granted	Rejected	Withdrawn
Total	4,186	271	145	1,955	668
1994-2003	251	14	13	50	39
2004	148	18	1	7	9
2005	410	9	13	79	29
2006	278	11	13	114	43
2007	717	13	9	86	62
2008	364	36	14	79	109
2009	324	70	22	994	203
2010	423	47	38	168	62
2011	1,011	42	20	277	90

Tables 2-11 presented in this section are indicative of demographic trends, along with the actual numbers of diaspora groups, in South Korea.

---

27 Data compiled from Statistics Korea – Government Website: www.index.go.kr (accessed 1.4.11).

28 www.index.go.kr/egams/stts/jsp/potal/stts/PO_STTS_IdxMain.jsp?idx_ cd=1534 &bbs=INDX_001 (accessed 29.8.12).

29 Data compiled from Korea Immigration Service: www.moj.go.kr (accessed 1.4.11).

Unprecedented Opportunities to Reach Receptive Diaspora Groups in South Korea

Due to the increase of foreigners and influx of diaspora groups in South Korea, unreached people groups are reachable in Korea. Table 12 shows a decade-long trend of the increase of foreigners in South Korea, including those from the Muslim country of Indonesia, communist countries of China and Vietnam, Buddhist countries such as Thailand and Cambodia, and the Catholic country of the Philippines. In addition to the 'presumed Muslims' coming from Indonesia in Table 12, 'about 130,000 of the 640,000 migrant workers in South Korea are Muslims'.[30] These Muslim migrants can be readily reachable with the gospel and the love of Christ in South Korea.

Table 12: Case Studies: Diaspora/Homogeneous Groups in South Korea

	TYPE	COUNTRY OF ORIGIN	CASE STUDY	PEOPLE GROUP
DIASPORA GROUPS	Communist	China 1,367,495	4, 9	Unreached people group
		Vietnam 114,849	9	
	Buddhist	Thailand 40,867	9	
		Cambodia 21,206	9	
	Muslim	Indonesia 31,448	1, 9	
	Catholic	Philippines 45,867	3, 7	
	Others	Mongolia 28,521	2,5	Reached people group
	Children of migrant workers[31]		2, 8	Homo-geneous group
	Interracial marriage and multicultural family		3, 8	
Korean	International students		8, 9, 10	
	Senior Christians		11	

Diaspora groups are more receptive to the gospel than those in their homeland. A case in point is the observation by the chief director of the Diaspora Mongolian Network: 'Evangelism to migrant workers in South Korea is more efficient than evangelism to people living in Mongolia...Mongolian migrant workers in South Korea are *seven times* more likely to become Christians than Mongolians in their home country'.[32]

---

[30] Lee, 'Migrant Workers' Churches', 376.

[31] For facts and tables of children of migrant workers and multicultural families, see Jun, 'A South Korean Case Study of Migrant Ministries', 206-9, where missions to them have been reported and strategized.

[32] Jun, 'A South Korean Case Study of Migrant Ministries', 378, italics added. For

The report of FAN (Friends of All Nations – Case Study #8) workers substantiates this phenomenon as well:

> There is greater openness and responsiveness from these foreign workers who are not held by the cultural and religious pressures from back home. This is especially true among those of Muslim background, where there is the greatest need of evangelism.[33]

Strategic Practice of Diaspora Missions in South Korea

In contrast to the 'sending and receiving' via a mission station in the traditional missiological paradigm, diaspora missiology is strategically fulfilling the Great Commission by means of missions to and through the diaspora. Christian workers go where God is believed to be providentially moving people spatially and spiritually. It is missiologically imperative and strategic to practice 'mission at our doorstep' by evangelizing diaspora groups. This section presents case studies of strategic practices in South Korea, organized according to the categories of diaspora ministry and diaspora missions (see also Table 1).

Diaspora ministry to the diaspora

'Ministry to the diaspora' fulfills the Great Commandment through pre-evangelistic practices of attending to the social and physical needs of diaspora groups.[34] Rev. Chon Eung Pak of the Ansan Immigrants Center reports that 'the four most frequent foreign workers' human rights violations are discrimination (27.7%), withholding identification (26.7%), violence (15.5%), and forced labor (14.3%)'.[35] Korean churches and

---

details of the Diaspora Mongolian Network, see: www.facebook.com/dmnetwork?sk=wall&filter=2 (accessed 29.6.12).

[33] Jun, 'A South Korean Case Study of Migrant Ministries', 215.

[34] Some helpful references for 'ministry to the diaspora' include: Tom Phillips, et al., *The World at Your Door: Reaching International Students in Your Home, Church, and School* (Minneapolis: Bethany House, 1997); Enoch Wan, *Missions Within Reach: Intercultural Ministries in Canada* (Hong Kong: Alliance Press, 1995); Thom Hopler and Marcia, *Reaching the World Next Door* (Downers Grove: InterVarsity Press, 1995); and Lausanne Committee for World Evangelization Issue Group No. 26 A and B: Diasporas and International Students, 'Lausanne Occasional Paper 55: The New People Next door', in David Claydon (ed), *A New Vision, a New Heart, a Renewed Call: Lausanne Occasional Papers from the 2004 Forum of World Evangelization Hosted by the Lausanne Committee for World Evangelization – Pataya, Thailand September 29 – October 5, 2004* (Pasadena: William Carey Library, and Delhi: Horizon Printers and Publishers, 2005), 75-137.

[35] Jun, 'A South Korean Case Study of Migrant Ministries', 211, quoting from C.E. Pak, 'The Present Reality of Foreign Workers and Multicultural Policy Agenda' (in Korean), presented at the 2006 Shinchon Forum.

missionary organizations can best minister to foreign workers in these areas related to human rights.

Since the 1990s, many churches and missionary organizations have ministered to foreign workers by addressing human rights violations and the social problems such generate. David Jun notes a case in point: 'Rev. Haesung Kim, Pastor at a missionary organization for Chinese Koreans, started his organization as a counseling place for migrant workers, mainly focusing on their human rights'.[36]

Myunghee Lee reports that when evangelizing diaspora Mongolians in Korea, Korean churches and Christians attempted to be 'holistic' by combining the Great Commandment with the Great Commission. These diaspora situations provide opportunities for church and mission workers to serve especially migrant workers, and others, 'through regularly scheduled visits to work places of migrant workers as well as providing shelter, medical treatment, job placement assistance or other social services to them. There have been many cases of migrant workers getting to know these churches and listening to the gospel through such social services'.[37] The following two case studies focus on ministry *to* the diaspora.

Case Study #1: Onnuri M Center in Ansan, ministering to global diasporas.[38] Onnuri Community Church in Seoul is one of the largest Presbyterian churches, with eight daughter churches, in South Korea.[39] It planted Onnuri M Center in December 2005 in the city of Ansan; the 'M' stands for 'Mission', in addition to 'Migrant, Mercy, Ministry, Mother, Missionary'.[40] As of February 2010, approximately 34,500 foreigners from 62 countries resided in Ansan. Among them were 3,900 foreign-born, Korean-married immigrants, and 2,800 children of multicultural families.[41] It is located in Won-Gok district of Ansan, which is known as 'Little Asia in Korea' because of the strong presence of the migrant populations from numerous countries. On Sunday, these foreign-language Christian worship services are offered at Onnuri M Center: Bangladesh, Mongolian, Russian, and Sri Lankan.[42] Missionally, the center serves various needs of migrant workers and the children of multicultural families while also working toward producing missionaries from those they are serving and disciplining. In addition, the facility provides a cultural, educational, and religious space for the city's migrant workers. Furthermore, it provides other social services including delivery of daily newspapers from home

---

[36] Jun, 'A South Korean Case Study of Migrant Ministries', 211.

[37] Lee, 'Migrant Workers' Churches', 370. More discussion on this issue is covered in case studies #8 and #9.

[38] www.news.cgntv.net/sub.aspx?pid=2135&vid=24453 (accessed 5.5.12).

[39] Onnuri Community Church: www.onnuri.or.kr (accessed 248.12).

[40] www.onnurimission.com/sub1_3.html (accessed 24.8.12).

[41] www.missionews.co.kr/lib/news/28163 (accessed 23.8.12).

[42] www.onnuri.or.kr/sub.asp?gubun=22 (accessed 24.8.12).

nations, medical services (especially for those who do not have medical insurance), work training, and a Korean language program.

Case Study #2: Da-Ae[43] *Multicultural School, ministering to children of migrant workers.* A number of important facts about children of migrant workers in South Korea should be noted. As of March 2008, it was estimated that 'of approximately 17,000 children, ages 16 or under, of undocumented migrant workers residing in South Korea, only 1,402 are receiving school educations (981 in elementary schools; 314 in middle schools; 107 in high schools). This means that approximately 16,000 children remain outside school systems'.[44]

The Da-Ae Multicultural School is an alternative middle school approved by Seoul City's Office of Education. The middle school, launched 10 March 2011 in Seoul, was established to 'educate children of multicultural families and migrant workers'.[45] In September 2011, it had 16 students: nine Chinese, five Mongolians, one Filipino, and one Japanese. Perhaps more surprisingly, at this same time the school had 17 teachers: three full-time, a few regular subject teachers, and a number of special education teachers. The school is supported by the Da-Ae congregation, which finances two-thirds of the school's budget. In addition, nine of the 17 teachers were members of Da-Ae Church. More about another aspect of Da-Ae's mission will be introduced shortly.

Diaspora ministry through *the diaspora*

'Ministry through the diaspora' is a strategic way of mobilizing diaspora Christians to serve others, both their own kinsman and other diaspora groups. One case study of such an endeavor is presented.

Case Study #3: Filipino congregations, ministering to kinsmen of 'marriage immigrants'. 'Marriage immigrants' refer to foreign women/men who were/are married to Korean men/women. In 2010, an average of 130 Filipino 'marriage immigrants' arrived in Korea every month.[46] Most of these marriages arranged between Filipina women and Korean men are made despite the fact that this is illegal in the Philippines according to the Philippines' Anti-Mail Order Bride Law. Statistics from the Korea Immigration Service showed as of 2011 that there were 8,367 Filipino

---

[43] *Da-Ae* means 'all love' or 'much love' in Korean.

[44] Da-Ae Multicultural School's website: www.allloveschool.or.kr/_board/bbs/board.php?bo_table=s1_01 (accessed 24.8.12).

[45] Ibid.

[46] www.filamstar.net/index.php?id=3982 (accessed 25.6.12); see also Chan Sik Park, 'Multicultural Society and Migrant Mission' [in Korean], in Chan Sik Park and Noh Hwa Jung (eds), *21 C New Nomad Era and Migrant Mission* [in Korean] (Seoul: Christian Industrial Society Research Institute Press, 2009), 118.

marriage immigrants living in Korea.[47] Based on the same data, the Philippines ranks fourth as the preferred source of foreign wives – after China, Vietnam, and Japan – for Korean men. There are more than 30 Filipino Christian churches and organizations in Korea that minister to fellow Filipinos, including marriage immigrants.[48]

Missions to *the diaspora*

'Missions to the diaspora' focuses on motivating and mobilizing diaspora individuals and congregations to heed the Great Commission and engage in evangelistic outreach and missions. According to Table 1, there are three types of diaspora missions: *to*, *through*, and *by and beyond*. 'Missions to the diaspora' refers to Koreans engaging in mission outreach to members of diaspora communities. In contrast to the traditional practice of geographically 'sending' missionaries abroad (involving complicated visa application and costly international travel), there are many advantages in missions to local diaspora groups within Korea.

Table 13: 'Missions to the Diaspora' as 'Mission at Our Doorstep'[49]

NO	YES
No visa required	Yes, door opened and given neediness
No closed door	Yes, people are accessible
No international travel required	Yes, missions at local doorsteps
No political/legal restrictions	Yes, ample opportunities
No political or legal restrictions to mission endeavors and methods	Yes, holistic ministries more easily accomplished

Table 14 (opposite) lists organizations and agencies engaging in 'missions to' and 'missions through' diaspora groups South Korea. One case study of 'mission to diaspora' is presented here.

Case Study #4: South Korea Leadership Training. An effective strategy of 'missions to diaspora' for Korean churches involves developing 'ethnic leadership through cooperative education programs with seminaries'.[50] Leadership development for each ethnicity is needed to minister to migrant workers of various ethnic groups. There is a partnership between Korean seminaries and Korean churches in leadership development for diaspora

---

[47] www.index.go.kr/egams/stts/jsp/potal/stts/PO_STTS_IdxMain.jsp?idx_ cd=2819 &bbs=INDX_001 (accessed 29.8.12).
[48] www.philembassy-seoul.com/filipino_community.asp (accessed 25.6.12).
[49] See Wan, *Diaspora Missiology*, 138.
[50] Lee, 'Migrant Workers' Churches', 380.

ministry and missions. Myunghee Lee notes: '12 ethnic leaders [have been] trained under this [seminary-sponsored, ethnic leadership] program from 2001. Some of them are currently serving as respective ethnic leaders in this church, while some have gone back to their respective countries to work for the gospel. It is noteworthy to see a migrant workers' church acting as the connecting link among migrant workers, South Korean churches and seminaries'.[51]

Table 14: Organizations/Agencies Focused on Cross-cultural Missions within Korea

TYPE	ORGANIZATION	DESCRIPTION
MISSIONS TO	Industrial Zone Mission Center	Located in the city of Si-Heung, Gyeong-Gi Province Focuses on holistic missions toward migrant workers Website: www.izmc.net
	Mission Center for Migrants in Daegu	Located in the city of Daegu Focuses on four specific ministries: (1) Evangelistic ministry toward migrant workers (2) Human rights ministry of migrant workers (3) Cultural ministry (4) Welfare ministry Website: www.mission4you.net
	Bangladesh Missions	Located in Incheon Focuses on migrant workers from Bangladesh Website: www.bmkorea.org
	Withee Missions	Located in An-Yang Focuses on migrant workers Website: www.withee.org
MISSIONS	Migrant Vision Center	Located in Ha-Nam Established to (1) evangelize migrant workers and children of multicultural families, (2) equip them to be disciples of Jesus, and (3) send some of them back to their homelands as evangelists Offers programs and services which include language, music, Korean culture, medicine, beauty, counseling, and theological education Website: www.hmigrant.org
THROUGH	Pharos Mission Center	Located in Si-Heung Church-based ministry toward migrant workers Focuses on migrant workers from Thailand Vision to evangelize, equip, and send workers to Thailand as church-planters Website: www.pharos1004.org

[51] Lee, 'Migrant Workers' Churches', 381.

Missions through *the diaspora*

'Missions through the diaspora' involves diaspora Christians and their congregations engaging in mission outreach not cross-culturally, but to kins-persons in homeland and elsewhere. For example, South Korea had 'about 30,000 Mongolian migrant workers...a little above 1% of the entire Mongolian population in Mongolia of 2.9 million' (as of August 2007).[54] Mongolian migrant workers' churches in South Korea are very effective and even successful in evangelizing fellow diaspora. Lee reports: 'The number of Mongolian migrant workers' churches was...60 in 2006, and it increased to 80 by the end of 2007'.[55]

I (Wan) was personally involved in training programs for the Chinese, sponsored by Korean congregations and a Christian university, before sending the trainees back to China. One such program was at a post-high school level (now defunct) and another one is at a Master's level (still in operation).

Case Study #5: Every Nation Church of Korea, Every Nation Church of Mongolia, and Crusades in Mongolia.[56] Every Nation Church of Korea was established in Seoul by Pastor Simon Suh and Pastor Jacob Lee in 2002. It is 'an international church that has people of different national, ethnic, and cultural backgrounds and is a community that pursues honoring God, loving people, and serving nations'.[57] In July 2003, Ulaanbaatur, the capital city of Mongolia, hosted Harvest Mongolia Crusade with Rev. Billy Kim as the main speaker. At that time Pastor Suh, then a Mission Pastor at Suwon Baptist Church, co-ordinated this event. 'It was the biggest gathering of Christians in Mongolian history, with over 30,000 people gathering in Central Stadium'.[58] It was during this event that Pastor Suh met Alliance N. Enkhbayar, commonly known as 'Pastor Joshua',[59] who was then President of Mongolian Evangelical Alliance. That meeting eventually led to planting Every Nation Church in Mongolia. In the midst of sufferings and trials, Every Nation Church in Mongolia strives to fulfill its purpose of being a center for reaching Mongolia and the world with the gospel.

---

[54] Lee, 'Migrant Workers' Churches', 378.

[55] Lee, 'Migrant Workers' Churches', 378.

[56] www.everynation.or.kr/2010_home/en_menu_01.php and www.everynation.org/church-directory/mongolia/mongolia/ (accessed 25.6.12).

[57] For details, see www.everynation.or.kr/2010_home/en_menu_01.php (accessed 25.6.12).

[58] From the Every Nation Church's website: www.everynation.or.kr/2010_home/en_menu_02_12.php (accessed 29.8.12.

[59] See Geraldine Fagan, 'Mongolia: Religious Freedom Oasis?' (part 2 of 2), 8 December 2013, available at httpwww.forum18.org/Archive.php?article_id=206 (accessed 29.8.12).

Missions by and beyond *the diaspora*

'Missions by and beyond the diaspora' happens when diaspora Christians/congregations cross-culturally evangelize other ethnic groups in the host society and beyond. A number of case studies are presented.

Case Study #6: Da-Ae Church in Seoul.[60] Rev. Soon-Keun Lee was an immigrant in the USA for 16 years. He brought his rich experience as an immigrant in a foreign land back to Seoul where he founded the Da-Ae Church. Approximately 50% of the congregation has had experiences abroad, and in particular as parents of children who had studied elsewhere, outside Korea.[61] Church members thus have been motivated to engage in ministry and mission in such environments. Lee and other key leaders therefore ensured that Da-Ae Multicultural School would serve as a missionary ministry to the diaspora groups, including their children, in Seoul. In addition, it is the plan and hope of the school that some of these foreign students would become 'future leaders of Korea, like Daniel and Esther, and diaspora leaders for their birth nations, like Ezra and Nehemiah'.[62]

Case Study #7: Filipino diaspora in Korea and missions to the Philippines. The Filipino ministry group in Sujeong Church was founded in May 1993 for migrant workers in the city of Incheon. Since then, the church's Filipino ministry has planted seven churches in the Philippines. The church's Filipino ministry strives to disciple Filipino Christians in Korea and to send them back to their homeland as missionaries.[63]

Case Study #8: Friends of All Nations (FAN). As an inter-denominational organization with a comprehensive ministry and mission vision, FAN has two dozen branches near industrial complexes throughout South Korea. 'The headquarters has five different language worship services: Filipino, Vietnamese, Thai, Indonesian, and English, with between 100 to 150 foreign workers usually in attendance'.[64] David Jun's summary of FAN shows that it exemplifies 'missions by and beyond the diaspora' in its reaching out to the migrant workers, foreign students, and multicultural families in Korea. FAN co-operates and networks with local churches and ministries in the area to foster one-to-one discipleship and shepherd new believers toward more mature faith. It also runs various programs that involve, train, and empower college students and young adults in different ministries. Further, FAN partners with overseas missionaries who have returned to Korea permanently or are on furlough,

---

[60] Soon-Keun Lee, 'Case Report: Da-Ae Multicultural School as a Missional Ministry of a Missional Church' (in Korean), presentation at Korea Diaspora Forum 2011 – Asia Region, at Da Nang, Vietnam, 11-14 October 2011; see also Case Study #2 for details of the congregation's school.

[61] Lee, 'Case Report: Da-Ae Multicultural School', 3.

[62] Lee, 'Case Report: Da-Ae Multicultural School', 4.

[63] Jun, 'A South Korean Case Study of Migrant Ministries', 216-7.

[64] Jun, 'A South Korean Case Study of Migrant Ministries', 215.

as well as connects foreign believers who are studying in Korea with foreign workers from the same country. Finally, with the support of local churches, FAN trains and sends out missionaries to plant churches overseas.[65]

Case Study #9: Migrant Mission Network in Korea (MMNK). MMNK is an interdenominational co-operative formed in 2008 by several mission organizations. It was featured at the '2009 Korean Migrant Mission Expo' when '200 migrant mission organizations and around 7,000 foreign workers gathered together for mission festival meetings'.[66] Tables 15 and 16 below provide a big picture of how the various organizations associated with the Network collaborate to serve diaspora groups in South Korea.

Table 15: Mission Organizations and Diaspora Groups in South Korea by Nationalities[67]

Nation	No. of groups	Region					Major Network
		Seoul	Gyeonggi	Youngnam	Honam	Chungcheong	
Mongolia	44	23	14	4	1	2	Mongolian Diaspora network
China	88	9	27	28	9	15	Han Jung Mission
Vietnam	42	5	21	11	3	2	Vietnam United Mission
Nepal	7	1	3	1		2	Nepali Worship
Thailand	21	2	18	N/A	1	N/A	Global Thai Mission Network
Indonesia	20	2	9	7	N/A	2	Antioch Inter-national Mission
Cambodia	9	1	5	2	1	N/A	Cambodia Mission
Sri Lanka	10	1	6	2	1	N/A	N/A
Bangladesh	8	2	6	N/A	N/A	N/A	Bangladesh Mission
Russia	31	10	12	5	N/A	4	Russia Mission
Philippines	16	5	10	1	N/A	N/A	N/A

[65] Jun, 'A South Korean Case Study of Migrant Ministries', 214-5.
[66] Jun, 'A South Korean Case Study of Migrant Ministries', 218.
[67] Jun, 'A South Korean Case Study of Migrant Ministries', 219.

Table 16: MMNK's Special Mission Organizations in South Korea[68]

Expertise	No.	Region					Major Networks
		Seoul	Gyeonggi	Youngnam	Honam	Chungcheong	
Foreign Students	9	1	2	3	3	N/A	International Student Fellowship; Han Jung Mission
Multi-cultural Family	18	2	6	5	4	1	Together Multi-cultural Network
Educational Mission [69]	8	1	5	1	1	N/A	N/A
Muslim	31	2	18	8	1	2	N/A
Shelter Ministry	28	2	13	5	4	4	N/A

Case Study #10: Korean International Students Overseas. As of April 2011 there were 262,465 Korean post-high school international students studying overseas (Table 17). Nearly all are temporary overseas residents. It is likely that a majority will return to South Korea with cross-cultural experiences.

Table 17: Number of South Korean Post-High School International Students in Overseas Context[70]

Country	USA	China	Australia	Japan	UK	Canada	NZ
Number of Students	72,153	62,957	33,929	25,692	17,310	15,808	10,289
Percentage	27.5	24.0	12.9	9.8	6.6	6.0	3.9

Upon the Christian international students' return back to Korea, Korean Christian leaders should encourage them to utilize their diaspora and cross-cultural experiences to engage in diaspora ministry and missions to diaspora groups in Korea. The ministry of Lee (see Case Study #6 above) at Da-Ae Church is a great example of this human resource implemented. Since there are also so many international students in South Korea (see also

[68] Jun, 'A South Korean Case Study of Migrant Ministries', 220.

[69] Educational mission includes training in computer, auto mechanics, tourism, and Taekwondo. Jun, 'A South Korean Case Study of Migrant Ministries', 220.

[70] 1 April 2011 data (total: 262,465), including college and post-college students in degree and non-degree programs: www.index.go.kr/egams/stts/jsp/potal/stts/PO_STTS_IdxMain.jsp?idx_cd=1534&bbs=INDX_001 (accessed 29.8.2012). Note: Table 17 is a partial list.

Tables 8 and 9), student ministry organizations should mobilize Korean students returning from abroad to engage in 'missions to and through' these diaspora groups in Korea.

Case Study #11: Mobilizing senior Christians. As one of the fastest-aging societies in the world, South Korea is 'expected to become a 'super-aged' society in 10 years, with the number of people over 65 forecasted to reach 20.8% of the estimated 48 million population'.[71] Given the fact that 'there are over 50,000 churches in Korea as well as nearly 10,000 Korean diaspora churches abroad',[72] many mission-minded senior Christians should be mobilized to become kingdom 'harvesters' serving the diaspora groups within Korea. In 2007, the First National Conference for the Mobilization of Senior Christians was held, followed by the second conference in 2009. Many of these seniors featured outstanding career profiles, were professionally trained in various ways, and had a strong passion for mission. This remains a largely untapped mission group which should be channeled to various types of mission work, including 'mission at our doorstep' to diaspora groups in their local areas. Those unhindered by health issues or familial obligations may even be interested in missionary services abroad.

Conclusion

Korean Christian churches are to be commended for being 'ranked second after the USA in numbers of overseas [Protestant] missionaries officially sent by [Protestant denominations and] mission agencies'.[73] In this study, the demographic trends of the increased presence of unreached diaspora groups in South Korea have been identified to show that they are reachable (see also Table 12). Strategic practices of diaspora missions in South Korea have been illustrated through the eleven case studies (categorized according to the framework of Table 1).

In a review of recent efforts in diaspora ministry/missions in Korea, David Jun gives a helpful summary:

> When we look at the 20 years of domestic migrant workers ministry, we have two main types: human rights-oriented and mission-oriented ministries. Within mission-oriented ministry, there are several models. Medium- to large-size Korean churches usually have a migrant workers' mission department and do the ministry...Initially, foreign workers are invited to participate in Korean churches' worship services aided by interpreters...some

[71] See-Young Lee, 'Mobilizing Senior Christians in Korea and among the Korean Diaspora for Mission', in Kim and Ma (eds), *Korean Diaspora and Christian Mission*, 260-63, quotation from 260.
[72] Lee, 'Mobilizing Senior Christians in Korea, 260.
[73] Lee, 'Migrant Workers' Churches', 376.

> other churches hire foreign pastors to minister to their own foreign workers with separate worship services.[74]

There are 'hundreds of migrant workers' churches in South Korea, although it is impossible to count the exact number'.[75] The migrant workers' churches 'help Christians in Korea see the reality that Korea is becoming a mission field, and challenge them to play their parts of world mission 'here' in Korea while overseas missionaries play their parts 'over there'.[76] Jun articulates well the missiological significance and strategic value of 'mission to diaspora' and 'mission through diaspora' in Korea:

> Therefore, if we want to make an impact through our migrant workers' mission, we have to train migrant Christian workers to become missionaries to their own people and train them to work with other missionaries already serving in their countries...The domestic migrant mission[' s] goal has to be training them to ...establish churches [in their countries after they return to their homelands].[77]

---

[74] Jun, 'A South Korean Case Study of Migrant Ministries', 213.
[75] Lee, 'Migrant Workers' Churches', 377.
[76] Lee, 'Migrant Workers' Churches', 383.
[77] Jun, 'A South Korean Case Study of Migrant Ministries', 221.

Diaspora Missiology and the Lausanne Movement at the Dawn of the Twenty-First Century

Sadiri Joy Tira

Introduction

The purpose of this chapter is to outline the development of diaspora missiology from the platform of the Lausanne Movement, and identify its goals at the dawn of the twenty-first century. Specifically, this chapter demonstrates the growing awareness of diaspora mission by the evangelical community, specifically represented by the Lausanne Movement. The significance of this study, therefore, is its contribution to mission educators and organizations on the historical development of diaspora missiology through the Lausanne Movement.

This chapter is organized in four parts. The first section, '*Kairos* Movement: Embracing the Global Trend of Diaspora', provides a description of the global trend of diaspora. This is followed, in 'Kingdom Collaborations: Early Proponents of Diaspora Missiology in the Lausanne Movement', by an historic overview of the diaspora initiative of the Lausanne Movement up until Cape Town 2010 and the launching of the Global Diaspora Network (GDN). In 'Kinetic Mission Models: Missiological Implications from Cape Town to Beyond', we discuss the implications raised by the 'borderless' world and present diaspora missiology as a non-spatial and 'moving' mission strategy model with some practical applications. I conclude with 'Recommendations and Conclusion' based upon the Lausanne *Cape Town Commitment Call to Action* published in 2010, with the goal of accelerating implementation of diaspora missiology by mission educators and practitioners.

At the outset, it is necessary to define key terms:

- 'Diaspora missiology': in this chapter, diaspora refers to 'the phenomenon of dispersion of any ethnic group'.[1] 'Diaspora in missions' is used to refer to 'dispersed ethnic groups who are actively engaged or actively involved in fulfilling the Great Commission; regardless of vocation and denominational affiliations of individuals involved'.[2] The Lausanne Seoul Declaration on

---

[1] Luis Pantoja Jr, Sadiri Joy Tira, and Enoch Wan (eds), *Scattered: The Filipino Global Presence* (Manila: LifeChange Publishing Inc., 2004), xxviii.

[2] Sadiri Joy Tira, 'Scattered with a Divine Purpose: A Theological and Missiological Perspective on the Filipino Diaspora', unpublished paper presented at the Christian Missionary and Alliance Asia Pacific Conference, Taipei, Taiwan,

Diaspora Missiology defines diaspora missiology as a missiological framework for understanding and participating in God's redemptive mission among people living outside their place of origin'.[3]

- '*Kairos* movement': *kairos* refers to what missiologists understand as divinely-appointed windows of opportunity. In God's providence and sovereignty, scattered peoples have been widely dispersed at a time of unprecedented opportunity. It is possible for diaspora Christians to engage and participate in the fulfillment of the Great Commission and the achievement of the ultimate goal of missions.[4]
- 'Kingdom collaboration': this refers to a consultative partnership forged by like-minded institutes, groups, or individuals having kingdom implications.[5]

The research methods I employed are case studies and participant observations. The case study approach proceeds 'over time through detailed, in-depth data collection involving multiple sources of information rich in context'.[6] Data is gathered from interviews and a review of literature on Lausanne diasporas, including documents from archives. Moreover, the participant observation methodology utilized reflects my immersion in the midst of what is being reported. This 'highest level of involvement...comes when [the authors] study a situation in which they are already ordinary participants'.[7] I am the first person appointed to the position of Lausanne Senior Associate for Diasporas and have been able to make systematic observations about the development of the Lausanne Movement's diaspora mission agenda.[8]

This chapter is limited to the diaspora advocates and initiatives of the Lausanne Movement from 1990, one year after Lausanne II in Manila, to July 2011, nearly one year after Lausanne III in Cape Town in 2010, unless specified otherwise.

April 1998.

[3] The Lausanne Seoul Declaration on Diaspora Missiology is available at www.lausanne.org/fr/eng/documents/all/175-consultation-statements/1112-the-seoul-declaration-on-diaspora-missiology.html (accessed 1.2. 13).

[4] This definition of '*kairos* movement' is based on Sadiri Joy Tira, 'Filipino International Network: A Strategic Model for Filipino Diaspora Glocal Missions', in Pantoja, Tira, and Wan (eds), *Scattered*, 149-72.

[5] See Tira, 'Filipino International Network', 157-58.

[6] J.W. Creswell, *Qualitative Inquiry and Research Design: Choosing Among Five Traditions* (Thousand Oaks, CA: Sage, 1998), 61.

[7] J.P. Spradley, *Participant Observation* (New York: Holt, Rinehart and Winston, Inc., 1980), 61.

[8] In Lausanne Diasporas documents from 2007 to 2010, the Lausanne Committee for World Evangelization (LCWE) refers to diaspora peoples as 'Diasporas'. In the 2010 Cape Town Commitment, published by the LCWE, now referred to as the Lausanne Movement (LM), diaspora people are referred to as 'scattered people'. Hereafter, diasporas will be referred to as scattered peoples.

Kairos Movements: Embracing the Global Trend of Diaspora

Unprecedented movements of diaspora groups, or 'scattered peoples', in large scale and higher frequency, have clearly set a 'global trend' in the twenty-first century. This complex movement, caused by multiple factors, both voluntary (e.g., educational, financial advancement) and involuntary (e.g., natural disasters, war, human trafficking), is increasingly changing regional demographics, societies, cultures, and economies.

In 1990, the United Nations estimated that there were more than 155 million international migrants (people living or working) outside of their country of birth.[9] In 2012, the International Organization for Migration (IOM) estimated the number of international migrants to be 214 million.[10]

Experts across disciplines are paying close attention to international migration patterns and their implications for politics, economics, law, religion, and other fields. Responding to these shifts in population, academics have increased their surveillance, and governments and international institutions have initiated changes in their policies. Further, missiologists and church planters are also monitoring and analyzing the recent mass movements of people, and recently the Third Lausanne Congress for World Evangelization (also referred to as Lausanne III, held in Cape Town, South Africa from 16-25 October 2010) has developed mission strategies to engage with this phenomenon.

In 'Finishing the Task: The Unreached Peoples Challenge', Ralph D. Winter and Bruce A. Koch write, 'As history unfolds and global migration increases, more and more people groups are being dispersed throughout the entire globe...Not many agencies take note of the strategic value of reaching the more accessible fragments of these "global peoples"'.[11] While it is true that many agencies are responding slowly to the realities of diaspora, there is a gradual realization regarding their strategic value for reaching the 'global peoples'. The diaspora mission initiative at Lausanne III is evidence of this growing awareness.

---

[9] See United Nations Department of Economic and Social Affairs, Population Division, 'Estimated Number of International Migrants at mid-year 1990 World', in *Trends in International Migrant Stock: The 2008 Revision* (United Nations database, POP/DB/MIG/Stock/Rev.2008), www.esa.un.org/migration/p2k0data.asp (accessed 28.6.12).

[10] IOM cites United Nations Department of Economic and Social Affairs (UN DESA), *Trends in International Migrant Stock: The 2008 Revision*, www.esa.un.org/migration/index.asp?panel=1.

[11] Ralph D. Winter and Bruce A. Koch, 'Finishing the Task', in Ralph D. Winter and Steven C. Hawthorne (eds), *Perspectives on the World Christian Movement: A Reader* (4th ed.; Pasadena: William Carey Library Publishers, 2002), 537.

Kingdom Collaborations: Early Proponents of Diaspora Missiology and the Lausanne Movement

As Christian individuals and mission organizations came to appreciate the challenges and *kairos* opportunities of the twenty-century diaspora, missiologists, mission practitioners, and theologians grappled to record the missiological implications. Their academic deliberations were collected in collaborative volumes and acted as early documentation of diaspora missions. This would later provide a framework for diaspora mission initiatives.

Early proponents of diaspora missions in the Lausanne Movement included Tom Houston, former International Director of the Lausanne Committee for World Evangelization (LCWE), who wrote about a 'Global Gospel', and Samuel Escobar, formerly of Palmer Theological Seminary, who proposed a 'Migration Model'.[12] Evangelical missiologists Enoch Wan of Western Seminary (Portland, Oregon) and Sadiri Joy Tira of the Filipino International Network then built on Houston's and Escobar's work when they articulated 'diaspora in missions' and 'diaspora missiology'.[13] Diaspora in mission refers to 'dispersed ethnic groups who are actively engaged or actively involved in fulfilling the Great Commission; regardless of vocation and denominational affiliations of individuals involved.' 'Diaspora missiology' refers to 'a missiological study of the phenomena of diaspora groups being scattered geographically and the strategy of gathering for the kingdom'.[14]

Gaining ground in missiological circles, 'Migration Challenge and Avenue for Christian Mission' was the designated topic at the annual

---

[12] See Tom Houston, 'Postscript: The Challenge of Diaspora Leaders for World Evangelism', in Pantoja, Tira, and Wan (eds), *Scattered*, 363-68, and Samuel Escobar, 'Migration: Avenue and Challenge to Mission', *Missiology* 31.1 (2003), 17-28.

[13] Enoch Wan and Sadiri Joy Tira have written extensively on diaspora missiology. See www.globalmissiology.org and www.?conversation.lausanne.org/en/home/diaspora for further discussions on the topic, plus their edited volume, *Missions Practice in the 21st Century* (Pasadena: William Carey International University Press, 2009). A case study discussion is in Wan and Tira, 'The Filipino Experience in Diaspora Missions: A Case Study of Christian Communities in Contemporary Contexts', in Enoch Wan and Michael Pocock (eds), *Missions from the Majority World: Progress, Challenges, and Case Studies* (Pasadena: William Carey Library, 2009), 387-411, but also available at www.edinburgh2010.org/fileadmin/files/edinburgh2010/files/Study_Process/EDINBURGH%20COMMISSION%20VII%20tira%20diaspora.pdf.

[14] See Tira, 'Scattered with a Divine Purpose', and Enoch Wan, 'Diaspora Missiology', *Occasional Bulletin of Evangelical Missiological Society* 20.2 (2007), 3-7, also available online at www.dake.com/EMS/bulletins/OB_Spring_ 07.pdf. Notably, two other prominent scholars outside of the Lausanne Movement, Andrew Walls of Edinburgh Seminary and Philip Jenkins of Pennsylvania State University, contributed heavily to the study of migration and mission.

gathering of the American Society of Missiology (AMS) in June 2002. The journal *Missiology*[15] published the proceedings of that annual gathering. Hence, missiologists are now recognizing the immense potential of Christians in diaspora as already-deployed 'kingdom workers', and are joining the growing body of academics tracking international migration.

The Lausanne 2004 Forum for World Evangelization held in Pattaya, Thailand, launched the Diaspora Issue Group. Ram Gidoomal, Patrick Tsang, Leiton Chinn, and T.V. Thomas led this group and produced the *Lausanne Occasional Paper 55 Diasporas and International Students: The New People Next Door.*[16] Further, *Scattered: The Filipino Global Presence*, edited by Luis Pantoja, Jr, Sadiri Joy Tira, and Enoch Wan, called for scattered peoples, particularly diaspora Filipinos, to be motivated, equipped, and mobilized for active participation in global missions. This book was distributed to all forum participants, showcasing the Filipino diaspora as diaspora missions in action. In it, historical demography, biblical theology, missiological methodology, and global strategy are discussed on the topic of the Filipino diaspora and its implications in global missiology. Luis Pantoja, Narry F. Santos, and Tereso C. Casiño are also credited for formulating the initial theological treatments of diaspora missiology in the same volume.

In 2007, under the leadership of Douglas Birdsall and Tetsunao Yamamori, Executive Chairman and International Director of the Lausanne Movement respectively, the LCWE appointed me as Senior Associate for Diasporas. And in 2008, I assembled the Lausanne Diasporas Leadership Team (LDLT), which included Elias Medeiros of Reformed Theological Seminary (Jackson, Mississippi), Greg Paek of Global Partners (USA), Vergil Schmidt of the Christian and Missionary Alliance (USA), T.V. Thomas of the Centre for Evangelism and World Mission (Canada), and Enoch Wan of the Evangelical Missiological Society (USA).[17] The LDLT committed itself to catalyzing collaborations between the blossoming diaspora movements (i.e., the Filipinos, Chinese, Koreans, Latinos).

---

[15] See *Missiology: An International Review* 31.1 (2003), a special issue devoted to 'Mission and Migration', edited by Terry C. Muck.

[16] Lausanne Committee for World Evangelization Issue Group No. 26 A and B: Diasporas and International Students, 'Lausanne Occasional Paper 55: The New People Next door', in David Claydon (ed), *A New Vision, a New Heart, a Renewed Call: Lausanne Occasional Papers from the 2004 Forum of World Evangelization Hosted by the Lausanne Committee for World Evangelization – Pataya, Thailand September 29 – October 5, 2004* (Pasadena: William Carey Library, and Delhi: Horizon Printers and Publishers, 2005), 75-137, also available at www.lausanne.org/docs/2004forum/LOP55_IG26.pdf (accessed 29.1.13). Material from the next few paragraphs has been adapted from the Lausanne Committee for World Evangelization booklet, *Scattered to Gather: Embracing the Global Trend of Diaspora* (Manila: LifeChange, 2010), 6-8, of which Sadiri Joy Tira was one of the principal authors.

[17] Tetsunao Yamamori assisted the LDLT as the Lausanne Senior Adviser.

Furthermore, the Lausanne leadership tasked the LDLT to formulate an evangelical diaspora theology and strategy to present at Lausanne III. The strategy that would be proposed was officially called 'diaspora missiology'.

At the November 2009 Lausanne Diaspora Educators Consultation held in Seoul, South Korea, participants produced 'The Seoul Declaration on Diaspora Missiology', which redefined diaspora missiology as 'a missiological framework for understanding and participating in God's redemptive mission among people living outside their place of origin'.[18] With diaspora missiology, the evangelical church would use the resources in place and strategically train diaspora Christians already on location both at formal and non-formal levels to mobilize a mission force that requires no 'missionary visa' and no mission agency-sponsored international travel. Moreover, diaspora kingdom workers would face no political restrictions and no technically 'closed doors'. Finally, the diaspora kingdom workers would not be self-sufficient, but would be sustained by kingdom collaborations and network partnerships, resulting in a synchronized approach to diaspora missions.

A crucial step in synchronizing the evangelical efforts to reach scattered peoples is through establishing effective global evangelism strategies grounded in a solid biblical and theological foundation, and moored in a sturdy missiological framework. Two consultations were convened in 2009 via the Lausanne platform to assist in accomplishing these steps: the Lausanne Diaspora Strategy Consultation held in Manila, Philippines, in May 2009, and the Lausanne Diaspora Educators Consultation held in Seoul, South Korea, in November 2009.

Greenhills Christian Fellowship, a fast-growing metropolitan congregation in Metro Manila, Philippines, with a passion to motivate their members for diaspora missions, partnered with the LDLT to organize the Manila Consultation. Participants came from governmental and non-governmental agencies, seminaries, and denominational and para-church organizations. The result of the consultation was the identification of diaspora peoples, various issues affecting diaspora peoples, and organizations and groups (and individuals) ministering specifically with diaspora peoples. Furthermore, a group of participants from academic institutions were tasked to form a committee to plan the Lausanne Diaspora Educators Consultation or Seoul Consultation to respond to the many questions raised regarding the future of diaspora missiology after Lausanne III.

These mission educators and missiologists then gathered in Seoul, hosted by the Torch Trinity Graduate School of Theology, a seminary

[18] See 'The Seoul Declaration on Diaspora Missiology' (14 November 2009), available at www.lausanne.org/en/documents/all/consultation-statements/ 1112-the-seoul-declaration-on-diaspora-missiology.html (accessed 31.8. 12); see also Appendix I later. 'Diaspora Missiology' was initially defined by Enoch Wan, and was redefined at the 2009 Seoul Consultation.

devoted to training diaspora leaders for ministry to diaspora peoples. The Seoul Consultation's culminating document, the previously referred to 'Seoul Declaration on Diaspora Missiology', summoned the church, including its mission agencies and academies, to motivate, equip, and mobilize diaspora kingdom workers. The consultation also formed Regional Diaspora Educators Teams.

Going forward with the Lausanne Diasporas agenda, the European Diaspora Educators Team, led by Thomas Harvey of the Oxford Centre for Mission Studies, convened the LCWE Diaspora Educators' Consultation (Europe) on 16 April 2010, in Oxford. The North American Diaspora Educators Team, led by Grant McClung, gathered on 22-23 September 2010, in Charlotte, North Carolina.

To cultivate awareness for mission among the scattered peoples, diasporas was featured during one of the Lausanne III plenary sessions, and was presented twice on separate multiplex sessions due to high public demand among participants. The LDLT also presented a position paper on the theology of diaspora entitled 'Diasporas and God's Mission' to develop understanding. This paper was included in *Scattered to Gather: Embracing the Global Trend of Diaspora* and distributed to participants of Lausanne III. Diaspora mission was affirmed in section IIC.5 of the *Cape Town Commitment Call to Action*,[19] the monumental declaration of the Lausanne Congress.

The LCWE leadership has recognized the tremendous task brought on by the diaspora mission vision. In particular, I addressed the need in 2012 by forming a wider and stronger organization, the Global Diaspora Network (GDN), dedicated to the agenda of Lausanne diasporas.[20] The GDN was organized during the conclusion of Lausanne III in order to broaden the diaspora network and project the diaspora agenda beyond the event. It officially replaced the former LDLT, which was a date and event-specific initiative devoted to preparation for Lausanne III. An International Board of Advisors composed of respected diaspora scholars and practitioners was formed in 2011. The GDN headquarters/secretariat office was established in Manila and officially registered under the Securities and Exchange Commission of the Philippines, providing the GDN with a legal identity. Its Advisory Board inaugural session took place in France in

---

[19] The Cape Town Commitment Call to Action can be accessed at www.lausanne.org/en/documents/ctcommitment.html. Section IIC.5 is reproduced in appendix II.

[20] The GDN operates under the Lausanne Movement and embraces its philosophy of ministry: 'Together we seek to bear witness to Jesus Christ and all his teachings, in every part of the world – not only geographically, but in every sphere of society and in the realm of ideas'. Its formation was announced on Lausanne Global Conversation at www.conversation.lausanne.org/en/conversations/detail/11347 (accessed 31.8. 12).

February 2011. In June 2011, the Lausanne leadership officially announced that a Global Diaspora Forum would take place in March 2015 in Manila.[21]

Under the umbrella of the Lausanne Movement, the GDN is committed 'to bear[ing] witness to Jesus Christ and all his teachings', in 'every sphere of society' and 'in the realm of ideas'.[22] The GDN gathered (Asian) regional educators for the Far East Asia Diaspora Educators Consultation held in Manila in August 2011 to continue the work of LDLT in nurturing networks of kingdom collaborations.

Diaspora missiology is gaining ground in academic and training institutions. In the winter of 2011, the Jaffray Centre for Global Initiatives at Ambrose University College (Calgary, Canada) introduced its diaspora missiology specialism and a series of diaspora courses offered at the college and seminary levels. In the spring of 2012, the Ukrainian Evangelical Theological Seminary launched the Eurasian Diaspora Study Centre; this was followed in the summer of 2011 with Alliance Graduate School in Manila unveiling its Institute of Diaspora Missiology. Finally, it ought to be recognized that there is an increasing number of evangelical students in doctoral programs of various seminaries who are writing diaspora-related dissertations. Their research and writing will be major contributions to the growing body of diaspora missiology literature.

The GDN Advisory Board convened again in Toronto on 2-5 July 2012. Deliberations included shaping the Lausanne diasporas agenda for the next three years, including the plotting of more regional educators consultations and organizing the Global Diaspora Forum in Manila in March 2015.

Kinetic Mission Models: Missiological Implications from Cape Town to Beyond

Missiologists and mission practitioners must admit that most current mission strategies are land-specific and geographically focused. Mission educators and practitioners must recognize that the world is becoming increasingly 'borderless', and that new non-spatial and moving or kinetic mission models are needed to effectively reach the millions of scattered peoples wherever they are.

In his paper, 'Diaspora Missiology', Enoch Wan discusses the four elements of 'traditional missiology vis-à-vis diaspora missiology', including perspectives and paradigms. Wan claims that the perspective of traditional missiology is:

> geographically divided, and its current paradigm is still based on Ralph Winter's ethnic blocks and accessibility to the Gospel [while] the perspective

[21] The Global Diaspora Forum was officially announced during the Lausanne Leadership Biennial Meeting in Boston, Massachusetts, in June 2011.

[22] From the Lausanne Movement, cited on the GDN's official website: www.globaldiaspora.org/.

> of diaspora missiology is non-spatial, 'borderless' or transnational and global, and its paradigm involves the twenty-first century reality of 'viewing and following God's way of providentially moving people spatially and spiritually.[23]

It is noteworthy to quote Winter's 2004 back cover endorsement of the book *Scattered*: '[Diaspora missiology] may well be the most important undigested reality in missions thinking today. We simply have not caught up with the fact that most of the world's people can no longer be defined geographically'. Indeed, there are some in the evangelical community who are still working hard to digest this reality.

Understandably, it is difficult to adjust one's thinking from the traditional linear mission paradigm of 'going from here to there', and 'foreign' versus 'local'. However, the GDN is invested in the truth espoused by diaspora missiology – the priority of the gospel is that *every person* outside of the kingdom (on land and on sea) and now the church has the ability and resources to reach many of these people due to increased accessibility as international migration populations.

Diaspora missiology promotes kinetic mission models, targeting moving people wherever they are and supplementing traditional missions by employing resources already in place. To accomplish this, diaspora missiology suggests strategically training diaspora Christians already on location or in preparation for deployment, both at formal and non-formal levels (not just career missionaries), with the potential of becoming a large mission force with dynamic mobility. Finally, diaspora missiology-based initiatives would be sustained by kingdom collaborations and extended networks of like-minded individuals and organizations giving them maximum accessibility.

Some question what diaspora missiology looks like practically. There are many examples of diaspora missions as evidenced by the growing body of literature, including anecdotal reports of the effects of migrant Christian workers.[24] It is true that many Christians start churches wherever they go. It is not only theologically-trained, mission-deployed missionaries who are starting these congregations, but also ordinary Christian workers who are naturally living out their faith.

Furthermore, expatriate congregations are reaching nationals of their host nations, thereby also impacting communities with the Christian message. In Canada, for example, Christian Sudanese refugees are taking evangelism and discipleship training to reach out to their Canadian neighbors.[25] In Japan, Filipino ex-nightclub workers who are now followers

---

[23] Enoch Wan, 'Diaspora Missiology', 6.

[24] See Pantoja, Tira, and Wan, *Scattered*, and Kim and Ma, *Korean Diaspora and Christian Mission*, for other examples.

[25] New Life Training Course was conducted from 14-15 June, 2010, with a Sudanese community in Brooks Alberta as reported in the *Enroute with the Spring 2010* prayer letter.

of Jesus Christ are using the *Jesus* film to introduce Jesus Christ to their contacts in the Yakuza, and to the families of their Japanese husbands.[26] In Qatar, overseas Filipino workers and Korean businessmen have partnered with Nepalese construction workers to initiate Bible studies with their international workmates.[27]

There is a growing sense of organization in these movements. A notable example is the movement to plant churches on the ocean, or 'churches at sea', as thousands of Christian seafarers witness to their shipmates. Specifically, Operation Mobilization, Seafarers Christian Friends Society, and the Filipino International Network have signed a Memorandum of Agreement to form the Alliance of Churches at Sea, and partner to train 500 Filipino Seafarers every year as 'church planters' on the ocean.[28] This seizes the opportunity presented by an overwhelmingly large community of Filipino seafarers, approximately 350,000-strong.[29]

There are countless stories like these. These examples are 'diaspora missiology in action'. The reality of the global diasporas and the potential of diaspora missiology to motivate and mobilize Christians to reach to and through scattered peoples cannot be underestimated. Never before has the church had so many opportunities to reach people with the message of Jesus Christ.

While there are growing initiatives in diaspora missiology, there is currently no synchronized effort in the evangelical academic community to train kingdom workers for diaspora mission. If the phenomenon of diaspora were a major issue in the twenty-first century, then would it not be essential to include diaspora missiology in the curricula of evangelical academic institutions? It is crucial that academic institutions embrace this field and recruit students to research on the various facets of diaspora missions.

The Lausanne Movement desires that a concerted effort be made to teach diaspora mission and diaspora missiology both at formal and non-formal levels. The goal is to train future pastors, international workers (missionaries), and lay leaders. Intentional diaspora training would prepare

---

26 See Venus Hannah Galvez, 'Ministry to Filipino Entertainers and Japinos', in Pantoja, Tira, and Wan (eds), *Scattered*, 251-371, and Jocelyn Dino, 'Transformed by God through Diaspora Mission', *Evangelicals Today* 37:1 (2011), 30.

27 See Sadiri Joy Tira, 'Indigenous Diaspora Workers: From Himalayan Mountains to Arabian Sands', *Advancing Indigenous Missions Newsletter* 9:1 (Spring 2012), 2.

28 See Martin Otto, 'Filipino Churches at Sea', *Evangelicals Today* 37:1 (2011), 29.

29 The Philippine Information Agency publishes the Marivic A. Alcover report, 'MARINA spearheads celeb of Day of 350,000 Seafarers' (22 June 2012), available at www.pia.gov.ph/news/index.php?article=1161340271675 (accessed 30.6.12), stating that there are 350,000 Filipino seafarers. Given a conservative estimate that 7% of these figures are evangelical Christians, Christian Seafarers become a powerhouse for the cause of world missions on the seas. See Sadiri Tira, *Filipino Kingdom Workers: An Ethnographic Study in Diaspora Missiology* (Pasadena: William Carey International University Press, 2012), 71.

workers for *kinetic mission* in the 'borderless world'. The GDN is tasked to see this actualized.

Recommendations and Conclusion

Diaspora mission is expected to accelerate as academics and the practitioners implement diaspora missiology following Lausanne III en route to the Global Diaspora Forum in 2015. To ensure a strategic and synchronous advance, the evangelical church must continue to embrace *kairos* opportunities, enhance kingdom collaborations, and employ kinetic mission models. I have derived these mission models and motifs from the *Cape Town Commitment Call to Action* (see appendix II for complete text of the *Cape Town Commitment Call to Action IIC.5)*:

A. 'Church and mission leaders' should be encouraged to embrace *kairos* opportunities by 'recogniz[ing] and respond[ing] to the missional opportunities presented by global migration and diaspora communities, in strategic planning, and in focused training and resourcing of those called to work among them' (IIC.5.A).
B. 'Christians who are themselves part of diaspora communities' should be encouraged to 'discern the hand of God, even in circumstances they may not have chosen, and to seek whatever opportunities God provides for bearing witness to Christ in their host community and seeking its welfare. Where that host country includes Christian churches, immigrant and indigenous churches together,' must be urged 'to listen and learn from one another, and to initiate co-operative efforts to reach all sections of their nation with the gospel' (IIC.5.C). These activities reflect what this chapter has called *kingdom collaborations*.
C. 'Christians in host nations which have immigrant communities of other religious backgrounds' must be encouraged to 'bear counter-cultural witness to the love of Christ in deed and word, by obeying the extensive biblical commands to love the stranger, defend the cause of the foreigner, visit the prisoner, practise hospitality, build friendships, invite into our homes, and provide help and services' (IIC.5.B). Doing so would be to employ *kinetic mission models*.

Diaspora mission is a *kairos* opportunity. Lausanne continues its discussions on diaspora issues via 'diaspora' at the Lausanne Global Conversation.[30] The Lausanne Movement's embrace of diaspora missiology has stimulated its vision of 'the Whole Church to take the Whole Gospel to the Whole World', particularly to the diasporas, the scattered peoples.

---

[30] www.conversation.lausanne.org/en/home/diaspora.

Appendix I
The Seoul Declaration on Diaspora Missiology

Convening as mission leaders, mobilizers, educators, trainers, and kingdom workers in the diaspora at the Lausanne Diaspora Educators Consultation on 11-14 November 2009 in Seoul, Korea – in partnership with and an extension of the Lausanne Diaspora Strategy Consultation held in Manila, Philippines, on 4-8 May 2009,

We Acknowledge

A. That the sovereign work of the Father, Son, and Holy Spirit in the gathering and scattering of peoples across the earth is a central part of God's mission and redemptive purposes for the world.
B. That the church, which is the body of Christ, is the principal means through which God is at work in different ways around the globe. We honor the uniqueness, dignity, and beauty in each person and culture, celebrating the collaboration of the church with the broader society.
C. That 'diaspora missiology' has emerged as a biblical and strategic field of missiology and is defined as: a missiological framework for understanding and participating in God's redemptive mission among people living outside their place of origin.

We Affirm

A. That our missional focus and ministry integrates and co-operates with the mission and vision of the Lausanne movement for world evangelization as published in The Lausanne Covenant and The Manila Manifesto.
B. That although we draw from various disciplines, our understanding and practice of the mission of God must be informed by, integrated with, and conformed to biblical and theological foundations.

We Appeal

A. To the whole people of God in local churches and church movements, mission agencies, the academy, and the marketplace to mobilize, train, deploy, support, work together with, and empower 'diaspora kingdom workers' for the diaspora fields ripe for harvest.
B. To church and mission leaders to recognize and respond to opportunities in world evangelization presented by the realities of the global diaspora.
C. To mission leaders and educators to give strategic priority in the funding and training of personnel and to provide space for the development of 'diaspora missiology' in training systems and curricula.

D. To the Lord of the harvest to send forth laborers into the harvest and raise up worldwide intercession for an unprecedented move of the Holy Spirit so that the Whole Church takes the Whole Gospel to the Whole World.

LCWE Diaspora Educators Consultation 2009
Torch Trinity Graduate School of Theology
Seoul, South Korea
November 11-14, 2009

Appendix II
The Cape Town Commitment
Part II – For the World We Serve: The Cape Town Call to Action
IIC. Living the love of Christ among people of other faiths
5. Love reaches out to scattered peoples

People are on the move as never before. Migration is one of the great global realities of our era. It is estimated that 200 million people are living outside their countries of origin, voluntarily or involuntarily. The term 'diaspora' is used here to mean people who have relocated from their lands of birth for whatever reason. Vast numbers of people from many religious backgrounds, including Christians, live in diaspora conditions: economic migrants seeking work; internally-displaced peoples because of war or natural disaster; refugees and asylum seekers; victims of ethnic cleansing; people fleeing religious violence and persecution; famine sufferers – whether caused by drought, floods, or war; victims of rural poverty moving to cities. We are convinced that contemporary migrations are within the sovereign missional purpose of God, without ignoring the evil and suffering that can be involved. [Footnote 75. Genesis 50:20]

A. We encourage church and mission leaders to recognize and respond to the missional opportunities presented by global migration and diaspora communities, in strategic planning, and in focused training and resourcing of those called to work among them.

B. We encourage Christians in host nations which have immigrant communities of other religious backgrounds to bear counter-cultural witness to the love of Christ in deed and word, by obeying the extensive biblical commands to love the stranger, defend the cause of the foreigner, visit the prisoner, practise hospitality, build friendships, invite into our homes, and provide help and services. [Footnote 76 – Leviticus 19:33-34; Deuteronomy 24:17; Ruth 2; Job 29:16; Matthew 25:35-36; Luke 10:25-37; 14:12-14; Romans 12:13; Hebrews 13:2-3; 1 Peter 4:9]

C. We encourage Christians who are themselves part of diaspora communities to discern the hand of God, even in circumstances they may not have chosen, and to seek whatever opportunities God provides for bearing witness to Christ in their host community and seeking its welfare. [Footnote 77 – Jeremiah 29:7] Where that host country includes Christian churches, we urge immigrant and indigenous churches together to listen and learn from one another, and to initiate co-operative efforts to reach all sections of their nation with the gospel.

Diaspora Mission and Bible Translation

S. Hun Kim

Change in World Mission Caused by Diaspora

Due to the explosive growth of the global church since the middle of the twentieth century, the nature of world mission is being changed. In addition, the acceleration of the global diasporas since the postcolonical era of the 1960s has become one of the most important factors related to world mission.[1] Therefore, it can be said that mission now is not 'going there from here', but is 'from everywhere to everywhere'; i.e., mission is 'at our doorstep'.

Bible translation[2] has historically been done by missionaries with linguistic knowledge of the language group in need of scriptural translation. Traditionally, Bible translation has been regarded as a part of frontier mission. A majority of Bible translations have been prioritized and completed for 'unreached and unwritten people groups' in mission fields.

However, at the turn of the twenty-first century, the number of diasporas from non-Western to Western countries has significantly increased, involving migrant workers, asylum seekers, refugees, international students, trafficked people, permanent immigrants, etc. *The Cambridge Survey of World Migration* has classified six patterns of migration based on various push and pull factors: (1) internal vs intercontinental/international migration, (2) forced vs free migration, (3) settler vs labor migration, (4) temporary vs permanent migration, (5) illegal vs legal migration, and (6) planned vs flight/refugee migration.[3]

Of the various diasporic migrants, asylum seekers or refugees have been identified as strategically significant for 'frontier mission' because of their unique situations. Most are of ethnic groups coming from regions generally inaccessible to Christian workers. Due to persecution, civil war, force

---

[1] In this paper, 'diaspora' is used as the same meaning as 'migration', which includes all sorts of people on the move. To Tereso C. Casiño, 'diaspora' refers to the overarching structure under which all forms of mobility take place, while migration serves as a tool to account for a diasporic process or condition; see Tereso C. Casiño, 'Why People Move: A Prolegomenon to Diaspora Missiology', in S. Hun Kim and Wonsuk Ma (eds), *Korean Diaspora and Christian Mission* (Oxford: Regnum, 2011), 45.

[2] 'Bible translation' is defined here as a translation work for vernacular languages without Bibles. Recent statistics indicate that 1,919 languages and 179 million people remain without the Bible in their own language – see www.wycliffe.net/resources/scriptureaccessstatistics/tabid/99/Default.aspx (accessed 29.4.14).

[3] See Robin Cohen, *Cambridge Survey of World Migration* (1995; reprint, Cambridge: Cambridge University Press, 2010).

majeure, and political instability, they are forced out of their homeland and moved to refugee camps. Many end up in cities of receiving countries, especially in Europe and North America.

I began my assignment with Wycliffe Global Alliance (formerly Wycliffe Bible Translators) in Europe in 1992. Since then, I have observed the landscape of the European populations change drastically. For example, almost half of London's population is of foreign origin and more than 300 languages are spoken in the city.[4] In this context, one could imagine Bible translation for specific ethnic groups being undertaken in the heart of London. In the same vein, Europe is a unique place for Bible translation since a huge influx of diaspora from Africa and other parts of the world began in the 1960s and have continued. In fact, even on the European continent there have been several Bible translation projects for ethnic language groups before and after the collapse of the former Soviet Union.

My translation task, hereafter called the 'Sura' language project,[5] was implemented in Europe. In 1990, several clusters of the Sura language group were scattered throughout Europe. They were found in London, Oslo, and Copenhagen, and some became dedicated Christians.

Here I discuss two similar cases of Bible translation in diaspora contexts: the Korean project in East Asia more than a century ago and the Sura language project. This brief study will enable us to explore the implications of diaspora mission and Bible translation.

Korean Bible Translation in the Early Stages of Protestantism in Korea

For Korean Bible translation, three different methods have been used.[6] First, the four Gospels and Acts were printed in Korean in Yokohama, Japan (1884); the New Testament in Fengtian, China (1897); and the complete Bible in Yokohama (1911). Based on current knowledge of Korean ethnic Bible translation in China, it is safe to assume that the 1911 Korean translation was done only for ethnic Koreans in China, not for Koreans in the Korean Peninsula. There were many other ethnic translations (e.g., into Manchurian, Mongolian, Xinjing, Kazakhstan Turkish, and Tibetan languages) in China during this period of time.

Second, another Korean Bible was translated by Scottish missionaries John Ross and John McIntyre and their Korean language helpers from the

---

[4] See www.en.wikipedia.org/wiki/London (accessed 25.6.12).

[5] For security reasons, I use a pseudonym for this language project. 'Sura' is one of the major language groups in Iran.

[6] Material in this section derives from Wang Weifan, 'The Bible in Chinese', *Nanjing Theological Review* 14/15 (1991), 75-90, and Keith Pratt and Richard Rutt, *Korea: A Historical and Cultural Dictionary* (London: Curzon, 1999); see also Timothy S. Lee, *Born Again: Evangelicalism in Korea* (Honolulu: University of Hawai'i Press, 2010), 10-11.

Korean Peninsula. When they began this process of translation, Ross, a cultural historian and linguist working in Manchuria, made contact with Korean diaspora merchants in order to learn the Korean language. The Korean merchants travelled between Korea and China, and traded herbal medicines. Ross met Lee Ungchan, who agreed to collaborate with him on a variety of translation works. Ross, with the help of Lee, published *The Korean Primer* (1877), *The Korean Language* (1878), *Yesu sunggyo mundap* (*Bible Catechism*, 1881), and *Yesu sunggyo yoryung* (*Outline of the New Testament*, 1881). In 1877, Ross and Lee began translating the New Testament, later aided by Mclntyre and several other Koreans, including Seo Sangyun and Paek Hongjun.

In 1882, Ross published the Gospels of Luke and John, the first Gospels to be translated into *Hangul (Korean).* Then, in 1887 under the initiative of Ross, the first complete translation of the New Testament was published in Korean. Once published, these translated materials were smuggled into Korea and used by a wide indigenous audience. It is reported that Sangyun, a team member of the translation team, risked his own life by carrying over 15,000 copies of the Korean Bible in his backpack over the border during a three-year period.[7] Many Koreans became Christians by reading the distributed Bibles even before foreign missionaries arrived in Korea. These developments laid the foundation for the early missionary movement in Korea, and the Korean Bible enabled the Korean church to grow rapidly as an indigenous church.

Third, the Gospel of Mark was independently translated by Lee Sujung, a Korean sojourning in Japan, and published in Japan. Copies of this translation were later taken to Korea by Horace G. Underwood and Henry Appenzeller, two North American missionaries. Underwood once reported to his mission board at home: 'Instead of sowing seed, we are already harvesting what has been already sown.'[8]

Bible Translation with Diaspora: The Case of the Sura Language

Displaced Translation as a Strategic Mission in Europe with Iranian Refugees

The Sura project was initiated by diaspora Christians from Iran in 1990. A cluster of diaspora Christians in the United Kingdom gathered together with Wycliffe Bible Translators in Cyprus and discussed the possibility of translation work for the Sura language in Iran. One dedicated Sura Christian volunteered to commit himself to this project. Our team set up the

[7] Jung Min-Young, 'Diaspora and Timely Hit: Towards a Diaspora Missiology', in Kim and Ma, *Korean Diaspora and Christian Mission*, 64.

[8] Jung Min-Young, 'Diaspora and Timely Hit', 64.

translation work (known as 'displaced translation') in the United Kingdom as a base because a Sura diaspora community existed in London to check and review the translated materials. (Note: Displaced translation refers to translation work that is undertaken in the context of diaspora due to hostile factors inhibiting Bible translation in the homeland, particularly for ethnic language groups in countries to which missionaries and Bible translators have restricted access.) Further, the wider Iranian Christian community in the region was ready to support the project.

When considering the escalated trends of the worldwide diaspora, there are many unreached people groups residing in Europe.[9] It is assumed that displaced translation strategy, working with people groups who resettle in free societies, could be an effective alternative in Bible translation mission. Otherwise, Christians seldom have contact with people in these hard-to-access areas. Evangelicals believe this diaspora phenomenon to be a 'divine conspiracy' through which God plans to redeem every nation in the world through scattered peoples.

Holistic Approach[10] Through the Sura Translation Process

I joined the project in 1994 while waiting for the new language assignment in the United Kingdom after finishing a linguistic training session with Summer Institute of Linguistics (SIL) in Singapore.[11] After several trips and long-term stays in the Republic of Azerbaijan (the former part of the Commonwealth of Independent States) and Istanbul, Turkey (where I gained some fluency in a dialect of the Sura language), in 1997 I moved to the southwestern part of London and began translation work with a native speaker.

'F', a Muslim-background believer from Iran, had already established himself as an important native translator through a 1994 production of the Gospel of John in audio format for the Sura. He and I translated the New Testament with the help of Sura community members in London, Oslo, and Copenhagen. We completed the first draft of the entire New Testament in 2003, and it was published in book format in 2009. Meanwhile, we

---

[9] 'Unreached people group' is a missiological term used by evangelicals referring to an ethnic group without an indigenous, self-propagating Christian church movement. Any ethnic or ethnolinguistic population without enough Christians to evangelize the rest of the nation is an unreached people group. The term is sometimes applied to ethnic groups with less than 2% evangelicals.

[10] 'Holistic' mission theory presumes that the church's mission is intrinsically 'integral': word and deed work together to complement each other; see C.R. Padilla, 'Holistic Mission', in John Corrie (ed), *Dictionary of Mission Theology: Evangelical Foundations* (Nottingham, UK, and Downers Grove, Ill.: InterVarsity Press, 2007), 157-62.

[11] SIL is a partner organization of Wycliffe Global Alliance that supports technical skills needed for the Bible translation, including linguistics.

developed a variety of media to enhance the accessibility of the translation on a website, with some books like the four Gospels in audio format. This site is designed in particular for diaspora Sura people outside Iran, although Sura people in Iran who are able to access the Internet can also benefit from it.

I served as a project co-ordinator and exegetical expert responsible for checking the accuracy of the translated materials based on the original text. Besides these routine processes, I also came to see that my relationships with the native translator and helpers invited other more conventional missionary activities as well. The life situation of Sura diaspora people in Europe was vulnerable and unstable, as well as financially stricken. In fact, I could empathize with them as a 'diaspora person' from a foreign land in the Far East. While building friendships with them, their real life concerns (e.g., jobs, Christian communities, family issues, legal status, etc.) became my own. In some cases, I painted and wallpapered the house of a language helper prior to resuming the translation work.

This kind of 'holistic approach' is central to the Christian mission. Mission is a holistic process that invites an incarnational lifestyle for those engaged with it.

Ultimate Partnership for the Kingdom of God

Bible translation in diasporic contexts poses challenges to many aspects of mission activity. One of the overriding concerns for the Sura project was the issue of partnership among stakeholders. In the early stages of the translation, I was involved with the northern dialect team of the Sura project in the Republic of Azerbaijan in order to get mutual co-operation between two similar dialect projects.

For that task, a partnership emerged between with the United Bible Society, the Institute of Bible Translation, the Kitab Sirketi (Azerbaijan Bible Society), Summer Institute of Linguistics (SIL), local churches in Baku, Azerbaijan, and an Iranian mission organization in the United Kingdom. In spite of several disagreements regarding policies and translation procedures among these organizations, in 2010 the whole Bible in the northern dialect of the Sura language was published.

Similarly, the Sura project also faced partnership issues among several organizations that were involved in the early 1990s in the United Kingdom, including SIL. To accomplish this task, however, every partner and person had to learn to share the burdens equally, according to his or her job description. For example, the indigenous Iranian mission organization took care of many issues on copyright and local church partnerships for the translation project, while SIL provided technical support and financial aids. In the real translation process, there were mother-tongue translators, several local reviewers, computer assistants, and so on. Some diaspora communities (e.g., Korean churches) in London supported the process with prayer and finances. One Baptist church in New Malden, Surrey, adopted this project as a part of their church mission. Through the synergized and voluntary efforts by each partner, the Sura New Testament was published in 2009. A Sura translation of the whole Bible is planned for 2012.

Mission is no longer the property of a single institution, organization, or mega-church with power and money. Mission emerges by the power of the Holy Spirit and with the ultimate co-operation of the whole body of Christ. Diaspora mission endeavors can facilitate the notion of mission-as-kingdom-partnership in the twenty-first century.

Missional Implications of Bible Translation and Diaspora Mission

The global diaspora has generated a 'theology of diaspora' and consequently, a 'diaspora missiology'. The Third Lausanne Congress in Cape Town in 2010 was a very encouraging occasion for the global diaspora mission movement. In fact, the issue of diaspora and its missiology were featured as one of the predominant themes of the whole program and acclaimed as a new paradigm for the next era of world evangelization. As Tereso C. Casiño notes:

> Missionary efforts among people on the move are biblically valid, theologically consistent, and historically grounded. Under the redemptive plan of God, people move because the migratory or diasporic flows and transitions provide them with opportunities to encounter more of God's redemptive acts.[12]

In order to fulfill God's redemptive plan for people on the move, Bible translation could be more effectively and strategically utilized if the 'displaced project' is mobilized in diasporic contexts for unreached and unwritten people groups. The following are missional implications of such an approach.

First, ethnic Bible translation in diasporic contexts may be an effective mission strategy for people groups who are not yet evangelized but live in limited access areas. As seen in the case of the Korean Bible translation, Koreans gained access to the Bible with the help of Korean diaspora in China and Japan, and they grew as self-feeding Christians by reading scripture on their own in the beginning.

Second, *ethnic Bible translation could be further mobilized in diasporic contexts*. Traditionally, Bible translation has happened in the physical locales in which ethnic languages were spoken and in many cases, for difficult-to-access and least-reached people groups, in frontier areas. However, considering a large scale of migration and mobility in this century, Bible translators now have more possibilities of implementing 'ethnic Bible translation' in the diasporic context, as seen in the Sura project executed in Europe.

---

[12] Casiño, 'Why People Move', 57.

Third, *ethnic Bible translation in the diasporic context may be a good example of the holistic approach to Christian mission.* The goal of translation is not only to produce a vernacular Bible in a certain language, but also to reproduce disciples of Jesus in the course of the translation work. Eventually, everyone who is involved in the translation has to grow together as the body of Christ. In the context of diaspora, ethnic people are perhaps more naturally dependent on others due to isolation, fear, insecurity, bereavement, trauma, and so on.

This vulnerable situation provides more opportunities for Christian workers to access them with practical aids, as well as spiritual ones. In this sense, Bible translation is an effective tool for engaging a 'holistic approach', as it is not only a long-term process of translation, but also a potentially life-transforming journey for one language community.

Fourth, *ethnic Bible translation in the diasporic context provides a symbiotic partnership for the Kingdom of God among participants.* As illustrated with the Sura project, Bible translation in its nature is not a task that an individual can accomplish. Rather, it is a collective product of many Christian bodies, under the supervision of the Holy Spirit. Therefore, ultimate partnership in translation should comprise local and other ethnic churches, Christian individuals, and interdenominational resources available in the region where translating work is executed. Consequently, diaspora contexts require new kingdom partnerships in mission.

Last, *ethnic and 'cluster' Bible translation will continue to play a key role for diaspora mission in multiethnic societies.* For example, in Europe a number of ethnic and social clusters have increased, and these clusters tend to characterize their own subcultures and communities. Recently, it was reported that a street kid's Bible in Amsterdam was published since many street kids were not able to understand the contemporary Dutch Bible.[13] Other examples of the 'cluster' Bible translations are Bike Bible and Metal Bible.[14] It will be essential to provide relevant materials like these for the people or cluster groups to be evangelized in diasporic mission environments.

Conclusion

The current century features unprecedented human migration from everywhere to everywhere. This phenomenon demands adjustments from Christian mission workers. Diaspora contexts involve developing new avenues of mission for those committed to participating in God's redemptive plan for all nations.

---

[13] See www.rnw.nl/english/article/bible-translated-dutch-slang (accessed 25 .6.12).

[14] The Bike Bible contains the whole New Testament and life stories of bikers, published by a group from the Christian Motor Cyclists Association and Bible for the Nations. The Metal Bible is for those who love hard rock and heavy metal music, published by Johannes Jonsson and Roul Akesson in Bible for the Nations.

The challenges of contemporary Bible translation for vernacular language groups invite reconsideration of conventional approaches and methodologies that have long been deployed. 'Displaced translation' or 'ethnic Bible translation' is one of the effectively strategic approaches for the unreached and unwritten vernacular language groups in the diasporic context. This approach has significant implications for 'holistic mission', 'discipleship' through the translation process, symbiotic 'kingdom partnership', and 'scripture in use'.

Diaspora Missions on Campuses: John R. Mott and a Centennial Overview of the International Student Ministry Movement in North America

Leiton Edward Chinn

International Student Ministry (ISM) As a Strategic Diaspora Mission

International students and scholars represent the diaspora category of those who voluntarily leave their homeland to reside in a host country, usually temporarily, for educational and professional advancement. Ministry among international students is highly strategic for numerous reasons, most obvious is that tertiary students will be the future leaders of the world and influence every sphere of society. The United States Department of State's Bureau of Educational and Cultural Affairs lists hundreds of world leaders today who studied in the USA. Many church and mission leaders have become Christians and were discipled while studying in another country and have returned home to contribute to the expansion of God's kingdom in their homeland and region.

International students are a global mission field already present on our campuses, in our communities, and often in our churches. International Student Ministry (ISM) is a classic example of 'glocal' missions, of global mission locally, and provides the opportunity for world missions at home and in our homes. International students who come from a context that is resistant to or ignorant about Christianity may appreciate the freedom to explore the Bible and learn of Jesus Christ. All members of a Christian fellowship or church, from children to grandparents, can engage in mutual cross-cultural friendship and extend sincere hospitality. Equally important are the reciprocal benefits of intercultural learning from international scholars who may also provide missional perspectives about their homeland and culture.

A tremendous benefit of ISM is the amount of funding not having to be spent to send missionaries to the multitude of nations represented by a group of international students who may be part of an outreach among foreign-born scholars. Pastors of local congregations with an ISM can attest that it is one of the best values for missions because of the extremely low costs associated with it and the tremendous potential for global impact. Additionally, ISM transcends personal mission involvement beyond prayer, financial support, and encouragement of missionaries, to actually being a missionary without leaving home. This opportunity has blessed many who felt called to traditional 'overseas' missionary service earlier in life, but did not go abroad.

Another strategic aspect of ISM is that Christian students who return home may serve as ready-made kingdom ambassadors to their own people, either as marketplace witnesses or as professional Christian workers. Returnees can also provide valuable networking connections and advocacy for further mission partnership endeavors in their homeland on behalf of Christians in their former host-country of study, or elsewhere. The large majority of Christians will not be called to relocate to another country to engage in Christian service, but will remain at home. Nevertheless, remaining at home provides the opportunity to be involved in reaching the world that God brings to nearby campuses.

Each year, more and more international students are arriving on more campuses around the world. In 2013, there were almost 4.3 million tertiary students studying in another country; since 2000, the number of international students increased by an average annual growth rate of almost 7%.[1] A projected growth of the international student population for 2025 is 7.2 million.[2]

As the number of globally mobile students increases, so do the opportunities to be involved in ISM. As Jesus told the disciples to lift their eyes to the fields ripe for harvest, so too are the multinational fields on our campuses ready for cultivation. But our churches, ministries, and laborers for the harvest must have eyes to see international students, open hearts and a hospitable spirit to welcome them with genuine friendship, a willingness to pray for and serve them, courage to appropriately share the love of God with them, and a desire to encourage them to be transformative agents for the welfare of their nations and the world, by and with the grace of God.

John R. Mott: Unrecognized Visionary and Founder of the ISM Movement

John Raleigh Mott's stellar leadership role as Chair of the famous 1910 World Missionary Conference (WMC) in Edinburgh, Scotland, has been recounted recently in association with the four global mission events commemorating the centennial of Edinburgh 1910: Edinburgh 2010, Tokyo 2010, Cape Town 2010, and Boston 2010.

But church historians and students of mission also remember the additional missional leadership achievements of Mott that are listed in his biography that was written when he received the 1946 Nobel Peace Prize. These achievements included serving as the first Chairman of the Student

---

[1] OECD, *Education at a Glance 2013: Highlights* (Location: OECD Publishing, 2013), 3.

[2] A. Bohm, D. Davis, D. Meares, and B. Pearce, *Global Student Mobility 2025* (Media Briefing by IDP Education Australia Limited, September 2002), 3.

Volunteer Movement for Foreign Missions (SVMFM); Chair of the International Missionary Council; the first General Secretary of the World's Student Christian Federation (WSCF); the National Secretary of the Intercollegiate YMCA; and several other leadership positions.[3]

What is not generally known by most mission enthusiasts is that Mott was the visionary who launched the first national Christian service ministry for international students, called the Committee on Friendly Relations Among Foreign Students (CFR). Mott undertook creating the CFR in April 1911, a month after returning from extensive evangelistic meetings in Europe and Egypt, and in the midst of very heavy demands to chair the Continuation Committee of the 1910 WMC. This was in addition to other leadership roles.

It should be noted that Mott's calling and passion was to promote the expansion of mission mobilization through student movements in the USA and globally, primarily through his long-term leadership with the SVMFM, WSCF, and YMCA and its International Committee. His resolute focus was on 'Carrying the Gospel to All the Non-Christian World' – the title of his keynote address and of the Report of Commission I, which he chaired, of the 1910 WMC.[4] Mott's gaze was outward from America to the other nations, and he traveled extensively overseas to raise up indigenous student missionary endeavors.

So how did it come about that Mott would even consider starting a new ministry or service in the USA – and to such a minority population of students? The establishment of the CFR was clearly the intervention of the sovereign and providential act of God that led Mott to adapt to the American context some preliminary ideas he had in 1907 to raise funds to establish Christian hostels in Japan which would not only serve Japanese students, but also those from China, Korea, and other Asian nations at the Imperial University in Tokyo.[5]

The seed idea of raising funds to benefit international students was planted in Mott's mind. In 1909, he helped to organize a service agency for Chinese students in the USA and provided funds from the Foreign Division of the YMCA. This very likely captured the thinking and interest of Mott, and he set out to spread the message of the need to serve the increasing number of foreign students in the USA.[6]

---

[3] Frederick W. Haberman (ed), *Nobel Lectures, Peace 1926-1950* (Amsterdam: Elsevier Publishing Company, 1972).

[4] World Missionary Conference 1910, *Report of Commission I, Carrying the Gospel to All the Non-Christian World* (Edinburgh and London: Oliphant, Anderson, and Ferrier; New York, Chicago, and Toronto: Fleming H Revell, 1910).

[5] Basil Mathews, *John R. Mott: World Citizen* (New York and London: Harper and Brothers, 1934), 412.

[6] Mary A. Thompson (ed), *Unofficial Ambassadors: The Story of International Student Service* (New York: International Student Service, 1982), 22.

So in April 1911, while Mott was in a New York meeting with Cleveland Dodge, Chairman of the International Committee of the YMCA, he spoke of the need to raise funds to help foreign students. Dodge offered to introduce Mott to Andrew Carnegie that afternoon; as a result, Carnegie made a gift of $10,000 and challenged Dodge to match it, which he did. On the way back to Dodge's home, they met a friend who also committed $10,000. The following night Mott was sharing the story of God's provision in a committee meeting, and a member contributed another $8,000. Thus, in two days nearly all the funds necessary to start the ministry among international students was raised, and the CFR was birthed.[7] Supplemental support came from the YMCA's International Committee.

Within a few years the CRF produced a handbook for foreign students, which listed a variety of foundational services that remain as essential good works of ISM a century later.[8] Besides the actual services rendered by the volunteers of the CFR (many of whom were recruited from churches via local YMCAs), the CFR motivated and substantially assisted other partners in the cause of caring for foreign students, with the result being the eventual establishment of numerous organizations and agencies.[9] Two such organizations indebted to the CFR are the NAFSA: Association of International Educators and the Institute of International Education.[10] After five decades, its magnanimous services and secondment of personnel had laid broad foundations for the care and service of scholars from abroad and the healthy beginnings of the ISM movement in North America. The CFR changed its name to International Student Service (ISS) in 1965.

Before continuing with a brief overview of the development of the ISM movement in North America, it would be insightful to get a glimpse of the growing vision Mott had for ministry among international students. A cursory review of some of the publications by and about him, as well as published records of some of his speeches and papers, reveal an increasing awareness of the gradually growing presence and needs of foreign-born scholars prior to and after the advent of the twentieth century. There were few foreign-born students before 1900 and Mott's references to them were scarce.

As the numbers increased in the new century, so did Mott's recognition of the new challenge and mission opportunity. His observations and comments about international students were found in at least 15

---

[7] Thompson, *Unofficial Ambassadors,* 23.

[8] Charles D. Hurrey, *Educational Guide: A Handbook of Useful Information for Foreign Students in the United States of America* (New York: The Committee on Friendly Relations Among Foreign Students, 1917), 7.

[9] Thompson, *Unofficial Ambassadors*, 14, 32, and 89-112.

[10] NAFSA was originally called National Association of Foreign Student Advisors. Later it was changed to the National Association of Foreign Student Affairs. It currently goes simply by NAFSA: Association of International Educators.

publications. The space limitations of this case study do not allow an exhaustive chronological demonstration of Mott's notice of and subsequent response to the expanding reality of the world's future leadership being educated in other countries. But here are a few examples of excerpts about or by Mott related to foreign students:

> It was undoubtedly out of this conference (Dwight L. Moody's summer conference in 1886 at Mt. Hermon/Northfield, MA) that the idea of a student volunteer organization to assist foreign students in the United States grew in the mind of Mott...But it was not to come to fruition for more than 25 years.[11]
>
> Shortly after the formation of the World's Student Christian Federation in Sweden in 1895, during which Mott was named general secretary, he wrote that the second goal of the Federation was 'to grapple successfully with the problem of the spiritual welfare of the large number of foreign students in different countries'.[12]
>
> After two previous trips to China had seen minimal response to his evangelistic messages in 1896 and 1901, Mott was surprised at the large turnout of students in Hong Kong in 1906. He noticed that on the platform of the largest theater in the country, there were 50 leading officials of the province, and that most had returned from studies in Japan or America. On a trip to Japan around the same time, he found that nearly all the professors at the Imperial University in Tokyo had attained degrees in Europe or America.[13]
>
> In 1907, Mott wrote, 'I have no hesitation in saying that I consider that this first generation of modern Chinese students (in America) presents to us the greatest opportunity that I have ever known. This first wave...will furnish a vastly disproportionate share of the leaders of the New China. I maintain that nothing could be more important than Christianizing these men...I am haunted with solicitude lest we miss this absolutely unique opportunity.[14]
>
> In an address given at the Student Volunteer Missionary Union Conference in Liverpool, England, in 1908, Mott said, 'Our hearts have been touched by the appeal of Dr. Datta this evening concerning Indian students in Britain. But possibly we have not been aware of the...scores of Indian students in Tokyo...nearly 700 Korean students there, also not a few students from the Philippines and Siam. There have been as many as 15,000 students there at one time from China. Without doubt Japan is leading the Orient educationally'.[15]

---

[11] Thompson, *Unofficial Ambassadors*, 18.

[12] Robert C. Mackie and Others, *Layman Extraordinary: John R. Mott 1865-1955* (New York: Associated Press, 1965), 30.

[13] John R. Mott, *The Present World Situation* (New York: Student Volunteer Movement for Foreign Missions, 1914), 45-49.

[14] Mathews, *John R. Mott*, 416.

[15] *Addresses and Papers of John R. Mott* (6 vols.; New York: Associated Press, 1946), I.329; hereafter *APJRM.*

> Mott's chairman's Report at the Sixth International Convention of the SVMFM in Rochester, New York, in 1910 cites, 'One opportunity, which comes to most of us but which many have overlooked, is that presented by the large and increasing number of students among us from Oriental and other non-Christian lands...These foreign students are in position to do more than some missionaries to extend the domain of Christ among their countrymen'.[16]

> The detrimental effects of negative experiences by international students are mentioned in Mott's brief referral to foreign students in his chairman's Report of Commission I for the 1910 WMC: 'On their return, some of them as teachers, editors, and Government officials constitute a great barrier to the spread of the Gospel. This has been notably true of many Chinese and Korean students on their return from Japan'.[17]

> In February of 1911, two months before organizing the CRF, Mott was on an extensive evangelistic tour of Europe, and declined an invitation to meet Germany's Kaiser at the Palace. Instead, he chose to 'give this time to the universities of Switzerland...the fact that more than half of them [students] were from Eastern Europe – Bulgarians, Serbs, Romanians, Czechs, and above all Russians...with a dominant misconception that Christianity must everywhere be synonymous with government oppression...a matter of forms and ceremonies and superstitions'.[18]

> At the Seventh International Convention of the SVMFM meeting in Kansas City in 1914, chairman Mott reminded the delegates that international students in North America who 'consecrate their lives to Christ's cause could do far more to advance His Kingdom among their peers than an equal number of foreign missionaries' and that relating with foreign students would 'make more vivid and real to us the meaning of the missionary enterprise'.[19]

> Also in 1914, Mott penned a comprehensive rationale for ISM and included, 'The best agency for dealing with foreign students is that of the Christian Student Movements...efficient and fruitful as has been their work in the past, the time has come when these organizations should plan more comprehensively to influence for Christ this important class of students...Possibly no one thing can be done by Christian forces which will do more to accomplish our great end'.[20]

Further commendations for involvement in ISM are found in Mott's reports and addresses at the SVMFM Conventions in Des Moines, Iowa (1920); Detroit, Michigan (1928); and Indianapolis, Indiana (1936).

---

[16] *APJRM,* I.139.

[17] World Missionary Conference 1910, 24.

[18] Mathews, *John R. Mott,* 165.

[19] *APJRM,* I.166.

[20] Mott, *The Present World Situation*, 140-46.

Post-World War II Expansion of Nationwide ISMs in North America

After the launch of the CFR in 1911, there was about a forty-year hiatus in the development of other national ISMs. The lone exception was the initial encouragement in 1944 by Inter-Varsity USA for its staff to include international students in their campus outreach. In addition to its General Secretary, C. Stacey Woods (who was himself a former international student from Australia at Wheaton College), two of the early Intervarsity USA leadership with overseas experience and mission responsibility, Christy Wilson and David Adeney, sought to increase the level of awareness for ISM. Adeney became the first Director for ISM for Inter-Varsity USA in 1952, and by the following year was engaging in partnerships with CFR.[21] Inter-Varsity Canada began its ISM in 1952.

The next national ISM to form was International Students Inc (ISI) in 1953 under the leadership of Bob Finley, who was forced out of missionary service in China after the Communist revolution in 1949. Finley noticed that many of the revolutionary Chinese leaders had become communist while studying abroad.[22]

The decadal growth and starting years of other national ISMs are summarized as follows:

Period	International Student Ministries and Their Starting Years
1950s	Southern Baptist Convention (1955)
1960s	Ambassadors for Christ with focus on Chinese (1963); Campus Crusade for Christ (now called Bridges International) (1968; restart 1983)
1970s	Navigators (1977); International Friendship Ministries (1979)
1980s	Association of Christians Ministering among Internationals (1981); Reformed University Fellowship-International (PCA denomination) (1983); International Student Ministries Canada (1984); China Outreach Ministries (1988); Chi Alpha (Assemblies of God) (1989)
1990s	Horizons International (1990); Japanese Christian Fellowship Network specializing in Returnee ministry (1990); InterFACE Ministries (1991); ISM Inc (Lutheran Church Missouri Synod) (1996)

In 1911, when Mott started the Committee on Friendly Relations among Foreign Students, there were only 4,856 foreign students in the USA.[23] A

[21] Stacey Bieler, 'The History of International Student Ministry in Inter-Varsity USA 1944-81' (unpublished paper, 2011), available at Resources on website of the Association of Christians Ministering among Internationals: www.acmi-net.net.

[22] Bob Finley, *Reformation in Foreign Missions* ([Charlottesville,] Virginia: Christian Aid Mission, 2010), 34.

[23] 'Quick Studies: A Brief History of the 20th Century and NAFSA, Selected Milestones Along the Way to the Golden Anniversary', *International Educator* 8:2-3 (Spring, 1998), 16.

century later in 2011, there were 723,277 international students in the USA.[24] The two largest groups of students were Chinese with 160,000, and Indians with nearly 104,000.

Among the four leading destination countries receiving international students, Canada saw the biggest percentage gains, with enrollments increasing by 67% (from 52,650 in 2002 to 87,798 in 2009).[25] Depending upon the parameters used in classifying international students (including undergraduate and graduate students, English language students, and post-doctorate researchers, etc.), it is conceivable that there are over one million international students and scholars in North America in 2014. The opportunities for engaging in diaspora missions on North American campuses have never been as great as they are now. The question is, *will the church actually see them, and if so, how will the people of God respond?* A century ago, John R. Mott had his eyes fixed on the world, not only out there beyond the seas, but also right here where students from other nations were coming ashore and enrolling in local colleges and universities. He saw them and did what he could. May we do the same.

---

[24] Patricia Chow and Rajika Bhandari, 'Fast Facts', *Open Doors 2011: Report on International Educational Exchange* (New York and Washington DC: Institute of International Education, 2011).

[25] Rahul Choudaha and Li Chang, *Trends in International Student Mobility* (New York: World Education Services, 2012), 6.

The Forsaken One: The Trafficked Woman as a Template for the Church's Identity and Mission

Myrto Theocharous

Introduction

After beginning my involvement in anti-trafficking street work in 2004, I came face to face with the worst expressions of an unjust society. I watched before my very eyes the increasing enslavement and exploitation of the alien, the widow, and the orphan (categories which usually sum up the profile of the trafficked woman[1]) in the streets and in the brothels of central Athens, Greece. I observed the commercialization of the individual and the stripping away of human dignity in its most brutal forms.

Recently, photographs of a dozen prostitutes were published on the Greek police website (www.hellenicpolice.gr), most of them non-Greeks. These women had HIV and were accused of intentionally spreading the disease to unsuspecting citizens. The discussions around this event were heated. Some condemned the public humiliation of these women by the authorities, stigmatizing them and violating their medical confidentiality while letting the clients off the hook. It was the clients who had demanded unprotected sex with the girls and, consequently, put their own families in danger. Others congratulated the authorities for the measures they had taken to protect the health of the customers and their families from these prostitutes who mercilessly spread the virus.[2] Even among Christians, opinions were divided, something which brought to light that there are various ways of perceiving the prostitute.

While we could point to numerous things which are wrong with the way prostitution is handled in Greece and elsewhere, I would like to focus on the way we as Christians perceive the prostitute.

The most common is to see the prostitute as something unrelated to ourselves, which we must either condemn or to which we show charity. I would like to argue that the Bible encourages an *identification* of God's

---

[1] Although there are various forms of human trafficking and the victims vary in age and gender, my references are primarily focused in trafficking of women for sexual exploitation. For the different forms of trafficking, see United Nations Office on Drugs and Crime, 'Human Trafficking', n.p. 8 August 2012, www.unodc.org/unodc/en/human-trafficking/what-is-human-trafficking.html (accessed 18.6.12).

[2] See the report by Derek Gatopoulos, 'Greece Prostitutes Arrested, 17 HIV-positive Women in Brothels', n.p. 18 June 2012], www.huffingtonpost.com/2012/05/03/greece-prostitutes-hiv-arrests_n_1473864.html (accessed 18.6.12).

people with the prostitute as a prerequisite for a just missiological approach toward these women and human trafficking in general. Numerous times, scripture takes a category which is perceived as foreign or much 'below' the reader and paints him or her with the same colors in an attempt to encourage identification. Its purpose is to eliminate the 'otherness'. One example of this literary technique is found in the book of Hosea and its identification of Israel with the category of the prostitute. Other categories are the 'alien' and the 'slave', with which the Israelites are exhorted to identify in order to deal with them justly (e.g., Ex. 22:21; 23:9; Lev. 19:34; Deut. 10:19; 15:13-15; 16:11-12; 23:7). It appears that justice toward another as *other* is inadequate. Treating another one fairly presupposes some sort of elimination of *otherness*, with the grandest example being that of the incarnation. Christ's becoming fully human earns him the role of the righteous judge (John 5:22).

Before examining a particular text from the book of Isaiah, we must listen to the woman called 'the prostitute'. One must empty the term 'prostitute' of the stereotypical content it usually carries and take a look at the actual person, her dreams and desires. Jenny, a woman I saw for the first time in a basement brothel, sent me the following letter which is indeed a window into her soul:

> I lost my father when I was really young. He was my great love. Then I had a failed marriage. I was 14 years old. I stayed with him for a year but he would beat me continually. Fortunately, we did not have a child together so I left him and I had to survive on my own with no help from anyone. I was looking for love so I got into another relationship. I gave all of myself into that relationship, for many, many years, but they never wanted me, his family. So they finally threw me out. Now I found my true love. A man who cares about me and loves me. He promised me I won't have to do this job forever, just until I repay all his debts, then he'll marry me. He doesn't take all the money I earn from me. He lets me have some. My dream is to be married and have a house. I want a house to take care of and I love flowers. I want the house to be full of flowers and gardens.

What we see in Jenny's story is the loss of the father's love very early on and then the pursuit of finding that lost love in cheap imitations, which were unable to fill the gap of the original loss. The vision of true covenantal love remains unquenched in her, regardless of the multiple disappointments and distortions of authentic care she had experienced. This is the prostitute, the forsaken woman. There are more painful stories and there are less painful ones, but overall, Jenny's narration represents the journey of numerous girls we meet on the streets of Athens every week.

Metaphor of the Forsaken Woman

In Isaiah 62, the author speaks of the story of a tormented city, Zion, or God's elect people, and he presents their story as that of a woman with a restless and painful history:

> For Zion's sake I will not keep silent, and for Jerusalem's sake I will not be quiet, until her righteousness goes forth as brightness, and her salvation as a burning torch. The nations shall see your righteousness, and all the kings your glory, and you shall be called by a new name that the mouth of the LORD will give. You shall be a crown of beauty in the hand of the LORD, and a royal diadem in the hand of your God. You shall no more be termed Forsaken, and your land shall no more be termed Desolate, but you shall be called My Delight is in Her, and your land Married; for the LORD delights in you, and your land shall be married. For as a young man marries a young woman, so shall your sons marry you, and as the bridegroom rejoices over the bride, so shall your God rejoice over you. (Isa. 62:1-5 ESV)

Metaphors make a point about what they are describing rather than about their origin. The purpose of the phrase 'the Lord is my shepherd' is to make a point about the Lord, not shepherds. However, the use of the word 'shepherd' presupposes a very good understanding of what a shepherd is and does.[3]

Similarly, in Isaiah 62:1-5, Zion is described as a forsaken woman, and, although the forsaken woman is just a metaphor, it presupposes a very good knowledge of the experience of such a woman. Isaiah must have encountered in his lifetime such an individual or must have had some idea of the destitute state she would have been in. He would have seen at least one point in her experience to which he was able to relate in order for him to turn her story into the template through which he would interpret the narrative and identity of the people of God (himself included). Through his description of Zion, we can discern how he conceives the forsaken woman.

The woman he describes did not have a bright and glorious appearance for the onlooker, as Isaiah desired for her, or an honorable position in society, but the prophet looks beyond appearances. Since he expects that she will one day again be the object of delight and be married, we can presume that this woman was rejected by her husband or lover, who no longer found any pleasure in her. The word used for 'pleasure, delight' in verse 4 (*ḥpṣ*) is commonly used in the context of marriage or to characterize someone's desire for marriage (e.g., Gen. 34:19). Lack of 'delight' in someone is used to describe lack of interest in marrying a particular person (e.g., Deut. 25:7-8; Ruth 3:13) and can be a reason for divorce or separation (e.g., Deut. 21:14). In other words, Isaiah's metaphor

---

[3] This falls in the realm of 'conceptual metaphor'. A conceptual metaphor consists of two domains, in which one domain is understood in terms of another. For example, we can think of life in terms of journeys. This means that 'we have coherently organized knowledge about journeys that we rely on in understanding life…The conceptual domain from which we draw metaphorical expressions to understand another conceptual domain is called source domain, while the conceptual domain that is understood this way is the target domain'. Life, for example, would be a target domain while journeys are source domains. Zoltán Kövecses, *Metaphor: A Practical Introduction* (2nd ed.; Oxford: Oxford University Press, 2010), 4.

is derived from a woman who has lost her man's affections (*ḥpṣ*) and been abandoned (*ʿzb*) by him.

Divorce was common in the ancient Near East and the reasons often centered on problems associated with infertility or illness.[4] R.N. Whybray understands that these are the conditions behind the names in our passage: 'Forsaken (*ʿᵃzûḇāh*) means "abandoned (by your husband)" as in 60:15 and in 54:6, from which the metaphor was taken. Desolate (read *šōmēmāh* for *šᵉmāmāh*) is to be understood as meaning "barren", as in 54:1'.[5] However, in the ancient world the husband would not normally need 'any more justification to divorce a wife than that he chose to do so for his own private purposes or possibly economic gain'.[6]

Just like marriage would have been formalized by the husband's declaration 'you are my wife' in her presence, the divorce was effected by pronouncing the opposite: 'You are not my wife'.[7] Although Deuteronomy 24:1-4 seeks to regulate divorces by demanding a written form of divorce so that a woman could remarry without being accused of adultery, women may have often found themselves in unfortunate situations such as that of Hagar when she was sent away with a child 'wandering in the desert' (Gen. 21:8-14).[8] It is also likely that a man would have gained economic profit out of selling a woman he no longer delighted in (hence the law in Deut. 21:14).

The sense that God's ideal is not found in divorce but in the union established in creation, as claimed by Jesus (Matt. 19:8), seems to be already expressed in the book of Malachi. Daniel Block recognizes Malachi 2:16 ('I hate divorce') as the basic biblical stance toward this issue, and in answering why divorce was so objectionable, he notes:

> Practically, in the ancient context, unless a woman was taken in by her father or her brothers, divorce put her in an extremely vulnerable economic position. Like the widow or the orphan, she would be without male provision and protection, and in many instances would turn to prostitution simply to earn a living.[9]

This resonates with Jenny's experience: loss of familial protection, rejection by in-laws, abandonment, and exploitation by men – circumstances far removed from what a woman would desire for her future.

---

[4] Victor H. Matthews, 'Marriage and Family in the Ancient Near East', in Ken M. Campbell (ed), *Marriage and Family in the Biblical World* (Downers Grove: IVP, 2003), 15.

[5] R.N. Whybray, *Isaiah 40-66* (The New Century Bible Commentary; Grand Rapids: Eerdmans, 1981), 248.

[6] Matthews, 'Marriage and Family in the Ancient Near East', 25.

[7] Matthews, 'Marriage and Family in the Ancient Near East', 25. Also, Daniel I. Block, 'Marriage and Family in Ancient Israel', in Campbell (ed), *Marriage and Family in the Biblical World*, 49.

[8] Block, 'Marriage and Family in Ancient Israel', 50.

[9] Block, 'Marriage and Family in Ancient Israel', 51.

Thus, the success of the metaphor used in Isaiah 62:1-5 begins with the attention the prophet pays to the phenomenon of the forsaken woman and his accurate reflection on her conditions. It is Isaiah's ability to observe and recognize her suffering, her deprivations, and her longings that teaches him about himself and his people.

The prophet's precise observation of her fallen humanity and his identification with her leads him to compassion and to the realization of the abnormality of the state she is in. It awakens his desire to see her condition reversed. Forsakenness could not be the ideal or permanent state of a woman. She is made to be received back and be the object of delight. The forsaken woman thus becomes the parable of Israel, a mirror for seeing the *self*.

Similarly, in today's global streets and brothels, if you are willing to look closely, you can meet living parables of yourself, the church, and humanity in general. In the face of the trafficked woman you can see the protagonist of salvation history and the life pattern on which the greatest narrative is built: the forsaken one to whom restoration is coming.

Zion, the Forsaken Woman

For the prophet, the life of the forsaken woman becomes the metaphor of the life of God's people, Zion. Zion has a long and painful history that makes one wonder: *why did God abandon her like this?* Instead of being the jewel for all the nations to marvel, she has become the disgrace of the nations, violated and brutally ravaged. Isaiah sees Jerusalem abandoned, not glorious. At times, she is described like Sodom and Gomorrah (Isa. 1:9-10). She opened up her most precious treasures, showed the holiest vessels of her temple to foreign kings (Isa. 39), and sold herself for false security and hope. Not only foreign armies, but even her own people continually defiled her (Isa. 1:21-23). She was abandoned by all, including her God who seemed to have turned his face away from her. Westermann says that '[T]he land's lying waste indicated that God had forsaken it'.[10]

Of course, God cannot be equated to a human husband or be faulted for the condition of the woman Zion (see Isa. 50:1). Whether it was through her own errors or due to the aggression of others, Zion's transgressions are not counted against her. The focus is on the devastation she has endured and its coming reversal. Only compassion, *not* blame, is appropriate at the sight of a destitute people and this is also obvious in the immediate context of our passage, verse 8: 'The Lord has sworn by his right hand and by his mighty arm: "I will not give your grain to be food for your enemies anymore, and foreigners shall not drink your wine for which you have

[10] Claus Westermann, *Isaiah 40-66* (Old Testament Library; trans. David M.G. Stalker; Philadelphia: Westminster Press, 1969), 376.

labored"'. God takes the role of her defender, *not* her accuser. He vindicates[11] her and restores her to the position of his wife.

The renaming (62:2-4) echoes the marriage ceremony[12] where the man's proclamation 'you are my wife' would have changed the status of a woman. Paul Hanson says that, 'Third Isaiah follows Hosea, Jeremiah, and Ezekiel in utilizing the marriage metaphor to express the new name, that is, the new status of the people in relation to God'.[13]

For women in prostitution, the name is particularly significant. They almost never give their real name to their clients. This serves as a defense mechanism where other personas are assumed to experience the suffering and the humiliation in an attempt to preserve the 'purity' of their true selves. The name of their childhood should not be found on the lips of strangers. This is how intimately linked their name is to their identity. Isaiah gives full authority to God as the one to determine the true identity of the woman Zion, the One to spell out her name. As with Naomi, an experience that overthrows one's whole life calls for a new name. For her it was Mara (Ruth 1:20). God's new name blots out the old experience and it marks a radical transformation in Zion's identity. It signifies a change that will be 'incisive, discontinuous with the oppressive structures of the past'.[14]

Christ's Identification with the Forsaken as his Mission

Not only was the forsaken woman the template through which Isaiah told Zion's story, but, in some sense, she became the parable of the Son of God in his earthly life. The Messiah's mission involved his full identification with the forsaken; it was her story that he chose to 'enact'. Such was the identification of God's son with the forsaken woman, with Zion, that he came to live and experience her pain and eventually attain to her much desired end, thus bringing that end to the realm of historical possibility for her. He lived a tormented life, rejected by his people, betrayed by his closest ones, but worst of all, abandoned by the Father.

On the cross, he became the 'Desolate', the 'Forsaken' (Matt. 27:46). The 'estranged' son was restored to life again and his broken body was remade into a glorious one. His ridiculed title written on the cross, 'This is the King of the Jews' (Luke 23:38), was indeed a royal status that was not

---

[11] Joseph Blenkinsopp notes that '[t]he passage from the ethical to the eschatological connotation of *ṣedeq* (here translated "vindication") and its variant *ṣĕdāqâ* corresponds to the passage from the forensic sense of vindication of innocence in a court of law to an ultimate vindication'; *Isaiah 56-66* (Anchor Bible 19B; New York: Doubleday, 2003), 235.

[12] Also Brevard S. Childs following Anderson's argument that the imagery is derived from the context of a wedding linked to the renaming ceremony. *Isaiah* (Old Testament Library; Louisville: John Knox, 2000), 512.

[13] Paul D. Hanson, *Isaiah 40-66* (Interpretation; Louisville: John Knox, 1995), 229.

[14] Hanson, *Isaiah 40-66*, 226.

apparent to the bystanders. It was a promise from his Father who had a throne waiting for him together with a new name, above every other name, that was waiting to be pronounced to him (Phil. 2:9). The Messiah took up the forsaken woman's suffering story and turned it into a monument that testifies to his work.

Now his body, the church, may look abandoned and forsaken but they are nothing more than heirs to the same story, Zion's story, indeed Jenny's story.[15] Luther says the following of the church:

> Note, however, that according to substance and appearance the church is a harlot, illegitimate and forsaken. But in the Word the church is seen as a bride, Hephzibah, and beloved son. In faith the heart must be convinced that it is Christ's Beulah, Hephzibah, and bride, and in the midst of tribulations such a person rejoices and is glad. For he knows that Christ's righteousness is his own. This produces cheerful hearts and consciences and good theologians, who are then in the best position to teach and console others.[16]

Prophetic Vision and Action

Our window to this perspective is the prophet. Prophecy has to do with having a fully formed picture of reality, from beginning to end, in order to be able to offer an interpretation of isolated moments in that history whose end and purpose do not seem apparent. Only in the light of the entire synchronic prophetic narrative is Isaiah in a position to find meaning in the momentary suffering of the broken community and to understand Zion's role in this narrative. It is the glorious vision of a coming restoration, a final reversal of the present state that injects him with the strength for survival so that he in turn can inspire his community with hope through his message.

Our prophet cannot 'keep silent'. He seems to have assumed the role of Zion's defender until the day of her restoration. Westermann says that the prophet 'was aware that he had been sent to counter God's silence and restraining of himself of which the state of things gave evidence.'[17] The prophet embodies the words of God in a context where God appears silent and distant. The persistent presence of the prophet as a preacher and an intercessor functions as a living sign of the presence of God among the

---

[15] Zion in Isaiah 62:1-5 is identified with the church by various church fathers such as Cyril of Alexandria, Jerome and Clement of Alexandria. See Robert Louis Wilken (ed), *Isaiah: Interpreted by Early Christian and Medieval Commentators* (The Church's Bible; Grand Rapids: Eerdmans, 2007), 484-87.

[16] Hilton C. Oswald (ed), *Luther's Works*: *Lectures on Isaiah, Chapters 40-66* (Vol. 17; Saint Louis: Concordia Publishing House, 1972), 346-47.

[17] Westermann, *Isaiah 40-66*, 374. John Oswald thinks this is God speaking: 'Thus God is depicted as responding to the charges that he has been silent to the pleas of his people (cf. 42:14; 45:15-19; 57:11; 64:12; 65:6)'. *The Book of Isaiah, Chapters 40-66* (New International Commentary on the Old Testament; Grand Rapids: Eerdmans, 1998), 578.

suffering people and breaks the apparent divine absence and silence. The prophet is animated by his vision of the royally married woman, and only through this glorious vision is he able to infuse hope into the ugly reality before his eyes.

Indeed, he beholds the forsaken woman through an already-and-not-yet lens. The present image has already begun its transformation. It is not a mere fantasy in his mind. The prophetic word has regenerative qualities. It was his words that sustained the community which preserved these words and passed them on. Light did appear when he spoke into the chaos.

Conclusion

The prophets of today, God's church, adopt this same vision, looking at the present reality as it should be or will be, not as it has come to be. Christians today have already seen the first fruits of the Abandoned One restored in the resurrection of Jesus. They have a precedent in which to ground their vision. In the light of the cross and resurrection, they refuse to accept that God's brides are forsaken.

Human trafficking projects a very ugly reality for women. They are abandoned, commodified, and expendable. Indeed, after visiting brothel after brothel in Athens, I see that there is nothing in the external appearance of a person or in her inner strength that promises a state different than the one she is already in. In the majority of cases, the person loses hope in expecting any other future and her willpower is crushed, so even if she did believe in it, she would not have the strength to pursue it.

It is here that the presence of the prophets is of utmost importance. They are the ones who will have to persist 'for Zion's sake'. The forsaken must be invited, many times over, to join the vision which the prophet both conveys and embodies. Until the forsaken begins to read herself in the prophet's narrative, the prophet must not keep silent. I believe that social action without the Christian theological background is inadequate. Charity from a privileged position is also inadequate and in danger of preserving inequality. Only the once-forsaken *owes* charity to the forsaken. Full identification accepts nothing less than everyone having equal access to the gift of restoration.

From my experience, I find that it is not enough to free trafficked women from their bondage. Girls can be easily deceived back into slavery or find themselves, out of economic necessity, in the same or similar position. Many, after having worked in prostitution for too long, whether they have been forced into it or not, have a deep sense of guilt and shame, thinking they are not worth anything better than this lifestyle. They can be like birds in a cage which refuse to fly away even if you leave the door open. Social action has to go deeper than opening the door, relocating and reintegrating these women to normal life and society. Freedom is secured only in the redefinition of the *self*.

Only in the adoption of a new narrative for their lives that reconstructs their humanity into the royal image they were meant to be, the divine image and likeness, can they begin to truly seek a renewed life. This is the freedom which normally precedes physical liberation: only once a woman discovers that her name is not 'Forsaken' but 'God's Delight' is she then able to shake off her fetters.

Paul's mission was inspired by this same vision (2 Cor. 11:2). He wanted to present the church as a pure bride to the groom, which is in fact the mission of Christ himself (Eph. 5:26-27): His word washed her clean so that he might present the church glorious to himself!

From Every Tribe, Language, People, and Nation: Diaspora, Hybridity, and the Coming Reign of God

Amos Yong

Growing up evangelical and Pentecostal, I had been taught that our cultural identities did not matter since we had converted to Christ and were now part of 'Christian culture'. This was a standard evangelical and Pentecostal understanding of what conversion entailed through the middle-third of the twentieth century.[1] Yet, I have come to see that the central acts of God's saving history actually invite us to think otherwise. That Jesus the Logos of God took on flesh means not only that he became biologically human, but also that he took up within himself first-century Palestinian languages, cultures, and even religions, transforming them in the process.[2]

Therefore, the outpouring of the Spirit upon all flesh on the Day of Pentecost means something similar: not just that men and women, young and old, slave and free from the Jewish diaspora around the Mediterranean world received the Spirit as individuals, but that their languages, cultures, and even religious traditions were being somehow redeemed in order to declare and speak 'about God's deeds of power' (Acts 2:11).[3] In short, Christian initiation and conversion involves not just a turning away from the world and a turning to God, but also constitutes God's ways of purifying, transforming, and redeeming the world in all of its complexity.

I have come to this theological conviction in part through reflecting upon my own journey. I was born to Pentecostal pastors who were also first-generation Chinese converts from a nominal form of Buddhism in postcolonical Malaysia. This aspect of my early life itself needs unpacking at least at three levels.

---

[1] E.g., as described among Pentecostal missionaries to Native Alaska in Kirk Dombrowski, *Against Culture: Development, Politics, and Religion in Indian Alaska* (Lincoln, NE: University of Nebraska Press, 2001), and among evangelical missionaries to West Africa in Birgit Meyer, *Translating the Devil: Religion and Modernity among the Ewe in Ghana* (Trenton, NJ: Africa World Press, 1999).

[2] As argued by Brian Bantum, *Redeeming Mulatto: A Theology of Race and Christian Hybridity* (Waco, TX: Baylor University Press, 2010).

[3] See my books, *Discerning the Spirit(s): A Pentecostal-Charismatic Contribution to Christian Theology of Religions* (Journal of Pentecostal Theology Supplement Series 20; Sheffield, UK: Sheffield Academic Press, 2000); *Beyond the Impasse: Toward a Pneumatological Theology of Religions* (Grand Rapids: Baker Academic, 2003); *The Spirit Poured Out on All Flesh: Pentecostalism and the Possibility of Global Theology* (Grand Rapids: Baker Academic, 2005).

First, Malaysia in the late 1960s and early 1970s – these were my growing up years, before our family emigrated to the USA – was a Muslim state attempting to find its bearings after achieving independence from the British in 1957. Even then, and until now, the slight majority population of indigenous Malays (the *bumiputra* or 'children of the soil'), all legally understood as Muslims, were politically privileged.

Yet, the fact that 20-25% of the Chinese population has always contributed a much larger percentage to the nation's GNP has meant that there have always been racial and ethnic tensions between Malays and Chinese. As Christians in Malaysia were mostly non-Malays (Chinese, but also South Indian Tamils, who make up about one-tenth of the population), they have always been a marginalized minority (around 10%), not only religiously, but also politically and socially. Yet, there are further complications, as when intermarriages occur. One example is my aunt, who married a Malay *datuk* (a chief and elite member of the Malay social hierarchy) and had three children with him. Her own religious identity, needless to say, has continuously been betwixt and between, neither Christian nor Muslim, at least not in any orthodox sense with regard to either tradition. I will return to this issue later.

Second, my parents believed that their being made new in Christ (cf. 2 Cor. 5:17) meant that they had left behind their Buddhist beliefs and practices once for all. However, growing up I learned about filial piety (a traditional Confucian value); about the importance of natural and herbal forms of health maintenance and healthcare, derived from the long history of indigenous and Daoist-based Chinese medicine; and about doing all things in moderation. This last one, while arguably a gloss on certain biblical proverbs, was also a clear Buddhist virtue, a central element of Buddhist teachings advocating a middle path between extremes.[4]

Of course, these aspects of my upbringing were always presented as common sense; I did not know of their cultural and religious backgrounds until I undertook graduate studies in comparative religion later in life. In any case, we celebrated a partially Christianized version of Chinese New Year (this was partly the case since not all of our relatives were converts). *But were we successful in leaving our (Buddhist) past behind, or were we right to desire to reject that past completely as the missionaries had taught us?*

Third, my parents were converts not to more established forms of Catholic or Protestant Christianity (the latter dominated by its Anglican and Methodist expressions in Malaysia), but to Pentecostalism. In the third quarter of the twentieth century, Pentecostalism was still viewed almost as a sectarian form of Christianity, the latter already a marginal religion in the

---

[4] I have explored this Buddhist path of moderation in my book, *Does the Wind Blow through the Middle Way? Pneumatology and the Christian-Buddhist Dialogue* (Studies in Systematic Theology 11; Leiden and Boston: Brill, 2012).

Muslim political context and amidst the Buddhist religious environment that most Malaysian Chinese inhabited.

My parents have told me of being persecuted at a young age for their Christian faith, even by their own family members. Eventually, their parents (my grandparents) also converted to Christianity. The point is that conversion in such situations has no doubt also contributed to the theological view that insisted on defining Christian faith over and against other religions. At the same time, given the small numbers of Christians in the Malaysian context, less and less was made of sectarian, denominational, or ecclesial differences over time, with most Christians thinking it more worthwhile to collaborate with others to achieve common goals, especially in the political venue. In that sense, in the Malaysian context, Pentecostals have remained distinctive, but not absolutely so from other Christians.[5]

My family immigrated to northern California when I was ten to pastor among other Chinese-speaking immigrants who were pouring into North America in the wake of the immigration reform laws passed in 1965. I was thus part of the Chinese diaspora twice removed – first in Malaysia and now in America.[6] Having spent the rest of my growing up years in the USA and having completed all of my graduate and post-graduate studies here, my education is thoroughly Western.

Along the way, I married a fifth-generation Mexican American woman, and together, we have had three children who continuously must decide if they should check 'Latino', 'Asian', or other boxes related to their ethnicity. Although I am now a naturalized Asian American citizen of the USA and a lifelong adherent to (and for the last 25 years a credentialed minister with) the Assemblies of God,[7] I remain very sensitive to the

---

[5] For an overview, see Tan Jin Huat, 'Pentecostal and Charismatic Origins in Malaysia and Singapore', in Allan Anderson and Edmond Tang (eds), *Asian and Pentecostal: The Charismatic Face of Christianity in Asia* (London: Regnum International, and Baguio City, Philippines: Asia Pacific Theological Seminary Press, 2005), 281-306.

[6] I reflect on my theological work in light of the experience of migration in my articles, 'The Im/Migrant Spirit: De/Constructing a Pentecostal Theology of Migration', in Peter C. Phan and Elaine Padilla (eds), *Theology and Migration in World Christianity: Contextual Perspectives*, vol. 2: *Theology of Migration in the Abrahamic Religions* (Christianities of the World; New York: Palgrave Macmillan, forthcoming), and 'Informality, Illegality, and Improvisation: Rethinking Money, Migration, and Ministry in Chinatown, NYC, and Beyond'", in Eleazar Fernandez (ed), *New Overtures: Asian North American Theology in the 21st Century* (Upland, Calif.: Sopher Press, 2012), 248-68, originally published in the *Journal of Race, Ethnicity, and Religion* 3:2 (2012) [http://www.raceandreligion.com/JRER/Volume_3_%282012%29.html].

[7] For reflections on how my scholarly vocation is intertwined with my ministerial vision, see my essay, 'The Spirit, Vocation, and the Life of the Mind: A Pentecostal Testimony', in Steven M. Fettke and Robby C. Waddell (eds), *Pentecostals in the Academy: Testimonies of Call* (Cleveland, Tenn.: CPT Press, 2012), 203-20.

dynamics of globalization, especially as these have impacted my own transnational, intercultural, and even interfaith experiences. As a theologian shaped by this history, then, I find myself continuously navigating between seven axes of tensions. Let me explicate on these in no particular order.

First, *I find myself always between East and West.* In some respects, I am comfortable in either world, but in other respects, I find myself belonging in neither.[8] This is in part because of my ethnic and racial identity, complicated certainly by the dominant black-white framework through which such issues are adjudicated in North America.[9] It is also in part because I now believe that various cultural aspects of my identity are constitutive of the goodness of creation and, in that sense, of the redemptive work of God.

This is not to say that all cultural realities are to be naively adopted into Christian faith. It is to say that there is much more to be considered about the cultural dimensions of Christian life than we have heretofore been open to. Beyond these factors, I ought to note that while I am grateful for the opportunities afforded to me and my immediate family in America, I know that part of my identity will always belong in Asia, with my extended family members and their children who remain there. As a person of Chinese descent, I will be on the margins of American life at least for the rest of my lifetime, even as my family members (and myself, if I were to ever return to Malaysia for more than a short-term visit) will remain at the margins of Malaysian life for the foreseeable future.

In short, neither can be an ultimate resting place. And I cannot even return to China: any relatives going back a few generations would not know me, not to mention that my American Chinese will be largely incomprehensible to native speakers. Some people might find this situatedness between East and West debilitating; perhaps it can be a resource for theological reflection instead.[10]

Second, *I live uneasily between a colonial and postcolonial world.* We are about a generation or two removed from independence of most colonized nations. At one level, as a Christian, there is much to be grateful

---

[8] Other Asian American theologians have also written about this sense of dual-exclusion and dual-belonging; see Peter C. Phan and Jung Young Lee (eds), *Journeys at the Margins: Toward an Autobiographical Theology in American-Asian Perspective* (Collegeville: Liturgical Press, 1999).

[9] See my chapter, 'Race and Racialization in a Post-Racist Evangelical World: A View from Asian America', in Anthony B. Bradley (ed), *Aliens in the Promised Land: Race and Evangelicalism* (Phillipsburg, NJ: P&R Publishing Company, 2013), 45-58 and 216-20; see also, e.g., Willie James Jennings, *The Christian Imagination: Theology and the Origins of Race* (New Haven and London: Yale University Press, 2011).

[10] See my articles, 'The Future of Asian Pentecostal Theology: An Asian American Assessment', *Asian Journal of Pentecostal Studies* 10.1 (2007), 22-41, and 'The Future of Evangelical Theology: Asian and Asian American Interrogations', *The Asia Journal of Theology* 21.2 (October 2007), 371-97.

for in how missionaries brought the gospel to the majority world, including, in my case, Pentecostal missionaries who went to Malaysia. While there were certainly missionaries around the world who were supported by and benefitted from the colonial enterprise, many were also politically motivated or at least indirectly implicated.

On the post-independence side of things, it is essential to note that the various countries of the world that have emerged from under colonial rule need to take responsibility for themselves and not blame the history of colonization for their woes. Many nations have made successful adjustments since independence, so others can as well. Still, the legacy of colonialism remains to this day, and its mechanisms, deeply embedded in countries and regions of the world across the global south, continue to reverberate in our shrinking global village.[11]

In the USA, the long history of slavery and Native American racism remain palpable in certain parts of this country, and continue to haunt our existence in a subterranean manner despite the gains made during the civil rights revolution in the 1960s. In this context and as a member of the Chinese diaspora (twice removed, as I indicated above), I wrestle with the fact that the dominant theological tradition has been implicated in the colonial enterprise. New postcolonial voices and perspectives are emerging, some resisting and rejecting the historic tradition, others (among whom I count myself) seeking to revise, retrieve, or reappropriate the Christian faith for a postcolonical – not to mention postmodern, post-Western, and post-Enlightenment – world. What does it mean to think Christianly and to reconceive Christian theology in light of the historical, social, and political realities after colonialism, not only for Malaysia, but for America as well? Can we preserve the gains of the Enlightenment while being open also to what late modernity has to offer through subaltern perspectives?[12]

Third, *I struggle strenuously with how my Christian faith commitments are not exclusive of other faiths*. This is my reality – I cannot deny that who I am as a person of Chinese descent is already a hybrid combination of the philosophical, cultural, and religious traditions of East and southeast Asia.

---

[11] See, e.g., my analysis of the violence that continues to blot the postcolonial landscapes of Nigeria and Sri Lanka in my *Hospitality and the Other: Pentecost, Christian Practices, and the Neighbor* (Faith Meets Faith series; Maryknoll, NY: Orbis Books, 2008), ch. 1.

[12] See also my musing about additional aspects of a postcolonial, post-Enlightenment, and postmodern theology and mission in 'Conclusion: The Missiology of Jamestown: 1607-2007 and Beyond–Toward a Postcolonial Theology of Mission in North America', in Amos Yong and Barbara Brown Zikmund (eds), *Remembering Jamestown: Hard Questions about Christian Mission* (Eugene, OR: Pickwick Publications, 2010), 157-67, and Yong and Peter Heltzel, 'Robert Cummings Neville and Theology's Global Future', in Yong and Heltzel (eds), *Theology in Global Context: Essays in Honor of Robert Cummings Neville* (New York and London: T & T Clark, 2004), 29-42.

In the West, we might think these various strands are detachable from one another and therefore that it might be acceptable to embrace the cultures but not the religions of the East. But in reality, these are overlapping domains.

Part of the challenge is that at least some traditions of Christianity consider any association with other religious traditions in negative terms as 'syncretism'. I am desiring neither an uncritical syncretism nor a bland lowest-common-denominator theology that is inclusive of other faiths.[13] Simultaneously, I also do not think that some versions of theological exclusivism can account for the complicated inter-religious lives and identities that are being formed through the gospel. While being for Christ will entail being against some aspects of other faiths, this does not necessarily involve complete repudiation. Can the tensions amidst these domains serve as a resource instead for rethinking Christian faith in global context?[14]

To see this more clearly, let me mention, fourth, *identity in Christ that is between ancient Israel and contemporary Judaism*. Is Christianity Jewish or not? Yes and yes. The issues are particularly urgent in light of the long history of Christian anti-Semitism culminating in the Holocaust. Post-Shoah Christian self-understandings cannot afford to ignore how Christian views of the Jews have had tragic political and historical consequences. Complicating contemporary Christian and Jewish relationships are the emergence of messianic Jews, certainly well received in evangelical Christian circles, but severely contested among Jews. On the one hand, many Christians insist upon the ongoing evangelization of Jews; on the other hand, our theological self-understanding is not as deeply informed by the Hebrew Bible as it ought to be.

In fact, there is a spectrum of response across the Christian community about how to understand the relevance of that portion of the biblical canon in relationship to the New Testament. Has the ancient covenant with Israel been subsumed into the Church or does it persist in some respects parallel to that of the new covenant in Christ? Therein lies part of the challenge about how Christians should relate to Jews in the contemporary world. No doubt, intermarriages between Jews and Christians have complicated this question of identity for both Christians and Jews. Does one have to be for or against Judaism today – or is the truth to be found in embracing the Jewish roots of Christian faith in a post-Holocaust world?[15]

---

[13] The way forward here would be something along the lines of what Walter Hollenweger calls a 'theologically responsible syncretism'; see Hollenweger, *Pentecostalism: Origins and Developments Worldwide* (Peabody, MA: Hendrickson, 1997), ch. 11.

[14] As I suggest in my essay, 'Between the Local and the Global: Autobiographical Reflections on the Emergence of the Global Theological Mind', in Darren C. Marks (ed), *Shaping a Global Theological Mind* (Aldershot, UK: Ashgate, 2008), 187-94.

[15] I struggle with this question in the final (eighth) chapter of my *In the Days of*

Fifth, *as a Pentecostal I ride the tension that persists between more evangelical and more ecumenical forms of Christianity today*. To be sure, such tensions are more relaxed today than at any time in the last century. Nevertheless, there are still debates between 'conservatives' and 'liberals', between 'orthodoxy' and 'progressivism', between confessional and mainline Protestantism (and Catholicism and Orthodoxy as well). In America, the lines between 'right' and 'left' are more hard and fast than in other parts of the Anglo-speaking world, even if the emergence of post-conservative forms of evangelicalism is erasing some of the rigidity.

Certainly, as I have indicated above, in some parts of the Majority World there is much more co-operation when confronted by the need to mobilize smaller numbers for common causes. This is not to say that Pentecostals and evangelicals need to give up on all of their theological convictions. It is to say that there may be better ways of holding to at least some of these convictions that more appropriately engages contemporary challenges. Again, maybe there is a way beyond either/or in this case.[16]

This leads, sixth, *to a discussion of how Pentecostal identity has existed in tension with the self-understanding of the broader Christian tradition from its emergence at the beginning of the twentieth century*. On the one hand, the Pentecostal belief in the baptism of the Holy Spirit that empowers Christian witness, as evidenced by speaking in tongues, suggests that those without such experiences are second-tier Christians (at best), if not members of non-vital churches from which they should depart (at worst). This view fosters a kind of Pentecostal elitism that, not surprisingly, rubs other Christians the wrong way. However, the fact that Pentecostals often attract nominal Christians from other churches has led also to concerns and accusations about Pentecostal proselytism and 'sheep stealing'.

In this context, how can I maintain my Pentecostal commitments on the one hand without perpetuating the triumphalism characteristic of Pentecostal attitudes from earlier eras? In addition, there is also the phenomenon of Oneness Pentecostalism – Trinitarian Pentecostals do not like to acknowledge this aspect of the modern renewal movement, but it is present nonetheless, especially in the ways that even Trinitarian Pentecostals count the demographics of global renewal.

Caesar: Pentecostalism and Political Theology – The Cadbury Lectures 2009 (Sacra Doctrina: Christian Theology for a Postmodern Age series; Grand Rapids and Cambridge, UK: William B. Eerdmans Publishing Company, 2010); see also the literature cited there.

[16] As urged in my 'Whither Asian American Evangelical Theology? What Asian? Which American? Whose *Evangelion*?', *Evangelical Review of Theology* 32.1 (2008), 22-37, and 'Asian American Historicity: The Problem and Promise of Evangelical Theology', *SANACS Journal* [*Society of Asian North American Christian Studies Journal*] 4 (2012-2013), 29-48; see also my response article, 'Beyond the Liberal-Conservative Divide: An Appreciative Rejoinder to Allan Anderson', *Journal of Pentecostal Theology* 16.1 (2007), 103-11.

Is it possible to consider Pentecostal Christianity as presenting certain gifts to the churches, even from the Oneness perspective,[17] while still inviting Pentecostals to be open to receiving the gifts of other churches? Can such a mutual gift exchange preserve the distinctiveness and uniqueness of the Pentecostal message across the Trinitarian and Oneness divide, while not demeaning those of other Christian traditions? Is this what it might mean to receive the many gifts of the Holy Spirit that are given through different members of the church?[18]

Perhaps the six tensions I have described so far participate in this last one: that of *living between now and eternity*. The New Testament does, in various places, identify followers of Jesus Christ as 'aliens and exiles' (1 Pet. 2:11, NRSV) who are seeking another, heavenly, city and country (Heb. 11:17). Thus we are sojourners, continuously living a diasporic existence, thrust into a world that is in some ways not our home. At the same time, the goal is not merely to escape from the world, as we anticipate a transformation of the present world and its remaking as a new one fit for the presence of God and the new city of God. Thus the Book of Revelation clearly indicates that 'the kings of the earth will bring their glory into it [the new Jerusalem that descends to the earth]', and that 'People will bring into it the glory and the honor of the nations' (Rev. 21:24, 26). In that sense, then, we live between the now and the not yet, between this world and the coming reign of God. There are certainly discontinuities between the present age and the world to come, but there are also continuities in how the redemption of this world will contribute to the glory of the one that is coming.

I am motivated also by the scenario in Revelation that there will be around the throne of the Lamb 'saints from every tribe and language and people and nation' (Rev. 5:9; cf. 7:9, 14:6). This tells me that God's final redemptive work will include not just 'souls' in the abstract, but real flesh-and-blood peoples in all of their linguistic, cultural, sociopolitical, and historical particularity. This is also consistent with the description of God's salvific work manifest through the Day of Pentecost narrative that lies at the center of my own Pentecostal faith. The outpouring of the Spirit was also not on ethereal souls, but on men *and* women, older *and* younger, free *and* slave, from various regions of the known world, and embodying different histories, experiences, and hopes. These pilgrims to Jerusalem,

---

[17] As done so brilliantly by David A. Reed, *'In Jesus' Name': The History and Beliefs of Oneness Pentecostals* (Journal of Pentecostal Theology Supplement Series 31; Blandford Forum, UK: Deo Publishing, 2008).

[18] As will be argued in Yong, with Jonathan A. Anderson, *Renewing Christian Theology: Systematics for a Global Christianity* (Waco, Tex.: Baylor University Press, 2014); see also my *The Bible, Disability, and the Church: A New Vision of the People of God* (Grand Rapids and Cambridge, UK: William B. Eerdmans Publishing Company, 2011), ch. 4, for an analysis of the how the charismatic fellowship of Christ is also constituted by people with disabilities.

while all Jews at varying depths of commitment, were encountered by the living God. Their lives in all their complexity were there and then recruited to declare the wondrous works of God.[19]

My claim would be that our status as aliens and strangers invites us to think about diaspora and hybridity not as marginal or incidental aspects of Christian faith, but as central to it. Historical identities are never pure. This does not mean that all languages, cultures, ethnic or racial aspects of human identity, and religious traditions are equal. The gospel comes to judge as well as to purify. But my account here suggests also that the gospel comes to redeem, which means literally to 'buy back'.

This means that in God's scheme of things, various aspects of our histories and life stories will find new meaning in light of our encounter with the God of Jesus Christ. This also means that we no longer have to be ashamed of our hybridized identities, neither as individuals nor as congregations, churches, and even as the church catholic. Instead, it is the nature of the church as the people of God, the body of Christ, and the fellowship of the Spirit to be constituted by manyness, difference, and plurality.

Further, any centering of the church portends its ossification. When this happens, voices from the margins, from the diasporas wherein the winds of the Spirit blows, will need to infuse new life into institutionalized forms of faith. The diaspora no longer remains the frontier when Christianity is expanding. Instead, diaspora captures the very heart of God's saving work, no matter when, where, or among whom. No tribes are too 'primitive'; no languages are too 'barbaric'; no peoples are too pagan or uncultured; and no nations are too 'marginal'. All are hybrids in some or other respect, and anyone, anywhere, anytime may represent the surprising work of the Spirit in anticipation of the coming reign of God.[20]

---

[19] As developed in my books, *Who is the Holy Spirit? A Walk with the Apostles* (Brewster, MA: Paraclete Press, 2011), and *Spirit of Love: A Trinitarian Theology of Grace* (Waco, TX: Baylor University Press, 2012).

[20] An earlier version of this chapter was presented at the Oxford Center for Mission Studies, Oxford, United Kingdom, 30 July 2013; thanks to Wonsuk Ma, David Singh, and David Jung for organizing this event, and to the audience for their reception and discussion of the text. Thanks also to my graduate assistant, Vince Le, for proofreading an earlier version of this article.

EPILOGUE

Chandler H. Im

For Christians, diaspora is a powerful metaphor for the spiritual journey. For diasporic Christians, 'in-between-ness' is the way of life and the reality they face. Diasporic believers are polycentric, multi-context Christians. As a product of the global Korean diaspora myself, I can testify to the reality that diasporic life often feels like simultaneously experiencing two parallel universes: both the old and the new. The diasporic person's mind and heart frequently move back and forth like a time traveler between the birth land and the newly-settled land. In general, the person in diaspora experiences the state of an in-between-ness.

Diasporic people and families face a litany of issues, concerns, and challenges, while striving to survive in and cope with (harsh) realities of 'the new world' as transplants/residents in unfamiliar settings: acquiring the new language, adapting to a different culture, maintaining their previous cultural heritage as a group, finding employment, navigating second-generation issues (e.g., identity crisis, learning the parents' language), working through psychological/emotional challenges like loneliness and homesickness, etc. There are other evolving and multifaceted aspects and implications that affect diaspora people which are not covered extensively in this volume, particularly in 'receiving' nations: (anti-)immigration laws; religious freedom and pluralism; discrimination, xenophobia, and ethnocentrism; brain drain (from the 'sending' nation) and brain gain (for the 'receiving' nation); poverty and economic/community developments; health care; social justice and human rights; and arts, sports, and entertainment industries, to name only a few.

Transnational migration and the establishment of diaspora communities around the world have been transforming the demographic landscapes globally. This includes Christians 'on the move' and worldwide Christian movements. In these global diasporas, one critical phenomenon has emerged in the context of the Christian world. As Andrew Walls maintains, the church in the West led Christendom until the last century, but in the twenty-first century and beyond the church in the global south (i.e., in Africa, Asia, and Latin America) is leading global Christianity,[1] in terms of numbers and influence. This assessment is one with which Philip Jenkins also strongly concurs.[2]

---

[1] Andrew F. Walls, presentation entitled 'The Rise of Global Theologies', Wheaton College, Illinois, 7 April 2011.

[2] Philip Jenkins, *The Next Christendom: The Coming of Global Christianity* (New York: Oxford University Press, 2002), 14.

In addition, according to Lamin Sanneh,[3] diaspora churches in the USA and around the globe 'hold a key to what happens in the resurgence of American Christianity and new global Christian movements'. He points out that the scattering of peoples around the world can be understood as one of God's mission plans or strategies – some even call it 'divine conspiracy' – to resuscitate and revitalize churches in many nations, Western in particular, through the global diaspora Christian churches. The global diaspora churches and movements will continue to play significant roles in affecting, encouraging, and catalyzing the hosting nations' churches and ministries: evangelism, global missions, church planting, discipleship programs, social services, justice and human rights issues, etc.

Furthermore, the dividing line that used to exist between home missions and overseas missions, particularly in Western countries, is no longer clear-cut and will get fuzzier, thanks to the global diasporas. As an example, the Southern Baptist Convention (SBC) had their national annual meeting in Phoenix in June 2011. One of the key agenda items was: how can SBC's International Mission Board and North American Mission Board work more closely and more effectively for the sake of evangelizing the unreached, especially those diaspora people groups in North America? The theme for their 2011 convention was 'A Great Commission People with a Great Commandment Heart'.[4] The Great Commission and the Great Commandment will not be fulfilled without intentionally engaging in cross-cultural missions to/with diaspora communities that have been popping up and will be expanding further around the globe, in our cities and communities.

The twenty-first century is truly an exciting time to be part of God's global mission movements. The numbers of immigrants, migrants, and other diasporic people groups around the world are increasing and historically unprecedented. Without paying attention to the people groups and the people on the move, Christian mission endeavors will never be complete. Many of the contributors to this volume believe that humanity's diaspora will not end until Jesus Christ comes back to the earth again. In the meantime, many missiologists believe that the Lord has been dispersing and gathering the nations (*ethne*) for his missional plans and purposes through the means of the global diasporas. In this perspective, diaspora is indeed an essential, God-orchestrated mission strategy for seeking the lost and nurturing the found.

Finally, Christians are increasingly recognizing and emphasizing the fact that they are part of the global church. The global church is not the church that's 'out there'. All belong to the same faith community, i.e., the body of Jesus Christ. Christians (e.g., national Christian leaders and churches, and

---

[3] Lamin Sanneh, presentation entitled 'Whose Religion is Christianity?', Wheaton College, Illinois, 9 April 2011.

[4] The Southern Baptist Convention in Phoenix, Arizona, 14-15 June 2011.

diaspora Christian leaders and churches) now understand that they must co-operate and collaborate more intentionally going forward. They must do more than simply tolerate and co-exist with each other. Even though their skin color and ethnic backgrounds differ, Christian unity and love for each other serve as a testament to the unbelieving world that they are indeed one in Christ. They are serving as co-laborers in God's kingdom and co-sojourners on earth on the way together to the City of God, their anticipated eternal home and resting place, where diaspora shall be no more.

Bibliography

Adogame, Afe. 'Betwixt Identity and Security: African Religious Movements and the Politics of Religious Networking in Europe'. *Nova Religio* 7:2 (2003), 24-41.

———. 'Up, Up Jesus! Down Down Satan! African Religiousity in the former Soviet Bloc – the Embassy of the Blessed Kingdom of God for All Nations'. *Exchange* 37:3 (2008), 310-36.

Adogame, Afe, and Cordula Weisskoeppel, eds. *Religion in the Context of African Migration.* Bayreuth: Eckhard Breitinger, 2005.

Adogame, Afe, and Jim Spickard, eds. *Religion Crossing Boundaries: Transnational Religious and Social Dynamics in Africa and the New African Diaspora.* Leiden: Brill, 2010.

Adogame, Afe, Roswith Gerloff, and Klaus Hock, eds. *Christianity in Africa and the African Diaspora: The Appropriation of a Scattered Heritage.* London: Continuum, 2008.

Ahn, J.J. *Exile as Forced Migrations: A Sociological, Literary, and Theological Approach on the Displacement and Resettlement of the Southern Kingdom of Judah.* Beihefte zur Zeitschrift für die alttestamentliche Wissenschaft 417. Berlin: Walter de Gruyter, 2011.

Aikman, David. *Jesus in Beijing: How Christianity Is Transforming China and Changing the Global Balance of Power.* Washington, DC: Regnery, 2003.

Antunes, Elias. 'Notas do Tradutor'. In *História da Emigração Japonesa para as Américas* [*History of Japanese Emigration to Americas*]. Ed. T. Tokunaga. S. Paulo: The Province of Miyazaki Association, 2009, 24.

Bailey, R.C., ed. *Yet With a Steady Beat: Contemporary U.S. Afrocentric Biblical Interpretation.* Semeia Studies, 42. Atlanta: Society of Biblical Literature, 2003.

Bantum, Brian. *Redeeming Mulatto: A Theology of Race and Christian Hybridity.* Waco, TX: Baylor University Press, 2010.

Barrett, David B., George T. Kurian, and Todd M. Johnson, eds. *World Christian Encyclopedia: A Comparative Survey of Churches and Religions in the Modern World.* Vol 2: *Religions, Peoples, Languages, Cities, Topics.* New York: Oxford University Press, 2001.

Barrett, David B., and Todd M. Johnson. *World Christian Trends, AD 30–AD 2200: Interpreting the Annual Christian Megacensus.* Pasadena, CA: William Carey Library Publication, 2003.

Bastide, Roger. *Les Religions Africaines au Brésil: Vers une Sociologie des Interpenetrations de Civilisations* [*African Religions in Brazil: Towards a Sociology of the Interpenetration of Civilizations*]. Paris: Presses Universitaires de France, 1960.

Bevans, Stephen. 'Mission among Migrants, Mission of Migrants: and Mission of the Church'. In *Promised Land, A Perilous Journey: Theological Perspectives on Migration.* Eds. Daniel Groody and Gioachhino Campese. Notre Dame, IN: University of Notre Dame Press, 2008, 90-94.

Blazejak, Janusz. *A Half of Century: The Missionary Oblates of Mary Immaculate – Assumption Province in Canada.* Toronto: Missionary Oblates of Mary Immaculate – Assumption Province, 2006.

Block, Daniel I. 'Marriage and Family in Ancient Israel'. In *Marriage and Family in the Biblical World.* Ed. Ken M. Campbell Downers Grove: IVP, 2003, 33-102.

Boer, R. *Last Stop Before Antarctica: The Bible and Postcolonialism in Australia.* The Bible and Postcolonialism 6. Sheffield: Sheffield Academic Press, 2001.

Boers, Hendrikus. *The Justification of the Gentiles: Paul's Letters to the Galatians and Romans.* Peabody: Hendrickson, 1994.

Boyarin, Daniel. *Border Lines: The Partition of Judeo-Christianity.* Philadelphia: University of Pennsylvania Press, 2004.

Brown, Peter. *Augustine of Hippo: A Biography.* London: Faber, 1967.

———. *Authority and the Sacred: Aspects of the Christianization of the Roman World.* New York: Cambridge University Press, 1995.

Callahan, A.D. *The Talking Book: African Americans and the Bible.* New Haven: Yale University Press, 2006.

Carroll, M. Daniel, Leiton Chinn, Chandler H. Im, and Sadiri Joy Tira. *Bibliographic Resources for The Cape Town Commitment, Diaspora (Scattered Peoples)* (available at www.lausanne.org/docs/ Bibliographic-Resources-for-CTC.pdf).

Carroll, M. Daniel. *Christians at the Border: Immigration, the Church, and the Bible.* Grand Rapids, MI: Baker Academic, 2008.

Casiño, Tereso C. 'Why People Move: A Prolegomenon to Diaspora Missiology'. In *Korean Diaspora and Christian Mission.* Eds. S. Hun Kim and Wonsuk Ma. Oxford: Regnum, 2011, 35-58.

Castles, Stephen, and Mark J. Miller. *The Age of Migration: International Population Movements in the Modern World.* 4th ed. New York: The Guilford Press, 2009.

Cha, Peter, Paul Kim, and Dihan Lee. 'Multigenerational Households'. In *Asian American Christianity Reader.* Eds. Viji Nakka-Cammauf and Timothy Tseng. Castro Valley, CA: The Institute for the Study of Asian American Christianity, 2009, 127-38.

Chang, Iris. *The Chinese in America: A Narrative History.* New York: Penguin, 2003.

———. *The Rape of Nanking.* New York: Penguin, 1997.

Chang, Roberta, and Wayne Patterson. *The Koreans in Hawaii: A Pictorial History, 1903-2003.* Honolulu: University of Hawaii Press, 2003.

Childs, Brevard S. *Isaiah.* Old Testament Library. Louisville: John Knox, 2000.

Choudaha, Rahul, and Li Chang. *Trends in International Student Mobility.* New York: World Education Services, 2012.

Chuck, James, ed. *Chinatown: Stories of Life and Faith.* San Francisco: First Chinese Baptist Church, 2002.

Chul, Han Jun David. 'A South Korean Case Study of Migrant Ministries'. In *Korean Diaspora and Christian Mission.* Eds. S. Hun Kim and Wonsuk Ma. Oxford: Regnum, 2011, 207-22.

———. 'World Christian Mission through Migrant Workers in South Korea and through the Korean Diaspora'. In *Tokyo2010 Global Mission Consultation Handbook.* Ed. Yong J. Cho. Seoul and Pasadena, CA: Tokyo 2010 Global Mission Consultation Planning Committee, 2010, 171-73.

Cogan, M. 'The Other Egypt: A Welcome Asylum'. In *Texts, Temples and Traditions: A Tribute to Menahem Haran.* Eds. M.V. Fox, et al. Wiona Lake: Eisenbrauns, 1996, 65-70.

Cohen, Robin. *Cambridge Survey of World Migration.* 1995. Reprint, Cambridge: Cambridge University Press, 2010.

———. *Global Diasporas: An Introduction.* Seattle: University of Washington

Press, 1997.
Cornille, Catherine. *Many Mansions? Multiple Religious Belonging and Christian Identity*. Maryknoll, NY: Orbis Books, 2002.
Covell, Ralph R. *The Liberating Gospel in China: The Christian Faith among China's Minority Peoples*. Grand Rapids: Baker, 1995.
Cox, Harvey G. *The Secular City: Secularization and Urbanization in Theological Perspective*. New York: Macmillan, 1965.
Creswell, J. W. *Qualitative Inquiry and Research Design: Choosing Among Five Traditions*. Thousand Oaks, CA: Sage, 1998.
———. *Research Designs: Qualitative and Quantitative Approaches*. Thousand Oaks, CA: Sage, 1994.
Dalby, David, David Barrett, and Michael Mann. *The Linguasphere Register of the World's Languages and Speech Communities*. 2 vols. Carmarthenshire, Wales: Linguasphere Press, 1999.
Dark, K.R. 'Large-Scale Religious Change and World Politics'. In *Religion and International Relations*. Ed. K.R. Dark. Hampshire: Palgrave, 2000, 50–82.
Davidson, Allan K. *Selwyn's Legacy: The College of St John the Evangelist, Te Waimate and Auckland, 1843-1992: A History*. Auckland: The College, 1993.
Dombrowski, Kirk. *Against Culture: Development, Politics, and Religion in Indian Alaska*. Lincoln, NE: University of Nebraska Press, 2001.
Droogers, André, Cornelis van der Laan, and Wout van Laar, eds. *Fruitful in this Land: Pluralism, Dialogue and Healing in Migrant Pentecostalism*. Geneva: WCC, 2006.
Dufoix, Stéphane. *Diasporas*. Trans. W. Rodarmor. Berkeley, CA: University of California Press, 2008.
Ekué, Amélé A. A. 'An den Ufern von Babylon saßen wir und weinten, wenn wir an Zion dachten…: Wahrnehmungen zur religösen Reinterpretation von Exil unter afrikanischen Christen und Christinnen in der Hamburger Diaspora'. In *Zwischen Regionalität und Globalisierung: Studien zu Mission, Ökumene und Religion*. Ed. Theo Ahrens. Hamburg: Ammersbek, 1997, 327-45.
Emerson, Michael, and Christian Smith. *Divided by Faith*. New York: Oxford University Press, 2001.
Escobar, Samuel. 'Migration: Avenue and Challenge to Mission'. *Missiology* 31:1 (2003), 17-28.
Estepa, Pio. 'The Asian Mission Landscape of the 21st Century'. *SEDOS* 43:5-6 (May-June 2011), 115-26.
Felder, C.H. *Troubling Biblical Waters: Race, Class, and Family*. Maryknoll: Orbis, 1989.
Felder, C.H., ed. *Stony the Road We Trod: African American Biblical Interpretation*. Minneapolis: Fortress Press, 1991.
Feldman, Louis H. *Jew and Gentile in the Ancient World: Attitudes and Interactions from Alexander to Justinian*. Princeton: Princeton University Press, 1993.
Finley, Bob. *Reformation in Foreign Missions*. Charlottesville, Virginia: Christian Aid Mission, 2010.
Fiorenza, E.S. *Rhetoric and Ethic: The Politics of Biblical Studies*. Minneapolis: Fortress Press, 1999.
Fischer, Moritz. *Pfingstbewegung zwischen Fragilität und Empowerment. Beobachtungen zur Pfingstkirche 'Nzambe Malamu' mit ihren transnationalen Verflechtungen*. Göttingen: VandR Unipress, 2011.
Fletcher, Richard A. *The Barbarian Conversion: from Paganism to Christianity*

374-1386 AD. New York: H. Holt and Co., 1997.
Foster, John. *The Church of the Tang Dynasty*. London, Society for Promoting Christian Knowledge, 1939.
Frend, W.H.C. *Martyrdom and Persecution in the Early Church*. Oxford: Blackwell, 1965.
Freyre, Gilberto. *Casa Grande e Senzala* [*Mansions and Shanties*]. 34th ed. Rio de Janeiro: Editora Record, 1998.
Galvez, Venus Hannah. 'Ministry to Filipino Entertainers and Japinos'. In *Scattered: The Filipino Global Presence*. Eds. Pantoja, Tira, and Wan. Manila: LifeChange Publishing Inc., 2004, 251-371.
George, K.M. *Development of Christianity through the Centuries: Tradition and Discovery*. Tiruvalla, India: Christava Sahitya Samithi, 2005.
George, Sam, and T.V. Thomas, eds. *Malalayi Diaspora: From Kerala to the Ends of the World*. New Delhi: Serials Publications, 2013.
Gerloff, Roswith. *A Plea for British Black Theologies: The Black Church Movement in Britain*. 2 vols. Frankfurt: Peter Lang, 1992.
Gillman, Ian and Klimkeit, H-J. *Christians in Asia before 1500*. Ann Arbor: University of Michigan Press, 1999.
Grim, Brian J., and Roger Finke. *The Price of Freedom Denied: Religious Persecution and Violence in the 21st Century*. New York: Cambridge University Press, 2011.
———. 'Religious Persecution in Cross-National Context: Clashing Civilizations or Regulated Economies?' *American Sociological Review* 72:4 (2007), 633–58.
Grimes, Barbara F. 'From Every Language'. In *Perspectives on the World Christian Movement: A Reader*. Eds. Ralph D. Winter and Steven C. Hawthorne. 4th ed. Pasadena, CA: William Carey Library, 2009, 565-67.
Groody, Daniel, and Gioachhino Campese, eds. *Promised Land, A Perilous Journey: Theological Perspectives on Migration*. Notre Dame, IN: University of Notre Dame Press, 2008.
Gungwu, Wang. 'Patterns of Chinese Migration in Historical Perspective'. In *The Chinese Overseas*. Ed. Hong Liu. Milton Park: Routledge, 2006, 34-41.
Haberman, Frederick W., ed. *Nobel Lectures, Peace 1926-1950*. Amsterdam: Elsevier Publishing Company, 1972.
Hanciles, Jehu. *Beyond Christendom: Globalization, African Migration and the Transformation of the West*. Maryknoll, NY: Orbis, 2008.
Hanson, Paul D. *Isaiah 40-66*. Interpretation. Louisville: John Knox, 1995.
Hastings, Adrian. *The Church in Africa 1450-1950*. Oxford: Clarendon Press, 1994.
Hattaway, Paul. *Back to Jerusalem*. Atlanta: Piquant, 2003.
Hattaway, Paul. *Operation China: Introducing All the Peoples of China*. Pasadena, CA: Piquant, 2000.
Hesselgrave, David. *Paradigms in Conflict: 10 Key Questions in Christian Missions Today*. Grand Rapids: Kregel Publications, 2006.
Hitti, P.K. *History of the Arabs*. New York: St. Martin's Press, 1968.
Hollenweger, Walter. *Pentecostalism: Origins and Developments Worldwide*. Peabody, MA: Hendrickson, 1997.
Holter, K. *Yahweh in Africa: Essays on Africa and the Old Testament*. Bible and Theology in Africa 1. New York: Peter Lang, 2000.
Holzmann, John, ed. *The Church of the East*. Littleton, CO: Sonlight Curriculum Ltd, 2001.

Hopler, Thom, and Marcia Hopler. *Reaching the World Next Door.* Downers Grove: InterVarsity Press, 1995.

Houston, Tom. 'Postscript: The Challenge of Diaspora Leaders for World Evangelism'. In *Scattered: The Filipino Global Presence.* Eds. Luis Pantoja Jr, Sadiri Joy Tira, and Enoch Wan. Manila: LifeChange Publishing Inc., 2004, 363-68.

Huntington, Samuel P. *The Clash of Civilizations and the Remaking of World Order.* New York: Simon and Schuster, 1996.

Hurrey, Charles D. *Educational Guide: A Handbook of Useful Information for Foreign Students in the United States of America.* New York: The Committee on Friendly Relations Among Foreign Students, 1917.

Ishii, Tadashi, ed. *Cem Anos da Imigração Japonesa no Brasil, através de Fotografias* [*One Hundred Years of Japanese Immigration to Brazil in Pictures*]. Fukyosha, Tokyo: Museu Histórico da Imigração Japonesa no Brasil, 2008.

Jackson, Darrell, and Alessia Passarelli. *Mapping Migration: Mapping Churches' Responses: Europe Study.* Brussels: Churches' Commission for Migrants in Europe, 2008.

Jenkins, Philip. *The Next Christendom: The Coming of Global Christianity.* Oxford: Oxford University Press, 2002.

Jennings, Willie James. *The Christian Imagination: Theology and the Origins of Race.* New Haven and London: Yale University Press, 2011.

Johnson, Todd M., ed. *World Christian Database.* Leiden, Netherlands: Brill, 2007.

Johnson, Todd M., and Brian J. Grim. *The World's Religions in Figures: An Introduction to International Religious Demography.* Oxford: Wiley-Blackwell, 2013.

Johnson, Todd M., and Brian J. Grim, eds. *World Religion Database.* Leiden, Netherlands: Brill, 2008.

Johnson, Todd M., and Gina A. Bellofatto. 'Immigration, Religious Diasporas, and Religious Diversity: A Global Survey'. *Mission Studies* 29 (2012), 1–20.

Johnson, Todd M., and Kenneth R. Ross, eds. *Atlas of Global Christianity.* Edinburgh: Edinburgh University Press, 2009.

Johnstone, Patrick. *The Future of the Global Church: History, Trends, and Possibilities.* Downers Grove: InterVarsity Press, 2011.

Jung, Min-Young. 'Diaspora and Timely Hit: Towards a Diaspora Missiology'. In *Korean Diaspora and Christian Mission.* Eds. S. Hun Kim and Wonsuk Ma.Oxford: Regnum, 2011, 59-71.

Kahl, Werner. 'Die Bezeugung und Bedeutung frühchristlicher Wunderheilungen in der Apostelgeschichte angesichts transkultureller Übergänge'. In *Religion und Krankheit.* Eds. Annette Weissenrieder und Gregor Etzelmüller. Darmstadt: WBG, 2010, 249-64.

———. 'Geh in ein Land, das ich dir zeigen werde: Biblische und theologische Aspekte der Identität von Migranten'. *Interkulturelle Theologie: Zeitschrift für Missionswissenschaft* 37:2-3 (2011), 204-22.

———. 'Paulus als kontextualisierender Evangelist beim Areopag'. In *Der eine Gott und die fremden Kulte: exklusive und inklusive Tendenzen in den biblischen Gottesvorstellungen*. Ed. Eberhard Bons, Biblisch-Theologische Studien 102. Neukirchen-Vluyn: Neukirchener, 2009, 49-72.

———. *Jesus als Lebensretter: westafrikanische Bibelinterpretationen und ihre Relevanz für die neutestamentliche Wissenschaft.* New Testament Studies in Contextual Exegesis 2. Frankfurt am Main and New York: Peter Lang, 2007.

———. *New Testament Miracle Stories in Their Religious Historical Setting: A Religionsgeschichtliche Comparison from a Structural Perspective*. Forschungen zur Religion und Literatur des Alten und Neuen Testaments 163. Göttingen: Vandenhoeck and Ruprecht, 1994.

Kasibante, Amos. 'The Ugandan Diaspora in Britain and Their Quest for Cultural Expression within the Church of England'. *Journal of Anglican Studies* 7:1 (2009), 79-86.

Kaufmann, Eric. *Shall the Religious Inherit the Earth? Demography and Politics in the Twenty-First Century*. London: Profile Books Ltd, 2010.

Kawano, Carmen, *João Yasoji Ito: A vida e a obra do missionário* [*João Yasoji Ito: The Life and Work of a Missionary*]. S. Paulo: Maluhy and Co. and Igreja Episcopal Anglicana do Brasil, 2010.

———. *Seikokai: A História da Primeira Construção Religiosa dos Japoneses no Brasil* [*Seikokai: The Story of the First Religious Building by Japanese People in Brasil*]. S. Paulo: Maluhy and Co., 2008.

Kellermann, D. '*gur*'. In *Theological Dictionary of the Old Testament*. Eds. G.J. Botterweck and H. Ringgren. Vol. 2 (Grand Rapids: Eerdmans, 1975) 439-49.

Kelly, Philip F. 'Filipino Migration and the Spatialities of Labour Market Subordination'. In *Handbook of Employment and Society: Working Space*. Eds. Susan McGrath-Champ, Andrew Herod, and Al Rainnie. Cheltenham, UK, and Northampton, MA: Edward Elgar, 2010, 159-76.

Khory, Kavita R., ed. *Global Migration: Challenges for the 21st Century*. New York: Palgrave Macmillan, 2012.

Kim, S. Hun, and Wonsuk Ma, eds. *Korean Diaspora and Christian Mission*. Eugene, OR: Wipf and Stock, 2011.

Kluj, Wojciech. 'Forms of Work of the Oblates of Mary Immaculate among Polish Immigrants in the Prairies of Canada (1898-1926)'. *Vie Oblate Life* [Ottawa] 56:3 (1997), 363-401, and 57:1 (1998), 27-76.

———. 'Początki pracy Misjonarzy Oblatów M.N. wśród polskich emigrantów na kanadyjskich preriach – parafia Ducha Świętego w Winnipeg 1898-1926 [The Beginnings of the Work of the Oblates of Mary Immaculate Among the Polish Immigrants on the Prairies of Canada – Holy Ghost Parish in Winnipeg 1898-1926]'. *Collectanea Theologica* [Warsaw] 70:2 (2000), 127-51.

Knitter, Paul F. *Without Buddha I Could Not be a Christian*. Oxford: OneWorld Publications, 2009.

Korean Mission Handbook 2006-2007. Seoul, Korea: Korean Research Institute for Mission, 2007.

Kosakiewicz, Frank. 'Polish Oblate ministry and immigration in Alberta'. In *Western Oblate Studies 1/Études Oblates de l'Ouest 1*. Ed. Raymond Huel. Edmonton: Western Canadian Publishers and Institut de Recherche de la Faculté Saint-Jean, 1990, 171-79.

Koshy, K. P. 'Christianity in the Arabian Gulf and Kuwait: The Role of Kuwait Town Malayalee Christian Congregation'. In *The Kuwait Town Malayalee Christian Congregation Golden Jubilee Souvenir*. Safat, Kuwait: published privately, 2003.

Kövecses, Zoltán. *Metaphor: A Practical Introduction*. 2nd ed. Oxford: Oxford University Press, 2010.

Kroeger, James H. 'Asia's Rich Diversity: Pathway into Mission'. *SEDOS* 43:5-6 (May-June, 2011), 100-14.

Lausanne Committee for World Evangelization Issue Group No. 26 A and B:

Diasporas and International Students. 'Lausanne Occasional Paper 55: The New People Next Door'. In *A New Vision, a New Heart, a Renewed Call: Lausanne Occasional Papers from the 2004 Forum of World Evangelization Hosted by the Lausanne Committee for World Evangelization – Pataya, Thailand September 29 – October 5, 2004.* Ed. David Claydon. Pasadena, CA: William Carey Library, and Delhi: Horizon Printers and Publishers, 2005, 75-137.

Lausanne Committee for World Evangelization. *Scattered to Gather: Embracing the Global Trend of Diaspora.* Manila: LifeChange Publishing Inc., 2010.

Lee, E.S. 'A Theory of Migration'. *Demography* 3 (1966) 47-57.

Lee, Helene, 'Hospitable Households: Evangelism'. In *Growing Healthy Asian American Churches: Ministry Insights from Groundbreaking Congregations.* Eds. Peter Cha, S. Steve Kang, and Helene Lee. Downers Grove: InterVarsity Press, 2006, 122-44.

Lee, Myunghee. 'Migrant Workers' Churches as Welcoming, Sending and Recruiting Entities: A Case Study of Mongolian Migrant Workers' Churches in Korea'. In *Missions from the Majority World: Progress, Challenges, and Case Studies.* Eds. Enoch Wan and Michael Pocock. EMS Series 17. Pasadena: William Carey Library, 2009, 371-85.

Lee, See-Young. 'Mobilizing Senior Christians in Korea and among the Korean Diaspora for Mission'. In *Korean Diaspora and Christian Mission.* Eds. S. Hun Kim and Wonsuk Ma. Oxford: Regnum, 2011, 260-63.

Lee, Timothy S. *Born Again: Evangelicalism in Korea.* Honolulu: University of Hawai'i Press, 2010.

LeRoux, M. *The Lemba: A Lost Tribe of Israel in Southern Africa?* Pretoria: University of South Africa, 2003.

Liamzon, Cristina. 'Accompanying and Journeying with Overseas Filipinos in Italy'. *SEDOS* 43:5-6 (May-June, 2011), 153-59.

Luck, Anne. *African Saint: The Story of Apolo Kivebulaya.* London: SCM Press, 1963.

Ludwig, F. '"Just Like Joseph in the Bible": The Liberian Christian Presence in Minnesota'. In *African Christian Presence in the West: New Immigrant Congregations and Transnational Networks in North America and Europe.* Eds. F. Ludwig and J.K. Asamoah-Gyadu. Religion in Contemporary Africa series. Trenton: Africa World Press, 2011, 357-80.

Mackie, Robert C. *Layman Extraordinary: John R. Mott 1865-1955.* New York: Associated Press, 1965.

Mandryk, Jason. *Operation World.* 7th ed. Colorado Springs: Biblica, 2010.

Mathews, Basil. *John R. Mott: World Citizen.* New York and London: Harper and Brothers, 1934.

Matsuoka, Fumitaka. *Out of Silence: Emerging Themes in Asian American Churches.* Cleveland: United Church Press, 1995.

Matthews, Victor H. 'Marriage and Family in the Ancient Near East'. In *Marriage and Family in the Biblical World.* Ed. Ken M. Campbell. Downers Grove: IVP, 2003, 1-32.

Matthey, Jacques. 'Mission und Macht – damals und heute'. *Interkulturelle Theologie* 4 (2009), 346-58.

Meyer, Birgit. *Translating the Devil: Religion and Modernity Among the Ewe in Ghana.* Edinburgh and London: Edinburgh University Press, 1999.

Min, Pyong Gap. 'The Structure and Social Functions of Korean Immigrant Churches in the United States'. *International Migration Review* 26:4 (Winter 1992), 1370-94.

Miranda, Dionisio. *Buting Pinoy.* Manila: Logos Publication, 1998.

Mizuki, John. *The Growth of Japanese Churches in Brazil.* Pasadena, CA: William Carey Library, 1978.

Moffett, Samuel H. *History of Christianity in Asia.* Vol 1. San Francisco: HarperSanFrancisco, 1992.

Mott, John R. *Addresses and Papers of John R. Mott.* 6 vols. New York: Associated Press, 1946.

———. *The Present World Situation.* New York: Student Volunteer Movement for Foreign Missions, 1914.

Mouw, Richard J. *Uncommon Decency: Christian Civility in an Uncivil World.* Downers Grove, IL: InterVarsity Press, 2010.

Mtata, K. '"How shall we sing the Lord's song in a foreign land?": African Diaspora Christianity as space and place of imagination'. In *African Christian Presence in the West: New Immigrant Congregations and Transnational Networks in North America and Europe*. Eds. F. Ludwig J. and K. Asamoah-Gyadu. Religion in Contemporary Africa Series. Trenton: Africa World Press, 2011, 335-55.

Nampo, Chieko and Liana Tatsumi Goya. *Monobe: Da Morte para a vida – Um missionário japonês no Brasil na década de 20* [*From Death to Life: A Japanese Missionary to Brazil in 1920s*]. S. Paulo: IEHB, 2006.

Nazir-Ali, Michael, *From Everywhere to Everywhere: A World View of Christian Mission.* Eugene, OR: Wipf and Stock Publishers, 2009.

Ng, Greer Anne Wenh-In. 'The Asian North American Community at Worship: Issues of Indigenization and Contextualization'. In *People on the Way: Asian North Americans Discovering Christ, Culture, and Community.* Ed. David Ng. Valley Forge: Judson Press, 1996, 147-74.

Ngai, Mae M. 'The Architecture of Race in American Immigration Law: A Reexamination of the Immigration Act of 1924'. *Journal of American History* 86 (June 1999), 67-92.

Noll, Mark A. *The New Shape of World Christianity: How American Experience Reflects Global Faith.* Downers Grove: InterVarsity Press, 2009.

Norris, Pippa, and Ronald Inglehart. *Sacred and Secular: Religion and Politics Worldwide.* Cambridge: Cambridge University Press, 2004.

Oh, Doug K., 'History of the Korean Diaspora Movement'. In *Korean Diaspora and Christian Mission.* Eds. S. Hun Kim and Wonsuk Ma. Oxford: Regnum, 2011, 181-96.

Olupona, Jacob K. and Regina Gemignani, eds. *African Immigrant Religions in America.* New York: New York University Press, 2007.

Oshima, Midori. *Vitória: Relatos dos primeiros anos do povo Metodista Livre no Brasil* [*Victory: Reports on Early Years of Free Methodist People in Brazil*]. S. Paulo: Igreja Metodista Livre, Concílio Nikkei, 2011.

Ositelu, Rufus. *African Indigenous Churches.* Langen: Alexander Verlag, 1984.

Oswald, Hilton C., ed. *Luther's Works Vol. 17: Lectures on Isaiah. Chapters 40-66.* Saint Louis: Concordia Publishing House, 1972.

Oswalt, John N. *The Book of Isaiah. Chapters 40-66.* New International Commentary on the Old Testament. Grand Rapids: Eerdmans, 1998.

Ott, Craig. 'Diaspora and Relocation as Divine Impetus for Witness in the Early Church'. In *Diaspora Missiology: Theory, Methodology, and Practice.* Ed. Enoch Wan. Portland, OR: Institute of Diaspora Studies at Western Seminary, 2011, 73-96.

Otto, Martin. *Church on the Oceans: A Missionary Vision for the 21st Century.* Carlisle, UK: Piquant, 2007.

Padilla, C. R. 'Holistic Mission'. In *Dictionary of Mission Theology: Evangelical Foundations.* Ed. John Corrie. Nottingham, UK, and Downers Grove, IL: InterVarsity Press, 2007, 157-62.

Pantoja, Luis Jr., Sadiri Joy Tira, and Enoch Wan, eds. *Scattered: The Filipino Global Presence.* Manila: LifeChange Publishing Inc., 2004.

Park, Chan Sik. 'Multicultural Society and Migrant Mission' (in Korean). In *21C New Nomad Era and Migrant Mission.* Eds. Chan Sik Park and Noh Hwa Jung. Seoul: Christian Industrial Society Research Institute Press, 2008, 18-48.

Park, Chan Sik, and Noah Jung, eds. *21C New Nomad Era and Migrant Mission.* Seoul: Christianity and Industrial Society Research Institute, 2010.

Park, Timothy Kiho. 'Korean Christian World Missions: The Missionary Movement of the Korean Church'. In *Missions from the Majority World: Progress, Challenges, and Case Studies*. Eds. Enoch Wan and Michael Pocock. EMS Series 17. Pasadena: William Carey Library, 2009, 97-120.

Pasura, Dominic. 'Modes of Incorporation and Transnational Zimbabwean Migration to Britain'. *Ethnic and Racial Studies* 36:1 (2013), 199-218.

———. 'Religious Transnationalism: The Case of Zimbabwean Catholics in Britain'. *Journal of Religion in Africa* 42:1 (2012), 26-53.

Patrick. *The Works of St Patrick.* Trans. Ludwig Bieler. Westminster, MD: Newman Press, 1953.

Payne, J.D. *Stranger Next Door: Immigration, Migration and Mission.* Downers Grove, IL: InterVarsity Press, 2012.

Perry, Cindy L. *Nepali around the World: Emphasizing Nepali Christians of the Himalayas.* Kathmandu: Etka Books, 1997.

Phan, Peter C. *Being Religious Interreligiously: Asian Perspectives on Interreligious Dialogue.* Maryknoll, NY: Orbis Books, 2004.

Phan, Peter C., ed. *Christianities in Asia.* Chichester: Wiley-Blackwell, 2011.

Phan, Peter C. and Jung Young Lee, eds. *Journeys at the Margins: Toward an Autobiographical Theology in American-Asian Perspective.* Collegeville: Liturgical Press, 1999.

Phillips, Tom, et al. *The World at Your Door: Reaching International Students in Your Home, Church, and School.* Minneapolis: Bethany House, 1997.

Pirouet, Louise. *Black Evangelists: The Spread of Christianity in Uganda.* London: Collings, 1978.

Pohl, Christine. 'Biblical Issues in Mission and Migration'. *Missiology* 31:1 (2003), 3-15.

Pratt, Keith, and Richard Rutt. *Korea: A Historical and Cultural Dictionary.* London: Curzon, 1999.

Prill, Thorsten. *Global Mission on Our Doorstep: Forced Migration and the Future of the Church.* Munster: MV-Wissenschaft, 2008.

Prior, M. *The Bible and Colonialism: A Moral Critique*. The Biblical Seminar 48. Sheffield: Sheffield Academic Press, 1997.

Raghuram, Parvati. 'Immigration Dynamics in the Receiving State: Emerging Issues for the Indian Diaspora in the United Kingdom'. In *Tracing an Indian*

Diaspora: Contexts, Memories, Representations. Eds. Parvati Raghuram, Ajaya Kumar Sahoo, Brij Maharaj, and Dave Sangha. New Delhi: Sage Publications, 2008, 171-90.

Rah, Soong-Chan. *The Next Evangelicalism: Freeing the Church from Western Cultural Captivity.* Downers Grove: InterVarsity Press, 2009.

Reed, David A. *'In Jesus' Name': The History and Beliefs of Oneness Pentecostals.* Journal of Pentecostal Theology Supplement Series 31. Blandford Forum, UK: Deo Publishing, 2008.

Riis, Ole. 'Modes of Religious Pluralism under Conditions of Globalization'. In *Democracy and Human Rights in Multicultural Societies.* Eds. Matthias Koenig and Paul de Guchteneire. Aldershot: Ashgate Publishing Limited, 2007, 251–65.

Saito, Hiroshi. *O Japonês no Brasil-Estudo de Mobilidade e Fixação* [*Japanese People in Brazil: A Study on Mobility and Settlement*]. S. Paulo: Editora Sociologia e Política, 1961.

Sanneh, Lamin. *Abolitionists Abroad: American Blacks and the Making of Modern West Africa.* Cambridge, MA: Harvard University Press, 1999.

———. *West African Christianity.* Maryknoll: Orbis Books, 1983.

Saunders, Doug. *Arrival City: How the Largest Migration in History is Reshaping Our World.* New York: Pantheon Books, 2010.

Scott, C.A.A. *Ulfllas: Apostle of the Goths.* Cambridge: Macmillan and Bowes, 1885.

Sherwood, Marika. *Pastor Daniels Ekarte and the African Churches Mission.* London: Savannah Press, 1994.

Simon, Benjamin. 'Christians of African Origin in the German Speaking Diaspora of Germany'. *Exchange: A Journal of Missiological and Ecumenical Research* 31:1 (2002), 23-35.

———. 'Leadership and Ministry in the Kimbanguist Church'. In *Church Ministry in African Christianity.* Eds. Ronilick E. K. Mchami and Benjamin Simon. Nairobi: Acton Publishers 2006, 126-42.

———. *From Migrants to Missionaries: Christians of African origin in Germany.* Frankfurt: Peter Lang, 2010.

Simon, Uriel. *Jonah.* The JPS Bible Commentary. Trans. Schramm. Philadelphia: The Jewish Publication Society, 1999.

Soerens, Matthew, and Jenny Hwang. *Welcoming the Stranger: Justice, Compassion and Truth in the Immigration Debate.* Downers Grove, IL: InterVarsity Press, 2009.

Spencer, Stephen, ed.*Mission and Migration.* Sheffield: Cliff College, 2008.

Spradley, J. P. *Participant observation.* New York: Holt, Rinehart and Winston, Inc., 1980.

Stake, R.E. *The Art of Case Study Research.* Thousand Oaks, CA: Sage, 1995.

Starke, Rodney, and Roger Finke. *Acts of Faith: Explaining the Human Side of Religion.* Berkeley: University of California Press, 2000.

Stendahl, Krister. *Final Account: Paul's Letter to the Romans.* Minneapolis: Augsburg, 1995.

Sundermeier, Theo. 'Konvivenz als Grundstruktur ökumenischer Existenz heute'. In *Ökumenische Existenz heute I.* Eds. Wolfgang Huber, Dietrich Ritschl, und Theo Sundermeier Muenchen: Kaiser, 1986, 49-100.

Takaki, Ronald. *Strangers from a Different Shore: A History of Asian Americans.* New York: Penguin, 1989.

Tamrat, Taddesse. *Church and State in Ethiopia.* Oxford: Clarendon Press, 1972.

Tan, Jin Huat. 'Pentecostal and Charismatic Origins in Malaysia and Singapore'. In *Asian and Pentecostal: The Charismatic Face of Christianity in Asia.* Eds. Allan Anderson and Edmond Tang. London: Regnum International, and Baguio City, Philippines: Asia Pacific Theological Seminary Press, 2005, 281-306.

Tanaami, Shimekiti. *Burajiru Fukuin Horinessu Kyodan: Senkyo Godjushunen Kinen [Brazil Evangelical Holiness Church: Fiftieth Anniversary*]. S. Paulo: Igreja Evangélica Holiness do Brasil, 1980.

Taylor, Paul M. *Freedom of Religion: UN and European Human Rights Law and Practice.* Cambridge: Cambridge University Press, 2005.

Ter Haar, Gerrie. *African Christians in Europe.* Nairobi, Kenya: Acton Publishers, 2001.

———. 'The African Diaspora in the Netherlands'. In *New Trends and Developments in African Religions.* Ed. Peter B. Clarke. London: Greenwood Press, 1998, 245-62.

———. *Half Way to Paradise: African Christians in Europe.* Cardiff: Cardiff Academic Press, 1998.

Ter Haar, Gerrie, ed. *Strangers and Sojourners: Religious Communities in the Diaspora.* Leuven: Peeters, 1998.

Thomas, Scott M. 'A Globalized God: Religion's Growing Influence in International Politics'. *Foreign Affairs* 89:6 (2010), 98.

Thompson, Andrew. *Christianity in the UAE: Culture and Heritage.* Dubai, UAE: Motivate Publishing, 2011.

Thompson, Mary A., ed. *Unofficial Ambassadors: The Story of International Student Service.* New York: International Student Service, 1982.

Tira, Sadiri Joy. 'Filipino International Network: A Strategic Model for Filipino Diaspora Glocal Missions'. In *Scattered: The Filipino Global Presence.* Eds. Pantoja, Tira, and Wan. Manila: LifeChange Publishing Inc., 2004, 149-72.

———. *Filipino Kingdom Workers: An Ethnographic Study in Diaspora Missiology.* Pasadena, CA: William Carey International University Press, 2012.

———. 'Indigenous Diaspora Workers: From Himalayan Mountains to Arabian Sands'. *Advancing Indigenous Missions Newsletter* 9:1 (Spring 2012), 2.

Tira, Sadiri Joy, and Enoch Wan, eds. *Missions in Action in the 21st Century.* Toronto: Prinbridge, 2008.

Turner, Harold W. *Religious Innovation in Africa: Collected Essays on New Religious Movements.* Boston: G. K. Hall, 1979.

Ustorf, Werner. *Bremen Missionaries in Togo and Ghana: 1847-1900.* Trans. James C.G. Greig. Legon, Ghana: Legon Theological Studies Series, 2002.

Währisch-Oblau, Claudia. 'From Reverse Mission to Common Mission…We Hope'. *International Review of Mission* 354 (2000), 467-83.

———. *The Missionary Self-Perception of Pentecostal/Charismatic Church Leaders from the Global South in Europe: Bringing Back the Gospel.* Leiden and Boston: Brill, 2009.

Walewander, Edward, ed. *Leksykon geograficzno-historyczny parafii i kościołów polskich w Kanadzie* [*Geographic-Historical Lexicon of Polish Parishes and Churches in Canada*]. Vol. 1. Lublin: KUL, 1992.

Walls, Andrew F. *The Cross-cultural Process in Christian History.* Maryknoll: Orbis Books, 2002.

———. *The Missionary Movement in Christian History.* Maryknoll: Orbis Books, 1996.

———. 'Towards a Theology of Migration'. In *African Christian Presence in the*

West: New Immigrant Congregations and Transnational Networks in North America and Europe. Eds. F. Ludwig and J.K. Asamoah-Gyadu. Religion in Contemporary Africa Series. Trenton: Africa World Press, 2011, 407-17.

Walton-Roberts, Margaret. 'Globalization, National Autonomy and Non-Resident Indians'. In *The Indian Diaspora: Historical and Contemporary Context.* Eds. Laxmi Narayan Kadeker, Ajaya Kumar Sahoo, and Gauri Bhattacharya. Jaipur, India: Rawat Publications, 2009, 209-31.

Wan, Enoch. 'Diaspora Missiology'. *Occasional Bulletin of Evangelical Missiological Society* 20:2 (2007), 3-7.

———. *Diaspora Missiology: Theory, Methodology, and Practice.* Portland, OR: Institute of Diaspora Studies at Western Seminary, 2011.

———. 'Global People and Diaspora Missiology'. In *Tokyo 2010 Global Mission Consultation Handbook.* Ed. Yong J. Cho. Seoul and Pasadena, CA: Tokyo 2010 Global Mission Consultation Planning Committee, 2010, 92-100.

———. 'Korean Diaspora: From Hermit Kingdom to Kingdom Ministry'. In *Korean Diaspora and Christian Mission.* Eds. S. Hun Kim and Wonsuk Ma. Oxford: Regnum, 2011, 101-16.

———. *Missions Within Reach: Intercultural Ministries in Canada.* Hong Kong: Alliance Press, 1995.

Wan, Enoch and Sadiri Joy Tira. 'The Filipino Experience in Diaspora Missions: A Case Study of Christian Communities in Contemporary Contexts'. In *Missions from the Majority World: Progress, Challenges, and Case Studies.* Eds. Enoch Wan and Michael Pocock. Pasadena, CA: William Carey Library, 2009, 387-411.

Wan, Enoch and Sadiri Joy Tira, eds. *Missions Practice in the 21st Century.* Pasadena, CA: William Carey International University Press, 2009.

Warner, R. Stephen. 'Coming to America: Immigrants and the Faith They Bring'. *Christian Century* 121 (10 February 2004), 20-23.

Warrior, R.A. 'A Native American Perspective: Canaanites, Cowboys, and Indians'. In *Voices from the Margin: Interpreting the Bible in the Third World.* Ed. R.S. Sugirtharajah. 3rd. ed. Maryknoll, New York: Orbis, 2006, 235-41.

Weifan, Wang. 'The Bible in Chinese'. *Nanjing Theological Review* 14/15 (1991), 75-90.

Weiner, Myron. 'International Migration and Development: Indians in the Persian Gulf'. In *Indian Diaspora in West Asia: A Reader.* Ed. Prakash C. Jain. New Delhi: Manohar Publisher, 2007, 124-41.

Weller, Paul, ed. *Migration Principles: Statement for Churches Working on Migration Issues.* London, Churches Together in Britain and Ireland and Churches' Commission for Racial Justice, 2007.

Westermann, Claus. *Isaiah 40-66.* Old Testament Library. Trans. David M. G. Stalker. Philadelphia: Westminster Press, 1969.

Wijsen, Frans. 'Intercultural Theology and the Mission of the Church'. *Exchange: A Journal of Missiological and Ecumenical Research* 30:3 (2001), 218-28.

Wild-Wood, Emma. *Migration and Christian Identity in Congo, DRC.* Leiden: Brill, 2008.

Wilken, Robert Louis, ed. *Isaiah: Interpreted by Early Christian and Medieval Commentators.* The Church's Bible. Grand Rapids: Eerdmans, 2007.

Wilson, Bryan R. *Religion in Secular Society: A Sociological Comment.* London: C. A. Watts and Co. Ltd, 1966.

Wilson, Dick. *China the Big Tiger: A Nation Awakes.* London: Abacus, 2000.

Wimbush, W.L. 'The Bible and African Americans: An Outline of an Interpretive History'. In *Stony the Road We Trod: African American Biblical Interpretation*. Ed. C.H. Felder. Minneapolis: Fortress, 1991, 81-97.

Wimbush, W.L., ed. *African Americans and the Bible: Sacred Texts and Social Textures*. New York: Continuum, 2000.

Winter, Ralph D. and Bruce A. Koch. 'Finishing the Task'. In *Perspectives on the World Christian Movement: A Reader*. Eds. Ralph D. Winter and Steven C. Hawthorne. 4th ed. Pasadena, CA: William Carey Library Publishers, 2002, 531-46.

Yamazaki, N. *A História dos 65 anos de Evangelização da Igreja Evangélica Holiness do Brasi* [*65 Years History of the Brazil Evangelical Holiness Church*]. S. Paulo: IEHB, 1998.

Yeo, Khiok-Khng. 'Christian Chinese Theology: Theological Ethics of Becoming Human and Holy'. In *Global Theology in Evangelical Perspective: Exploring the Contextual Nature of Theology and Mission*. Eds. Jeffrey P. Greenman and Gene L. Green. Downers Grove: InterVarsity Press, 2012, 102-15.

Yin, Robert K. *Case Study Research: Design and Methods*. 4th ed. Thousand Oaks, CA: Sage, 2009.

Yong, Amos. 'Asian American Evangelical Theology'. In *Global Theology in Evangelical Perspective: Exploring the Contextual Nature of Theology and Mission*. Eds. Jeffrey P. Greenman and Gene L. Green. Downers Grove: InterVarsity Press, 2012, 195-209.

———. 'Asian American Historicity: The Problem and Promise of Evangelical Theology'. *SANACS Journal* [*Society of Asian North American Christian Studies Journal*] 4 (2012-2013), 29-48.

———. 'Between the Local and the Global: Autobiographical Reflections on the Emergence of the Global Theological Mind'. In *Shaping a Global Theological Mind*. Ed. Darren C. Marks. Aldershot, UK: Ashgate, 2008, 187-94.

———. *Beyond the Impasse: Toward a Pneumatological Theology of Religions*. Grand Rapids: Baker Academic, 2003.

———. 'Beyond the Liberal-Conservative Divide: An Appreciative Rejoinder to Allan Anderson'. *Journal of Pentecostal Theology* 16:1 (2007), 103-11.

———. *The Bible, Disability, and the Church: A New Vision of the People of God*. Grand Rapids and Cambridge, UK: William B. Eerdmans Publishing Company, 2011.

———. 'Conclusion: The Missiology of Jamestown: 1607-2007 and Beyond – Toward a Postcolonial Theology of Mission in North America'. In *Remembering Jamestown: Hard Questions about Christian Mission*. Eds. Amos Yong and Barbara Brown Zikmund. Eugene, OR: Pickwick Publications, 2010, 157-67.

———. *Discerning the Spirit(s): A Pentecostal-Charismatic Contribution to Christian Theology of Religions*. Journal of Pentecostal Theology Supplement Series 20. Sheffield, UK: Sheffield Academic Press, 2000.

———. *Does the Wind Blow through the Middle Way? Pneumatology and the Christian-Buddhist Dialogue*. Studies in Systematic Theology 11. Leiden and Boston: Brill, 2012.

———. 'The Future of Asian Pentecostal Theology: An Asian American Assessment'. *Asian Journal of Pentecostal Studies* 10:1 (2007), 22-41.

———. 'The Future of Evangelical Theology: Asian and Asian American Interrogations'. *The Asia Journal of Theology* 21:2 (October 2007), 371-97.

———. *Hospitality and the Other: Pentecost, Christian Practices, and the Neighbor.* Faith Meets Faith series. Maryknoll, NY: Orbis Books, 2008.

———. 'The Im/Migrant Spirit: De/Constructing a Pentecostal Theology of Migration'. In *Theology and Migration in World Christianity: Contextual Perspectives*, vol. 2: *Theology of Migration in the Abrahamic Religions.* Eds. Peter C. Phan and Elaine Padilla. Christianities of the World. New York: Palgrave Macmillan, forthcoming.

———. *In the Days of Caesar: Pentecostalism and Political Theology – The Cadbury Lectures 2009.* Sacra Doctrina: Christian Theology for a Postmodern Age series. Grand Rapids and Cambridge, UK: William B. Eerdmans Publishing Company, 2010.

———. 'Informality, Illegality, and Improvisation: Rethinking Money, Migration, and Ministry in Chinatown, NYC, and Beyond'. In *New Overtures: Asian North American Theology in the 21st Century.* Ed. Eleazar Fernandez. Upland, Calif.: Sopher Press, 2012, 248-68.

———. 'Race and Racialization in a Post-Racist Evangelical World: A View from Asian America'. In *Aliens in the Promised Land: Race and Evangelicalism.* Ed. Anthony B. Bradley. Phillipsburg, NJ: P and R Publishing Company, 2013, 45-58 and 216-20.

———. *Spirit of Love: A Trinitarian Theology of Grace.* Waco, TX: Baylor University Press, 2012.

———. *The Spirit Poured Out on All Flesh: Pentecostalism and the Possibility of Global Theology.* Grand Rapids: Baker Academic, 2005.

———. 'The Spirit, Vocation, and the Life of the Mind: A Pentecostal Testimony'. In *Pentecostals in the Academy: Testimonies of Call.* Eds. Steven M. Fettke and Robby C. Waddell. Cleveland, TN: CPT Press, 2012, 203-20.

———. 'Whither Asian American Evangelical Theology? What Asian? Which American? Whose *Evangelion*?'. *Evangelical Review of Theology* 32:1 (2008), 22-37.

———. *Who is the Holy Spirit? A Walk with the Apostles.* Brewster, MA: Paraclete Press, 2011.

Yony, Amos, with Jonathan A. Anderson. *Renewing Christian Theology: Systematics for a Global Christianity.* Waco, TX: Baylor University Press, 2014.

Yong, Amos, and Peter G. Heltzel. 'Robert Cummings Neville and Theology's Global Future'. In *Theology in Global Context: Essays in Honor of Robert Cummings Neville.* Eds. Amos Yong and Peter G. Heltzel. New York and London: T and T Clark, 2004, 29-42.

Yune, In-Jin. 'Korean Diaspora: Immigration, Accommodation, Identity of Overseas Korean'. *The Society of Social Study in Korea* 6 (2003), 101-42.

Zehnder, M. *Umgang mit Fremden in Israel und Assyrien: Ein Beitrag zur Anthropologie des 'Fremden' im Licht antiker Quellen.* Beiträge zur Wissenschaft vom Alten und Neuen Testament 8. Stuttgart: W. Kohlhammer, 2005.

Ziel, Machado. 'Pequenas Iniciativas podem gerar transformação' ['Small Initiatives May Generate Transformation']. In *Igreja: Agente de Transformação* [*Church: Agent of Transformation*]. Eds. René Padilla and Péricles Couto. Buenos Aires: Curitiba, Missão Aliança and Kairos, 2011, 235-57.

INDEX

List of Contributors

Tereso C. Casiño is Professor of Missiology and Intercultural Studies at the School of Divinity at Gardner-Webb University (Boiling Springs, North Carolina, USA), and serves as Executive Chair of the North America Diaspora Educators' Forum of the Global Diaspora Network.

Leiton Edward Chinn (Indian Land, South Carolina, USA) is Lausanne Senior Associate for International Student Ministries.

Knut Holter is Professor of Old Testament Studies at the MHS School of Mission and Theology (Stavanger, Norway) and Extraordinary Professor at Stellenbosch University (Stellenbosch, South Africa).

Chandler H. Im is Director of Ethnic America Network and Director of Ethnic Ministries at the Billy Graham Center at Wheaton College (Wheaton, Illinois, USA), and Adjunct Professor of Mission at Faith Evangelical Seminary (Tacoma, Washington, USA).

Todd M. Johnson is Associate Professor of Global Christianity and Director of the Center for the Study of Global Christianity at Gordon-Conwell Theological Seminary (South Hamilton, Massachusetts, USA).

Werner Kahl is Professor of New Testament at the University of Frankfurt (Frankfurt, Germany) and Head of Studies at the Academy of Mission (Hamburg, Germany).

S. Hun Kim is a Wycliffe Diaspora Consultant in Europe and Director of Korean Research Institute for Diaspora (Oxford, England).

Wojciech Kluj, OMI, is Assistant Professor of Missiology at Cardinal Wyszynski University (Warsaw, Poland).

Andrew G. Recepcion is Director of the Caceres Mission Office (Naga City, Philippines) and President of International Association of Catholic Missiologists.

Benjamin Simon is Secretary for Mission and Ecumenism in the Church of Baden (Karlsruhe, Germany).

Myrto Theocharous is Professor of Old Testament at Greek Bible College (Athens, Greece).

T.V. Thomas is Director of the Centre for Evangelism and World Mission (Regina, Canada), and Chair of Ethnic America Network.

Sadiri Joy Tira is Lausanne Committee for World Evangelization Senior Associate for Diasporas, Vice President for Diaspora Missions at Advancing Indigenous Missions, Director of the Institute of Diaspora Missiology at Alliance Graduate School (Manila, Philippines), and Diaspora Missiology Specialist at the Jaffray Centre for Global Initiatives at Ambrose University College (Calgary, Canada).

Andrew F. Walls is Honorary Professor at the University of Edinburgh (Edinburgh, Scotland), Professor of the History of Mission at Liverpool Hope University (Liverpool, England), and Professor at the Akrofi-Christaller Institute for Theology, Mission and Culture (Akropong-Akuapem, Ghana).

Enoch Wan is Director of the Institute of Diaspora Studies-USA at Western Seminary (Portland, Oregon, USA).

Emma Wild-Wood is Director of the Henry Martyn Centre and teaches at Cambridge University and the Cambridge Theological Federation (Cambridge, England).

Jenny Hwang Yang is Director of Advocacy and Policy for the Refugee and Immigration Program at World Relief (Baltimore, Maryland, USA).

Allen Yeh is Associate Professor of Intercultural Studies and Missiology at Cook School of Intercultural Studies at Biola University (La Mirada, California, USA).

Amos Yong is Professor of Theology and Mission and Director of the Center for Missiological Research at Fuller Theological Seminary (Pasadena, California, USA).

Key Yuasa is Senior Pastor of Liberdade Evangelical Holiness Church (São Paulo, Brazil) and served as President of the Evangelical Holiness Church of Brazil denomination.

Gina A. Zurlo is a Research Associate at the Center for the Study of Global Christianity at Gordon-Conwell Theological Seminary (South Hamilton, Massachusetts, USA) and a PhD student at Boston University's School of Theology (Boston, Massachusetts, USA).

REGNUM EDINBURGH CENTENARY SERIES

David A. Kerr, Kenneth R. Ross (Eds)
Mission Then and Now
2009 / 978-1-870345-73-6 / 343pp (paperback)
2009 / 978-1-870345-76-7 / 343pp (hardback)

Daryl M. Balia, Kirsteen Kim (Eds)
Witnessing to Christ Today
2010 / 978-1-870345-77-4 / 301pp (hardback)

Claudia Währisch-Oblau, Fidon Mwombeki (Eds)
Mission Continues
Global Impulses for the 21st Century
2010 / 978-1-870345-82-8 / 271pp (hardback)

Brian Woolnough and Wonsuk Ma (Eds)
Holistic Mission
God's Plan for God's People
2010 / 978-1-870345-85-9 / 268pp (hardback)

Kirsteen Kim and Andrew Anderson (Eds)
Mission Today and Tomorrow
2010 / 978-1-870345-91-0 / 450pp (hardback)

Tormod Engelsviken, Erling Lundeby and Dagfinn Solheim (Eds)
The Church Going Glocal
Mission and Globalisation
2011 / 978-1-870345-93-4 / 262pp (hardback)

Marina Ngurusangzeli Behera (Ed)
Interfaith Relations after One Hundred Years
Christian Mission among Other Faiths
2011 / 978-1-870345-96-5 / 338pp (hardback)

Lalsangkima Pachuau and Knud Jørgensen (Eds)
Witnessing to Christ in a Pluralistic Age
Christian Mission among Other Faiths
2011 / 978-1-870345-95-8 / 277pp (hardback)

Beth Snodderly and A Scott Moreau (Eds)
Evangelical Frontier Mission
Perspectives on the Global Progress of the Gospel
2011 / 978-1-870345-98-9 / 312pp (hardback)

Rolv Olsen (Ed)
Mission and Postmodernities
2011 / 978-1-870345-97-2 / 279pp (hardback)

Cathy Ross (Ed)
Life-Widening Mission
2012 / 978-1-908355-00-3 / 163pp (hardback)

Beate Fagerli, Knud Jørgensen, Rolv Olsen, Kari Storstein Haug and Knut Tveitereid (Eds)
A Learning Missional Church
Reflections from Young Missiologists
2012 / 978-1-908355-01-0 / 218pp (hardback)

Emma Wild-Wood & Peniel Rajkumar (Eds)
Foundations for Mission
2012 / 978-1-908355-12-6 / 309pp (hardback)

Wonsuk Ma & Kenneth R Ross (Eds)
Mission Spirituality and Authentic Discipleship
2013 / 978-1-908355-24-9 / 248pp (hardback)

Stephen B Bevans (Ed)
A Century of Catholic Mission
2013 / 978-1-908355-14-0 / 337pp (hardback)

Robert Schreiter & Knud Jørgensen (Eds)
Mission as Ministry of Reconcilation
2013 / 978-1-908355-26-3 / 382pp (hardback)

Petros Vassiliadis, Editor
Orthodox Perspectives on Mission
2013 / 978-1908355-25-6 / 262pp (hardback)

Orthodox Perspectives on Mission is both a humble tribute to some great Orthodox theologians, who in the past have provided substantial contribution to contemporary missiological and ecumenical discussions, and an Orthodox input to the upcoming 2013 Busan WCC General Assembly. The collected volume is divided into two parts: Part I: The Orthodox Heritage consists of Orthodox missiological contributions of the past, whereas Part II includes all the papers presented in the Plenary of the recent Edinburgh 2010 conference, as well as the short studies and contributions prepared, during the Edinburgh 2010 on going study process.

Pauline Hoggarth, Fergus MacDonald,
Bill Mitchell & Knud Jørgensen, Editors
Bible in Mission
2013 / 978-1908355-42-3 / 317pp (hardback)

To the authors of Bible in Mission, the Bible is the book of life, and mission is life in the Word. This core reality cuts across the diversity of contexts and hermeneutical strategies represented in these essays. The authors are committed to the boundary-crossings that characterize contemporary mission – and each sees the Bible as foundational to the missio Dei, to God's work in the world.

Wonsuk Ma, Veli-Matti Kärkkäinnen
& J Kwabena Asamoah
Pentecostal Mission and Global Christianity
*2014 / 978-1908355-43-0 / 397pp (*hardback)

Although Pentecostalism worldwide represent the most rapidly growing missionary movement in Christian history, only recently scholars from within and outside the movement have begun academic reflection on the mission. This volume represents the coming of age of emerging scholarship of various aspects of the Pentecostal mission, including theological, historical, strategic, and practical aspects.

Afe Adogame, Janice McLean & Anderson Jeremiah, Editors
Engaging the World
Christian Communities in Contemporary Global Societies
*2014 / 978-1908355-21-8 / 235pp (*hardback)

Engaging the World deals with the lived experiences and expressions of Christians in diverse communities across the globe. Christian communities do not live in a vacuum but in complex, diverse social-cultural contexts; within wider communities of different faith and social realities. Power, identity and community are key issues in considering Christian communities in contemporary contexts.

Peniel Jesudason Rufus Rajkumar, Joseph Prabhakar Dayam
& IP Asheervadham, Editors
Mission At and From the Margins
Patterns, Protagonists and Perspectives
*2014 / 978-1908355-13-3 / 283pp (*hardback)

Mission At and From the Margins: Patterns, Protagonists and Perspectives revisits the 'hi-stories' of Mission from the 'bottom up' paying critical attention to people, perspectives and patterns that have often been elided in the construction of mission history. Focusing on the mission story of Christian churches in the South Indian state of Abdhra Pradesh this collection of essays ushers its readers to re-shape their understanding of the landscape of mission history by drawing their attention to the silences and absences within pre-dominant historical accounts.

REGNUM STUDIES IN GLOBAL CHRISTIANITY

David Emmanuel Singh (Ed)
Jesus and the Cross
Reflections of Christians from Islamic Contexts
2008 / 978-1-870345-65-1 / 226pp

Sung-wook Hong
Naming God in Korea
The Case of Protestant Christianity
2008 / 978-1-870345-66-8 / 170pp (hardback)

Hubert van Beek (Ed)
Revisioning Christian Unity
The Global Christian Forum
2009 / 978-1-870345-74-3 / 288pp (hardback)

Young-hoon Lee
The Holy Spirit Movement in Korea
Its Historical and Theological Development
2009 / 978-1-870345-67-5 / 174pp (hardback)

Paul Hang-Sik Cho
Eschatology and Ecology
Experiences of the Korean Church
2010 / 978-1-870345-75-0 / 260pp (hardback)

Dietrich Werner, David Esterline, Namsoon Kang, Joshva Raja (Eds)
The Handbook of Theological Education in World Christianity
Theological Perspectives, Ecumenical Trends, Regional Surveys
2010 / 978-1-870345-80-0 / 759pp

David Emmanuel Singh & Bernard C Farr (Eds)
Christianity and Education
Shaping of Christian Context in Thinking
2010 / 978-1-870345-81-1 / 374pp

J.Andrew Kirk
Civilisations in Conflict?
Islam, the West and Christian Faith
2011 / 978-1-870345-87-3 / 205pp

David Emmanuel Singh (Ed)
Jesus and the Incarnation
Reflections of Christians from Islamic Contexts
2011 / 978-1-870345-90-3 / 245pp

Ivan M Satyavrata
God Has Not left Himself Without Witness
2011 / 978-1-870345-79-8 / 264pp

Bal Krishna Sharma
From this World to the Next
Christian Identity and Funerary Rites in Nepal
2013 / 978-1-908355-08-9 / 238pp

J Kwabena Asamoah-Gyada
Contemporary Pentecostal Christianity
Interpretations from an African Context
2013 / 978-1-908355-07-2 / 194pp

David Emmanuel Singh and Bernard C Farr (Eds)
The Bible and Christian Ethics
2013 / 978-1-908355-20-1 / 217pp

Martin Allaby
Inequality, Corruption and the Church
Challenges & Opportunities in the Global Church
2013 / 978-1-908355-16-4 / 228pp

Paul Alexander and Al Tizon (Eds)
Following Jesus
Journeys in Radical Discipleship – Essays in Honor of Ronald J Sider
2013 / 978-1-908355-27-0 / 228pp

Cawley Bolt
Reluctant or Radical Revolutionaries?
Evangelical Missionaries and Afro-Jamaican Character, 1834-1870
2013 / 978-1-908355-18-8 / 287pp
This study is based on extensive research that challenges traditional ways of understanding some evangelical missionaries of nineteenth century Jamaica and calls for revision of those views. It highlights the strength and character of persons facing various challenges of life in their effort to be faithful to the guiding principles of their existence.

Isabel Apawo Phiri & Dietrich Werner (Eds)
Handbook of Theological Education in Africa
2013 / 978-1-908355-45-4 / 1110pp
The *Handbook of Theological Education in Africa* is a wake-up call for African churches to give proper prominence to theological education institutions and their programmes which serve them. It is unique, comprehensive and ambitious in its aim and scope.

Hope Antone, Wati Longchar, Hyunju Bae, Huang Po Ho, Dietrich Werner (Eds)
Asian Handbook for Theological Education and Ecumenism
2013 / 978-1-908355-30-0 / 675pp (hardback)
This impressive and comprehensive book focuses on key resources for teaching Christian unity and common witness in Asian contexts. It is a collection of articles that reflects the ongoing 'double wrestle' with the texts of biblical tradition as well as with contemporary contexts. It signals an investment towards the future of the ecumenical movement in Asia.

Bernhard Reitsma
The God of My Enemy
The Middle East and the Nature of God
2014 / 978-1-908355-50-8 / 206pp
The establishment of the State of Israel in 1948 for the Church in the West has been the starting point of a rediscovery of its own roots. In the Middle East the effect has been exactly the opposite: Christians have become estranged from their Old Testament roots, because they have been expelled from their land exactly because of an appeal to the Old Testament. The concept of Israel changed from a nation in the Bible, with which they could associate, to an economic, political and military power that was against them

Pantelis Kalaitzidis, Thomas Fitzgerald, Cyril Hovorun, Aikaterini Pekridou, Nikolaos Asproulis, Dietrich Werner & Guy Liagre (Eds)
Orthodox Handbook on Ecumenism
Resources for Theological Education
2014 / 978-1-908355-44-7 / 962pp (hardback)
We highly recommend the publication of this new *Orthodox Handbook* for Teaching Ecumenism edited by a group of orthodox theologians in collaboration with WCC/ETE Program, the Conference of European Churches, Volos Academy for Theological Studies in Greece, and Holy Cross Greek Orthodox School of Theology in Brookline, Massachusetts.

REGNUM STUDIES IN MISSION

Kwame Bediako
Theology and Identity
The Impact of Culture upon Christian Thought in the Second Century and in Modern Africa
1992 / 978-1870345-10-1 / 507pp

Christopher Sugden
Seeking the Asian Face of Jesus
The Practice and Theology of Christian Social Witness in Indonesia and India 1974–1996
1997 / 1-870345-26-6 / 496pp

Keith E. Eitel
Paradigm Wars
The Southern Baptist International Mission Board Faces the Third Millennium
1999 / 1-870345-12-6 / 140pp

Samuel Jayakumar
Dalit Consciousness and Christian Conversion
Historical Resources for a Contemporary Debate
1999 / 81-7214-497-0 / 434pp
(Published jointly with ISPCK)

Vinay Samuel and Christopher Sugden (Eds)
Mission as Transformation
A Theology of the Whole Gospel
1999 / 978-18703455-13-2 / 522pp

Christopher Sugden
Gospel, Culture and Transformation
2000 / 1-870345-32-3 / 152pp
A Reprint, with a New Introduction, of Part Two of Seeking the Asian Face of Jesus

Bernhard Ott
Beyond Fragmentation: Integrating Mission and Theological Education
A Critical Assessment of some Recent Developments in Evangelical Theological Education
2001 / 1-870345-14-9 / 382pp

Gideon Githiga
The Church as the Bulwark against Authoritarianism
Development of Church and State Relations in Kenya, with Particular Reference to the Years after Political Independence 1963-1992
2002 / 1-870345-38-x / 218pp

Myung Sung-Hoon, Hong Young-Gi (Eds)
Charis and Charisma
David Yonggi Cho and the Growth of Yoido Full Gospel Church
2003 / 978-1870345-45-3 / 218pp

Samuel Jayakumar
Mission Reader
Historical Models for Wholistic Mission in the Indian Context
2003 / 1-870345-42-8 / 250pp
(Published jointly with ISPCK)

Bob Robinson
Christians Meeting Hindus
An Analysis and Theological Critique of the Hindu-Christian Encounter in India
2004 / 987-1870345-39-2 / 392pp

Gene Early
Leadership Expectations
How Executive Expectations are Created and Used in a Non-Profit Setting
2005 / 1-870345-30-9 / 276pp

Tharcisse Gatwa
The Churches and Ethnic Ideology in the Rwandan Crises 1900-1994
2005 / 978-1870345-24-8 / 300pp
(Reprinted 2011)

Julie Ma
Mission Possible
Biblical Strategies for Reaching the Lost
2005 / 978-1870345-37-8 / 142pp

I. Mark Beaumont
Christology in Dialogue with Muslims
A Critical Analysis of Christian Presentations of Christ for Muslims from the Ninth and Twentieth Centuries
2005 / 978-1870345-46-0 / 227pp

Thomas Czövek,
Three Seasons of Charismatic Leadership
A Literary-Critical and Theological Interpretation of the Narrative of Saul, David and Solomon
2006 / 978-1870345-48-4 / 272pp

Richard Burgess
Nigeria's Christian Revolution
The Civil War Revival and Its Pentecostal Progeny (1967-2006)
2008 / 978-1-870345-63-7 / 347pp

David Emmanuel Singh & Bernard C Farr (Eds)
Christianity and Cultures
Shaping Christian Thinking in Context
2008 / 978-1-870345-69-9 / 271pp

Tormod Engelsviken, Ernst Harbakk, Rolv Olsen, Thor Strandenæs (Eds)
Mission to the World
Communicating the Gospel in the 21st Century:
Essays in Honour of Knud Jørgensen
2008 / 978-1-870345-64-4 / 472pp (hardback)

Al Tizon
Transformation after Lausanne
Radical Evangelical Mission in Global-Local Perspective
2008 / 978-1-870345-68-2 / 281pp

Bambang Budijanto
Values and Participation
Development in Rural Indonesia
2009 / 978-1-870345-70-4 / 237pp

Alan R. Johnson
Leadership in a Slum
A Bangkok Case Study
2009 / 978-1-870345-71-2 / 238pp

Titre Ande
Leadership and Authority
Bula Matari and Life - Community Ecclesiology in Congo
2010 / 978-1-870345-72-9 / 189pp

Frank Kwesi Adams
Odwira and the Gospel
A Study of the Asante Odwira Festival and its Significance for Christianity in Ghana
2010 /978-1-870345-59-0 / 232pp

Bruce Carlton
Strategy Coordinator
Changing the Course of Southern Baptist Missions
2010 / 978-1-870345-78-1 / 273pp

Julie Ma & Wonsuk Ma
Mission in the Spirit:
Towards a Pentecostal/Charismatic Missiology
2010 / 978-1-870345-84-2 / 312pp

Allan Anderson, Edmond Tang (Eds)
Asian and Pentecostal
The Charismatic Face of Christianity in Asia
2011 / 978-1870345-94-1 / 500pp
(Revised Edition)

S. Hun Kim & Wonsuk Ma (Eds)
Korean Diaspora and Christian Mission
2011 / 978-1-870345-89-7 / 301pp (hardback)

Jin Huat Tan
Planting an Indigenous Church
The Case of the Borneo Evangelical Mission
2011 / 978-1-870345-99-6 / 343pp

Bill Prevette
Child, Church and Compassion
Towards Child Theology in Romania
2012 / 978-1-908355-03-4 / 382pp

Samuel Cyuma
Picking up the Pieces
The Church and Conflict Resolution in South Africa and Rwanda
2012 / 978-1-908355-02-7 / 373pp

Peter Rowan
Proclaiming the Peacemaker
The Malaysian Church as an Agent of Reconciliation in a Multicultural Society
2012 / 978-1-908355-05-8 / 268pp

Edward Ontita
Resources and Opportunity
The Architecture of Livelihoods in Rural Kenya
2012 / 978-1-908355-04-1 / 328pp

Kathryn Kraft
Searching for Heaven in the Real World
A Sociological Discussion of Conversion in the Arab World
2012 / 978-1-908355-15-7 / 142pp

Wessley Lukose
Contextual Missiology of the Spirit
Pentecostalism in Rajasthan, India
2013 / 978-1-908355-09-6 / 256pp

Paul M Miller
Evangelical Mission in Co-operation with Catholics
A Study of Evangelical Tensions
2013 / 978-1-908355-17-1 / 291pp

Alemayehu Mekonnen

Culture Change in Ethiopia

An Evangelical Perspective

2013 / 978-1-908355-39-3 / 199pp

This book addresses the causes and consequences of culture change in Ethiopia, from Haile Selassie to the present, based on thorough academic research. Although written from an evangelical perspective, this book invites Ethiopians from all religions, ideological, and ethnic backgrounds to reflect on their past, to analyse their present and to engage in unity with diversity to face the future.

Godwin Lekundayo

The Cosmic Christ

Towards Effective Mission Among the Maasai

2013 / 978-1-908355-28- 7 / 259 pp

This book reveals a complex interaction between the Christian gospel brought by western missionaries and the nomadic Massai culture of Tanzania … an important insider's voice courageously questioning the approach to condemn some critical Maasai practices, particularly polygamy, and its missionary consequences. This is a rare study from a Maasai Christian leader.

Philippe Ouedraogo

Female Education and Mission

A Burkina Faso Experience

2014 / 978-1-908355-11-9 / 263pp

This volume is the result of six years research in 'Overcoming Obstacles to Female Education in Burkina Faso'. It narrates how Christians and religious groups can speed up female education and contribute to the socio-economic growth of Burkina Faso. Religious culture and traditions were seen as a problem to female education. However, the evidence from this research shows that Christianity is also part of the solution to a quality female education, thus a key factor of socio economic growth of the country.

Haw Yung

Mangoes or Bananas?

The Quest for an Authentic Asian Christian Theology

(Second Edition)

2014 / 978-1-908355-47-8 / 232pp

Over the past few decades there has been a growing awareness of the need for contextual theologies throughout Asia. But how genuinely contextual are these? Based on the premise that theology and mission are inseparable, the author applies four missiological criteria to representative examples of Protestant Asian writings to assess their adequacy or otherwise as contextual theologies.

Daniel Taichoul Yang

Called Out for Witness

The Missionary Journey of Grace Korean Church

2014 / 978-1-908355-49-2 / 167pp

This book investigates the theological motivation for GKC's missions: Reformed theology, Presbyterian theology, and mission theology. The book also shows the extent of the church's mission engagement by continents. Finally, the book turns its attention to the future with an evaluation of the church's missionary journey.

REGNUM RESOURCES FOR MISSION

Knud Jørgensen
Equipping for Service
Christian Leadership in Church and Society
2012 / 978-1-908355-06-5 / 150pp

Mary Miller
What does Love have to do with Leadership?
2013 / 978-1-908355-10-2 / 100pp

Mary Miller (Ed)
Faces of Holistic Mission
Stories of the OCMS Family
2013 / 978-1-908355-32-4 / 104pp

David Cranston and Ruth Padilla DeBorst (Eds)
Mission as Transformation
Learning from Catalysts
2013 / 978-1-908355-34-8 / 77pp

This book is the product of the first Stott-Bediako Forum, held in 2012 with the title *Portraits of Catalysts*. Its aim was to learn from the stories of Christian leaders whose lives and work have served as catalysts for transformation as each, in his or her particular way, facilitated the intersection between the Good News of Jesus Christ and the context in which they lived, in particular amongst people who are suffering.

Brian Woolnough (Ed)
Good News from Africa
Community Transformation Through the Church
2013 / 978-1-908355-33-1 / 123pp

This book discusses how sustainable, holistic, community development can be, and is being, achieved through the work of the local church. Leading African development practitioners describe different aspects of development through their own experience.

Makonen Getu (Ed)
Transforming Microfinance
A Christian Approach
2013 / 978-1-908355-31-7 / 264pp

"This book highlights the important role that Christian-based organisations bring to the delivery of financial services for the poor. It is times, significant and important and deserves a wide circulation".

Lord Carey of Clifton, former Archbishop of Canterbury

Jonathan Ingleby, Tan Kand San, Tan Loun Ling, (Eds)
Contextualisation & Mission Training
Engaging Asia's Religious Worlds
2013 / 978-1-908355-40-9 / 109pp

Contextualisation & Mission Training, offers "contextual frameworks" and "explorations" in order to enhance deeper engagement with the complexity of Asian social, cultural and religious systems.

On Eagle's Wings
Models in Mentoring
2013 / 978-1-908355-46-1 / 105pp

David Cranston writes unashamedly as a Christian for whom no account of mentoring would be complete without placing it in the biggest context of all – that of the relationship between humans and God.

John Lennox, Professor of Mathematics, University of Oxford
Fellow in Mathematics and Philosophy of Science

GENERAL REGNUM TITLES

Vinay Samuel, Chris Sugden (Eds)
The Church in Response to Human Need
1987 / 1870345045 / xii+268pp

Philip Sampson, Vinay Samuel, Chris Sugden (Eds)
Faith and Modernity
Essays in modernity and post-modernity
1994 / 1870345177 / 352pp

Klaus Fiedler
The Story of Faith Missions
1994 / 0745926878 / 428pp

Douglas Peterson
Not by Might nor by Power
A Pentecostal Theology of Social Concern in Latin America
1996 / 1870345207 / xvi+260pp

David Gitari
In Season and Out of Season
Sermons to a Nation
1996 / 1870345118 / 155pp

David. W. Virtue
A Vision of Hope
The Story of Samuel Habib
1996 / 1870345169 / xiv+137pp

Everett A Wilson
Strategy of the Spirit
J.Philip Hogan and the Growth of the Assemblies of God Worldwide, 1960 - 1990
1997 /1870345231/214

Murray Dempster, Byron Klaus, Douglas Petersen (Eds)
The Globalization of Pentecostalism
A Religion Made to Travel
1999 / 1870345290 / xvii+406pp

Peter Johnson, Chris Sugden (Eds)
Markets, Fair Trade and the Kingdom of God
Essays to Celebrate Traidcraft's 21st Birthday
2001 / 1870345193 / xii+155pp

Robert Hillman, Coral Chamberlain, Linda Harding
Healing & Wholeness
Reflections on the Healing Ministry
2002 / 978-1- 870345-35- 4 / xvii+283pp

David Bussau, Russell Mask
Christian Microenterprise Development
An Introduction
2003 / 1870345282 / xiii+142pp

David Singh
Sainthood and Revelatory Discourse
An Examination of the Basis for the Authority of Bayan in Mahdawi Islam
2003 / 8172147285 / xxiv+485pp

REGNUM AFRICA TITLES

Kwame Bediako
Jesus in Africa, The Christian Gospel in African History and Experience
(2000) (Theological Reflections from the South series)
SECOND EDITION FORTHCOMING 2013

Mercy Amba Oduyoye
Beads and Strands, Reflections of an African Woman on Christianity in Africa
(Theological Reflections from the South series)
2002 / 1-870345-41-X / 114pp

Kä Mana
Christians and Churches of Africa Envisioning the Future, Salvation in Christ and the Building of a new African Society
(Theological Reflections from the South series)
2002 / 1-870345-27-4 / 119pp

Ype Schaaf
On Their Way Rejoicing, The History and Role of the Bible in Africa
2002 / 1-870345-35-9 / 252pp

E.A.W. Engmann
Kpawo-Kpawo Toi Kpawo – Vol. 1, Adesai, Oboade, Lalai, Ajenui ke Shwemoi (Folklore of the Ga People)
(Gbotsui Series - Indigenous Sources of Knowledge in Ghanaian Languages)
2009 / 978-9988-1-2296-6 / 70pp

Philip Tetteh Laryea
Yesu Homowo Nuntso (Jesus, Lord of Homowo)
(Nyamedua series in Mother-tongue Theology)
(reprinted 2011) / 1-870345-54-1 / 176pp

E.A.W. Engmann
Kpawo-Kpawo Toi Kpawo – Vol. 2, Kusumii (Folklore of the Ga People)
(Gbotsui Series - Indigenous Sources of Knowledge in Ghanaian Languages)
2012 / 978-9988-1-2294-2, 186pp

Philip T. Laryea
Ephraim Amu: Nationalist, Poet and Theologian (1899–1995)
2012 / 978-9988-1-2293-5, 425pp

Jon P. Kirby
The Power and the Glory, Popular Christianity in Northern Ghana
(Trends in African Christianity Series)
2012 / 978-9988-1-2295-9, 350pp

For the up-to-date listing of the Regnum books visit www.ocms.ac.uk/regnum

Regnum Books International
Regnum is an Imprint of The Oxford Centre for Mission Studies
St. Philip and St. James Church
Woodstock Road
Oxford, OX2 6HR

Made in the USA
San Bernardino, CA
01 March 2017